THE NEW CAMBRIDGE SHAKESPEARE

GENERAL EDITOR
Brian Gibbons, *University of Münster*

ASSOCIATE GENERAL EDITOR
A. R. Braunmuller, *University of California, Los Angeles*

From the publication of the first volumes in 1984 the General Editor of the New Cambridge Shakespeare was Philip Brockbank and the Associate General Editors were Brian Gibbons and Robin Hood. From 1990 to 1994 the General Editor was Brian Gibbons and the Associate General Editors were A. R. Braunmuller and Robin Hood.

TIMON OF ATHENS

Karl Klein's edition of *Timon of Athens* introduces Shakespeare's play as a complex exploration of a corrupt, moneyed society, and Klein sees the protagonist not as a failed tragic hero, but as a rich and philanthropic nobleman, surrounded by greed and sycophancy, who is forced to recognise the inherent destructiveness of the Athenian society from which he retreats in disgust and rage.

Klein establishes *Timon* as one of Shakespeare's late works, arguing, contrary to recent academic views, that evidence for other authors besides Shakespeare is inconclusive. The edition argues that the play is neither tragedy, satire nor comedy, but a subtle and complete drama whose main characters contain elements of all three genres.

Karl Klein, who died in 1997, was Professor of English Literature at the Universität des Saarlandes, Germany. His research and publications were in the fields of Renaissance literature, the nineteenth-century English novel, and contemporary poetry. This edition of *Timon of Athens* was near completion at the time of Professor Klein's death. It was prepared for publication by colleagues; an account of the Royal Shakespeare Company production of 1999 was written by A. R. Braunmuller.

THE NEW CAMBRIDGE SHAKESPEARE

All's Well That Ends Well, edited by Russell Fraser
Antony and Cleopatra, edited by David Bevington
As You Like It, edited by Michael Hattaway
The Comedy of Errors, edited by T. S. Dorsch
Coriolanus, edited by Lee Bliss
Hamlet, edited by Philip Edwards
Julius Caesar, edited by Marvin Spevack
King Edward III, edited by Giorgio Melchiori
The First Part of King Henry IV, edited by Herbert Weil and Judith Weil
The Second Part of King Henry IV, edited by Giorgio Melchiori
King Henry V, edited by Andrew Gurr
The First Part of King Henry VI, edited by Michael Hattaway
The Second Part of King Henry VI, edited by Michael Hattaway
The Third Part of King Henry VI, edited by Michael Hattaway
King Henry VIII, edited by John Margeson
King John, edited by L. A. Beaurline
The Tragedy of King Lear, edited by Jay L. Halio
King Richard II, edited by Andrew Gurr
King Richard III, edited by Janis Lull
Macbeth, edited by A. R. Braunmuller
Measure for Measure, edited by Brian Gibbons
The Merchant of Venice, edited by M. M. Mahood
The Merry Wives of Windsor, edited by David Crane
A Midsummer Night's Dream, edited by R. A. Foakes
Much Ado About Nothing, edited by F. H. Mares
Othello, edited by Norman Sanders
Pericles, edited by Doreen DelVecchio and Antony Hammond
The Poems, edited by John Roe
Romeo and Juliet, edited by G. Blakemore Evans
The Sonnets, edited by G. Blakemore Evans
The Taming of the Shrew, edited by Ann Thompson
Timon of Athens, edited by Karl Klein
Titus Andronicus, edited by Alan Hughes
Twelfth Night, edited by Elizabeth Story Donno
The Two Gentlemen of Verona, edited by Kurt Schlueter

THE EARLY QUARTOS
The First Quarto of Hamlet, edited by Kathleen O. Irace
The First Quarto of King Henry V, edited by Andrew Gurr
The First Quarto of King Lear, edited by Jay L. Halio
The First Quarto of King Richard III, edited by Peter Davison
The Taming of a Shrew, edited by Stephen Roy Miller

TIMON OF ATHENS

Edited by
KARL KLEIN
Universität des Saarlandes

CAMBRIDGE
UNIVERSITY PRESS

PUBLISHED BY THE PRESS SYNDICATE OF THE UNIVERSITY OF CAMBRIDGE
The Pitt Building, Trumpington Street, Cambridge, United Kingdom

CAMBRIDGE UNIVERSITY PRESS
The Edinburgh Building, Cambridge CB2 2RU, UK   www.cup.cam.ac.uk
40 West 20th Street, New York, NY 10011-4211, USA www.cup.org
10 Stamford Road, Oakleigh, Melbourne 3166, Australia
Ruiz de Alarcón 13, 28014 Madrid, Spain

First published 2001

Printed in the United Kingdom at the University Press, Cambridge

Typeface Ehrhardt 10/12 pt.   *System* PageMaker [BT]

A catalogue record for this book is available from the British Library

Library of Congress Cataloguing in Publication data

Shakespeare, William, 1564–1616.
Timon of Athens / Karl Klein.
   p.   cm. – (New Cambridge Shakespeare)
Includes bibliographical references.
ISBN 0-521-22224-9 – ISBN 0-521-29404-5 (pbk.)
   1. Timon of Athens (Legendary character) – Drama.   I. Klein, Karl, 1928–   II. Title.
PR2834.A2 K57   2000
822.3′3 – dc21   00–027899   CIP

ISBN 0521 22224 9 hardback
ISBN 0521 29404 5 paperback

CONTENTS

ILLUSTRATIONS

Illustrations 1, 2, 3, 4, 7, 8 and 10 are reproduced by permission of the Shakespeare Centre Library, Stratford-upon-Avon.

ACKNOWLEDGEMENTS

The following expressions of appreciation and gratitude are meant for everyone who has directly or indirectly contributed to the creation and completion of this edition, be they mentioned here in name or not. Special thanks are due – to the late Philip Brockbank for his invitation to undertake this edition and his inspiring example; to Silvia Carvalho, Maria Fett, Andreas Jaeger, Martina Mangasser, Angelika Michelis, Susanne Krugmann, and Karin Lothschuetz for their support; to Becky van Gelder Deutsch and Anne Charlton for their generous contributions concerning linguistic issues. Monika Bins, Britta Graeber and Saskia Schabio have been especially helpful with research, data processing, preparing of visual materials and other editorial chores. Saskia Schabio has not least contributed with her judgement, inspiration and friendship, as have Gisela Kreissig, Sandy Cunningham, Tim Mares, Mary Winkler, Alan Grob, Meredith Skura, M. Gilbert Porter and Detlev Gohrbandt. Special thanks are due furthermore to the Universität des Saarlandes permitting leaves of absence and research visits in the US and UK, to the Department of English at the Universität des Saarlandes, to Rice University, Houston, Texas and its English Department, to the Huntington Library, the Folger Shakespeare Library and the Shakespeare Institute, University of Birmingham, whose staff were so hospitable and helpful; to the General Editor, Brian Gibbons, to Lydia Remke, Angela Stock, Anne-Julia Zwierlein, Christian Krug and Sabine Burkard. At Cambridge University Press I thank Paul Chipchase and Sarah Stanton.

GUDRUN KLEIN

ABBREVIATIONS AND CONVENTIONS

1. Shakespeare's plays

Shakespeare's plays, when cited in this edition, are abbreviated in a style modified slightly from that used in the *Harvard Concordance to Shakespeare*. Other editions of Shakespeare are abbreviated under the editor's surname (Rowe, Maxwell) unless they are the work of more than one editor. In such cases, an abbreviated series title is used (Cam.). When more than one edition by the same editor is cited, later editions are discriminated with a raised figure (Collier[2]). All quotations from Shakespeare, except those from *Timon of Athens*, use the text and lineation of *The Riverside Shakespeare*, under the general editorship of G. Blakemore Evans.

Ado	*Much Ado About Nothing*
Ant.	*Antony and Cleopatra*
AWW	*All's Well That Ends Well*
AYLI	*As You Like It*
Cor.	*Coriolanus*
Cym.	*Cymbeline*
Err.	*The Comedy of Errors*
Ham.	*Hamlet*
1H4	*The First Part of King Henry the Fourth*
2H4	*The Second Part of King Henry the Fourth*
H5	*King Henry the Fifth*
1H6	*The First Part of King Henry the Sixth*
2H6	*The Second Part of King Henry the Sixth*
3H6	*The Third Part of King Henry the Sixth*
H8	*King Henry the Eighth*
JC	*Julius Caesar*
John	*King John*
LC	*A Lover's Complaint*
LLL	*Love's Labour's Lost*
Lear	*King Lear*
Luc.	*The Rape of Lucrece*
Mac.	*Macbeth*
MM	*Measure for Measure*
MND	*A Midsummer Night's Dream*
MV	*The Merchant of Venice*
Oth.	*Othello*
Per.	*Pericles*
R2	*King Richard the Second*
R3	*King Richard the Third*
Rom.	*Romeo and Juliet*
Shr.	*The Taming of the Shrew*
Son.	*Sonnets*
STM	*Sir Thomas More*
Temp.	*The Tempest*

TGV	*The Two Gentlemen of Verona*
Tim.	*Timon of Athens*
Tit.	*Titus Andronicus*
TN	*Twelfth Night*
TNK	*The Two Noble Kinsmen*
Tro.	*Troilus and Cressida*
Wiv.	*The Merry Wives of Windsor*
WT	*The Winter's Tale*

2. Other works cited and general references

Works mentioned once in the Commentary and the Introduction appear there with full bibliographical information; others are either cited by the shortened titles below or may be found in the Reading List.

Abbott — E. A. Abbott, *A Shakespearian Grammar*, 3rd edn, 1919 (references are to numbered paragraphs)

Adelman — Janet Adelman, *Suffocating Mothers: Fantasies of Maternal Origin in Shakespeare's Plays, 'Hamlet' to 'The Tempest'*, 1992

Alexander — *Works*, ed. Peter Alexander, 1951

Armstrong — E. A. Armstrong, *Shakespeare's Imagination*, 1946

Barber — C. L. Barber and Richard P. Wheeler, *The Whole Journey: Shakespeare's Power of Development*, 1986

Bayley — John Bayley, *Shakespeare and Tragedy*, 1981

Beckerman — Bernard Beckerman, *Shakespeare at the Globe, 1599–1609*, 1962

Berry — Ralph Berry, *Shakespearean Structures*, 1981

Bevington — *Works*, ed. David Bevington, 1980

Blunt — A. Blunt, 'An echo of the Paragone in Shakespeare', *Journal of the Warburg Institute* 2 (1938–9), 260–2

Bowers — Fredson Bowers, *On Editing Shakespeare*, 1966

Bradbrook, 'Comedy' — M. C. Bradbrook, 'The Comedy of Timon: a revelling play of the Inner Temple', *Renaissance Drama* 9 (1966), 83–103

Bradbrook, *Craftsman* — M. C. Bradbrook, *Shakespeare the Craftsman*, 1969

Bradbrook, *Pageant* — M. C. Bradbrook, *The Tragic Pageant of 'Timon of Athens'*, 1966

Brockbank — Philip Brockbank, *On Shakespeare: Jesus, Shakespeare, and Karl Marx, and Other Essays*, 1989

Brownlow — F. W. Brownlow, *Two Shakespearean Sequences: 'Henry VI' to 'Richard II' and 'Pericles' to 'Timon of Athens'*, 1977

Bullough — *Narrative and Dramatic Sources of Shakespeare*, ed. Geoffrey Bullough, 8 vols., 1957–75, VI, 1966

Burke — Kenneth Burke, *Language as Symbolic Action*, 1966 ('Timon of Athens and misanthropic gold', pp. 115–24)

Butler — Francelia Butler, *The Strange Critical Fortunes of Shakespeare's 'Timon of Athens'*, 1966

Cam. — *Works*, ed. W. G. Clark, J. Glover and W. A. Wright, 1863–6 (Cambridge Shakespeare)

Cam.² — *Works*, ed. W. A. Wright, 1891–3

Campbell	Oscar James Campbell, *Shakespeare's Satire*, 1943
Capell	*Comedies, Histories, and Tragedies*, ed. Edward Capell, 1768
Capell, *Notes*	*Notes and Various Readings to Shakespeare*, 3 vols., 1779–83
CH	*Shakespeare: The Critical Heritage*, ed. Brian Vickers, 6 vols., 1974–81
Chambers	*Works*, ed. E. K. Chambers, 1908 (Red Letter Shakespeare)
Chambers, *Shakespeare*	E. K. Chambers, *William Shakespeare: A Study of Facts and Problems*, 2 vols., 1930
Charney	*Timon of Athens*, ed. Maurice Charney, 1965 (Signet Classic Shakespeare)
Chew, 'Fortune'	S. C. Chew, 'Time and Fortune', *ELH* 6 (1939), 83–113
Chew, *Pilgrimage*	S. C. Chew, *The Pilgrimage of Life*, 1962
Clemen	W. H. Clemen, *The Development of Shakespeare's Imagery*, 1951
Collier	*Works*, ed. John Payne Collier, 1842–4
Collier²	*The Plays*, ed. John Payne Collier, 1853
Collier³	*Comedies, Histories, Tragedies and Poems*, ed. John Payne Collier, 2nd edn, 1858
Colman	E. A. M. Colman, *The Dramatic Use of Bawdy in Shakespeare*, 1974
conj.	conjecture
Craig, H.	*The Complete Works of Shakespeare*, ed. Hardin Craig, 1951
Craig, W. J.	*The Oxford Shakespeare*, ed. William James Craig, 1894
Davidson	Clifford Davidson, '*Timon of Athens*: the iconography of false friendship', *HLQ* 43 (1979–80), 181–200
Deighton	*Timon of Athens*, ed. K. Deighton, 1905 (Arden Shakespeare)
Delius	*Werke*, ed. Nicolaus Delius, 1855
Dent	R. W. Dent, *Shakespeare's Proverbial Language*, 1981 (references are to numbered proverbs)
Dessen	Alan C. Dessen, *Recovering Shakespeare's Theatrical Vocabulary*, 1995
Diogenes Laertius	Diogenes Laertius, *Lives of Eminent Philosophers*, trans. R. D. Hicks, Loeb Classical Library, 2 vols., 1925
Dyce	*Works*, ed. Alexander Dyce, 1857
Dyce²	*Works*, ed. Alexander Dyce, 2nd edn, 1864–7
EC	*Essays in Criticism*
ELH	*ELH: A Journal of English Literary History*
Elliott	Robert C. Elliott, *The Power of Satire: Magic, Ritual, Art*, 1960
Ellis-Fermor	Una Ellis-Fermor, '*Timon of Athens*: an unfinished play', *RES* 18 (1942), 270–83
Empson	William Empson, *The Structure of Complex Words*, 1952
F	*Mr. William Shakespeares Comedies, Histories, and Tragedies*, 1623 (First Folio)

F2	*Mr. William Shakespeares Comedies, Histories, and Tragedies*, 1632 (Second Folio)
F3	*Mr. William Shakespeares Comedies, Histories, and Tragedies*, 1663–4 (Third Folio)
F4	*Mr. William Shakespeares Comedies, Histories, and Tragedies*, 1685 (Fourth Folio)
Farnham, 'Beast theme'	W. Farnham, 'The beast theme in Shakespeare's *Timon*', *Essays and Studies by Members of the Department of English, University of California* 14 (1943), 49–56
Farnham, *Frontier*	W. Farnham, *Shakespeare's Tragic Frontier: The World of His Final Tragedies*, 1950
Fly, 'Ending'	R. D. Fly, 'The ending of *Timon of Athens*: a reconsideration', *Criticism* 15 (1973), 242–52
Fly, *World*	R. D. Fly, *Shakespeare's Mediated World*, 1976
Franz	W. Franz, *Die Sprache Shakespeares in Vers und Prosa*, 1939 (references are to numbered paragraphs)
Fulton	R. C. Fulton, 'Timon, Cupid and the Amazons' *S.St.* 9 (1976), 283–99
Globe	*Works*, ed. W. G. Clark and W. A. Wright, 1864
Gomme	A. Gomme, '*Timon of Athens*', *EC* 9 (1959),107–25
Greek Anthology	*The Greek Anthology*, trans. W. R. Paton, Loeb Classical Library, 5 vols., 1916–18
Greg	W. W. Greg, *The Shakespeare First Folio: Its Bibliographical and Textual History*, 1955
Handelman	Susan Handelman, '*Timon of Athens*: the rage of disillusionment', *American Imago* 36 (1979), 45–68
Hanmer	*Works*, ed. Thomas Hanmer, 1743–4
Harbage	*Works*, gen. ed. Alfred Harbage, 1969 (Pelican Shakespeare revised)
Harrison	*Works*, ed. G. B. Harrison, 1934
Hauser	Arnold Hauser, *Mannerism: The Crisis of the Renaissance and the Origin of Modern Art*, 1965
Herford	*Works*, ed. C. H. Herford, 1899–1900
Hibbard, 'Sequestration'	G. R. Hibbard, '"Sequestration into Atlantick and Eutopian polities": Milton on More', *Renaissance and Reformation* 4 (1980), 209–25
Hibbard, *Timon*	*Timon of Athens*, ed. G. R. Hibbard, 1970 (New Penguin Shakespeare)
Hinman	*Timon of Athens*, ed. Charlton Hinman, 1964 (Pelican Shakespeare)
Hinman, *Printing*	Charlton Hinman, *The Printing and Proof-Reading of the First Folio of Shakespeare*, 2 vols., 1963
HLQ	*Huntington Library Quarterly*
Honigmann, *Shakespeare's Text*	E. A. J. Honigmann, *The Stability of Shakespeare's Text*, 1965
Honigmann, 'Stage direction'	E. A. J. Honigmann, 'Re-enter the stage direction: Shakespeare and some contemporaries', *S.Sur.* 29 (1976), 117–25
Honigmann, 'Timon'	E. A. J. Honigmann, 'Timon of Athens', *SQ* 12 (1961), 3–20

Merchant, *Shakespeare*	W. M. Merchant, *Shakespeare and the Artist*, 1959
Merchant, 'Timon'	W. M. Merchant, 'Timon and the conceit of art', *SQ* 6 (1955), 249–57
MLN	*Modern Language Notes*
MLQ	*Modern Language Quarterly*
MLR	*Modern Language Review*
MP	*Modern Philology*
Nevo	Ruth Nevo, *Shakespeare's Other Language*, 1987
N&Q	*Notes and Queries*
Nowottny	Winifred M. T. Nowottny, 'Acts IV and V of Timon of Athens', *SQ* 10 (1959), 493–7
Nuttall	A. D. Nuttall, *Timon of Athens*, 1989
OED	*The Oxford English Dictionary*, ed. James A. H. Murray *et al.*, 12 vols. and supplement, 1933
Oliver	*Timon of Athens*, ed. H. J. Oliver, 1959 (Arden Shakespeare)
Onions	C. T. Onions, *A Shakespeare Glossary*, rev. Robert D. Eagleson, 1986
Oxford	*The Complete Works*, gen. eds. Stanley Wells and Gary Taylor, 1986
Oxford Companion	William Shakespeare. *A Textual Companion*, ed. Stanley Wells and Gary Taylor, 1987
Painter	William Painter, *The Palace of Pleasure* (1566), in Bullough, VI, 293–5
Partridge	Eric Partridge, *Shakespeare's Bawdy*, rev. edn, 1955
Patch	H. R. Patch, *The Goddess Fortuna in Mediaeval Literature*, 1927
Plutarch, *Lives*	*The Lives of the noble Grecians and Romanes, compared together by . . . Plutarke . . . ; translated out of Greeke into French by J. Amyot . . . and out of French into Englishe by Thomas North*, 1579
PMLA	*Publications of the Modern Language Association of America*
Pope	*Works*, ed. Alexander Pope, 1723–5
PQ	*Philological Quarterly*
Rabkin	Norman Rabkin, *Shakespeare and the Common Understanding*, 1967
Rann	*Dramatic Works*, ed. Joseph Rann, 1978–94
Reid	S. A. Reid, ' "I am misanthropos" – a psychoanalytic reading of Shakespeare's *Timon of Athens*', *Psychoanalytic Review*, 56 (1969), 442–52
RES	*Review of English Studies*
Riverside	*The Riverside Shakespeare*, textual ed. G. Blakemore Evans, 1974
Rowe	*Works*, ed. Nicholas Rowe, 1709
Rowe³	*Works*, ed. Nicholas Rowe, 1714
Ruszkiewicz	John J. Ruszkiewicz, *Timon of Athens. An Annotated Bibliography*, 1986
SAB	*Shakespeare Association Bulletin*
SB	*Studies in Bibliography*
Schmidt	Alexander Schmidt, *Shakespeare-Lexicon*, rev. Gregor Sarrazin, 2 vols., 1923

SD	stage direction
SH	speech heading
Singer	*Works*, ed. Samuel Weller Singer, 1826
Sisson	*Works*, ed. Charles Jasper Sisson, 1954
Sisson, *Readings*	C. J. Sisson, *New Readings in Shakespeare*, 2 vols., 1956
SJ	*Shakespeare Jahrbuch*
Skura	M. A. Skura, *Shakespeare the Actor and the Purposes of Playing*, 1993
Smith	G. G. Smith (ed.), *Elizabethan Critical Essays*, 2 vols., 1904
Soellner	R. Soellner, '*Timon of Athens': Shakespeare's Pessimistic Tragedy*, 1979
Spevack	Marvin Spevack, *A Shakespeare Thesaurus*, 1993
Spurgeon	Caroline F. Spurgeon, *Shakespeare's Imagery and What It Tells Us*, 1935
SQ	*Shakespeare Quarterly*
S.St.	*Shakespeare Studies*
S.Sur.	*Shakespeare Survey*
Stampfer	Judah Stampfer, *The Tragic Engagement*, 1968
Staunton	*The Plays*, ed. Howard Staunton, 1858–60
Steevens	*see* Johnson/Steevens[2]
Swigg	R. Swigg, '"Timon of Athens" and the growth of discrimination', *MLR* 62 (1967), 387–94
Theobald	*Works*, ed. Lewis Theobald, 1733
Theobald[2]	*Works*, ed. Lewis Theobald, 1740
Tilley	M. P. Tilley, *A Dictionary of the Proverbs in England in the Sixteenth and Seventeenth Centuries*, 1950 (references are to numbered proverbs)
Timon Comedy	*Timon*, ed. J. C. Bulman and J. M. Nosworthy, The Malone Society, 1980
TLN	Through Line Numbering
Tudor Translations	*The Tudor Translations*, 1st series, ed. W. E. Henley, 44 vols., 1967
Var. 1821	*Works*, ed. James Boswell, 1821
Warburton	*Works*, ed. with notes by Pope and William Warburton, 1747
Williams	Gordon Williams, *A Dictionary of Sexual Language and Imagery in Shakespearean and Stuart Literature*, 3 vols., 1994
Wright	George T. Wright, *Shakespeare's Metrical Art*, 1988

INTRODUCTION

Date

Since we have no knowledge of *Timon of Athens* having been performed in Shakespeare's lifetime, dating it will always remain a matter of conjecture. Arguments have been based on various assumptions. One possibility is to consider the play's sources. Shakespeare used Thomas North's translation of Plutarch for *Coriolanus* and *Antony and Cleopatra*. For *Timon*, Shakespeare used the *Lives* of Antony and Alcibiades, whom Plutarch coupled with Coriolanus. Thus he may have composed *Timon* within the same period of time – that is, 1607–8.[1] Bullough places the play after *Antony and Cleopatra* and before *Coriolanus*, on the hypothesis that Shakespeare may have realised the thinness of the Timon subject matter and then turned away from it to work on *Coriolanus*.

Another point of orientation is provided by the play's thematic affinity with *Lear*, but it is an open question whether to place it before this play or after it. Maxwell lists a majority of critics favouring an earlier dating of *Timon*, amongst them J. Dover Wilson and P. Alexander, who considered *Timon* to be 'a tentative treatment of the theme so majestically handled in *Lear*'.[2]

Reflections on the comparatively 'free' versification and the rough nature of the blank verse[3] have led some scholars to place it close to the romances. Bertram and Brownlow take it to be Shakespeare's last play, written after 1614, and think that its unfinished state is due to Shakespeare's death.

The play and its themes

ASPECTS OF FORTUNE

In the play's first scene the Poet's description of Fortune is conventional, recalling the Goddess Fortuna in medieval writing.[4] The most common attribute is the picture of Fortune's Wheel with four riders sitting on its spokes, signifying the stages of their rise and fall. The concept of the hill with Fortune's throne on top of it, signifying inaccessibility and adversity, is also not uncommon.[5] These portrayals of Fortune's impact on people's lives are both sombre and stereotyped; the fact that the Poet adopts such a model emphasises the conventional nature of his art: the stereotypical *de casibus*

---

[1] These points were made by Honigmann, 'Timon', and by Oliver, p. xli.

[2] Maxwell, pp. xii–xiii.

[3] See Textual Analysis, pp. 193–5 below.

[4] An extensive account is given by Patch, ch. 2. For a representative view of Fortune's power at this period see Sackville's 'Induction' in *The Mirror for Magistrates*, ed. Lily B. Campbell, 1938, pp. 298–317.

[5] See Patch, pp. 132–6, and Chew, *Pilgrimage*, pp. 53–4. However, Chew, 'Fortune', says that 'the image of Fortune seated upon a hill is one that does not occur . . . anywhere in the graphic arts'.

tale; the mechanistically conceived patterning of an individual's life; and the didactic stance of a narrator telling a cautionary tale.

Frederick Kiefer has demonstrated how the portrayals of Fortune were modified during the latter part of the fifteenth century.[1] What had formerly been essential implements of her activity – above all, the wheel – were discarded. Many conventional features signifying Fortune's absolute authority over men's lives were replaced by others which allowed man scope to choose and to decide for himself which course to take.[2] These modifications in the iconographic representation of Fortune have their correlative in new descriptions of her power and influence. Machiavelli devoted chapter 25 of *The Prince* to the problem of 'How much Fortune can do in Human Affairs, and in what Mode it may be opposed'. He strongly argued against the belief 'that worldly things are so governed by fortune and by God, that men cannot correct them with their prudence'.[3] The way to exercise one's prudence was to act out flexible responses to changing situations, and not cling to absolute and rigid norms of conduct.

Telling the story of a man's life with these considerations in mind would require far greater complexity, and far less rigidity, since it would have to accommodate his own initiatives, all the measures and countermeasures which someone takes against Fortune's dealings. Only then could he be judged prudent or imprudent.

Montaigne, too, asserts that we should not attempt to find excuses in external determinants such as Fortune for things turning out badly for us. 'Our good, and our evill hath no dependancy, but from our selves. Let us offer our vowes and offerings unto it; and not to fortune. She hath no power over our manners.'[4] Francis Bacon, in his essay 'Of Fortune', also argues in favour of man's ability to control his own fortune: 'It cannot be denied, but Outward Accidents, conduce much to *Fortune*: Favour, Opportunitie . . . But chiefly, the Mould of a Mans *Fortune*, is in his owne hands. *Faber quisque Fortunae suae*; saith the Poet.' And he goes so far as to claim that 'the Exercised *Fortune* maketh the Able Man'.[5]

This concept of Fortune, which does not completely rule out Fortune's power over man's life, but expresses confidence in man's ability to meet adversities and at least partly shape his own fortune, is 'new' when compared with the medieval concept which makes man acquiesce far more in what Fortune has in store for him. In an article on the impact of the Christian idea of Providence, disseminated by Boethius's *De Consolatione Philosophiae*, upon the concept of Fortune, F. P. Pickering observes that 'there was some notable advance from *simple* medieval ideas towards a final sophistication in the Renaissance'.[6] The driving force in this development is a growing determination to

---

[1] Kiefer, 'The conflation of Fortuna and Occasio in Renaissance thought and iconography', *Journal of Medieval and Renaissance Studies* 9 (1979), 1–27.

[2] *Ibid.*, pp. 3–5.

[3] Machiavelli, *The Prince*, trans. H. C. Mansfield, 1985, p. 98.

[4] Montaigne, *Essays*, 1.50 ('Of Democritus and Heraclitus'), trans. John Florio, ed. G. Saintsbury, 3 vols., 1892–3, I, 349 f.

[5] Francis Bacon, *The Essayes or Counsels, Civill and Morall*, ed. Michael Kiernan, 1985. The author of 'Each man is maker of his own fortune' is either Plautus (see *ibid.*, p. 264) or Sallust (see Harry Levin, *Christopher Marlowe: The Overreacher*, 1961, p. 206).

[6] Pickering, *Literature and Art in the Middle Ages*, 1970, pp. 182–91, p. 185.

diminish the idea of Fortune's power and authority. 'The old tag that a man may "fashion" his own fortune (as *faber fortunae suae*) becomes an influential philosophy. This is, in a way, a return to the classical conception of Fortune . . .'[1] Juvenal's Satire X gives a striking example: 'Thou wouldst have no divinity, O Fortune, if we had but wisdom; it is we that make a goddess of thee, and place thee in the skies.'[2]

These changes in the conception of Fortune's power have repercussions on Elizabethan and Jacobean drama. The focus shifts away from Fortune's dominance and man's submission and stresses instead man's ingenuity and scope in creating his own identity and shaping his own life. The dramatic hero negotiates new relationships to society and to metaphysics. In turn new and different responses are prompted from audiences and readers. There is a wide range of alternatives in the approach and interpretation of a text: to assume that Fortune has a governing power over men's lives will lead to a corresponding view of the text's cohesion, thereby reducing the significance of other features of the dramatic action. The dramatic function of the Poet might be – has been – taken as a guide to interpreting the whole dramatic action. The Poet certainly does impart a schematised picture of the course of man's life, modelled after the rise-and-fall pattern of medieval tradition. The Poet's message, also, is that his poem should be understood as a warning. This didactic impact is corroborated by the Painter's reaction: 'A thousand moral paintings I can show, / That shall demonstrate these quick blows of Fortune's' (1.1.93–4). Yet as we have seen, the original Jacobean audience had an alternative idea, in which man had freedom to choose, and from this point of view the Poet must appear rigidly dogmatic and old-fashioned. It is therefore rather surprising that the Poet has so frequently been accepted by critics as making sense of Timon's career. His 'moral' poem, corroborated by the Painter's 'thousand moral paintings', provides easily applicable terms, and there are copious examples of critics reading the Poet's concept of Fortune as a straightforward guide. Maurice Charney understands the Poet's speech on Fortune as 'the central fable of the play',[3] and, correspondingly, he reads the whole play as a 'dramatic fable like an allegory or morality play, the structure of which is schematic'.[4] Kenneth Muir, writing 'In defence of Timon's Poet', maintains that the 'rough work' that the Poet has composed 'consists of an allegory of Fortune, designed, apparently, to warn Timon . . . The Poet . . . presents the moral of Shakespeare's play.'[5] Other critics writing in this vein simplify character and action so that they fit into a schematised concept denying the possibility of self-determination to characters: 'many of the play's peculiarities result from Shakespeare's attempt to demonstrate the operations of the goddess through dramatic action . . .';[6] '[t]he emphasis is not on what Timon does or has done, but rather on what Fortune does to him and what she causes to be done by others . . .'[7]

---

[1] *Ibid.*

[2] 11.365–6, in *Juvenal and Persius*, trans. G. G. Ramsay, Loeb Classical Library, 1918.

[3] Charney, p. 136.

[4] *Ibid.*, p. 136.

[5] Muir, 'In defence of Timon's Poet', *EC* 3 (1953), p. 121.

[6] Lewis Walker, 'Fortune and friendship in *Timon of Athens*', *Texas Studies in Literature and Language* 18 (1976), p. 577.

[7] *Ibid.*, p. 578.

Interpersonal relations, such as Timon's relations with his so-called friends, are also seen as determined by Fortune: 'Shakespeare is showing how Fortune affects relationships between human beings by presenting a thorough perversion of the ideal of true friendship.'[1]

A modern recasting of this rigid view of Fortune and her role in the play by Kahn and Adelman emerges in readings that explore the psychological dimension of her impact.[2] In these readings, Fortune's traditional role of shaping human destinies is seen as infused with the notion of Fortune as a mother-figure, with a mother's nurturing capacities. The conventional qualities of the medieval Fortune are retained in the mother's dual role of both dispensing bounty and practising betrayal. From this vantage point, the Poet's account of Fortune's residence on a 'high and pleasant hill' (1.1.66), with all kinds of people thronging to catch her attention, turns into the notion of a female body, which 'all kind of natures . . . labour on' (68–9) to get their share of nurture.[3] Lord Timon, as Fortune's elect, at first takes on the role of a child '[t]o climb his happiness' (79) and is thus portrayed as being completely dependent on Fortune/ mother.[4] In the Poet's account, this phase of Timon's dependence is followed by one in which he deals out favours to other people; that is, he has created for himself the image that he most enjoys: that of Fortune/mother dealing out favours and nurturing others. This deep-structure reading sees Timon casting himself in the role of a nurturing mother as a way of becoming independent of Fortune's unreliable and treacherous dealings, even going so far as to excise all signs of women's presence and of female nurture.[5] As the Poet's fable shows, however, this attempt to overturn Fortune's female domination ends in disaster: Fortune's elect is spurned (87–8), but this means that Timon fails to play the role of a nurturing and all-sustaining mother.

These psychoanalytical readings are in their own way deterministic, structurally similar both to the medieval concept of Fortune having power over men's lives and to the critical assumption that the Poet's fable provides the key to Timon's history. In his attempt to usurp the mother's nurturing role, Timon is just as doomed as any of Fortune's elect. Viewed within these modern parameters, the history of Timon closely resembles the conventional rise-and-fall pattern and still lends itself to being read as a cautionary tale. An altogether different view of both the Poet's and the Painter's frame of reference is given by David Bevington. According to him, 'both Painter and Poet take as their most axiomatic assumption the ability of art to communicate through fixed correspondences connecting signifier and thing signified. This correlation depends on readily understood truisms about human behavior.'[6] What results is 'that their fine neoplatonic truisms have encouraged the Painter and Poet to bring forth works that are hollow ceremonial forms. Their ability to achieve a "pretty mocking of the life" (1.1.36) takes on a double meaning, of imitation and of travesty.'[7] In short,

---

[1] *Ibid.*, p. 598.
[2] See Kahn, *passim*; Adelman, ch. 7.
[3] Kahn, pp. 36–7, and Adelman, pp. 167–8.
[4] See Kahn, p. 37.
[5] Adelman, pp. 166–8.
[6] Bevington, p. 28.
[7] *Ibid.*, pp. 28–9.

their generalised and simplified interpretations of life cast in the form of allegorical frames cannot be taken as a guideline for an audience's reaction. Bevington points out that '[w]hen Shakespeare most wishes to criticize the myth of correspondences, he chooses allegory as the kind of art most given to complacent generalities'.[1]

MONEY/GOLD

The play gives special emphasis to wealth in the form of money/gold and the language is full of allusions to commerce, cash and finance, but nowhere is this done in the explicit manner of Marlowe's *Jew of Malta* or Jonson's *Volpone*.

In *The Jew of Malta*, Barabas is introduced to us counting his gold and expatiating on the ethical implications of his amassing of riches: 'And thus methinks should men of judgment frame / Their means of traffic from the vulgar trade, / And, as their wealth increaseth, so inclose / Infinite riches in a little room' (1.1.34–7).[2] Volpone holds forth in a similarly declamatory fashion on his veneration of gold and wealth – 'Thou art virtue, fame, / Honour and all things else! Who can get thee, / He shall be noble, valiant, honest, wise' (1.1.25–7)[3] – which, by way of inversion, has much in common with Timon's curses on gold. The Merchant praises Timon's moral eminence (1.1.10–12), using expressions like 'goodness' and 'He passes', which, however, simultaneously signal solvency and credit-worthiness.[4] The same applies to the Poet when he speaks of 'minds' who 'tender down / Their services' (1.1.54–7), and to the Old Athenian using 'thrift' in its double sense (1.1.122) and sealing his deal with Timon, about giving away his daughter, by asking for Timon's honour as a 'pawn' (1.1.151). Alcibiades when defending his case in the Athenian senate is ready to 'pawn [his] victories, all [his] honour' to the Senators (3.5.82).[5] The Senators are particularly infected with these habits of language, as can be seen in 5.1.133–45, when one of their ambassadors speaks to Timon of 'their sorrowed render', and uses terms like 'recompense', 'weigh', 'dram', 'heaps and sums of love and wealth'. Even this group of characters who give the impression of being non-calculating are in fact deeply immersed in such language. Examples of this are Flavius's complaint about Timon's reckless generosity (1.2.180–92; in particular 187), and Timon's assurances to the flattering Lords: 'I weigh my friends' affection with mine own' (1.2.204).

The only character in the play who takes issue with these superficially harmless and inoffensive turns of speech is Apemantus. He reveals, at least in linguistic terms, what he regards as the state of this society governed by cupidity, veiling avarice behind a mask of courteously correct behaviour.

Our perception of Apemantus as diagnosing the darker sides of the rituals and linguistic courtesies is at its strongest in 1.1 and 1.2 when he disturbs the smooth

[1] *Ibid.*, p. 29.
[2] Christopher Marlowe, *The Complete Plays*, ed. J. B. Steane, 1969.
[3] Ben Jonson, *Volpone*, ed. Philip Brockbank, 1968.
[4] 'A most incomparable man, breathed, as it were, / To an untirable and continuate goodness; / He passes.' For a detailed account of the ambiguities see the Commentary.
[5] See 3.5.81 and 83 nn.

linguistic surface of his various interlocutors, saying to the Merchant 'Traffic's thy god, and thy god confound thee' (1.1.239); commenting on the lords present at the reception 'to see meat fill knaves, and wine heat fools' (1.1.261); and generally on Timon himself throughout 1.1 and 1.2.

Given the structural importance of the money/gold theme in the rituals and language of Timon's society, one might assume that in it human and personal values are not only obstructed in their growth, but infected at their very roots. As early as the beginning of the sixteenth century this issue was raised by Thomas More in his *Utopia* (1516), when he made Hythloday expatiate on the social effects of valuing gold more highly than human qualities: 'They [i.e. the Utopians] wonder, too, that gold, which by its very nature is so useless, is now everywhere in the world valued so highly that man himself, through whose agency and for whose use it got this value, is priced much cheaper than gold itself. This is true to such an extent that a blockhead who has no more intelligence than a log and who is as dishonest as he is foolish keeps in bondage many wise men and good men merely for the reason that a great heap of gold coins happens to be his.'[1] Almost a century and a half later, Thomas Hobbes analysed human value or worth in terms of how these qualities can be seen functioning in response to patterns of interest at work in society: 'The *value* or WORTH of a man is as of all other things, his price; that is to say, so much as would be given for the use of his power: and therefore is not absolute; but a thing dependent on the need and judgement of another . . . The manifestation of the value we set on one another, is that which is commonly called honouring, and dishonouring. To value a man at a high rate, is to *honour* him.'[2] Thus, human qualities like personal worth or honour are not seen as having an intrinsic value, but, like money or gold, their estimation is a matter of pure expediency.[3]

Apart from Apemantus's caustic remarks, there is no other character who reveals a clear awareness of the power factor that resides in the possession of riches ('Riches, are honourable; for they are power'),[4] nor of the manipulative implications in the rituals of bestowing gifts. 'To give great gifts to a man, is to honour him; because it is buying of protection, and acknowledging of power . . . Magnanimity, liberality . . . are honourable; for they proceed from the conscience of power.'[5] Flavius, for all his criticism of his master's liberal spending, is not aware of the human damage caused by Timon's way of being sociable. He is only concerned about Timon's imminent bankruptcy.

It is only with Timon's diatribes against Athenian society in the second part of the play that the perverting influence of gold and money on society is brought into the

[1] Thomas More, *Utopia*, in *The Complete Works of Thomas More*, ed. E. Surtz and J. H. Hexter, IV, 1965, p. 157. Hibbard ('Sequestration') exposes the damage that money was supposed to be doing to a commonwealth by quoting another passage from More's *Utopia*: 'where moneye beareth all the stroke, it is hard and almoste impossyble that there the weale publyque may iusteloye be gouerned and prosperouslye floryshe' (p. 217).

[2] Thomas Hobbes, *Leviathan*, ed. M. Oakeshott, nd, p. 57. See also Ulysses' manipulative way of arguing in *Troilus and Cressida* 3.3.95–102 and 115–23.

[3] A striking example is the discussion between Timon and the Jeweller about the value of the jewel in 1.1.168–77.

[4] Hobbes, *Leviathan*, p. 59.

[5] *Ibid.*, pp. 58, 59.

open. Timon is the principal spokesman for these ideas. He speaks in high anger. But however emotionally overstated in manner it may be, it remains valid in matter – indeed, his anger actually functions positively, enabling him to focus on the disarray in Athenian society to which he had previously been blind. There are two passages in 4.3 in which his indictments of gold and its uses in society are concentrated. In the first passage (26–45) he places emphasis on the transforming power of gold, turning negative qualities like 'black', 'foul', 'wrong', 'base', 'old' into what seem to be their positive counterparts (29–30). Ethical values supposedly fixed and ideal are exposed as actually contingent on the fluctuations of material interest.

The second passage (377–88) like the first focuses on the disruptive effects that gold and the desire for gold can have. The examples given of gold's disruptive energies culminate in the vision of human society being transformed into an empire of beasts (387–8).

Karl Marx quoted Timon's speeches, using them (together with a passage from Goethe's *Faust*)[1] as show-cases for his notions of the alienating effects of gold and money in early capitalist societies.[2] He asserts that in this play's money-dominated society, as in all societies of this type, there is a disjunction between what an individual is capable of doing by virtue of his own personality, and what he can achieve through the power of money:

That which is for me through the medium of *money* – that for which I can pay (i.e. which money can buy) – that am *I myself*, the possessor of the money. The extent of the power of money is the extent of my power. Money's properties are my – the possessor's – properties and essential power. Thus, what I *am* and *am capable of* is by no means determined by my individuality . . . Does not my money, therefore, transform all my incapacities into their contrary?[3]

And in a different context, Marx focuses on the same idea: 'How little connection there is between money, the most general form of property, and personal peculiarity, how much they are directly opposed to each other was already known to Shakespeare.'[4]

Marx sums up by asserting that 'Money is the alienated *ability of mankind*.'[5] One might say that money's power is both alienated and alienating: what human beings can accomplish through the power of money is alienated from their personal capabilities and characteristics. By the same token, money has self-alienating effects on those who utilise its power as a substitute for their personal faculties.

'Shakespeare', Marx maintains, 'stresses especially two properties of money: it is the visible divinity – the transformation of all human and natural properties into their

[1] Mephistopheles argues that whatever money can buy adds to its owner's personal capabilities. 'Six stallions, say, I can afford, / Is not their strength my property? / I tear along, a sporting lord, / As if their legs belonged to me' (J. W. v. Goethe, *Faust* I, iii, trans. Philip Wayne, 1949, p. 91).

[2] Marx's comments on the money/gold complex in the play have been widely discussed by, amongst others, Kenneth Muir, '*Timon of Athens* and the cash-nexus', *Modern Quarterly Miscellany* I (1947), 67–76 (repr. in K. Muir, *The Singularity of Shakespeare and Other Essays*, 1977, pp. 56–75); Lerner, pp. 106–22; Berry, ch. 7; and Brockbank, ch. 1.

[3] Marx, *Economic and Philosophic Manuscripts of 1844*, in *Collected Works*, 1976, III, 324.

[4] Marx, *The German Ideology*, in *Collected Works*, V, 230. This is followed up by quotations from the two passages mentioned above.

[5] Marx, *Economic and Philosophic Manuscripts*, p. 325.

contraries, the universal confounding and distorting of things.'[1] In Timon's speeches, gold is addressed as the 'visible god' (4.3.382), and its divine power is realised in several acts of perversion which suggest that its divinity is itself of a perverted nature. Thus it is addressed as a 'king-killer', but a 'sweet' one (377); it brings about a 'divorce / 'Twixt natural son and sire', but this divorce is 'dear' (377–8); it is a 'defiler / Of Hymen's purest bed', but a 'bright' one (378–9). This listing of acts of perversion finally leads to the climax 'that beasts / May have the world in empire' (387–8). Marx's idea that money has an enormous potential for perverting people's realisation of their social selves provides a criterion for assessing the social structures of this 'moneyed city'.[2] Money's distorting influence on the fabric of the social interactions of characters becomes apparent all through Act 1. Not that they themselves appear in their words or actions to be aware of these perversions; rather, their self-knowledge does not extend beyond what they see as opportune for furthering their moneyed existence. So, whilst the Poet's remarks in 1.1.57–60 may be intended by him to extol Lord Timon's superior status, the nature of this relationship is evidently alienated: 'His large fortune, / . . . Subdues and properties to his love and tendance / All sorts of hearts . . .' The Lords' comments on their host's generosity in 1.1.276–81 may be not quite as portentous as the Poet's utterance, since they may be thought to be informed by a shot of cynical awareness: 'no meed but he repays / Sevenfold above itself; no gift to him / But breeds the giver a return exceeding / All use of quittance'. This is then topped by the remark of First Lord, whose designation of Timon's mind as 'noble' may be as sincere as it is unconsciously revealing:[3] 'The noblest mind he carries / That ever governed man.' The implicit cynicism becomes blatantly explicit in the behaviour of the three Lords in 3.1–3.3, whom Timon approaches for a loan.[4]

It is not only Timon's entourage who induce this atmosphere of alienation; he himself is most active in generating it. Shakespeare orchestrates Timon's first entrance in 1.1, preceding it by the attention-focusing remarks of his expectant guests. Timon's gracious public manner gives the impression that what matters most is belonging to this elect group, seeing and being seen on occasions like this. Shakespeare's emphasis is on the requests for money the guests make to Timon – for instance, by the messenger of Ventidius and, more indirectly, in the complaints of the Old Athenian. The Jeweller hopes to find in Timon a financially reliable customer; the Poet and the Painter hope that he will be a liberal patron of the arts. All, including the Lords with their obsessions about gifts, fix their attention on Timon as a magnate and a social tycoon, not as an individual. They address his alienated self, alienated from his individual personality. Timon himself does everything to present his alienated self to them, calling this friendship. Paradoxically, in his speech on friendship (1.2.81–96) he formulates an image of his guests that suits his own needs: 'I have told more of you to myself than you can with modesty speak in your own behalf' (84–5); that is, he produces a stylised picture of what he considers friends should be; in this picture,

---

[1] *Ibid.*, p. 324.
[2] The phrase is Brockbank's, p. 12.
[3] *Ibid.*
[4] See Brockbank's interpretation of Sempronius's cultivation of hypocrisy (*ibid.*).

there is no understanding of the 'otherness' of a friend, nor is there any positive recognition of a friend's idiosyncrasies; rather it tends to make the other subject to Timon's 'needs'.

The second point that Marx makes in his comments on Timon concerns the condition of general venality and prostitution which is consequent on money being the 'alienated ability of mankind'. In a marginal note on *Timon* 4.3.26–33, he calls gold 'the universal agent of corruption and prostitution'.[1] In the *Preparatory Materials* to *Capital*, he quotes the same passage after having analysed the nature of money and its impact on man's potential: 'Money, as purely abstract wealth – in which every specific use value is extinguished, and hence also every individual relation between possessor and commodity – comes under the power of the individual likewise as an abstract person, relating to his individuality as totally alien and extraneous. At the same time, it gives him universal power as his private power . . .' And after the *Timon* quotation 4.3.26–33 he concludes: 'That which yields itself to all, and for which all is yielded, appears as the universal means of corruption and prostitution.'[2] Shakespeare in *Timon*, however, gives prominence to the sexual aspects of prostitution, whereas Marx does not. In Marx prostitution is placed in the wider context in which almost everything, women included, can be procured by the power of money. Timon denounces gold's perverting power comprehensively but he reserves special venom for prostitution and women's debauched sexuality, which, he says, spread all kinds of disease, disorder and disruption.[3] In 4.3.43, Timon addresses gold as 'Thou common whore of mankind'. For him gold represents the personification of a prostituted self, alienated in its doings from private incentives and subjected to other-directed interests. It is a self that does not even have a language of its own, 'that speak'st with every tongue / To every purpose' (4.3.384–5). This is what Timon's friends have been doing all along, throughout their 'better days' (4.2.27). Although they spoke of and to Timon in language full of admiration, veneration and gratitude, they were concerned with setting up a flattering glass. Timon, for his part, was as hungry for praise as his friends were eager to dispense it. What Phrynia and Timandra say very bluntly – 'Believe't that we'll do anything for gold' (4.3.151) – Timon's friends prefer to disguise under polite forms of discourse, but with a comparable attitude of complaisance and venality.[4] There is no difference in kind between prostituting acts in the service of friendship and those in the service of whoring.

---

[1] In his *Outlines of the Critique of Political Economy* (1857–8), Marx argues: 'The exchangeability of all products, activities, relationships for a third, *objective* entity, which in turn can be exchanged for everything *without distinction* – in other words, the development of exchange values (and of monetary relationships) is identical with general venality, with corruption. General prostitution appears as a necessary phase in the development of the social character of personal inclinations, capacities, abilities, activities.'

[2] Marx, *Collected Works*, XXIX, 451–2.

[3] 4.3.38–42, 4.3.84–6, 4.3.152–67. An act of prostitution occurs only in the verbal exchanges between Timon and Phrynia and Timandra, in the sense of demanding and complying with venal services; 4.3.49–177, in particular 134, with Phrynia and Timandra imploring him 'Give us some gold, good Timon; hast thou more?'; 150–1: 'Well, more gold! What then? / Believe't that we'll do anything for gold' and 168: 'More counsel with more money, bounteous Timon'.

[4] It would be worthwhile considering playing the role of Timon's friends as if they were saying: 'We'll do anything for gold.'

Shakespeare's dramaturgy in *Timon* exhibits alienation in many ways, and characterisation in particular seems comparatively schematic and flat even when set beside that other great study in alienation, composed in the same phase of Shakespeare's career, *Coriolanus*. This issue of characterisation has been a subject of debate among the critics. In a recent study A. D. Nuttall argues that the opening scene sets a style, Shakespeare creating characters that offer resistance 'to the more ordinary modes of imaginative sympathy'. 'The Poet and the Painter in the opening scene of *Timon* begin to take on a distinctively inhuman concreteness . . . They are not so much talking persons as walking texts, speaking pictures . . .'[1]

Nuttall considers this to be a mode of representation in which emphasis is placed on 'the pictorial character of figures', an example of what he calls 'Renaissance alienation'.[2] The characters represented in this play, Timon himself included, seem to be modelled not so as to mirror life directly, but to mirror life that has already been transformed into art. Nuttall uses the term 'ecphrastic' to describe their condition – an 'ecphrasis' being a poem which describes a work of art. What prevails in this play, he writes, is 'an ecphrastic atmosphere, in which (especially with Timon himself) we are uncertain whether we are looking at a man or at a simplified picture of a man'.[3] And he further qualifies the ecphrastic image of Timon by saying that it 'never brightens into life and colour. Instead, the seemingly living protagonist dies into the two-dimensional world of incised letters.' Nuttall gives a 'catalogue of things *not* done in this play'. 'Timon's period of liberality is unenlivened by any distinct relation of human love . . . his sojourn in the wilderness is never fired by any positive affection of a higher order . . . Timon finds in his seclusion no divine lover . . . we are given, not a Jacob wrestling with the Angel, but a vanishing figure, lost in water and air, forming at the last not substance but words.'[4] This might have been a different and more sympathetic play, but would it be Shakespeare's play as it stands?

Nuttall's 'alienation' is mainly an aesthetic term, and is here used to identify and explain shortcomings in the dramatic rendering of characters in *Timon*. There are, however, wider ranges of meaning for 'alienation', and Arnold Hauser gives a detailed account of this term used by Hegel, Marx and Freud;[5] it marks for him 'the crisis of the Renaissance'. Starting from Marx's notion that money has acquired the power of reducing values to an impersonal common denominator, thereby introducing dehumanising factors into man's social life, Hauser considers what art could and should achieve under such conditions:

Mannerism is not so much a symptom and product of alienation . . . as an expression of the unrest, anxiety, and bewilderment generated by the process of alienation of the individual from society and the reification of the whole cultural process.[6]

When an artist sets out to represent a state of 'alienation', to what extent will his mode of representation itself take on characteristics of alienation? How far can he distance

---

[1] Nuttall, p. 16.
[2] *Ibid.*
[3] *Ibid.*, p. 139.
[4] *Ibid.*, pp. 140–1.
[5] Hauser, p. 95.
[6] *Ibid.*, p. 111.

himself from such features and represent 'alienation' as 'raw material', as something to be observed from a critical distance?[1]

Doubts have been raised about Marx's alienation concept, as far as its explanatory function for the individual and social conditions in *Timon* is concerned. Ralph Berry contends that Marx's model of the alienating power of money can be stood on its head, since money could just as well be viewed as 'the social bond that unites a community'.[2] As proof, he puts forward Timon's situation – in his period of wealth he was linked to society by money, whereas in his poverty he was not. But if 'alienation' means that the conditions found in a society tend to move the scope of personal action from individual motivation to self-alienated substitutes, then Timon in his period of wealth was living in an alienated form of society.

Laurence Lerner takes issue with Marx's contention that the gold passages in *Timon* can be applied to illustrate his theory of the power of money in a bourgeois society and that 'Shakespeare . . . excellently depicts the real nature of money.'[3] He argues instead 'that for Shakespeare money is not the mechanism that keeps society functioning, it is what causes malfunctioning . . . What we have in Shakespeare is a pure version of the moral view of money.'[4]

It is worth pursuing this question of whether Shakespeare had in mind a moral or a systemic view of the impact of money. There are two lines of approach: to consider what the characters are themselves aware of – that is, what they themselves mean when using words and doing things (this is the representational model of understanding), and to assess the play on the evidence of what determines behaviour but may be considered outside the range of the characters' awareness in historical, political or psychological terms. There is no firm demarcation between the two. In the first or ceremonial part of the play, gold or money makes up an essential component of Timon's life, and he regards money as if it were limitlessly available. Timon is certainly adept at this kind of life and at attracting and entertaining his social circle, but he does not show any critical awareness, he does not question the conditions of his lifestyle, and his repeated refusals even to listen to his Steward show how little he can be bothered with such things. The audience is prompted by Shakespeare to an awareness, in the first part of the play, of the social implications of human riches, in the form of the moralising account of the Poet's fable. But he does not refer it to the reality of Timon's circle, nor does Timon show any signs of ever having read the Poet's work. Ironically, the Poet conducts himself in complete conformity with the social conventions Timon and his guests abide by – the guests making obeisance to Timon and offering him presents and gifts, and Timon generously playing the role of host by providing entertainment and liberally dispensing gifts and money. The gift-giving and courtesy-exchanging ritual in 1.2.145–222 is a poignant example. What gives it its mechanical impact is the rapid succession of incidents, with Timon either at the giving or the receiving end, allowing no time for reflection on personal matters. It culminates

---

[1] Similar questions have been raised with regard to Samuel Beckett and whether or not his representations of *ennui* necessarily take on its features.
[2] Berry, p. 111.
[3] Lerner, p. 121.
[4] *Ibid.*, pp. 121–2.

in an exchange of half-completed thank you formulas (216–22), some of them delivered as short lines giving the impression of swelling, hectic agitation. Looked at from Marx's and Hauser's vantage points, what they are all doing, without being aware of it, is fetishising material objects and presents, money included – that is, endowing these with the qualities of a personal attachment, of friendship or affection. Thus, exchanging these material objects takes the place of developing genuine human sentiments; the mechanical character of their exchange shows how far this has turned into a substitute for personal relationships. That Shakespeare presents these episodes in a deliberately critical spirit is confirmed by the role he assigns Apemantus, the only character who does not conform.

Apemantus consciously perceives himself, or his role, to be different from all the rest; rather than be bound to the social norms of Timon's circle, he prefers to be an outcast (1.2.25). He seems to need this distance since he is determined to observe (1.2.34) what is going on around him, where all the gestures of conviviality which are proper to social decorum are at variance with people's real feelings, so that what starts off as an expression of personal affection may all of a sudden turn into its opposite (1.2.130–1). This is, ironically, what was shown in the Poet's fable, but Apemantus exposes Timon's guests as false flatterers. He also declares he will not be 'bribed' (1.2.230) by Timon, implying that Timon's circle of servile flatterers are created and encouraged by Timon himself. It is a moral and not a systemic diagnosis that Apemantus offers: if only people in general could change their conduct – Timon's guests their ridiculous flattery and Timon his coaxing them into it – (and there is no cogent reason why they could not) then all would be well.

Whereas Shakespeare's dramatic presentation offers systemic as well as moral criticism, the characters' perception of their own situation shows no such systemic awareness later in the play: when Timon finally listens to his Steward and realises the seriousness of his financial situation, he says 'Unwisely, not ignobly, have I given' (2.2.168); and 'No villainous bounty yet hath passed my heart' (167). He attempts self-exoneration on moral grounds, and acts as if his venial mistakes can be reversed simply by upholding the moral principle of friendship and relying on others to do the same.

With extraordinary rapidity Timon's former 'friends' perceive the shift in his fortunes, and just as rapidly they draw their own conclusions. Their elaborate regrets at not being able to help Timon out seem to show that they are well aware of how to play this game, in both its phases: in the first phase, by trading material goods with Timon, as substitutes for affection; in the second phase (however much they pretend otherwise), by stripping money of its alleged qualities of affection, de-fetishising it and dealing with it in its economic aspect. Their conduct is alienated from any feeling of personal allegiance, any concern for sustaining continuity in personal relations. Timon's former friends have an attitude to money which not only allows, but demands abrupt change according to circumstances.

To an alert spectator this highlights the underlying system governing Timon's world. When staging the mock banquet, Timon ironically works with the same principles of alienated conduct. He whets his guests' appetites only to plunge them into acute frustration. The system is the same as in Act 1; Timon can simply reverse it, employ it strategically to expose what he has learnt of their attitudes: what is not clear is whether Timon's understanding is only moral, or whether he grasps the fuller structural implications of a moneyed society.

When he takes on the role of a radical misanthrope, Timon utilises his newly found gold similarly to further the self-destructive tendencies of his society (4.3.28–45)[1] and to help finance Alcibiades' campaign against Athens. Now Timon has learnt how to employ the system of alienated values to punish those whom he previously chose as arbitrary favourites. The question arises of whether he is by now aware of his own involvement in this system: he can see well enough its perverting effects on others, but does he recognise his own complicity? One might conclude that Shakespeare's concern is to show Timon caught between two levels of awareness; one reinforces his stance of moral censor, the other a systemic view of society in which human relations are subject to alienating conditions.

Increasingly, Timon's mind becomes preoccupied by the second one. His desire to blame his situation on others (which is in part a sick desire for self-defence and self-pity, in part a sound desire to close himself off from a sick environment) decreases, while at the same time existence itself, his own and that of others, becomes hateful to him. There is no way out, either through the salvation of individual love (as in *King Lear*) or through finding a viable mode of living (this is as inconceivable as in the plays of Beckett).

This is a bleak picture – a publicly respected and admired man turning into a relentlessly determined misanthrope, great human energies turning self-destructive – so that Shakespeare's tragedy of *Timon of Athens* may be found nihilistic to its depths, incapable of offering any life-affirmation. Yet such an interpretation needs to take account of the critical impetus in the play's design, its generic affinity to Juvenalian satire and its Jacobean dramatic context of experiments in generic hybridisation by Shakespeare and his contemporaries Jonson, Middleton, Marston and Webster. And the mode of satire would be restrictive. In a satiric play the dramatist's creativity is necessarily restricted by comparison with heroic tragedy. The central character, and the play, will be constituted differently, restricted by the alienated structures of the society he lives in and turns away from. Nevertheless Timon, after having turned misanthrope, is the only character in the play who attains an awareness of the profound rottenness of Athenian society; he is also the only one who during this phase rejects the old game of substituting material values for human affections; nor, being different from the rest, does he use his gold for purposes of personal enrichment.[2] He adopts a stance of repulsion, but his force is undeniable.

USURY

Judging by the listing of 'The Actors Names', which is attached to the printing of *Timon* in F, there are more usurers in this play than in any other by Shakespeare. However, most of them do not appear in person, but achieve their dramatic impact

---

[1] Nowottny calls it 'substituting the myth of Prostitution for the myth of Order' (p. 496).
[2] This is what Apemantus thinks would be the proper way for Timon to conduct himself (4.3.212–20 and 248–9). Lucian actually has Timon use his treasure only for himself.

through their servants 'Caphis, Varro, Philotus, Titus, Lucius and Hortensius', and we must add Isidore. Of the creditors themselves only one, a Senator, has a brief appearance in 2.1, when he charges his servant to urge Timon to repay his loans. The same is done by the other, anonymous, 'usurers', whose servants in 2.2 and 3.4 press Timon to have their masters' bonds cashed.

According to *OED* the term 'usurer' means 'One who practises usury or lends money at interest', with the addition 'esp. in later use one who charges an excessive rate of interest'. However, during the latter half of the sixteenth century and the beginning of the seventeenth, the delimitation of 'usury' and 'interest' was fuzzy, owing to conflicting opinions concerning the moral and economic legitimacy of the practice of usury. In the pamphlet literature of the time,[1] money-lending with the aim of gaining interest was denounced as usurious, i.e. as damnable on religious and moral grounds.[2] In his pamphlet *A Discourse Upon Usury* (1572) Thomas Wilson has one of the partners in the dialogue, the 'Advocate' or 'Civilian', set up a rigorous distinction between usury and interest:

> to shewe . . . the difference betwixt interest and usurie . . . you muste understande, that usurie is onely given for the onelye benefite of lendynge for time, whereas interest is demaunded when I have susteyned losse through an other mans cause, and therefore *interest mea*, that is to saye, it behoveth me, or it belongeth to mee, or it is for mine avail, or it is reason, that I bee aunswered all losses and dammages that I have susteyned thoroughe an other mans cause, aswell for the gayne that els I myghte have had by my moneye, if touche had beene kepte, as for the losses susteyned thoroughe an other mans faulte, that hathe not paide mee myne owne in due tyme . . . And the name of interest is laweful, as the whyche seketh onelye equalytye: whereas the name of usurye is odyous, ungodly, and wycked, as that whych seeketh al inequalitie . . .[3]

If the economic needs of society are taken more fully into account, the need for capital and loans for purposes of economic growth becomes immediately obvious. The various statutes that were passed in the period from 1545 to 1571 mirror in their different orientations the confusion of attitudes to credit facilities. In his introduction to Wilson's pamphlet, Tawney has detailed these legislative attempts of 1545, 1552 and 1571.[4] In the Act of 1571 the rigorous condemnation of usury as a crime, as it had been set down in the Act of 1552, was supplanted by a more pragmatic set of regulations, thus making allowance for economic demands and necessities, and also for the subsistence problems of the nobility.[5] As to the legitimacy of taking interest, the statute of 1571 set down that

---

[1] John W. Draper ('The theme of *Timon of Athens*,' *MLR* 29 (1934), 20–31, here pp. 25–6) lists Thomas Lodge, *An Alarum Against Usurers* (1584); Thomas Dekker, *English Villanies* (1651); Thomas Powell, *The Art of Thriving. Or, The plaine path-way to Preferment* (1635–6); Thomas Acheley, *The Massacre of Money* (1602); Philip Caesar, *A General Discourse Against the Damnable Sect of Usurers* (1578). To these should be added: George Whetstone, *The Enemie to Unthryftinesse* (1586), and Roger Fenton, *A Treatise of Usurie* (1612).

[2] See *The Merchant of Venice*, ed. M. M. Mahood, 1987, pp. 20–1. Mahood refers to Luke 6.35 ('Lend, looking for nothing again') as well as to Aristotle's idea 'that to make money breed was against the course of nature'. Francis Bacon expresses the same idea 'That it is against nature for money to beget money' (*Essays*, no. 41).

[3] Thomas Wilson, *A Discourse Upon Usury*, ed. R. H. Tawney, repr. 1962, p. 319.

[4] Tawney, pp. 155 ff.

[5] For an account of the scale of borrowing and its financial consequences see Lawrence Stone, *The Crisis of the Aristocracy 1558–1641*, repr. with corr. 1979, pp. 538–46.

interest must not exceed ten per cent.[1] Thus, provision was made to set up a distinction between 'interest' (legal) and 'usury' (illegal, and immoral into the bargain), but on different grounds from those provided for by merely moral and religious arguments; the borderline was shifted towards an economically viable solution – one that makes allowance for urgent public demands for capital and legally sanctions a rate of interest that could give money-owners sufficient incentive to lend out capital.

A similar line was taken by Francis Bacon in his essay 'Of Usury'.[2] He balances the 'incommodities' and 'commodities' of lending out money; since 'to speak of the abolishing of usury is idle', he favours a regulated system of lending, thus removing it from arbitrary speculation.

The popular opinion of money-lenders and their practices was, however, governed by irrational fears and prejudices rather than by economic considerations. Elizabethan playwrights accordingly developed the usurer-figure into a vicious and odious stereotype.[3] One of the reasons why he grew to become such a loathsome character was that, at the time, the terms 'usurer' and 'usury' had much broader connotations than today's sense of excessive interest on a loan of money. 'Any unpopular character', R. H. Tawney maintains, 'might be called by the average man a usurer, and any bargain from which one party obviously gained more advantage than the other . . . was regarded as usurious.'[4] Taken in this broad sense, money-lending for interest is only the most conspicuous amongst other practices of taking advantage of someone else for personal gain. Since such practices can easily be extended to forms of social bonding, such as flattery and the dissembling of friendship, Thomas Acheley grouped together 'gold-entombing hellish usurers' and 'foule, dissembling frye of flatterers'.[5] Thus, the term 'usury' in its broader sense becomes applicable to all sorts of malpractice in social conduct. By the same token, these forms of social conduct seem to be contaminated with the loathsome connotations of the notion of usury, and the language of the time reflects this. Roger Fenton explains about euphemistic replacements for the term 'usury':

whatsoever the matter is, the more that men have been in love with the thing itself, the more have they purposely declined and avoided this name. They will not call it Usurie, lest the word should be offensive, or make the thing odious. But it shall be termed Use or Usance in exchange, which are smooth words as oil . . . Or it shall be called interest, or Consideration, which are civil and mannerly terms . . .[6]

In *Timon of Athens*, it is not usury in the form of taking an excessive rate of interest which gives offence. Timon's anger is stirred up by his creditors' pressing demands to have their loans repaid, which is, at the worst, a breach of trust, and by his friends' refusal to save him from bankruptcy by granting him more loans. These acts of denial are nevertheless in a wider sense forms of usury in that their perpetrators use Timon as long as he serves their own advantage; what they consider to be their gain is commensurate with the interest made from a loan of capital.

[1] Tawney, p. 131.
[2] *Essays*, no. 41.
[3] Mahood (ed.), *MV*, p. 21 says that by 1642 'some sixty usurers had been hissed from their stages'.
[4] Tawney, p. 122.
[5] Quoted by Draper, 'The theme of *Timon*', p. 26.
[6] Roger Fenton, *A Treatise of Usurie* (1612), p. 4.

Usury in this wider sense is conspicuous in the play, contaminating all areas of life. Viewed from this vantage point, gestures of friendship, such as gift-giving or dealing out favours, as practised by Timon and many other characters in the first two scenes of the play, may be seen as conscious or subconscious attempts to gain profit – that is, as forms of conduct structurally similar to money-lending and taking interest. At the end of 1.2, when saying goodbye to his noble guests, Timon deals out valuable gifts to Lords 1, 2, and 3 with a conspicuous persistence; this leads to protestations of thanks, brought forward with a similar persistence, from the recipients of these gifts, who eventually fall into such a hectic excitement that sentences are left incomplete (216 ff.). Earlier on, by way of anticipation, these gift-givings are represented as problematical: '. . . no meed but he repays / Sevenfold above itself; no gift to him / But breeds the giver a return exceeding / All use of quittance' (1.1.276–9). The use of the term 'breed' insinuates that gift-giving has overtones of 'usury'; giving away gifts may mean showing friendship, but at the same time may conceal the giver's expectation of an advantageous return, as of course happens with flattery too.[1] This is what the three Lords are practising. But what also needs to be seen is that Timon tolerates their flattery and thus connives consciously or unconsciously in shaping relationships which have the appearance of friendship, but which are undermined by usury.[2] By Act 4, Scene 3 Timon doubts whether Flavius's conduct is 'a usuring kindness' (4.3.502) – that is, whether he is taking advantage of him, either in monetary or in human terms.[3] Alcibiades, in his anger, addresses the senate as 'usuring senate' (3.5.111), and again the sense is ambiguous, referring to their money-addiction, and also to the senate having 'used' (that is, exploited) him and his services to their own advantage, gaining a surplus over what they had originally invested.

Apemantus, the Fool and the three Servants in 2.2.50 ff. jestingly insinuate associations between 'usury', 'sexual debauchery' and bawdry. The Fool uses the term 'usurer' as referring to a money-lender as well as to a bawd (2.2.96–9); with either of these, something or someone is used as an object for further gain. When Apemantus speaks of 'Poor rogues, and usurers' men, bawds between gold and want' (2.2.62–3), the sense of 'want' is extended beyond 'want of money' to insinuate 'sexual need' as well: the practice of usury is related, linguistically and otherwise, to sexual debauchery.

A further aspect of usury takes effect in what has been called 'verbal usury'.[4] By analogy with the increase or 'breeding' of capital in the form of interest, surplus verbal

---

[1] See 1.1.277–8 n. and the reference to *MV*. Maxwell, 'Timon', p. 199, places emphasis on the evocative qualities of the term 'breed'; '[it] evokes all the traditional doctrines about "barren metal". In this sense of the guilt shared both by lender and borrower, and infecting all transactions in a usurious society, lies the advance in complexity in Shakespeare's treatment of usury since *MV*.'

[2] For the overlap of usurers and flatterers see also the quotation above from Thomas Acheley, p. 15, n. 5. In the 'List of Characters' as given in f, the term 'usurer' is restricted to creditors; the designations of 'Flattering Lords' and 'False Friends', however, are interchangeable. This proves the mechanical character of this nomenclature; it makes no allowance for the linguistic complexities of these designations.

[3] See also 4.3.502 n.

[4] '"[V]erbal usury" is an important technical term in the Jewish Talmud, in the Christian church fathers, and in the Islamic traditions. There it refers to the generation of an illegal – the church fathers say unnatural – supplement to verbal meaning by use of such methods as punning and flattering' (Marc Shell, *Money, Language, and Thought*, 1982, p. 49).

meanings can be generated by way of punning or by creating ambiguities. This may occur when a convergence of terms affects their individual meanings, such as in the many punning contests of Apemantus with others, or when a single term evinces different meanings on various levels of reference. The euphemistic use of terms, as mentioned above by Roger Fenton, is a case in point. The most outstanding instance in the play is the use of 'use', with meanings oscillating between 'employing a thing for any . . . purpose' (*OED* Use *sb* 1) and utilising someone or something to one's own advantage. A succinct example is 3.1.28–9, where either meaning is applicable and where the usurious way of 'using time' is pretty obvious.[1] In other instances, like 1.2.79, or 3.2.42, or 4.3.298, ambiguity is not certain, but, once the probability is established, the susceptibility for such a reading will increase.[2]

Critical approaches

The history of the play's interpretation shows that *Timon* has prompted widely different, even contrary explications. Its representation of characters has been viewed as too narrow, too little elaborated and too flat. Precisely because the characters' self-presentation seems to indicate no great powers of self-awareness, nor psychological complexity, critics have felt the need to supply those aspects themselves, sometimes with over-interpretation. Similarly, the plot has been found deficient in complexity and coherence, which again has prompted critics to find more indirect and subtle dramaturgy than the straightforward speech and action of characters, especially when characters explicitly declare their intentions.

Without aiming at a full coverage of critical assessments, I want to give a structured overview. I shall begin by surveying character criticism, then discuss genre and structure, then imagery and psychoanalytic readings.

CHARACTER CRITICISM

Timon

There is a type of criticism focusing on the moral qualities of the play's protagonist. John W. Draper's study is of this order. In his view, 'Shakespeare expected his audience to admire Timon's very prodigality, to feel outraged at his ruin and to sympathise with his . . . seemingly unbalanced ravings.'[3] In order for the audience to have the chance of establishing such a rapport, he claims, 'Timon is ruined through the virtue of generosity',[4] and, to a still larger degree, by usury, by the high rates of interest he has to pay. Thus, to extol Timon's generosity is to relieve Timon of responsibility for his downfall; it is a reading that safeguards the image of the hero.[5] Ruth L.

---

[1] See 3.1.29 n.
[2] Sonnets 4 and 6 help to focus on the meanings of 'use' (together with 'abuse') and 'usury'/'usurer'.
[3] Draper, 'The theme of *Timon*', p. 21.
[4] *Ibid.*
[5] This policy can be followed right through Draper's readings of single passages. For instance, he takes Flavius's and Timon's servants' comments (1.2.187; 4.2.39; 4.2.6) as proof of Timon's virtuous generosity, following Dr Johnson's model. He further reads Apemantus's comment in 1.2.227 as 'a sort of praise' ('The theme of *Timon*', p. 21), not really taking into account his highly satirical manner of speaking. That is, he does not take into account the speakers' self-interests when assessing their utterances.

Anderson[1] argues on a similar line, and bases her arguments on comparisons with other tragic heroes of Shakespeare, like Brutus and Coriolanus, whom she sees as victimised by their own nobility.

Such readings suffer from a comparatively narrow focus on qualities of character, and moral qualities at that. Readings where the scope of vision is wider allow more light in. G. Wilson Knight's various interpretations of the play[2] aim at an understanding of Timon's personality by viewing him within the wider context of his world – that is, the circles of society in which he moves. This social world of Act 1 Knight describes as 'sensuous and erotic, yet not vicious or ignoble'.[3] It is an atmosphere of brilliance and richness comparable with that of *Antony and Cleopatra*, and seen within this context, 'the true erotic richness of Timon's soul'[4] will become apparent. What other critics take as an indication of a moral flaw and, on Timon's part, as irresponsible prodigality, Knight interprets as a picture of 'an idealized perfected civilization'.[5] How can such widely different estimations of Timon's world come about? Knight claims as a basis for his approach that the 'true interpretative faculty in the reader must be the bride of the poet's imagination, since only so can it give birth to understanding'.[6] By tuning in to Shakespeare's and Timon's imaginative world, we will learn to appreciate that Timon 'would build a paradise of love on earth'.[7]

Knight proposes particular contexts. Firstly, there is the Nietzschean perspective. Knight claims that Timon is Shakespeare's 'superman', and that Timon's rejection of decadent Athens is like summoning to account 'the future civilization of the western world'.[8] Thus, his hate is to be understood as being 'nearer prophecy than neurosis', and it is, 'in the Nietzschean sense, a love'.[9] Timon's withdrawal from human society and human purposes, to be 'more truly at home with a wild nature, a surging ocean, and imagery of sun and moon', is seen to be analogous to Nietzsche's Zarathustra and his withdrawal from the life of the city, and also to Christ's withdrawal into the desert.[10] Knight is not blind to the differences that exist between these personalities, and particularly to the fact that Timon's 'original error in judgment' is shared neither by Christ nor by Zarathustra; but classing him with them releases him from petty considerations of a moral order and lends him universal stature.[11]

Other critics have questioned this aggrandising view of Timon. W. Moelwyn Merchant sets out to explore Timon's character by relating him to the two dominant themes of the play: deceitful appearance is a theme developed by the Poet and the Painter in the first scene of the play and by Timon himself when he hints darkly at the

---

[1] Ruth L. Anderson, 'Excessive goodness a tragic fault', *SAB* 19 (1944), 85–96.
[2] Knight, *Wheel*, 1930, ch. 10: 'The pilgrimage of hate: an essay on *Timon of Athens*'; *The Olive and the Sword*, 1944; *Christ*, 1948; *Shakespeare's Dramatic Challenge: On the Rise of Shakespeare's Tragic Heroes*, 1977; '*Timon of Athens* and Buddhism', *EC* 30 (1980), 105–23.
[3] Knight, *Wheel*, p. 209.
[4] *Ibid.*, p. 210.
[5] *Ibid.*
[6] *Ibid.*
[7] *Ibid.*, p. 211.
[8] Knight, *Christ*, p. 224.
[9] *Ibid.*, pp. 228, 225.
[10] *Ibid.*, p. 228.
[11] 'All three, Christ, Zarathustra, Timon, are universal lovers' (*ibid.*, p. 229).

potential of deceitfulness in pictorial art.[1] The other theme is 'the betrayal of trust and friendship'; it is 'related to the scriptural theme of an ideal of charity and its denial'.[2] Merchant's evidence for this is the large number of scriptural references in the text.[3] He argues that Timon is involved in both themes, concluding that since he is not what he seems, his likeness to Christ[4] need not be regarded as unambiguous either. Merchant would see 'a moral ambiguity in the texture of the character', and Timon is therefore not to be identified with Christ.[5] Merchant's line of argument was continued by Winifred M. T. Nowottny. Examining Timon's curses in Acts 4 and 5, she finds that Timon 'preaches a doctrine of despair in words that almost openly invert the message of Christ'.[6] Richard Fly goes a good step further than this, calling Timon's consorting with his friends in 1.2 an 'outrageous blasphemy' and interpreting it 'as the measure of his need to transcend his fellow men'.[7]

Knight's ennobling picture of Timon has been disputed on other counts as well. Andor Gomme takes issue with Knight's notion of the 'aristocratic brilliance and richness of entertainment' and points out 'the lack of depth beneath the rich surface'.[8] Timon's generosity, which Knight uncritically accepted as such, is viewed by Gomme against the backdrop of Athenian society in all its shallowness and materialistic obsessions. To practise generosity in such surroundings can only show 'a narrowness of outlook, a failure of intellectual awareness, which finally appears as moral weakness'.[9] Timon in Gomme's interpretation never makes the effort to look beneath this smooth surface but instead complies with its conventions. What may appear to be pure generosity, if viewed in isolation, will be seen to involve complacency and self-satisfaction, when due consideration is given to the impact of his actions on his society. Gomme argues that our view of the society affects our view of Timon, and comes to the conclusion that 'Timon has failed to achieve a proper response to his situation: his failure is at once an intellectual and a moral one.' This points in the same direction as Maxwell, who sees 'subtle corruption exercised by the materialistic spirit of Athens'. 'Timon cannot really overcome it; he can only outbid it in its own currency of gold.'[10]

Cyrus Hoy places Timon in a line with Hamlet, Othello and Lear, who 'must pick their way through a maze of conflicting appearances that have been wilfully erected by the unscrupulous to confound the image of truth'.[11] Timon is betrayed by his flattering friends, as is Othello by Iago and Lear by his false daughters; they all fall prey to the manipulators and deceivers, and are therefore victims, not accomplices. Hoy then explores what this betrayal has done to Timon: Timon is alienated from a deceiving society; he remains alone in his exile with his hatred for mankind, 'staring relentlessly

---

[1] See 1.1.161–4 and the two readings I suggest.
[2] Merchant, 'Timon', p. 253.
[3] *Ibid.*
[4] The main references are 1.2.39–41, with the imagery suggesting the Last Supper, and 3.2.59 with the Judas allusion.
[5] Merchant, 'Timon', p. 254.
[6] Nowottny, p. 494.
[7] Fly, *World*, p. 130.
[8] Gomme, p. 111; the citation from Knight is from *Wheel*, p. 209.
[9] *Ibid.*, p. 114.
[10] *Ibid.*, p. 115; Maxwell, 'Timon', p. 198.
[11] Hoy, 'Tragedy', p. 58.

into the image of his hate', and his visitors in the woods of Athens, like Apemantus and Alcibiades, serve as nothing more than partners in shouting matches. '[T]he psychology of alienation is narcissism; and there is something distinctly narcissistic about Timon's misanthropy.'[1] Hoy interprets Timon's misanthropic stance as showing that Timon is 'bent on making his actions square with his words' and that these words are the expression of his inner desire and represent what he really feels.[2] Hoy does not see Timon as the accomplice of those people who turn away from him.

J. Dillon's view is in certain respects the reverse of Hoy's.[3] She views the play in the context of Shakespeare's late plays, like *Macbeth* and *Coriolanus*, in which the protagonists are presented as hero and villain at once.[4] All of them are solitary in the sense that they withdraw from society into psychological and physical isolation. In Dillon's analysis Timon comes off worse than others, Timon being an 'archetypal solitary, his very name a synonym for solitude'.[5] This brings the play close to morality plays, with a clearly defined division of good and bad characters.[6] Timon, by defining himself within the limits of his own subjectivity – 'I am Misanthropos' – 'cuts himself off from life in cutting himself off from society', with the result that 'in rejecting the framework of natural absolutes . . . [he] destroys not the framework but himself'.[7]

G. K. Hunter sets the play amongst a group of plays which he calls 'plays of exile'.[8] Comparing Lear's exile speech to Timon's, he finds that whereas Lear's attitude is not restricted to feelings of revenge alone, but opens up the potential for creating a society based on a new and more humane set of values, Timon's mind in exile is trapped by his hatred of his society, and there is no sense in which he might want to explore new and positive concepts. His stance as a misanthrope does not admit of the possibility that he himself has been an accomplice in creating this materialistically minded society; instead, he is incapable of doing other than attributing all the blame to the evil society of Athens.

Harry Levin concentrates on the literary tradition of misanthropy in assessing Timon. He refers to 'the archetypal "Timonist" of Elizabethan allusion',[9] according to

---

[1] *Ibid.*, p. 59.

[2] *Ibid.* Hoy takes no account of the instances in the shouting matches which disclose how ambivalent Timon's feelings are. (See 4.3.255–73, and in particular notes on 4.3.265 and 266.) To see a parallel between Timon and Cordelia in this respect seems to be rather dubious.

[3] Janette Dillon, *Shakespeare and the Solitary Man*, 1981, pp. 152–65.

[4] In this she follows Willard Farnham's contention that there are no villains as such in these plays and that the heroes' noble features are inseparable from their flaws (Farnham, *Frontier*, pp. 8–10).

[5] Dillon, *Solitary Man*, p. 154.

[6] Dillon makes reference to a late morality play, *Liberality and Prodigality* (1601), which 'may help to suggest how Timon should be judged' (*Solitary Man*, p. 155). In this scheme, Flavius is equated with Liberality, showing discernment, whereas Timon has features in common with Prodigality.

[7] Dillon, *Solitary Man*, p. 160. The outcome, with Alcibiades reaching a compromise with the corrupt senators, corroborates this view.

[8] G. K. Hunter, *Dramatic Identities and Cultural Tradition: Studies in Shakespeare and his Contemporaries*, 1978. The plays in question are *Lear*, *Macbeth*, *Coriolanus* and *Antony and Cleopatra*.

[9] Levin, p. 90. Farnham provides a detailed survey of such allusions, mentioning Robert Greene, Thomas Lodge and Montaigne (*Frontier*, pp. 64–7). For further references to the Timon figure of popular tradition, see Draper, 'The theme of *Timon*', pp. 20–31, 22; among other sources he mentions Shakespeare's reference to the popular Timon figure in *Love's Labour's Lost* 4.3.168 ('And critic Timon laugh at idle toys'). Thomas Nashe spoke of 'Timonists' with reference to those men who were hurt by their riches (*Christs Teares ouer Jerusalem*, in *The Works of Thomas Nashe*, ed. R. B. McKerrow, 5 vols., 1904–10, II, 93).

which the misanthrope's role was laid out for him. Timon's solitude is 'antisocial by definition',[1] a trait that lends itself to an individual not really making an effort to change the society that he or she hates, but merely expressing distaste for it. Robert Burton mentions 'Timons' in his account of solitariness and of misanthropic types: 'These wretches do frequently degenerate from men, and of sociable creatures become beasts, monsters, inhuman, ugly to behold, *misanthropi*; they do even loathe themselves, and hate the company of men, as so many Timons . . .'[2] In assessing the character of this misanthrope, Levin tends to focus on the play's dramatic weaknesses. Against the backdrop of a clear-cut morality-play structure, Levin notes the absence of any of the components of psychological insight; there is no process of introspection; what we find instead is a 'lightning change from one state of mind to its polar opposite'.[3] There is no attempt made in the play to recreate Timon's earlier personality so as to register his various stages of alienation.

Following the same line of placing Timon within the Renaissance tradition of the misanthrope, Clifford Davidson undertakes a more balanced assessment of Timon's misanthropy. He bases his arguments on the ambivalent nature of the iconographic representations of the magnanimous person whose 'pouring out from a cornucopia' – which matches Second Lord's comment on Timon's liberality in 1.1.275 ('He pours it out') – may be seen either as 'a sign of immense goodness and nobility' or as 'unpardonable folly'.[4] Davidson concludes that, in Timon, 'goodness and prodigality are inseparably bound together in one character'.[5] It follows that "Timon's openness is at once a great virtue and a great fault.'[6] Going one step further, Davidson attempts to gauge these ambivalent character traits by invoking the readers' (the audience's) most likely response. Viewing the faults of Timon's 'friends' side by side with Timon's own, he presumes that an audience response will be more sympathetic to Timon, since 'the qualities of this misanthropic man, living a bestial existence, nevertheless impress us as somehow preferable to the false appearances, the hypocrisy, and the acquisitiveness in the society he has left'.[7]

Timon and Apemantus

Timon and Apemantus are closely related characters, and in either phase of the play they are clearly set off against each other. The earlier critical estimations of Apemantus contrast him as a merely cavilling figure with the heroic figure of Timon. Dr Johnson remarks on the 'subtilty of discrimination with which Shakespeare distinguishes the present character of Timon from that of Apemantus, whom to vulgar eyes he would now resemble' – which implies that to cultivated eyes Timon will appear as superior to Apemantus.[8] Hazlitt speaks of Apemantus's 'sordid licentiousness' and says that he

---

[1] Levin, p. 90.
[2] *The Anatomy of Melancholy*, Everyman, repr. 1948, I, 248–9.
[3] Levin, p. 92.
[4] Davidson, p. 187.
[5] *Ibid.*
[6] *Ibid.*
[7] *Ibid.*, p. 199.
[8] *CH*, V, p. 531.

'turns everything to gall and bitterness'.[1] In view of his interferences in 1.1 and 1.2, Campbell regards him as a 'buffoonish commentator',[2] and Kernan impugns his railing attacks on Timon for having no virtue and for lacking understanding of the intensity of Timon's vision.[3] M. C. Bradbrook follows suit by saying that Apemantus 'does not understand the irreversible nature of [Timon's] mutation'.[4] Referring to the encounter of Timon and Apemantus in the woods of Athens (4.3), Brownlow judges Apemantus to be 'an intellectual brute' who is full of 'vanity and self-interest' and who has no clue as to the nature of Timon's misanthropy.[5]

All of these negative assessments of Apemantus are based on the premise that his character can be determined in unequivocal terms – an approach which does not take into account the character responding to shifting situational contexts.

Joan Rees, on the other hand, views the play as being structured on contrasts, the most interesting being the considerable disparity, notwithstanding their similarities, between Timon and Apemantus. The focal point is their shared role as satirist. 'The satirist is by definition unbalanced in his view, uncharitable in his judgment, directing his eye to one side of experience only.'[6] Right from the beginning of the play Apemantus takes on this role of satiric commentator. He is not, however, likely to win the sympathy of the audience through his behaviour in this role, because he appears 'comfortably domesticated in the world he professes to challenge';[7] he is 'content to live without ideals or expectations'.[8] '[H]is way of life is compromise';[9] thus he preserves a symbiotic relationship with the society he consistently criticises. By contrast, Timon makes no concessions. 'In the magnitude of his gestures of repudiation, and his confronting of intolerable pain, he is almost but not quite, a tragic hero.'[10] The suffering Timon undergoes from his diverse frustrations (i.e. being perturbed by the disloyalties of his friends and his self-contempt) determines his deep and personal involvement in his role as misanthrope and almost lends him tragic stature, whereas Apemantus, who has been a misanthrope since birth (this is Timon's view, at least – see 4.3.275–6), lacks this element of being personally involved when carping at the manners of Timon and his friends.

In his keen analysis of the Timon–Apemantus debate, J. C. Maxwell moves still further away from a rigid classification of their characters. Maxwell thinks Apemantus cherishes a romantic view of Timon's nature and of human nature generally. 'Apemantus for all his cynicism has a picture of a finely incorruptible "nature"

[1] *The Complete Works of William Hazlitt*, ed. P. P. Howe, 1930, IV, 211.
[2] Campbell, p. 187.
[3] Kernan, p. 202.
[4] Bradbrook, *Pageant*, p. 22.
[5] Brownlow, p. 225.
[6] Joan Rees, *Shakespeare and the Story: Aspects of Creation*, 1978, p. 131.
[7] *Ibid.*, p. 224.
[8] *Ibid.*, p. 126.
[9] *Ibid.*, p. 224.
[10] *Ibid.*

refusing to flatter man – a picture made in his own image, and one to which, in turn, he strives to approximate even more closely.'[1]

L. P. de Alvarez[2] calls attention to the view that different characters in the play have different judgements of Apemantus and that none of them can be taken as the only true and comprehensive one. He contests the First Lord's estimation that Apemantus is 'opposite to humanity' (1.1.273); instead, he considers Apemantus's aggressive verbal behaviour in the first two scenes as an expression of his desire 'that human vanity be seen for what it is' and not as an expression of a 'general hatred of humanity'.[3] As far as his relationship with Timon is concerned, Apemantus counsels him in different ways, depending on the conditions of Timon's way of life. In Act 1 he accosts him in a biting and aggressive manner to make him see through the hypocrisies of his friends; during their meeting in the woods (4.3) he argues with him to make him see his warped attitude to mankind so that he can realise what it means to live in tune with '[t]the middle of humanity' (4.3.307). However, none of this reaches Timon's ear; he is full of 'irredeemable prejudice' against Apemantus,[4] believing himself far superior to him.

GENRE AND STRUCTURE

Una Ellis-Fermor considers that the play is basically unfinished[5] and finds fault with Shakespeare's representation of the character of Timon: 'our complaint concerning Timon is not that we do not see enough of him, but that, in spite of the length of time during which he occupies the stage, he fails to leave a deep, coherent impression of his personality'.[6] This, she says, has to do with the way the play is structured. Although we are offered single aspects of Timon, 'the action does not knit together his fate and that of the other people in the play'.[7] What is missing is any sense that the protagonist is connected to other dramatic figures, to society, and to his own previous life. We learn nothing about his blood relations, his career or his age. In other words, 'we have here a character which has not been deeply imagined'.[8]

Ellis-Fermor's criticism derives from her expectation of a many-faceted and fully represented dramatic personality. John Bayley agrees. For him, a fully represented tragic personality materialises in the process of his consciousness being unfolded, and this is what happens with Macbeth, Hamlet and Othello. In Timon, however, we are confronted with states of mind, and with 'obsessive and monotonous states of mind' to boot, which curb the development of a live personality.[9] For Bayley, the dramatic speaker 'is not thinking, or expounding in the manner native to his present mood';[10]

[1] Maxwell, 'Timon', p. 207.
[2] Leo Paul de Alvarez, 'Timon of Athens', in John Alvis and T. G. West (eds.), *Shakespeare as a Political Thinker*, 1981, pp. 157–79. His interpretation is based on a political reading of the play, following Howard B. White, *Copp'd Hills Towards Heaven: Shakespeare and the Classical Polity*, 1970.
[3] Alvarez, 'Timon', p. 169.
[4] *Ibid.*, p. 171.
[5] See p. 65 below.
[6] Ellis-Fermor, p. 280.
[7] *Ibid.*, p. 282.
[8] *Ibid.*, p. 283.
[9] Bayley, p. 76.
[10] *Ibid.*

Timon's speeches, which are packed with rhetoric, are always expressive of the same state of mind, his generosity in the first part and his misanthropy in the second. 'Timon is not someone whose consciousness can be entered', says Bayley;[1] we never get a sense that his character is in any way elusive. Thus the play is set against the backdrop of a concept of tragedy and its corresponding expectations, but these *Timon* cannot fulfil. In Bayley's view, Timon has no life in the sense of evoking 'deep psychological echoes'; he has no past;[2] his transformation into Misanthropos is not made acceptable.[3] '[W]e lack the inwardness in the play',[4] and the dramatic speeches do not convey a real picture of the speaker. Throughout his critique of Timon, Bayley relies on his own 'big idea'[5] of what tragedy with Shakespeare is and should be like, and if he is not willing to suspend this idea, all the undercurrents of meaning and the echoes of the unconscious, which do in fact make issues elusive, will escape him.

Stampfer's assessment of the play's structure bears some resemblance to Bayley's, but she does not find the structural characteristics dramatic shortcomings. She considers *Timon* to be an episodic play, the episodes unfolding 'in an artful balance; but they are not caused by what preceded them'. She sees it as a 'choreography, unfolding static example without dramatic engagement';[6] that is, these episodes are not meant to reveal inward aspects of the dramatic characters, and the play is not made up of characters engaging in conflicts. Instead, we have tableaux of different topics – 'Act 1, Scene 1, is a tableau of munificence; Act 1, Scene 2, one of extravagant folly; Act 2 a tableau of hard-pressed innocence, destitution, and blind trust . . .',[7] and so forth. These episodes are symmetrically arranged, and they give the impression of a 'stylized abstraction' – abstracted from bourgeois life, from marital and family situations.[8]

In his account of *Timon* Norman Rabkin applies his concept of complementarity in an untypically inflexible fashion.[9] This is a term borrowed from physicists of the 1950s, and states that complex phenomena like light will yield to different, even contrary explanations, depending on the set-up of the experiment. It follows that certain phenomena cannot be elucidated if one only applies a single concept, so that there is no equivalent to an ultimate 'truth' concerning that phenomenon. Rabkin applies this concept to equally complex phenomena – that is, the representation of human experience in imaginative literature. Approached with this concept of complementarity in mind, one would have to concede that two or more interpretations, even if opposed, are equally valid and objective. However, when addressing himself to *Timon*, Rabkin takes a surprising turn. He finds *Timon* a failure, because it

---

[1] *Ibid.*, p. 74.

[2] *Ibid.*, p. 83.

[3] Bayley argues that 'it may be that the play itself never manages to accept – and therefore to make us accept – the transformation of this Timon into *misanthropos*' (*ibid.*, p. 82).

[4] *Ibid.*, p. 90.

[5] Bayley states that 'the "big idea" does not go with Shakespearean tragedy', and in *Timon* this idea 'seems . . . tyrannical' (*ibid.*, pp. 74 and 75). One might just as well apply this to his own critical stance.

[6] Stampfer, p. 188.

[7] *Ibid.*, p. 193.

[8] From this Stampfer draws tentative conclusions regarding the staging problems of the play; see Stampfer, pp. 204–5 and my remarks about the play's stage history, pp. 35–47 below.

[9] Rabkin, pp. 19–26.

is not complementary. Shakespeare assumes a simple moral position and he never gets down to the unresolvable conflicts of human experience. The play's universe displays a simplicity that is typical of the 'angry self-confidence of the satirist'. Timon is a 'passive hero'; 'he is scarcely individualized'.[1]

Rabkin sees in *Timon* the satirist at work, which for him is an indication of the play's lack of complementarity. Other satiric readings of the play seem to be at least partly in accord. O. J. Campbell sees the play as an attempt at 'tragical satire'.[2] He describes Timon as someone 'veering between folly and madness',[3] not being in control of what will become of him. Campbell does not regard Timon's violent reactions to his disillusionment as the expression of a noble mind's indignation, as other critics of satire have done, but as 'wild automatic surrenders to irrational misanthropy'.[4] Timon's outbursts in Acts 4 and 5 can only arouse strong disapproval, since they are not meant to improve conditions in Athens or to reform individuals.[5] The consequence is that his gestures and speeches in the second phase of his career 'represent all that the Renaissance critics, and Shakespeare among them, believed to be false, presumptuous, and ugly in satire'.[6] One of the outcomes of 'tragical satire' is that there is no catharsis; thus, Timon remains deprived of human dignity.

Alvin Kernan gives a much more positive account of the play as a tragical satire. He considers Timon at the beginning of the play to be 'the incarnate spirit of love itself', and the banquet in 1.2 is for him truly 'the feast of earthly love, of generosity'.[7] After his transformation into a satirist he becomes 'the heroic denouncer of vice'; his rage is 'for truth' and his desire is 'to escape hypocrisy'.[8] In contrast to Campbell's estimation, Kernan thinks that Timon's satire 'has a moral force behind it'[9] and goes as far as maintaining that Timon's satiric stance is 'raised to heroic proportions', and that 'in Timon's titanic loathing of the world there is a romantic grandeur'.[10] It is only in Timon's final phase that satire and tragedy part company. In contrast to Lear, who 'passes through satiric outrage with the world to tragic perception', Timon persists in his unyielding hatred'.[11] Thus, he remains within the confines of satire which is, in the last resort, a failure to acknowledge man's full potential.

R. C. Elliott concentrates more than others on the reading of single passages, listening to the undertones of the text. He maintains that the Lords in the first part 'use the language of virtue . . . perversely'; that '[e]veryone talks alike'; that the 'hill of Fortune allegory' is 'deliberately trite', and that the 'fortune–equals–money equation [is] constantly present'.[12] Analysing the misanthropic part, Elliott comes to surprising conclusions. There is dignity, Elliott says, in Timon's first curse upon the city of

[1] *Ibid.*, p. 194.
[2] Campbell, p. 196.
[3] *Ibid.*, p. 194.
[4] *Ibid.*
[5] Campbell claims that these are 'the only two impulses toward satire approved by the critics' (*ibid.*, p. 192).
[6] *Ibid.*
[7] Kernan, p. 199.
[8] *Ibid.*, p. 200.
[9] *Ibid.*, p. 203.
[10] *Ibid.*, p. 201.
[11] *Ibid.*, p. 203.
[12] Elliott, p. 150.

Athens (4.1). In his brawl with Apemantus, however, which Elliott describes as 'a conventional wit-combat in invective',[1] Timon forfeits his moral authority and turns himself into an object of ridicule. But his utterly misanthropic view of man is not the last thing to be commented upon, something usually done either admiringly or with disgust; Elliott lifts the problem to another level by claiming that there is another satirist, Shakespeare himself, who sheds a satiric light on Timon and his railing at society, suggesting that 'Timon's indiscriminate love and his indiscriminate hate are shown dramatically to be folly.'[2]

IMAGERY

In Shakespeare's tragedies images function as a rhetorical means of placing emphasis. As W. H. Clemen says: 'In Shakespeare's great tragedies we can observe time and again how the imagery takes its cue from some real event taking place on the stage, this event then being symbolically interpreted by the imagery.'[3] We can collect and read images so that a motif or theme can be made apparent. In these cases, images may open up new interpretative vistas. The most conspicuous and thematically focused image cluster in the play is its all-pervasive beast imagery. Farnham sees in this cluster 'the essence of the tragedy' of Timon.[4] Although *Timon* and *Lear* resemble each other in expressing the theme of monstrous human ingratitude through an extended variety of beast images, what distinguishes them is that '[u]nder the impact of human beastliness Lear does not himself become a beast, but Timon does'.[5] 'Beasthood' and 'manhood' are according to Farnham the normative perspectives for measuring the soundness of a society, and the widely diversified imagery of beasts[6] serves to unfold and emphasise the idea that many members of this society are indeed characterised by beasthood. Farnham further points out that beastliness in the shape of a man is much worse than the beastliness of beasts, because it shows man's perverted nature.[7] The 'figure of devouring beastliness in cannibal man'[8] is a more specific image of beastly behaviour. The notion of Timon being eaten by his flatterers had been already broached in Lucian's report.[9] In *Timon* it is resumed in many places;[10] the most conspicuous one is where Apemantus likens the Lords' flattering manners to their devouring Timon (1.2.39–40). With reference to 1.1.206–7, R. C. Fulton flatly concludes that for Apemantus, 'dining *with* Timon is equivalent to dining *on* Timon'.[11] And with reference to 1.2.39–40, he remarks 'seen through his [i.e. Apemantus's] eyes the banquet is a cannibals' feast'.[12]

[1] *Ibid.*, p. 159.
[2] *Ibid.*, p. 167.
[3] Clemen, p. 174.
[4] Farnham, *Frontier*, p. 68. There is an earlier essay ('Beast theme') of 1943 in which he first compiled the various beast images.
[5] Farnham, *Frontier*, p. 45.
[6] The most frequent one is 'dog'; others are 'baboon', 'monkey', 'wolves', 'bears' and 'ass'.
[7] A pertinent passage is 4.3.35–6.
[8] Farnham, *Frontier*, p. 71.
[9] 'When they had finally eaten him down to the bone, and sucked the marrow, they left him dry and stripped from top to toe . . .' (Lucian, quoted in Bullough, VI, 265).
[10] 1.1.205–6; 1.1.252–3; 1.1.273; 1.2.39–40; 1.2.111–14; 3.1.45–8; 3.4.86–8.
[11] Fulton, p. 293.
[12] *Ibid.*

W. H. Clemen describes the dissemination of such images over wide parts of the play as 'subterraneous'; Ralph Berry speaks of an 'underground narrative'.[1] '*Eating* is the figure for relationship', says Berry; and Clemen contends that the imagery of eating and food contradicts and corrects an impression of the 'apparently trustworthy attitude of the friends' and reveals that 'the core of the relationship between them and Timon is unsound'.[2]

Kenneth Burke develops this interpretation of the image cluster. He sees it as all of a piece with violent and brutish behaviour. 'We are invited to think of eating, not as the pleasant gratifying of a peaceloving appetite . . . but as rending, tearing, biting, destroying. Eating here is the rabid use of claws and jaws, a species of hate.'[3] Another spin off of this cluster is the expansion of food imagery into that of poison,[4] connected with images of surfeit and vomiting.[5] Thus, the idea of sickness displaces the notion of eating/consuming, and this leads on to another prominent image cluster: the imagery of disease. This is connected with Timon's wish to curse, and his determination to destroy, the society that has inhumanely rejected him. Disease, in this context, is 'the strongest force of destruction';[6] 'the primary verb of transmission is *infect*'.[7] Thus, Timon invokes diseases of all imaginable kinds to extinguish mankind: first and foremost the plague,[8] followed by leprosy, consumption, sciatica, fever, ulcerous sores, canker and sickness. 'Timon takes disease as the figure for the human condition', says Berry,[9] and calling down these diseases on humanity is a way of bringing home to people what their condition really is.

In these instances imagery was perceived as having illustrative and rhetorically embellishing functions. A remarkable breakthrough in a different direction was made by William Empson with his interpretation of the dog images:[10] 'Apemantus is continually called "dog" . . . with the sense, "snarling and envious critic" . . . Contrariwise, Apemantus continually calls the courtiers of Timon "dogs" with the sense of "flatterers".'[11] Neither identification, however, has a stable or normative meaning. The variant 'critic' by itself offers a wide scale of possible meanings, from the truth-telling critic showing up the insincerities of others – Empson points out the 'respected figure of the Fool'[12] – to the figure of the disappointed idealist venting his dissatisfaction with existing conditions. An equally wide range of meaning applies to the dog metaphor. To call someone a dog may indicate that one wishes to expose him as a deceiving flatterer, a false friend or a cynic; on the other hand, the fawning dog may turn out to be the most faithful of animals and this may accordingly be taken as a term

---

[1] Clemen, p. 170; Berry, p. 105.
[2] Berry, p. 102 (Berry's emphasis); Clemen, p. 169.
[3] Burke, p. 123.
[4] The relevant lines are 3.1.47–8; 4.1.31–2; 4.3.25; 4.3.304; 4.3.422–6.
[5] 3.1.44–52; see Berry, p. 104.
[6] Clemen, p. 172.
[7] Berry, p. 108 (Berry's emphasis).
[8] 2.2.53; 4.3.74–5; 4.3.110; 4.3.163; 4.3.349–50; 5.1.127; 5.1.179; 5.1.211; 5.4.71.
[9] Berry, p. 108.
[10] Empson, pp. 175–84.
[11] Empson, p. 176.
[12] *Ibid.*

of praise. 'Timon's generosity was a way of begging for affection, and it makes him the same kind of dog as the spaniels.'[1] Another variation of the dog image occurs in Ovid's story of Actaeon being devoured by his own dogs.[2] Timon may consequently be seen as having become the victim of those whom he has fed, whom indeed he calls 'dogs' in the course of the mock banquet.

It is in psychoanalytic interpretation that the most conspicuous changes in reading images have occurred, proposing refocused and rearranged relationships between images and providing new perspectives.[3] An impressive example is provided by the dog-licking-candy-melting image cluster 'called up . . . by the thought of false friends or flatterers'.[4] Meredith Skura analyses the interconnections of the individual elements. 'The cluster is a node, like the dream nodes Freud identified, the umbilical cord of the dream, the mycelium from which signifiers spread metaphorically and metonymically outward into a net of signifiers. "Candy" thus leads not only to "sweet" . . . but, because "candied" means "covered in crystals", it also leads to "ice" and "glass" – and thus to the disreputable double of the mirror in dramatic theory: the untrustworthy "flattering glass".'[5] The most compressed passage of this cluster is 4.3.256–76, where Timon rejects being called 'miserable' by Apemantus. Here we find in a condensed form most of the components of this cluster: 'dog'; 'sweet'; 'melted'; 'icy'; 'sugar'd'; 'confectionary'; the theme of flattery, with further ramifications in 4.3.227–8 ('the cold brook, / Candied with ice') and in 1.1.60 ('the glass-faced flatterer').

Clusters of images, carrying Timon's fantasies, are also propounded by Adelman. Among other things, she pinpoints Timon's fantasy of self-generated male bounty and unconstrained giving, the fantasy of a magically bountiful male body that can replace the female body by taking on its nurturant qualities – i.e. his replacement of the female's 'plenteous bosom' with his own.[6] Here, more than anywhere else, the path to attributing meanings to image clusters starts from reading (and interpreting) single images in new and unconventional combinations.

PSYCHOANALYTIC READINGS
Psychoanalytic approaches have recently increased in number and impact. Like interpretations which identify cultural and social contexts and influences, they attend to determinant influences, of which a character may not be aware – in this case from within, from the character's unconscious. The character's unconscious is taken to be

---

[1] Empson, p. 182. Empson (p. 177) quotes Erasmus's *Praise of Folly* to show that 'flattery was not mere lying but belonged to the valuable kind of fool': 'What is more fawning than a spaniel? Yet what more faithful to his master?'

[2] Ovid, *Metamorphoses*, III, 301. Davidson (pp. 189–90) describes this analogy. He maintains that ingratitude was 'symbolized in Renaissance iconography by Actaeon's dogs' (p. 190). Skura holds Actaeon's dogs to be flatterers, sycophants (p. 293, n. 4).

[3] See Skura, in particular ch. 6, pp. 202–16.

[4] Spurgeon, pp. 194–5.

[5] Skura, p. 166.

[6] Adelman, pp. 167–8. Fulton at first suggests reading 'bosom' as a metonym for Timon's sumptuous tables; later, when confronted with the cannibalistic image cluster, he expresses doubts as to 'whether "bosom" is a figure of speech at all' (Fulton, pp. 290 and 293).

as important for an understanding of his actions and motivations as his self-knowledge. This line of enquiry does not, however, aim to override literal and referential meanings, but to shed a different light on their authenticity; and once this authenticity has been questioned, a more open, speculative view of characters may be possible.

Clearly the crucial problem for psychoanalytic critics is how to gain access to the supposed unconscious of a given fictional character in a play without imposing preconceived notions taken from the store of psychoanalytic knowledge. In my account I will focus on those critics who engage in the effort of balancing psychoanalytic readings with literary-critical approaches.

Psychoanalytic critics following Lacan do not conceive of the conscious and the unconscious as mutually exclusive, but hold that 'the unconscious speaks as something other from within the speech of consciousness, which it undercuts and subverts'.[1] Thus, discourse is diversely structured, containing fantasy and dream as well as rationally ordered elements. 'Unconscious signification' is found in the 'rifts at the realist-rational level of plot, character and diction'.[2]

Meredith Skura advocates the psychoanalytic approach because it 'fosters openness and encourages the reader . . . to look at details that have not traditionally been given a role in interpretation . . . that have seemed too obvious to deserve attention or too trivial to bear the weight of interpretation'.[3] She wants to direct attention towards what 'was always there but not seen before, or what was almost there'.[4]

A select number of topics dominates the critical history of the play. One is Timon's generosity and bounty, with a question of whether his liberality is genuine or whether it functions as a mask to hide darker desires. Connected with this topic is the role attributed to Fortune, since the Poet's account of Fortune (1.1.66–91) is often taken as exemplary of Timon's fate.[5] A second topic is Timon's misanthropy, his self-imposed exile and his towering rage. A third topic, related to the two previous ones, is imagery and its modes of interpretation. All three topics play a central role in conventional as well as in psychoanalytic criticism. In traditional criticism, Timon's generosity and bounty are discussed in terms of motivation: we ask whether his generosity is unselfish or whether it is to be seen as a camouflage for gaining other ends. Psychoanalytic critics approach the play with very different questions in mind: they will not focus on the ethics of Timon's conduct but on Timon's psychic condition, on aspects of which the dramatic characters themselves are unaware, the life of their unconscious and its influence. One such approach interprets Timon himself in terms of Freud's concept of narcissism. Susan Handelman sees in narcissism a dual and conflicting orientation; one side is 'the drive to recapture the primal feeling of undifferentiated unity with the original object', which is 'one's own body and that of the nurturant mother'; and the other is 'the opposing drive to assert one's own

---

[1] Nevo, p. 24.

[2] *Ibid.*, p. 8. Shoshana Felman speaks of the 'attempt to disrupt this monologic, master–slave structure' to sidestep the subordination of literary analysis to psychoanalysis ('To open the question', in *Literature and Psychology*, ed. S. Felman, *Yale French Studies* 6 (1977), 55–6).

[3] Skura, p. 273.

[4] *Ibid.*, p. 204.

[5] Brockbank, e.g., sees it as a 'fable that shapes the play' (p. 8).

separate ego'.¹ To resolve this dualism, that primal loss of an all-embracing unity has to be redeemed, and this is done by means of projecting a symbolic world of substitutions and idealisations. These, when confronted with a conflicting reality, are vulnerable to being disillusioned. This posits a primal experience of loss which produces a trauma, but also carries a creative potential, for what we do to redeem that loss creates 'the public monuments and myths of our culture'.² By this theory Shakespeare's plays deal with characters whose 'dreams of omnipotence' conflict with an opposing reality.³ They may be seen as documents of a cultural substitution, achieving what art is expected to bring about: to 'help us to accept loss'.⁴

Handelman considers *Timon* to have failed on all these counts. In the first place, Timon abandons himself to a rage that shows his inability to accept loss. The play, she says, 'is a breakdown of all those ways in which rage, pain, and loss can somehow be accepted, made sense of, transformed into life-affirming energies'.⁵ In order to meet the expectations Handelman assigns to art, Timon would have had to find acceptable substitutes for his loss; he would have had to relinquish his hate on the strength of a substitute ideal; instead, he engages in a heightened and lasting rage. 'Shakespeare does not believe in his own art, and that is why the play is unfinished.'⁶

Timon's idea of friendship and of communion with others, viewed from this perspective, is not evidence of Timon's magnanimous and high-minded personality but a defence mechanism, launched by the impulse to recover loss.⁷ Handelman reads it as a dream of omnipotence resulting from his infantile narcissism. This, in its way, is a deterministic view. Timon's dispensing gifts to everybody is interpreted as an attempt to take over the role of the nourishing Mother. Gestures of Timon's such as those in 1.2.9–11 and 1.2.83–7 that could be viewed as evidence of his almost boundless generosity are seen by Handelman as Timon's unconscious attempts to substitute himself in the role of woman as nourisher and to assume her nurturant functions. Accordingly, the role of women in the play is given a new focus. Whereas earlier critics simply mentioned the fact that women play a very reduced role,⁸ Handelman can see this lack as an outcome of Timon's unconscious desire to excise women altogether by taking over their functions and trying to attain an independence

---

¹ Handelman, pp. 45–6.
² *Ibid.*, p. 46.
³ *Ibid.*, p. 45.
⁴ *Ibid.*, p. 48.
⁵ *Ibid.*
⁶ *Ibid.*
⁷ Reid adopts a similar approach when he sets out to understand and define the roots of Timon's excessive beneficence and misanthropy. In both parts of the play he sees defence mechanisms against depression at work; they provide otherwise missing information about the motives for Timon's conduct.
⁸ Kenneth Burke, for example, remarked: 'there are no mothers, sisters, or wives in this play. Timon is an almost brutally end-of-the-line character' (*Language as Symbolic Action*, p. 118). He makes no attempt to place this lack within any other context. So also Richard Fly: '*Timon*'s world is unique in its strict avoidance of wives, children, or even kinsmen. In fact, the only women in the play, aside from the masculine Amazons . . . are the two diseased prostitutes who accompany Alcibiades' (*World*, p. 127). Knight gives it still another turn of meaning: 'Timon himself has no individual love of either sex . . . He is, really, supersexual, as Nietzsche's Zarathustra is supersexual . . . He is rather a universal lover' (Knight, *Christ*, p. 227).

and autonomy that will save him from further loss and frustration caused by female fickleness. The fable of Fortune, with the elect being brought low, is a case in point (1.1.87–91). Timon's misanthropy defines itself to a large degree through his denial of the female; 'the man who denies the female divides his own self and like Timon becomes his opposite, Misanthropos'.[1] Finally, money or gold is made to serve as a substitute, as a means to deny loss. Handelman refers extensively to Marx to demonstrate that money can only convert human values to market values, and that it can never be a genuine compensation for the experience of loss. Money acquires a binding power in the play. 'Timon's acts of beneficence bind other men to him, defend against separation . . .'[2] Timon's attempts to utilise the power of money to safeguard his omnipotence are, like the other substitutions, doomed to failure.

More recent psychoanalytic approaches to *Timon* build upon Handelman's and her predecessors' analyses: Coppélia Kahn, Janet Adelman, and C. L. Barber and R. P. Wheeler.[3] Kahn and Adelman centre their interpretations on what they consider to be the 'core fantasy' of the play. Kahn identifies it as the 'fantasy of maternal bounty and maternal betrayal'; Adelman sees the play as Shakespeare's 'most extreme vision of scarcity and his most ruthless exposure of the fantasy of male bounty'.[4] Although outwardly contradictory, both focus on the same dramatic constituents, the exertion of social power channelled through the concepts of patronage and gift-giving, and male power vying with and wanting to outdo women's bounteousness.

Putting forth a 'core fantasy' as the nucleus of understanding is different from focusing on the motivations of characters. In the first place, 'fantasy' is not something that the characters would openly acknowledge and be aware of.[5] Since it is not directly referred to, the technique is to discover what Skura calls 'the presence of primitive material and structures':[6] 'the analyst reminds us that there is always more in a text than we normally see, and much that would surprise us. These unnoticed elements are not unconscious secrets but merely the details and patterns that become available only if we are willing to be flexible in the sort of consciousness we bring to bear on texts.'[7]

To Adelman, Timon's numerous gestures of generosity in the play's first two scenes are an exposition of his fantasy 'of an infinite male nurturance'.[8] The fact that there is no indication in the play of the source of Timon's wealth, together with his insistence

---

[1] Handelman, p. 49.

[2] *Ibid.*, p. 57. See also 1.1.108 and n.

[3] Coppélia Kahn, 'Magic of bounty: *Timon of Athens*, Jacobean patronage, and maternal power', *SQ* 38 (1987), 34–57; Janet Adelman, *Suffocating Mothers: Fantasies of Maternal Origin in Shakespeare's Plays, 'Hamlet' to 'The Tempest'*, 1992; C. L. Barber and Richard P. Wheeler, *The Whole Journey: Shakespeare's Power of Development*, 1986.

[4] Kahn, p. 35; Adelman, p. 165.

[5] Skura, p. 274.

[6] *Ibid.*, p. 273.

[7] *Ibid.*, pp. 273–4.

[8] Adelman, p. 166. Her textual substantiation for this idea begins with the Poet's admiring remark in 1.1.6 ('Magic of bounty'); it is continued when Timon pays the ransom for Ventidius (1.1.103–7) and subsequently refuses to have it repaid (1.2.8–11); and finally, in the performance of the masque, he can recognise only his 'own device' (1.2.137).

on denying reciprocity, is given special significance as expressing his 'fantasy of self-generating abundance'.[1] A further step in Adelman's argument is that 'both Timon and the play initially make that wealth identical with Timon's body'.[2] For Adelman, this finds support first in the fact that his wealth is not located in his social context – that is, in that there is a gap in his social background; and second in the images and metaphors of feeding that straightforwardly are expressions of veneration for Timon, indirectly pertaining to the play of fantasy, and that seem to suggest that 'a magically bountiful male body . . . can replace the female body by taking on its nurturant qualities'.[3] Metaphors of feeding range from Alcibiades' 'I feed / Most hungrily on your sight' (1.1.252–3) to the Lords who attend Timon's banquet to 'taste Lord Timon's bounty' (1.1.273) and to Apemantus's remark 'What a number of men eats Timon, and he sees 'em not' (1.2.39–40). Adelman is keen – probably too keen – to prove that Timon himself participates in this fantasy of his wealth/body being unlimited. To illustrate this, she takes Cupid's speech of welcome (1.2.110–13), in which Cupid speaks of Timon's 'plenteous bosom'. The only time Timon himself uses this phrase is when he addresses the 'Common mother' that she may supply him with 'one poor root' from her 'plenteous bosom' (4.3.188). There is indeed no indication that Timon would consider himself to be furnished with a 'plenteous bosom'.

These two aspects of the core fantasy of the play – Kahn's propagated fantasy of maternal bounty and maternal betrayal and Adelman's concept of Timon's attempted realisation of male bounty ending up in an exposure of male scarcity – are shown most clearly in the Poet's representation of the myth of Fortune. Both critics read the text of the Poet's rendering of his poem and its metaphors as mirroring characteristic elements of this fantasy: 'the female body is imagined as a "high and pleasant hill"' which, being 'coterminous with the earth itself', promises abundance.[4] Men labouring 'on the bosom of this sphere' are anxious to avail themselves of Fortune's wealth; however, all the resources are dependent on Fortune's – i.e. the woman's – benevolence. This shows that man cannot prosper on his own authority: his utter dependence on Fortune is evident.[5]

Man's dependence on Fortune's caprices also has its threatening side. Expanding on this, Adelman detects another facet of the fantasy, which consists of the 'immense generative appetite of women' which threatens to swallow men up,[6] and she finds proof of it in the Painter's remark that moral paintings can show the quick blows of Fortune 'More pregnantly than words', which to her shows 'an overdetermined language of pregnancy'.[7]

Concurring with Kahn and Adelman on the topic of interpreting Timon's conduct as compensating for maternal nurturance, Barber and Wheeler see Timon 'engaged in a strategy of altruistic defense that joins potential rivals to him in apparent love'.[8] This

---

[1] *Ibid.*
[2] *Ibid.*, p. 167.
[3] *Ibid.*
[4] *Ibid.*, p. 168.
[5] Kahn, pp. 36–7.
[6] Adelman, p. 168.
[7] *Ibid.*
[8] Barber, p. 306.

idea sheds new light on Timon's ostentatious declarations of friendship, as well as on his insistence on feeding his friends and giving gifts; underlying the social aspect of these acts is an infantile need to be acknowledged by his chosen group – that is, his expressions of love and friendship could be seen to have self-serving aspects running counter to what is openly confessed.

The picture of Timon that we are offered in these readings contrasts with those in more orthodox character criticism. Especially perhaps in the case of this Shakespeare tragedy, *Timon of Athens*, with its uniquely hybrid dramatic style and its strongly dialectical structure, character criticism is often prone to oversimplification, especially when an overall interpretation of the play takes a strongly positive or negative view of Timon himself. The critic who is most exuberant in praising Timon is Knight, who sees in him the 'flower of human aspiration' and the paragon of humanism.[1] In his later chapter on Timon he even exalts Timon's hatred, calling it noble and identifying it with love.[2] In a similar vein R. L. Anderson views Timon as a character 'undone by goodness' and 'brought low by his own heart', thus following Flavius's estimation of his master (4.2.37–9 and 4.3.452–8); she also scrutinises classical and Renaissance texts, including plays like *King Lear*, *Julius Caesar* and *Coriolanus*, that provide evidence for the notion that noble persons are liable to fall victim to their own nobility.[3] Following a similar method, G. Bullough bases his estimation of Timon's conduct on Timon's own statement in 2.2.167–8, 'No villainous bounty yet hath passed my heart; / Unwisely, not ignobly, have I given', implying that Timon speaks the 'truth', which means that this truth is induced by the speaker's sincerity.[4] Bullough does not consider that even a statement of subjective truth might be seen from different vantage points as self-delusion. With a slightly different focus, H. S. Wilson speaks of Timon as 'a lofty if impractical idealist who believes that the practice of virtue lies in giving, and who is innocent enough to suppose that other men share his feelings and his aims, who is blind to human self interest because he has little or none of it himself'.[5]

Another group of critics stress Timon's negative qualities, his reckless prodigality, his self-indulgence, self-satisfaction and complacency.[6] A third group of critics see instead a blend of opposing qualities in him, or make the point that, for a critical estimation, one has to discriminate from amongst mixed motives.[7]

When the 'other' side of the text, the textual unconscious, is invoked, a particular

[1] Knight, *Wheel*, p. 210.
[2] *Ibid.*, p. 225.
[3] Anderson, 'Excessive goodness'.
[4] Bullough, vi, 248.
[5] Wilson, *On the Design of Shakespearean Tragedy*, 1957, p. 146.
[6] Campbell exposes Timon's selfish ostentation: he is deprived of human dignity and worthy of satirical scorn. G. B. Harrison (*Shakespeare's Tragedies*, 1951) writes of Timon in the same vein; he is a reckless prodigal and shows the rottenness of human nature. Gomme takes issue with Knight's laudatory criticism and, again using Flavius's assessment of his master, but a different one from that used by Anderson – namely 2.2.1–5 – brings out the excessive aspects of Timon's conduct, blaming him for his complacency and self-glorification.
[7] Swigg sees the characters of the play living within a civilisation that carries within itself the germ of its decay. Therefore, Timon's affirmations and acts of friendship will have to be viewed in this context as being flawed, and 'the validity of the spoken word . . . is weakened by its divorce from reality' (p. 389). Davidson asserts the ambivalence of Timon's gestures of magnanimity and concludes 'that Timon's openness is at once a great virtue and a great fault' (p. 187).

idea of implicit meaning deriving from post-Freudian psychoanalytic theory is applied to dramatic fiction. It is the diminished attention to the play as a whole system of codes and conventions that makes such a critical approach vulnerable to objection. As Ruth Nevo says, critics should not lock up the interpretation of literature 'within the exclusive domain of the repressed':[1] psychoanalytic criticism of a Shakespearean tragedy is not an inclusive explanatory system either.

There are objections to the psychoanalytic readings by Handelman, Kahn and Adelman. Adelman tends to disregard the rules of reading: she argues as though Cupid's welcoming speech for Timon (1.2.110–13) were delivered by Timon himself, and as if Cupid's references to his 'bounties' could be read as Timon 'posing his own body as the source of an infinite nurturance'. It is Cupid, not Timon, who refers to Timon's 'plenteous bosom'; and Adelman writes as if Timon himself were replacing the female body's 'plenteous bosom' with his own.[2] Her reading of Second Lord's remark 'Joy had the like conception in our eyes, / And at that instant like a babe sprung up' (1.2.98–9) shows a similar bias; she obliges the reader to understand it, irrespective of the fact that Second Lord is the actual speaker, as if it were said by Timon himself: 'as he contemplates his friends, they dissolve into the babes that spring up in his eyes as he weeps . . .'[3] Such readings are liable to serve a self-validating view: even if one accords characters the dramatic function of voicing arguments beyond their personal interests, this does not justify falsifying the evidence about who says what; nor can structural features of the play be interpreted as Adelman does ('The undeveloped characters and shadowy social relations of the play . . . replicate Timon's own condition . . .'),[4] as if there were no alternative explanation for this 'undeveloped' state of the text. The moderate view of Meredith Skura is worth quoting:

I am not suggesting that these fantastic reversals and equivalences replace the more rational distinctions which 'really' make up the action but that they enrich and complicate an already ambiguous world. Fantasy material is always present.[5]

A second critical issue is Timon's abrupt turn-about from philanthropy to mis-anthropy. The abruptness of this change is one of the standard critical objections to the characterisation of Timon as well as to the play's overall structure.[6] Viewed in the light of fantasy concepts, however, Timon's change may not seem so abrupt. If one assumes that the unstated core of the play lies in Timon's attempt to do 'without maternal nurturance by trying to be himself an all-providing patron',[7] his failure to

[1] Nevo, p. 23.
[2] Adelman, p. 167.
[3] *Ibid.*
[4] *Ibid.*
[5] Skura, p. 98.
[6] Levin speaks of a 'lightning change from one state of mind to its polar opposite' (p. 92). 'Instead of psychological insight . . . we are confronted with overt theatricalism' – and Levin compares it to Leontes being 'overcome by jealousy in a single instantaneous seizure' (p. 91). Fly extends this issue to a criticism of the play's overall design: 'we are confronted with a dramatic texture characterized by stark oppositions and abrupt noncommunicative contrasts and by disturbing disjunctions and harsh antitheses'. This disjunctive impulse in the play at large also shows in 'the schizoid personality of his protagonist' (Fly, *World,* p. 125).
[7] Barber, p. 305.

keep up this fantasy of being himself the source of maternal nurture will, without entailing a disjunctive personality structure, result in violent rejections of what has rejected him. Both Timon's patronising and his misanthropic stance are products of the same fantasy. Timon's two stances are interpreted as defensive measures, his abrupt change as 'the absolute breakdown of one defense structure and the immediate adoption of another . . .'[1]

A third issue is the near absence of women from the play, together with Timon's attitude toward women. Though this near absence has long been recognised,[2] until the recent diversification of psychoanalytic approaches it had not been made a critical issue in the sense of opening up an interpretative space and establishing a resonance between it and other features of the play. Viewed from the vantage point of psycho-analytic readings, the role and presentation of women in the play becomes telling in various respects. The only women in the play are Amazons and whores. 'Ladies as Amazons' partake in the masque performed in Timon's honour. They are announced by Cupid, and after having been welcomed, they dance and play 'with lutes in their hands'. Finally, the 'Lords rise from table' and 'each single out an Amazon, and all dance . . .' This arrangement does not give us any clue as to why the ladies should mask as Amazons, and Apemantus's comment on them does not shed any light on this either. However, assuming in Timon an unconscious anxiety about the power of the female and his fantasy of himself taking on women's nurturant role, the presence of women as Amazons will be no threat to him: Amazons may be cruel, warriorlike and aggressive against males, even male children, but Timon's anxieties are focused on women who show caring and nurturant attributes. Amazons are no threat to Timon's unconscious desires.

With Phrynia and Timandra the tendency to degrade women in the play is more openly dramatised. As companions of Alcibiades in his attempt to enlist an army, they meet Timon in the woods and are immediately exposed to his scathing abuse. But it is not only Timon calling them 'whores' in his misanthropic fit who paints this sordid picture; it is also they who represent themselves as complying with venal services and thus prostituting themselves.[3] The revolting picture they offer ties in with Timon's desire to erase women from his life.

The play on the stage

There is no evidence that *Timon of Athens* was ever performed at the time it was written or shortly afterwards.[4] The first registered performance based on Thomas Shadwell's adaptation, *The History of Timon of Athens, the Man-Hater*, was mounted

[1] Reid, p. 447.
[2] See p. 23 above.
[3] Their meeting takes place in 4.3.49–177; they offer their services by saying 'Well, more gold! What then? / Believe't that we'll do anything for gold' (150–1).
[4] M. C. Bradbrook's hypothesis which regards *The Comedy of Timon* as a burlesque of Shakespeare's play presupposes that the latter had indeed been acted before, since without a known play for the audience to refer to, it would be pointless to regard *The Comedy of Timon* as a parody. She dates the *Comedy* around 1611 (Bradbrook, 'Comedy', p. 13 and *passim*).

in London with the Duke's Company in 1678, Thomas Betterton playing the leading role. Part of the music for this production was composed by Louis Grabu. In most of the revivals from 1694 onward, newly composed music by Henry Purcell was chosen. Shadwell's adaptation enjoyed considerable popularity; it was, in fact, the most favoured of all subsequent adaptations. During the period from 1701 to 1750 there were 89 listed performances of the play and in the popularity-ranking it occupied fifteenth place of all Shakespeare plays.[1] In the second half of the eighteenth century, the popularity of Shadwell's version declined; Richard Cumberland's adaptation had eleven performances in 1771–2, and Thomas Hull's only one in 1786.

The first revival of the play in the nineteenth century was at Drury Lane in October 1816, with an adaptation by George Lamb. The fame (and distinction) of this version is probably due to the fact that Edmund Kean played the leading role. Kean's powerful performance was described in a review in the *New Monthly Magazine* for December 1816: 'It is certainly one of those parts in which his peculiarity of manner, his rapid transition of countenance, and the harshness of his voice, are employed to great advantage . . .' And with reference to the conclusion of the third act:

When he called on his persecutors to 'cut out his heart in sums' to 'tell out his blood' in the liquidation of their demands, his eyes flashed fire, his frame seemed convulsed with passion, and his utterance choked with the violence of his rage.[2]

Leigh Hunt gave a similar description, emphasising the intensity and impact of Kean's acting style:

the energy with which he gave the execrations of Timon, the intense thought which he infused into every word of his parting address to Athens . . . His burst of impatience, 'Give me breath,' and the manner in which he reprobated the guests at the empty feast, were electrical.[3]

The next noteworthy production was by Samuel Phelps in 1851, with a revival in 1856. The picture of Timon that he conveyed met with great applause, being one which gave full play to the inherent nobility and dignity of the character. Williams gives a detailed account of Phelps's production and points out that the text was 'the most complete yet to have been produced'.[4]

This was the last London production of the play in the nineteenth century. There were several others elsewhere, the most remarkable one Frank Benson's production at the Shakespeare Festival at Stratford-upon-Avon in 1892.[5]

Thus far the stage history of the play is inevitably tied up with what were regarded as its inadequacies and with efforts to improve on what Shakespeare had left incomplete. These efforts resulted in a variety of adaptations; and also in the assumption that

[1] The figures are taken from Charles Beecher Hogan, *Shakespeare in the Theatre 1701–1800*, 1952, Appendix B.
[2] Cited by Stanley T. Williams, 'Some versions of *Timon of Athens* on the stage,' *MP* 18 (1920/1), 269–85, 273.
[3] *Ibid.*, p. 274.
[4] Gary Jay Williams, 'Stage history, 1816–1978', in Soellner, p. 167.
[5] Benson's version of the play was compressed into three acts. It was played only three times, with different endings. See S. T. Williams, 'Some versions', p. 277, and G. J. Williams, 'Stage history', in Soellner, p. 172.

1 Woodcut of John Philip Kemble as Timon in Act 4, Scene 3, 1785 (RST)

2 Edmund Kean as Timon in the 1816 revival at Drury Lane Theatre, London

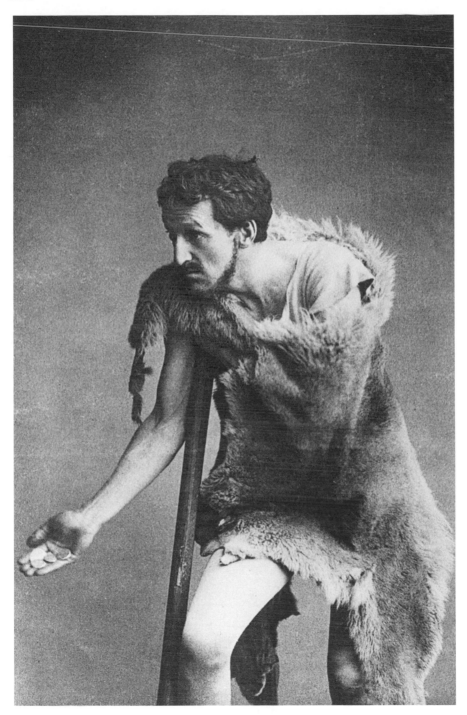

3 Frank Benson as Timon in his 1892 production for the Shakespeare Festival at Stratford-upon-Avon

the text had to be expurgated to suit decorum, which largely meant clearing it of sexual allusions and Timon's most savage curses. This resulted in major cuts and rearrangements of the text.

It was only in 1922 and 1928 that some producers turned away from the traditional pictorial settings of the nineteenth century and the conventions of a declamatory style and based their productions on a text that was neither altered nor reduced. These producers were Robert Atkins, who staged the play at the Old Vic, London (1922), and W. Bridges-Adams, who staged it at Stratford-upon-Avon (1928). Both were disciples of William Poel who held the view that the staging of Shakespeare's plays should be largely free from scenic embellishments and that they should be played uncut.[1]

From this time onward productions became more frequent.[2] In 1935, Nugent Monck produced *Timon* at the Westminster Theatre, London; the music was composed by Benjamin Britten. Monck cut the Fool scene, which he thought was not by Shakespeare, as well as 'other repetitive scenes'.[3] He added a ballet for the masque. In 1947 came a production by Willard Stoker at the Birmingham Repertory Theatre. It was a modern-dress production, with the characters as contemporary Athenian business men. It was an attempt to establish a connection with post-war Birmingham society. In 1952 Tyrone Guthrie staged *Timon* at the Old Vic, London. Guthrie conceived *Timon* as a social satire on Timon as well as on the society of Athens. Kenneth Tynan pointed out that 'Mr Guthrie sets us down in Ben Jonson territory': 'he never lets us overlook the upstart element in Timon's too genial distributions of largesse'.[4] The option of presenting Timon as an idealised figure, particularly in the first half of the play, was not chosen; in the second half Guthrie did not try for 'the most intense and imaginative expressions of rage and despair',[5] so important dramatic possibilities were left unexplored.

Only a few years later, in 1956, the Old Vic saw Michael Benthall's production, for which the text was heavily cut: 500 of its 2300 lines were omitted, including the opening dialogue between the Poet and the Painter. Timon's exchanges with Apemantus were reduced, as well as Apemantus's and the Fool's dialogue with the creditors. The role of Timon (played by Sir Ralph Richardson) was geared towards replacing fury with irony.[6] The ending of the play was remodelled so as to give a meaning to, and a future perspective on, Timon's death: resolved to have his vengeance on Athens, Alcibiades begins to feel pity on hearing Timon's epitaph.

Michael Langham's 1963 production at the Festival Theatre in Stratford, Ontario,[7] was in modern dress; Duke Ellington's music composed on themes of the play

---

[1] The first German version following the original was a production at Munich in 1910 by Paul Heyse (who also did the translation) and Eugen Kilian ('Timon von Athen auf der heutigen Bühne', *SJ* 49 (1913), 124–36).

[2] The productions until 1978 are listed and described by G. J. Williams in Soellner; productions until 1964 are described by J. C. Trewin in *Shakespeare on the English Stage 1900–1964*, 1964.

[3] G. J. Williams, 'Stage history', p. 175.

[4] Kenneth Tynan, *Curtains*, 1961, pp. 23–4.

[5] G. J. Williams, 'Stage history', p. 177.

[6] *Ibid.*, p. 179.

[7] Peter Coe, co-director, resigned shortly after the première.

4 John Schlesinger's Royal Shakespeare Company production in 1965, with Paul Scofield in the title role

reinforced this concept.[1] The Timon of Athens suite consists of the 'Banquet Theme', followed by a number entitled 'Skillipoop' which Ellington explains is an American colloquialism, 'skillipooping' – what the young ladies brought out to dance before the wealthy guests in the banquet scene must do to hide the fact that they are amateurs.[2] The last number is the 'March' written for Alcibiades and his army.

In 1965 John Schlesinger directed the Royal Shakespeare Company production with Paul Scofield in the title role. Influenced by Brecht's anti-illusionistic concepts, the RSC under the directorship of Peter Hall, Peter Brook and Michel Saint-Denis developed a new mode of interpreting plays in contemporary contexts, both dramatic and philosophical. Sets were designed by Ralph Koltai. In Acts 1–3, red-tiled walls opened up for the scenes within Timon's house. Timon's cave 'was set in a barren waste with a single gnarled tree, reminiscent for audiences of Samuel Beckett's *Waiting for Godot*'.[3]

[1] It would be wrong to consider Duke Ellington's musical contributions as merely part of a fashionable trend. Ellington's connection with Shakespeare dates back to 1956 when at Stratford, Ontario, the Shakespeare Festival included a jazz session together with its regular presentation of Shakespearean plays. At the Festival in 1957, Duke Ellington presented his suite 'Such Sweet Thunder'. Included in this suite are pieces like 'Sonnet in Search of a Moor', 'The Star-Crossed Lovers', 'Madness in Great Ones', 'Lady Mac' and others ('Such Sweet Thunder – Duke Ellington and his Orchestra', CBS 52421).
[2] See *Duke Ellington: Day by Day and Film by Film*, arranged by Klaus Strateman; Jazz Media 1992.
[3] G. J. Williams, 'Stage history', p. 182.

In 1973 an important production appeared, directed by Peter Brook at the Théâtre des Bouffes-du-Nord, Paris, in a French prose translation by Jean-Claude Carrière. This production has been called 'the most important Shakespeare production seen in the West in recent years'.[1] Brook understood the play to have a genuine relevance for his own time in that it deals with 'money and inflation, expressed in waste, credit, consumption, prices and abundance'.[2] Thus, his undertaking was not simply a modern-dress production; it was based 'not on analogies of person . . . but on profound analogies of situation' to our own time.[3]

The theatre at Les Bouffes-du-Nord is more than a hundred years old – it opened in 1876 – and had been in a state of dilapidation for at least the last twenty years, with crumbling walls, a deep cavity in the place that was originally the stage, and with a catwalk running along the back wall. According to Georges Banu's account, Brook's production revealed a twofold effort: to rescue a decaying theatre building and to retrieve a play never truly completed.[4] There was an intense correspondence between the state of deterioration of the house and the imaginative atmosphere created right at the beginning of the play – the Painter, standing high up in an aperture of one of the side stage walls, answers the Poet's question of 'how goes the world' by saying 'It wears, sir, as it grows' (1.1.2–3) – where the words matched exactly the wall's crumbling surface. The acting space displays certain elements of the Elizabethan theatre without being a reconstruction of the Elizabethan model. The main acting space, part of which was originally occupied by the front stalls, advances into the audience after the pattern of the Elizabethan Swan Theatre. However, unlike the Swan, it is not an elevated stage; actors and audience remain on the same level. In addition, Brook had two elevated levels which were used for theatrical effects; one consisted of the two apertures in the side walls, and the other was the less elevated catwalk on the rear wall. There were no special lighting arrangements; actors and audience remained in the same full light.

According to Banu, two different yet complementary principles govern the acting process: contiguity and distance. Contiguity was achieved in various ways: there was the equal level proximity of actors and audience; during the interval, the public was invited to move about the acting area. Further, in Acts 1 and 2, actors often adopted the role of spectators; depending on the situation, they changed from actors to viewers and back again. During the first banquet, seated on their cushions in a circle, they set up an acting space within a larger one; and with Timon in a slightly elevated position, they assumed the role of spectators within their own spectacle. Apemantus was the exception; he seated himself outside this inner acting space; he observed the profligacy either from a bench outside the circle or sitting in a balcony amongst the audience. Certain scenic components were vertically distanced in the apertures high up on the side walls. These included the Poet and the Painter's meeting right

[1] Ralph Berry, *On Directing Shakespeare: Interviews With Contemporary Directors*, 1977, p. 131.
[2] From an interview given by Brook and translated by Berry in *On Directing Shakespeare*, p. 131.
[3] *Ibid.*, p. 132.
[4] The best and most detailed accounts of Les Bouffes-du-Nord and Peter Brook's production are by Georges Banu, 'L'écriture spatiale de la mise en scène', and by Richard Marienstras, 'La représentation et l'interprétation du texte', both in *Les Voies de la création théâtrale* 5, 1977.

5 Peter Brook's 1973 production of Carrière's French translation performed at the Théâtre des Bouffes-du-Nord, Paris

at the start, the rumours of Timon's bankruptcy, Timon's plan for the mock banquet, and the Senators announcing the impending attack of Alcibiades. A less spectacular elevation, the cat-walk across the rear wall, was where the servants watched the mock banquet and where Alcibiades appeared as a figure of authority in the last scene.

In 1980 Ron Daniels directed *Timon* at The Other Place, Stratford-upon-Avon. 'The play presents the actor with a path towards a journey of redemption', wrote Richard Pasco, who played the role of Timon, describing Ron Daniels's vision of the play.[1] It is a journey, Pasco says, referring to the play's second half, through steps of

[1] Richard Pasco, '*Timon of Athens*', in Philip Brockbank (ed.), *Players of Shakespeare: Essays in Shakespearean Performance by Twelve Players with the Royal Shakespeare Company*, 1985, p. 134.

6 Brook's production of Carrière's translation at the Théâtre des Bouffes-du-Nord, Paris (1973)

regression, from Timon's 'dawning realization of the state of his world'[1] to a state of 'spiritual abnegation', which shows that he 'has passed beyond worldly hate and misanthropy, to an almost trance-like willingness for death'.[2] Thus Timon is lifted up beyond the level of meddling with the play's affairs to a nirvana-like state of being.[3] In the first part of the play, Pasco considered it his task to make visible the 'psychology

[1] *Ibid.*, p. 135.
[2] *Ibid.*, p. 137.
[3] Compare G. Wilson Knight's idealising view of Timon discussed at p. 18 above.

7 *Timon of Athens* at The Other Place, Stratford-upon-Avon, directed by Ron Daniels (1980)

of misanthropy' and to show elements of Timon's 'imbalance of personality' right from the start.[1] Timon's character was perceived to be central to the play; 'the conflict lies in Timon's inner soul'.[2] Critics claimed the production met 'the modern appetite for emotional extremes', the first part showing in Timon more noble innocence than neurotic prodigality, the second part offering 'a concerto for bile'. 'When he finally expires under a huge net, it seems the only logical end for a character who finds life a mortal sickness.'[3] This assessment of the production seems to be a long way from Daniels's concept of the play as a journey of redemption. Another reviewer found fault with the conflict between stylised features like the kimono costumes of Timon and the Senators (possibly Noh-influenced) and the realist-illusionistic presentation of the seaside, 'with a very intrusive sound-track of waves . . . and a violent thunderstorm'.[4]

1990 saw Frank Patrick Steckel's production in Bochum, Germany, on strongly anti-naturalistic principles.[5] The characters presented themselves in masks which were not meant to deceive or to conceal individual features, but rather to present what

[1] Pasco, '*Timon*', p. 133.
[2] *Ibid.*, p. 132.
[3] Michael Billington in *Guardian Weekly*, 21 September, 1980, p. 21.
[4] Roger Warren, 'Shakespeare in performance, 1980', *S.Sur.* 34 (1981), 149–60, 153.
[5] Stampfer depicts the play's episodic structure as unfolding in a succession of tableaux. She remarks: 'only semiabstraction would suffice in the staging of *Timon of Athens*, to balance its symmetries with a muted, meditative tone' (p. 205).

8 Richard Pasco as Timon (1980)

the characters really are, or are projected to be. Timon's mask resembled a bone-like structure with two differently-coloured sides; Apemantus's mask was oversized and looked like a black box; Alcibiades wore a rusty-coloured mask matching the colour of his soldier's costume. There were expressive features inscribed in these masks, but they were features that pertain to a role, not individualised expressions of actions and reactions.[1] In keeping with this effacement of individualised expression was the suspension of interactive gestures between characters. Accordingly, dramatic figures, when talking with each other, would look in different directions; when the three Lords took their leave (1.2.216ff.) they did so with ritualised gestures of adulation behind Timon's back. The choreography of the dance (1.2) deserves a mention, since it differed from other productions. Steckel's concept derived from Apemantus's comment 'I should fear those that dance before me now / Would one day stamp upon me' (1.2.130–1). The correlation of 'dancing' and 'stamping' stresses the double-faced nature of such rituals, both civilised and barbarically violent, suggested by spears, shields and torches, and erotic gestures by the two male and three female dancers.[2]

In 1991 Trevor Nunn directed *Timon* for the Young Vic, in a modern-dress version. Nunn shifted the action from ancient Athens to contemporary London, a thuggish, lawless place of private affluence and public squalor. Timon, played by David Suchet, was a 1990s city magnate, surrounded in the first act by sharks and tycoons; Apemantus was one of London's homeless, scavenging in dustbins for food. In the second half Timon retreated to a battered car in a scrap yard, memorably designed by John Gunter.

Michael Billington in the *Guardian* praised Nunn's provocative and witty comment on London mercantile society, but regretted the loss of the play's symbolic strangeness. Others criticised more sharply the emasculation of the play to this simple modern analogy. Suchet himself, however, won much praise for the seemingly effortless slide from confidence and charm in the first half to misanthropic rage in the second.

Timon at the Royal Shakespeare Theatre, 1999

The Royal Shakespeare Company's first *Timon of Athens* since 1980 (when Ron Daniels directed at The Other Place) and the first Royal Shakespeare Theatre ('main house') production since 1965 (when it was directed by John Schlesinger) entered repertory in August 1999 with the added distinction of Duke Ellington's incidental music for Acts 1–3. This excellent score, newly arranged by Stanley Silverman, had

---

[1] A detailed and interpretative account of the production, to which I am indebted, is Walter Bachem, 'Das Maskenspiel der Repräsentation: Shakespeares *Timon von Athen* in der Inszenierung von Frank-Patrick Steckel', in *Theater im Revier: Kritische Dokumentation – Spielzeit 1990–91*, vol. 2, 1991.

[2] This warlike atmosphere is also prominent in the illustrations of the play by Wyndham Lewis in 1911–12. Originally, they had been scheduled to appear in a special edition of the play which, however, was never published. In 1913 these drawings and water-colours were published by the Cube Press as a portfolio. Timon is shown surrounded by figures wearing armour and helmets and carrying spears.

9 David Suchet as Timon in Trevor Nunn's 1991 production with the Young Vic

been commissioned for Michael Langham's 1963 Stratford, Ontario, production, and it seems to have had a decisive effect on Stephen Brimson Lewis's designs and Gregory Doran's direction in 1999, particularly on the first banquet scene (1.2) with the masque of Cupid and the Amazons and on Act 3, Scene 2, imagined as a symmetrically arranged set of massage tables in a steam-bath, a staging that also originated in Langham's 1963 production.

As part of the RST's continuing architectural experiments, the stage – initially a large, grey, shallowly raked circle with an expansive area for entrances along the back and blacked-out walkways left and right in front of the still-obtrusive proscenium arch – thrust so deeply into the auditorium that the first three rows of stalls seats were removed. During the play's first half, tall double doors to Timon's house, upstage centre, dominated the almost bare stage, as similar doors had done in Michael Benthall's 1956 Old Vic production. A number of smaller scenes were played downstage with deep black curtains closing off most of the playing space. A few large props – tables and benches for the banquets, for example – were carried on and off; such changes were often covered by dialogue or silent interpolated action. When Timon abjures his native city, Coriolanus-like, these doors are flung open to make a gaunt central frame and all the curtains and drops were withdrawn to reveal a slightly decoratively enhanced brick wall – in fact, the theatre's own back wall. After a single interval, the stage's grey turned sandy yellow and a single black backcloth very far upstage remained throughout. On this backcloth appeared a vibrant yellow-orange

ring surrounding a smaller black disc – many audiences understood, and some ap-
plauded, an allusion to the total solar eclipse visible in parts of Britain (11 August
1999), though the more appropriate reference was, presumably, to the dimming of
Timon's bright fortunes and promise of others' fortunes. Recorded sounds of the sea's
surges echoed a shallow jagged line (breaking waves?) in the sun's yellow-orange
colour that extended across the backdrop's base just above the stage's rear perimeter.
Timon's 'cave' was a sand-walled trap very close to the audience; it produced parsnip-
like roots and gilt rocks as required and came equipped with a serviceable short-
handled spade. This half of the play demands few props, and received few. Twirling
parasols, Timandra (Nadine Marshall) and Phrynia (Kemi Baruwa) arrived in litters –
it is, emphatically, a hot and sunny seaside as Timon's flyting with Apemantus was
soon to prove – and Alcibiades' final threats to Athens found him suspended on a
stage-wide gantry, speaking in a dictator's mechanically enhanced voice amidst the dry
ice clouds of impending theatrical chaos.

As so often in productions of *Timon*, the masque provided the most obvious
occasion for spectacle, and Gregory Doran, abetted by Ellington's music, grasped the
opportunity gratefully. Apemantus (Richard McCabe, also Iago in this Stratford
season and Thersites and Webster's Flamineo in the 1996 season) harangued the
guests in text that apparently included some lines from his otherwise omitted dialogue
with the Fool (Act 2, Scene 2), proceeded to deliver 'Apemantus' Grace' (announcing
its title as if reciting a party-piece), and then delivered his 'Hoy-day, / What a sweep
of vanity comes this way' satiric attack while acting first as master of ceremonies –
black shirt, black suit, dark glasses, wireless microphone – and then as nightclub
pianist from a keyboard in a gallery above stage left. McCabe described Apemantus as
'half-entertainer, half-philosopher' and found the central performance issue how to
keep the focus on Apemantus here.[1] And what a show the 'half-entertainer' had to
present! Cupid, recognisably Sam Dastor's Poet from Act 1, Scene 1, descended a
little creakily from the heavens to shoot Timon with a most unfatal-looking arrow and
was then followed by four ostentatiously male Amazons, also armed with toy bows,
who arrived in swings and proceeded to dance to Ellington's music, first *ensemble* and
then, as the Folio directs, with 'The Lords', who by now appeared quite drunk and
very amorous.

Drag Amazons, Lords and Senators all exited with varying amounts of pantomimed
sexual horseplay to allow the act to conclude with Apemantus's foreboding 'O that
men's ears should be / To counsel deaf, but not to flattery.' Between the acts an
Amazon crossed the stage, paused, looked off, and exited, stalked by a dishevelled
reveller, one we had seen drinking copiously from a flask, who drew a dagger as he
pursued his quarry. This pursuer returned as a penitent presence in Act 3, Scene 5,
evidently the murderer-for-honour whom Alcibiades (Rupert Penry-Jones) defends
unsuccessfully in a set that intimates a gentlemen's club. (The accused's silent presence echoes similar business in Benthall's 1956 production.) Alcibiades' final denun-

---

[1] Richard McCabe, in discussion with University of California students, 'Shakespeare in Performance'
programme, 19 August 1999.

ciation of Athens takes place against a backdrop of the accused man, now hanged from an upstage gallows.

Making his first Stratford appearance since his excellent Hamlet in 1980, Michael Pennington first strode onto the stage as a commanding and eagerly greeted Timon, wearing a long silky robe over simple white shirt and trousers enlivened by a precious-looking jewelled pendant. Amidst a swirl of exaggeratedly costumed and becoiffed Senators, who seemed vaguely North African in dress, and Lords, who appeared in Velasquez-like robes with elaborate over-the-arm trains, Pennington made a comparatively restrained central figure, though the expensive garb and rock-musician-like flowing hair-style also suggested wealthy self-indulgence. Successively petitioned, Timon paused slightly at each request before awarding his gifts and glanced around to see first how the requests and then how the grand, perhaps excessive, responses were received. The overall effect was one of strain, of theatre: leeches vying for notice any way they might, benefactor seeking to make an *effect* and anxious to know he had succeeded.[1] Intended or not, Pennington's portrayal and the stagy surroundings made his 'We are born to do benefits' both sentimental and deluded.

Almost at once, of course, Timon must seek help from his supposed friends, but they are 'Feast-won, fast-lost', as his Steward says, and Timon's 'I am wealthy in my friends' is delivered in near-Pollyanna tones. As Pennington speaks them, Timon's demands – 'fifty talents', 'A thousand talents', 'five talents' – strongly recalled his seeming off-handedness an act before. Directors and actors enjoy the satirical scenes that follow, and this production offered rather campy scenes of self-indulgent Lords and Senators: stage business included a bravura performance by Lucius (Geoff Francis) as he rejected Timon's requested help while receiving a muscle-stretching and joint-cracking massage (Act 3, Scene 2), all timed to Ellington's music, and by Sempronius (David Hobbs), who worked himself into a faked rage at being asked last for assistance, a rage sufficient to lift him from his nineteenth-century wheelchair (Act 3, Scene 3).

When John Woodvine's Steward entered *with many bills in his hands* (Act 2, Scene 2), his conservatively dressed grey hair, severely tailored grey but rather rich-appearing garb, and his upright posture all silently rebuked the luxurious excess of the first act and conveyed a probity he maintained throughout the play. Deep-voiced and deeply loyal, Woodvine never conveyed a hint of *Schadenfreude*, never implicitly criticised his master, and managed the potentially saccharine dismissal of Timon's few remaining servants – 'All broken implements of a ruined house . . . fellows still, / Serving alike in sorrow' (4.2.16, 18–19) – with stern sympathy, no self-pity. He was, effectively, the prudent master Timon was not, though of course without Timon's social status and weight of responsibility. When Timon soon exempts his Steward, 'So true, so just, and now so comfortable', from 'general and exceptless' condemnation (Act 4, Scene 3), he reaches a Lear-like recognition of universal wrong and particular right that Pennington and Woodvine sustained superbly; attempting to institute, perhaps even to discover, a place where human relations mean more than financial ones, Timon offers, 'conditioned', gold to the Steward. Woodvine quietly returned the poisonous gift.

[1] 'Even when he is acting the sole [*sic*] of conviviality, the rousing heartiness of this Timon feels obscurely remote and narcissistic' (Paul Taylor, *The Independent*, 27 August 1999).

10 Michael Pennington as Timon and Richard McCabe as Apemantus in Gregory Doran's 1999 production at the RST

For the actor of Timon, the play's severely reduced second half – when he has abandoned the city, 'a forest of beasts' that bled and then abandoned him – tempts him to rant – loud, monotone and finally boring, no matter how just and potentially affecting. As Richard Pasco, the splendid Timon in Ron Daniels's 1980 production, said, 'From here [Act 4, Scene 3] to the end of the play the actor's problem is to prevent each set scene from becoming one long shouting-match between Timon and his visitors in the wilderness.'[1] This fate Pennington's Timon largely escaped, though the margin was sometimes narrow, especially in his attacks on society and on the natural relations and forces he seems to hold responsible for his and all others' unhappiness. Just as it is hard to keep Timon *agonistes* from sounding a single note, it is difficult for a production to distinguish his successive and potentially over-abstract or overly allegorical meetings with Alcibiades (now in camouflage trousers and modern military boots), Apemantus, the Bandits and (a concluding indignity here powerfully portrayed) with the Poet and Painter who had introduced us to Timon's grandeur and folly.

Timon's rejection of Alcibiades' manifest personal concern elegantly prepared the way for the later meetings. Richard McCabe's Apemantus demonstrated his suspicion of Timon's true misanthropy by arriving ready for a funereal seaside vacation. Still in black, but now barefoot with shoes in hand, he was costumed in lightweight trousers rolled above the knee, unbuttoned short-sleeved shirt, and straw sunhat – an urban

[1] Philip Brockbank (ed.), *Players of Shakespeare*, 1985, p. 134.

satirist at the beach. Apemantus announced his arrival by tossing a coin onto the stage, admired the odd pieces of gold lying about and asked Timon where he could find the real Timon – 'Men report / Thou dost affect my manners'; his business was to unfurl a beach towel (very white) and apply suntan lotion as he prepared to get a tan while castigating near-naked Timon. Warming to Timon's plight and truthfulness, Apemantus eventually offers the metaphorically charged 'medlar for thee'. By now, Timon and Apemantus were seated at opposite ends of the sandy pit that served for Timon's 'cave', and they tossed, ate, tossed, ate the 'medlar' back and forth in a comic-angry game recalling the stage business in earlier RSC performances of Lear and his Fool.[1] The moment is wholly affecting – tenderness amidst the ruins of Timon's generosity and the present rebuke to Apemantus's blanket condemnations. Michael Pennington answered Apemantus's seemingly unanswerable desire to return the world to beasts with a superb delivery of the astonishing speech beginning 'If thou wert the lion, the fox would beguile thee . . .' So powerful was it, the production asked us to believe, that Apemantus, having exited (it seemed), slowly returned from upstage during Timon's speech on gold as 'Thou visible god'. Timon now converted the Banditti from their ways – 'I'll believe him as an enemy, and give over my trade' – and faced his Steward in the scene described before. The same Senators who earlier condemned Alcibiades' friend now arrived to plead for Athens's survival, and while they did so, Timon carved his epitaph, speaking of his 'long sickness / Of health and living'. His cave or theatrical trap now became his grave, and he gave a long slow look at the audience while an Ellingtonian saxophone wailed amid the sound of sea-surges. The Steward returned to collect the wooden board upon which Timon had carved his epitaph.

Simplifying the Folio's conclusion, this production ended with the Steward producing Timon's 'gravestone' and reciting the second epitaph, 'Here lies a wretched corse . . .' Alcibiades, conqueror, remained aloof on his gantry, and the stage emptied, leaving him above, the Steward on the main stage, and Apemantus, silent, downstage left. Gregory Doran, the play's director, called *Timon* 'a very simple parable' and said the second half was 'very astonishing . . . a man and a tree in a wilderness . . . like *Waiting for Godot*'.[2] Whatever the director thought, this production of *Timon* was neither a simple parable nor merely Beckett *avant la lettre*. It was, however, a worthy and popular successor to the company's 1965 and 1980 productions.

Narrative and dramatic treatments of the Timon legend

FROM LUCIAN TO *THE COMEDY OF TIMON*

Before Lucian, Timon is only a stereotype, but with Lucian's dialogue *Timon, or the Misanthrope*,[3] he is placed within a variety of contexts and acquires personal complexi-

---

[1] For example, Michael Gambon (Lear) and Fool (Anthony Sher), RSC, Stratford, 1982. Producers often invent similar business with Yorick's skull in *Hamlet*.

[2] Gregory Doran, interview, BBC Radio 3, 10 August 1999.

[3] Lucian of Samosata lived from *c.* AD 115 to after AD 180. There existed no English translation of his Timon dialogue in the sixteenth century; there was, however, a Latin version by Erasmus, as well as an Italian and a French translation. The latter, by Filbert Bretin, *Les Oeuvres de Lucian* (Paris 1582–3), is, according to Honigmann ('Timon', p. 9), Shakespeare's likeliest source. A complete English translation of the Greek text is available in the Loeb Classical Library (by A. M. Harmon, in *Lucian*, II, 1915, pp. 325–93). Bullough, VI, 263–77, gives a partial translation of the Italian version of 1536.

ties instead of stereotypical fixities. As to whether Timon's spending is out of generosity or prodigality – a vexed question about Shakespeare's Timon – in Lucian it is
first broached by Timon himself. He holds forth, accusing Jove of having shown
neglect in the guidance of human affairs and in ensuring that justice be done. Timon
represents himself as unjustly dealt with by those Athenians whom he rescued from
poverty but who no longer recognise him when he loses his wealth. He also accuses
Jove of irresponsibly permitting this injustice. Timon's viewpoint is that he himself is
generous and liberal.

A new note is struck when Mercury points to the inherent ambivalence in Timon's
conduct: 'He was brought to this by his bounty, humanity and compassion towards
all in want; or rather, to speak more correctly, by his ignorance, foolish habits, and
small judgement of men, not realizing that he was giving his property to ravens and
wolves.'[1]

Other viewpoints on this problem are offered when the question of the identity of
Riches comes up[2] – whether, for a man to become and stay rich, it calls for parsimo-
nious or for prodigal behaviour on his part. Riches herself argues for a moderate
position: that a rich person should neither squander his wealth nor keep it in a miserly
fashion. From Riches' perspective, Timon's fate was brought about by his unwise and
prodigal use of Riches.

Riches' perspective is, however, not completely reliable, since she is a shape-
changing figure, with a mask on her face, sometimes blind and limping, and sometimes
swift of foot, depending on the mission she undertakes. Moreover, she lets in all kinds
of evils like 'Pride, Ignorance, Arrogance, Sloth, Violence, Fraud' to whomever she
visits.[3] The influence of such a complex, self-contradictory figure on Timon may be to
induce self-contradictory instability.

Lucian also presents a view of Timon's self-appointed misanthropic stance. After
having reluctantly consented to be rich once more, he starts digging and finds gold.[4]
This is a new trait added to the stereotypical features of his conduct as a misanthrope,
generating the new question of how a misanthrope copes with newly acquired wealth.[5]
Lucian's Timon first addresses his treasure in exuberant terms[6] and then decides to
keep his riches to himself; he desires to be solitary, 'not to know anyone, to despise all
other men';[7] he will please only himself. This contrasts with Shakespeare's treatment,

---

[1] Bullough, VI, 265.
[2] In the Loeb translation of Lucian, Riches, in accordance with the Greek *Plutos*, is male; in the Italian
translation of 1536 as well as in Bretin's French translation, Plutus is transformed into a woman, and a
prostitute at that. Thus, 'the long discussion of the corrupting love of money consequently centres not on
a man but a woman' (Honigmann, 'Timon', p. 11). In *Timon of Athens*, the reference in the first part is to
'Plutus, the god of gold' (1.1.275); it is only in Act 4 that gold, prostitution and sexual debauchery of
women are shown to be implicated.
[3] Bullough, VI, 268.
[4] Bullough, VI, 271–2.
[5] Comparable problems are put forward by Apemantus in 4.3.219–20 and 4.3.248–9.
[6] 'O gold, the best prosperity of men [a phrase from Euripides' *Danae*], you shine like flaming fire by day
as by night. Come my dearest friend and lover . . . What maiden would not open her lap to receive so
beautiful a lover . . .' (Bullough, VI, 272). This ties in with Timon's apostrophes of gold in 4.3.31–45 and
4.3.377–88; it also touches on the relation of gold and prostitution as it is further elaborated in connection
with the academic *Comedy of Timon*.
[7] Bullough, VI, 272.

where Timon expresses hatred of others as well as of himself[1] and puts his gold to use by contriving the downfall of Athens and of all humanity. In Lucian's version gold only serves to satisfy Timon's egoistic needs. When his former friends and acquaintances come and visit him, obviously with the intention of getting their share of Timon's wealth, Timon demonstrates his resolution to let nobody share his wealth, which is solely for his own well-being. Again, Shakespeare's treatment is darker than Lucian's – as Shakespeare puts it, Timon is friendly neither with others nor with himself.[2]

M. M. Boiardo's version of the Timon story, *Timone Comedia*,[3] is in large part a dramatised version of Lucian's dialogue, although Boiardo places the emphasis differently and adds a new theme to the Timon legend. Timon's hatred of mankind is set in motion through his drudgery 'for other's profit and my own great hurt';[4] it finds expression in his desire that everything growing may prove inimical and deadly to mankind, therein anticipating Shakespeare's Timon when he curses about nature (*Timon* 4.3.178–98).

Boiardo adds the beast theme to the Timon legend. In classical times it was Pliny who asserted that man has nothing in his nature to be proud of, and that he is not superior to the nature of beasts.[5] Men are worse than beasts in that they act cruelly against their own kind.[6] Boiardo's Timon uses beast references to magnify his disgust of human beings, finding that human cruelty exceeds that of wild beasts.[7] The man–beast analogy has since become an essential part of the Timon legend. While Richard Barckley in *A Discourse of the Felicity of Man* (1598) uses it in the same way as Boiardo, other writers reverse the application of the beast analogy to Timon himself, saying that

[1] See 4.3.20–2.

[2] The question of whether or not Shakespeare was aware of Lucian's dialogue of *Timon* can only be answered hypothetically. It has often been placed in the foreground of critical enquiries, sometimes too much so. T. W. Baldwin, enquiring into Shakespeare's reading and investigating the grammar school curricula in the late Tudor period, supposed that since quite a few of Lucian's dialogues had been translated into Latin by Erasmus, 'Shakspere would have been considered capable of reading Lucian's Dialogues in Latin translation before he completed the lower school, and consequently his ultimate borrowings from Lucian may well be direct ones, occasioned by his having read some of Lucian either in or out of school' (*William Shakspere's Small Latine and Lesse Greeke*, 2 vols., 1944, I, 735). Christopher Robinson's remarks on the relationship between Lucian and Shakespeare (*Lucian and his Influence in Europe*, 1979, p. 103) are unconvincing about detailed correspondence: most of the images in Mercury's remarks (Bullough, VI, 265) are *not* used by Shakespeare; on no grounds can Gnathonides (Bullough, VI, 273) be taken as the source for the Poet; nor is it sensible to derive Alcibiades' remarks on Timon's qualities as a military leader (*Timon* 4.3.93–6) from Demeas's hilariously fantastic and ungrounded inventions (Bullough, VI, 274–5).

[3] The date is *c.* 1487. Bullough gives a partial translation in VI, 277–93. Boiardo's relation to Shakespeare's *Timon* is discussed by R. W. Bond, 'Lucian and Boiardo in *Timon of Athens*', *MLR* 26 (1931), 52–68.

[4] Bullough, VI, 281.

[5] Pliny, *Natural History*, VII.i.1–5; trans. H. Rackham, Loeb Classical Library, II, 1942. It was first translated into English by Philemon Holland in 1601.

[6] Pliny, *Natural History*, VII.i.5. In the same book Pliny refers to particular persons who, by showing an unbending severity of nature and a lack of emotion, were called 'apathetic'; they were founders of schools of philosophy, like Diogenes the Cynic and others, and among these he mentions one by the name of Timo, of whom he says that he went so far as 'to hate the whole human race' (VII.xix.80) – a reference in which the philosopher Timon of Phlius (*c.* 320–*c.* 230 BC) is most probably conflated with Timon the misanthrope.

[7] Bullough, VI, 280–1.

it is he who lives like a beast. This is so in Pedro Mexia's account *La silva de varia lección* (1540),[1] as well as in W. Painter's tale 'Of the straunge and beastlie nature of Timon of Athens, enemie to mankinde, with his death, buriall, and Epitaphe'.[2] Painter takes great pains to expand on Timon's 'beastlie nature' by placing emphasis on the fact that he 'dwelt alone', lived 'separated', and 'could not abide any other man'. Paradoxically, however, he also asserts the sociable nature of beasts ('Al the beastes of the worlde do applye theimselves to other beastes of theyre kind'), so that Timon appears to be not only singular among humans but unnatural even as a beast. There is a third, more ambiguous way of applying the beast theme. P. Boaistuau, *Theatrum Mundi*, trans. John Alday (1581), has Timon resort to the wilderness to live a life with the beasts because this is to him the better alternative.[3]

In *The Comedy of Timon*, Timon expresses his desire that his human shape be removed and that he be transformed into a beast, so that he can have his revenge upon mankind.[4] In Shakespeare's play, these various uses of the beast theme are turned into competitive arguments in the Timon–Apemantus debate in 4.3.200–393.

In Boiardo's account, the topic of Timon finding gold acquires a new dimension. Boiardo partly follows Lucian in having Timon give praise to the godlike power of gold and its seductive potential with women;[5] but Boiardo then strikes a different note when his Timon realises that gold also tends to corrode his own strength and that he feels he has become its slave.[6] Having struck this moralistic note Boiardo shows Timon struggling to free himself from the snare of his own treasures. He is no longer complicit in gold's corruptive effect. Timon turns with a clear conscience to his misanthropic and solitary way of life.

The anonymous Timon play, usually called *The Comedy of Timon*, collects together various threads of earlier versions and adds new features. Its authorship and date are uncertain;[7] the most urgent questions – whether it was written before or after Shakespeare's *Timon*, and whether Shakespeare drew upon it or vice versa – are also matters of conjecture. A manuscript copy of the play is preserved as MS 52 in the Dyce collection of the Victoria and Albert Museum, London. It was edited in a bowdlerised version by Alexander Dyce for the Shakespeare Society in 1842, and a reprint was included in Hazlitt's *Shakespeare's Library*, vol. VI, in 1875. It was newly edited by J. C. Bulman and J. M. Nosworthy for the Malone Society Reprints, 1978 (1980). The editors provide a detailed account of the manuscript and the critical

---

[1] For details see Farnham, *Frontier*, pp. 55–6.
[2] Painter; in Bullough, VI, 293 5.
[3] Bullough, VI, 296.
[4] J. C. Bulman and J. M. Nosworthy (eds.), *Timon*, The Malone Society, 1980, 4.2.1791–9.
[5] Boiardo's Timon speaks of its 'divine power' (Bullough, VI, 285), Shakespeare's Timon addresses it as 'visible god' (4.3.382); following Lucian (see p. 53 n. 3 above), who in his turn was following Euripides, Boiardo's Timon remarks on the effects of gold: 'Where can there be a damsel so unwilling / As not to open her lap to such a lover . . .' (Bullough, VI, 285); Shakespeare rendered it dramatically in Phrynia's and Timandra's greed for gold: 'Believe't that we'll do anything for gold' (4.3.151).
[6] Bullough, VI, 286. Shakespeare's Timon does not refer to the effects that gold may have on himself but he does elaborate on its effect on people from different strata of society.
[7] Thomas Middleton was suggested as its author by Bulman and Nosworthy (eds.), *Timon*, p. xv.

opinions concerning its date, what audience it was meant for, and, most important, its relation to Shakespeare's *Timon of Athens*.

Critical consensus exists as to the play having been written to be performed at one of the Inns of Court.[1] As to the play's date, the critical majority holds that the *Comedy of Timon* precedes Shakespeare's *Timon* and was written about 1602–3. Bulman and Nosworthy point out the play's echoes of Ben Jonson's comical satires and Shakespeare's romantic comedies.[2] This theory allows for the possibility (not the certainty) of Shakespeare having made use of the *Comedy*, advanced by R. H. Goldsmith[3] and J. C. Bulman.[4] The opposite view, taken by M. C. Bradbrook, holds that the *Comedy* was conceived as a burlesque of Shakespeare's play and presented at the Inner Temple Christmas Revels of 1611.[5] Between these two falls a third highly speculative theory by H. J. Oliver, based on material supplied by Georges Bonnard:[6] since it is unlikely that Shakespeare knew the unpublished *Comedy* or that the anonymous author of the *Comedy* knew Shakespeare's unprinted play, elements common to both plays but not shared by other sources could only be derived from another as yet unidentified source.

The *Comedy* can be placed within the tradition of the legend. Ever since Lucian's account, the generosity/prodigality problem has figured prominently. In contrast to Lucian's markedly ambiguous treatment of this theme, in the *Comedy* Timon boasts of his liberal and unmiserly handling of his riches, going so far as to proclaim that he would scatter his gold among the people (1.1.9–12). This brings him closer to the wastrel type, and he is judged to be a wastrel by Laches, the type of faithful servant who sees through other people's hypocrisy better than his master can, and who rebukes him for his spendthrift conduct.[7]

Timon boasts about his wastefulness, calling it bounty: 'It is to me a Tryumph and a glorye / that people fynger poynt at me and saye / this, this is he, (th)at his lardge wealth and store / scatters among the Commons & the poore' (1.1.40–3).

Both aspects – Timon's wastefulness and his egoistic desire for glory – are focused on in two scenes: 1.2, where Timon redeems a young man from his debts; and 2.4, where he bails out the orator Demeas.[8] The first incident has its analogue in Shakespeare's *Timon* 1.1.98–113. But whereas in *Timon* much is made of the debtor being a gentleman 'that well deserves a help' (1.1.106), in the *Comedy*, it is all rather degrading, the debtor a 'dissolate young man' who, after having been rescued from his usurer,

---

[1] See Bradbrook, 'Comedy', p. 83, and J. C. Bulman, 'The date and production of "Timon" reconsidered', *S. Sur.* 27 (1974), 111–27, pp. 113–19.

[2] Bulman and Nosworthy (eds.), *Timon*, pp. xiii–xiv.

[3] Goldsmith, 'Did Shakespeare use the old *Timon* comedy?' *SQ* 9 (1958), 31–8.

[4] Bulman, 'Shakespeare's use of the *Timon* comedy', *S. Sur.* 29 (1976), 103–16.

[5] Bradbrook, 'Comedy', pp. 83–103. Bradbrook argues for this late date on the basis of revelling plays' conventions.

[6] Oliver, pp. xxxviii–xl; G. Bonnard, 'Note sur les sources de *Timon of Athens*', *Études Anglaises* 7 (1954), 59–69, 63–9.

[7] Flavius's prudent perception of Timon's weakness has its analogue in Laches, although in the *Comedy* the split between Timon and Laches is carried to extremes, in that Laches is dismissed by Timon and, like Kent in *Lear*, re-enters Timon's service in disguise.

[8] In Lucian, the orator Demeas is one of Timon's flattering visitors.

falls to singing a drinking song. This, together with his expression of his sexual desires, finds Timon's approval. The second scene is also modelled on comic lines; Demeas is taken into custody for having stolen all the words he speaks. Timon intervenes and pays sixteen talents, adding 'I doe desire / A gratefull minde, thats all that I require. / I putte my talents to strange vsury / To gaine mee freinds . . .' (2.4.857–60).[1]

In conclusion, whereas, in the *Comedy*, Timon is unambiguously a wastrel using his wealth to buy friendship, in the corresponding scenes in Shakespeare's play Timon's moral profile is ambivalent. This connects with another topic, the relation of money and usury to love and sexuality. In the *Comedy*, Timon embarks on a love affair with Callimela.[2] He competes with another suitor and Callimela is drawn to him because '[w]ho doth possesse most golde shall mee possesse / Let womans loue bee neuer permanent' (3.2.1263–4). Timon finds himself dismissed just as fast, and on the same grounds, as soon as he loses his wealth (3.5). After having found gold in the end, he is just as naturally seen once more as worth having as a husband.

In Shakespeare's *Timon* the relationship of money to love is an equally important feature, but it is focused not in main characters but minor ones, and not in terms of plot but in insinuations in the dialogue and bawdy imagery – for instance, in the greedy conduct of the two whores, Phrynia and Timandra ('Believe't that we'll do anything for gold' (4.3.151)), and in the bawdy exchanges of Apemantus, the Fool and the three Servants (2.2.50 ff.), where usury and desire for gold are coupled with sexual debauchery.[3]

In the *Comedy* a banquet is staged on the occasion of Timon's and Callimela's proposed wedding (3.4 and 3.5), which lends it a different focus from the banquet in *Timon* 1.2, where the focus is on friendship. The mock banquet in 4.5 of the *Comedy*, however, is more like the one in *Timon* 3.6. Timon wishes to be revenged on his former friends and followers; he feasts them on stones painted to resemble artichokes and then beats them up. And again as in Shakespeare he expresses his hatred of man's society and banishes himself from 'this inhumane City' (4.5.2098).

There are a few conspicuous verbal affinities which do not occur in the other treatments of the Timon legend. In the *Comedy*, the 'dissolate young man' Eutrapelus, when he is trying to escape the notice of the usurer Abyssus, says of himself 'my cloake / muffled my face' (1.2.70–1); in *Timon* 3.4.38, a stage direction presents the Steward Flavius '*in a cloak, muffled*' and Lucius says of him 'Ha! Is not that his steward muffled so?' After having helped Eutrapelus to pay his debt, Timon endorses his act of giving by saying 'I will not see my ffreinds to stand in neede' (*Comedy* 1.2.122); Timon, when bailing out Ventidius, endorses his act by saying 'I am not of that feather to shake off / My friend when he must need me' (1.1.104–5). In the *Comedy* Stilpo, one of the 'lying Philosophers', and others put pressure on Timon, now wealthy again: 'it is better to giue than receaue' (*Comedy* 5.5.2578–9); Timon, to confirm his giving out of

---

[1] For the play's inconsistencies about the value of a talent, cf. Supplementary Notes, 1.1.99.

[2] Callimela is the daughter of Philargurus, who is described as 'a Couetous churlish ould man' ('The Actors Names'). There is no direct equivalent to Shakespeare's *Timon* on the level of the plot. The circumstances rather remind one of Lucilius's love for the daughter of the Old Athenian in 1.1.114–56.

[3] See also 2.2.62–3 n.

selfless love, says '. . . there's none / Can truly say he gives, if he receives' (1.2.10–11).[1] Timon, in his distress, and lying on the ground, repeatedly declares life futile. 'Nothing . . . Nothing (I say) nothing / All things are made nothing' (*Comedy* 4.2.1773–6). In Shakespeare, Timon expresses his sense of futility by saying 'My long sickness / Of health and living now begins to mend, / And nothing brings me all things' (5.1.176–8).

Finally, John Lyly's play *Campaspe* (1584) has been listed as a 'possible source'.[2] The subplot is centred on Diogenes of Sinope, living with other philosophers at the court of Alexander the Great. Diogenes chooses a position in his community similar to Apemantus in his, and he is treated by his companions in a similar way: as a curiosity with whom it is possible to communicate only in the form of banter. Throughout, one of Diogenes' characteristics is his biting repartee, wherein he resembles Apemantus. Both 'dog' and 'beast' as forms of address are prominent; 'dog' being used by others to address Diogenes, 'beast' being used by either side as a degrading term to humiliate one's partner. In *Timon* we have similarly derisive remarks, by Apemantus in 1.1.204 and by Timon in 4.3.343–4 and 362, and this adds to the impression of there being some kind of link between the two plays. There is also in *Campaspe* the topic of 'eating' and 'being eaten'. One of the company remarks of Diogenes and his servant that 'nowe do they dine one upon another';[3] in *Timon* there is Timon's remark to Alcibiades about 'a breakfast of enemies' and 'a dinner of friends' (1.2.72–3) and many other references to this image cluster.[4]

TIMON'S DESCENDANTS

There is no evidence that Shakespeare's *Timon*, despite being printed in the Folio of 1623 and in subsequent editions of the seventeenth and eighteenth centuries, was performed then.[5] The play has, however, attracted an unusually large number of writers who adapted it in conformity with the literary taste of their times.

The first and most far-reaching adaptation is Thomas Shadwell's *The History of Timon of Athens, the Man-Hater* (1678).[6] While giving credit to 'the inimitable hand of *Shakespear*' Shadwell makes the claim that he has made it into a 'Play', implying that

---

[1] See also the Commentary on these lines.

[2] Bullough, VI, 339–45.

[3] Bullough, VI, 341.

[4] E.g. 1.1.205–6; 1.1.252–3; 1.1.273; 3.2.58–9; 3.4.48. Other verbal and thematic echoes between Lyly's and Shakespeare's plays include the following: while they are bandying insults, the question arises of whether or not Diogenes should 'flye' to escape their hateful company; Apemantus does the same in *Timon* 1.1.271: 'I will fly like a dog, the heels o'th'ass.' References to being 'honest' occur in Lyly's play – 'unlesse thou be honest' (Bullough, VI, 343) – as well as in *Timon* 1.1.185 and 1.1.257. In *Campaspe* 4.1 (Bullough, VI, 342–4) Diogenes hurls a sustained curse against Athens. In Shakespeare's play, this is repeatedly done by Timon. But in contrast to Timon's curses, Diogenes distinguishes between being a 'hater of menne', which he is not, and a 'hater of your maners', which he says he is. Making such a distinction would show that Diogenes' hatred is not to be understood as a general disposition of misanthropy, but as a criticism of the Athenian corruption of manners.

[5] There are, however, hypotheses about early productions, based on theories about the nature of the play; as e.g. by Bradbrook, whose claim that the *Comedy of Timon* was conceived as a burlesque of Shakespeare's play requires 'that Shakespeare's play must have been given on the stage, since burlesque would be pointless unless the original were generally familiar' ('Comedy', pp. 83–4).

[6] *The Complete Plays of Thomas Shadwell*, ed. Montague Summers, 5 vols., III, 1927.

Shakespeare's 'Masterly strokes' were a jumble and had not attained the structural coherence that a good play demands (p. 194).[1]

Shadwell aims to do this first by breaking up Shakespeare's rigorous focus on the figure of the misanthrope; second, by placing Timon in more varied configurations to show more of his human potential, both in its positive and its negative aspects. In doing this, Shadwell is following and developing elements in the *Comedy of Timon*, particularly the relationship of love and sexuality to wealth and luxury. Shadwell introduces two women figures (in the *Comedy* there is one): one of them, Melissa, the daughter of a Senator, allows herself to be played for by rich suitors; the other, Evandra, a subdued and faithful type, follows Timon in his exile and serves him to the very end. Shadwell's Timon has a different moral stature, since he is not only profligate with his wealth but gives rein to lust for Melissa and shows ingratitude to Evandra.

Shadwell also attempts a strengthening and reshaping of the link between the main plot and the Alcibiades subplot. His Alcibiades functions as Timon's rival for Melissa; concurrently, Timon shows his friendship for him by petitioning the Senators to lift their ban on Alcibiades.

Above all, in the play's closure, Shadwell enhances Alcibiades' heroic stature by adding suitable incidents: Alcibiades gets the opportunity to punish Apemantus for his aggressiveness, but forbears to do so. He also forbears to take his revenge on the Senators for having dealt unjustly with him. Again, he spares the citizens, even though he knows that they have treated him badly.

Quite a few passages of Shakespeare's *Timon* reappear in Shadwell's play either verbatim or with slight changes. But many of them are assigned to other speakers or addressed to a different character. Flavius's words of self-justification in *Timon* 2.2.151–7 and 2.2.162–4 are assigned by Shadwell to Apemantus (p. 219), which gives Apemantus a completely different quality. The meeting of the truthful woman Evandra and Timon, during his exile (pp. 251–60), follows a similar plot pattern to that of the meeting of Flavius and Timon in Shakespeare (4.3.450 ff.), Evandra using words similar to those used in Shakespeare by Flavius. Conversely, Shadwell's Timon uses words in speaking to Evandra (p. 253) that are similar to those used by Shakespeare's Timon to Flavius (*Timon* 4.3.516–18). Evandra in Shadwell has taken on Flavius's role of the loyal follower – the Steward as well as the servants having adopted a hostile attitude towards Timon.[2] Shadwell's changes add to the play's alienating effect.[3]

---

[1] See also Brian Vickers, *Returning to Shakespeare*, 1989, pp. 216–17.

[2] Evandra's role in Shadwell's play is still further upgraded by her being assigned words in Act IV (p. 254) originally spoken by Timon in *Timon* 4.3.179–86. Furthermore, she serves as Timon's dialogue partner in the context of important speeches, like the one on the power of gold in *Timon* 4.3.26–42, which carries the thrust of a monologue, whereas in Shadwell's play, Timon's words are tied up in a dialogue with Evandra and thus take on a more conversational quality (p. 253).

[3] The question of Shadwell having blended Shakespeare's *Timon* with Molière's *Le Misanthrope* (1666) has been raised. However, apart from more superficial resemblances such as the introduction of two major female roles, Alceste's misanthropy is very different from Shakespeare's and Shadwell's *Timon*. Alceste's disdain of his society is rooted in his moral claim to a life of absolute honesty, which clashes with the vested interests of others who are either hypocritical or temperately pragmatic and conformist. Alceste applies his moral principles with equal rigour to his private life: he expects the woman he loves (Célimène) to accept his views. In the end, he presses her to make a decision about whether to follow him in his self-imposed exile or risk the break-up of their relationship (cf. John Edmunds, '*Timon of Athens* blended with *Le Misanthrope*: Shadwell's recipe for satirical tragedy', *MLR* 64 (1969), 500–7).

The next version to appear was the one by James Love in 1768; he reduced the role of women by dropping Melissa, but he kept Evandra. In his adaptation of 1771, Richard Cumberland broke completely with the fashion of representing Timon as being entangled in the snares of women's love. Instead, Timon is provided with a daughter, Evanthe, who becomes the love object of both Alcibiades and Senator Lucius, with Alcibiades prevailing through his honesty. When these plot supplements are integrated into a mainly Shakespearean text, they produce jarring effects. But except for these additions, Cumberland follows the words of Shakespeare's *Timon* much more closely than Shadwell. The closure, however, goes off at a tangent, with justice being served out to the hypocritical and flattering Lords, and Timon, in the presence of his daughter and Alcibiades, dying a long and wordy death. There is a further adaptation by Thomas Hull of 1786, in which Shadwell's emphasis on the role of women is continued.

In 1816, George Lamb made an attempt to restore Shakespeare's text for stage presentation, 'with no other omissions than such as the refinement of manners has rendered necessary'.[1] The omissions include: removing Cupid from the banquet in 1.2; the dropping of Apemantus and the Fool in 2.2; Phrynia's and Timandra's non-appearance in 4.3 and the dropping of all references to them; as well as the Poet's and Painter's scene in 5.1. But the omissions also include some verbal bowdlerising, affecting either coarse passages in dialogues such as 4.3.278–81, where Timon enlarges on Apemantus's origin; or obscure and punning passages such as Apemantus's speech 4.3.248–54, and parts of Timon's and Apemantus's banter 4.3.286–91. Also cancelled are the extended references to beasts 4.3.326–48. The most drastic encroachment on Shakespeare's play comes, however, at the play's closure, when Lucius, Lucullus, Sempronius and other friends of Timon's are 'brought in bound'; when justice at last prevails and their treasures are taken from them.

TIMON IN GERMANY

The most remarkable, albeit abortive, attempt to dramatise the subject of the misanthrope in Germany was made by Friedrich Schiller. He could draw on various treatments of the subject: Christoph Martin Wieland, who was well versed in the classic portrayal of Timon, had translated Lucian into German and had produced a prose translation of Shakespeare's play in 1763; Johann Joachim Eschenburg had supplied another prose translation in 1777. In his commentary on the translation, Eschenburg had expressed his high estimation of the play, setting it against other plays in the canon: 'Without doubt, *Timon of Athens* belongs to the best Shakespearean plays, and is, on the whole, one of the most instructive.'[2] Thus, Schiller found abundant interpretation and commentary to provide a basis for his own attempts at tackling the problem of Timon and misanthropy. He started out with a very high appreciation of Shakespeare's *Timon*:

[1] George Lamb, *Timon of Athens*, a facsimile published by Cornmarket Press, 1972, with an introduction by T. P. Matheson. Advertisement.
[2] J. J. Eschenburg, 'Über Timon von Athen', in *William Shakespear's Schauspiele. Neue Ausgabe*, x, Zürich, 1777, pp. 424–44, p. 430 (my translation).

Sure as I am that I would look for stage representations of man in Shakespeare above all other places, I am just as unfailingly aware that there is no play in the Shakespeare canon where I could meet man more truthfully, where he could speak to my heart with a louder and more eloquent voice, and where I could learn more of life's wisdom, than in *Timon of Athens*.[1]

With regard to his own creative plans, he wrote in the same year: 'Our theatre will and must have a reinforcement of many new and excellent plays through myself, and amongst them are Macbeth and Timon.'[2] The Timon adaptation envisaged here never came to pass. Instead, he set out to compose a new play – a tragedy – on the theme of the misanthrope. His early comments on the play's growth are quite positive; he even thought that his play would surpass his previous writings.[3] However, in 1788 he realised that the subject was proving to be intractable: 'after having carefully and critically considered the matter, I had to abandon the plan after repeated and abortive attempts. This type of misanthropy is far too general and philosophic a concept to be treated in the tragic manner.'[4] In his judgement, his failure in writing the play seems to be intrinsic to the subject. The play remained a fragment and was published with the title 'Der versöhnte Menschenfeind' ('The reconciled misanthrope').[5] It remains a matter for conjecture whether one can draw parallels from the fact that two eminent playwrights have each left uncompleted a play on a comparable topic.[6]

Authorship

Dr Johnson's general criticism of the play's structural deficiencies – that 'in the plan there is not much art' and that 'many passages [are] perplexed, obscure, and probably corrupt'[7] – influenced subsequent editors, as well as critics, and gave rise to what may

[1] 'Was kann eine gute stehende Schaubühne eigentlich wirken?' (1784): '. . . so gewiss ich den Menschen vor allem andern zuerst im Shakespear aufsuche, so gewiss weiss ich im ganzen Shakespear kein Stück, wo er wahrhaftiger vor mir stünde, wo er lauter und beredter zu meinem Herzen spräche, wo ich mehr Lebensweissheit lernte, als im Timon von Athen' (lecture; first published in *Thalia* 1 (1785), 1–27, 13–14) (my translation). This passage was deleted in 1802 when the lecture was re-edited, under the title 'Die Schaubühne als moralische Anstalt betrachtet', in *Kleinere prosaische Schriften*, IV.

[2] Letter to Dalberg 24 August 1784: 'Durch mich allein wird und muss unser Theater einen Zuwachs an vielen vortreflichen neuen Stükken bekommen, worunter Makbeth und Timon . . . sind' (*Schillers Werke. Nationalausgabe*, XXIII: *Schillers Briefe 1772–1785*, 1956, p. 155) (my translation).

[3] See letter to Göschen 3 March 1787 (*Schillers Werke. Nationalausgabe*, XXIV: *Schillers Briefe 1785–1787*, 1989, pp. 83–4).

[4] Letter to Körner 26 November 1790: 'diesen Gedanken habe ich nach der reifsten kritischen Überlegung und nach wiederholten verunglückten Versuchen aufgeben müssen. Für die tragische Behandlung ist diese Art Menschenhass viel zu allgemein und philosophisch' (*Schillers Werke. Nationalausgabe*, XXVI: *Schillers Briefe 1790–1794*, 1992, p. 58) (my translation).

[5] For an analysis of the fragmentary character of the play and his reasons for abandoning it, see Käte Hamburger, 'Schillers Fragment "Der Menschenfeind" und die Idee der Kalokagathie', *Deutsche Vierteljahrsschrift für Literaturwissenschaft und Geistesgeschichte* 30 (1956), 367–400.

[6] The reasons that Schiller adduced for his unsuccessful handling of the subject matter bear a certain resemblance to Oliver's and Craig's hypotheses regarding Shakespeare's unsuccessful treatment of the Timon story – that Timon is 'not right for great tragedy' (Oliver, p. li) and that 'there is no drama in mere non-participation, where it arises from avoidance of the conflict or from definite refusal to participate' (H. Craig, *An Interpretation of Shakespeare*, 1948, p. 246; cited by Oliver, p. li).

[7] *Johnson on Shakespeare*, ed. Walter Raleigh, 1908, pp. 165–6.

not have been Johnson's objective at all: doubt about Shakespeare's sole authorship of the play.

One result has been to exonerate Shakespeare from charges of poor performance by attributing parts of the play to another playwright, to an 'inferior' author. Charles Knight[1] was the first to do this, on metrical and structural evidence: he regarded certain scenes such as 3.5 as completely unmetrical; in particular, the 'offensive recurrence of the couplet' confirmed his opinion that an inferior playwright must have been involved. He also identified several scenes as not integrated into the play's overall movement.[2]

This 'inferior-second-author' theory was developed by both editors and critics in the second half of the nineteenth century and the first two decades of the twentieth. Gulian C. Verplanck[3] conjectured the existence of traces of an inferior hand, although he considered the play to be substantially Shakespeare's. Henry N. Hudson and R. Grant White[4] provided detailed attributions of Shakespearean and non-Shakespearean passages.[5]

Frederick G. Fleay and Ernest Hunter Wright[6] took great pains to differentiate in detail between Shakespeare's authentic passages and those which they thought could not be his. Couplets as well as irregular and unscannable lines were considered to be unworthy of Shakespeare. This method of portioning out the play in terms of dramatic craftsmanship and metrical art is unconvincingly carried out.[7]

Just as inadequate were the attempts to identify the 'inferior' playwright whose work supposedly served as a draft that Shakespeare had used or whose work, conversely, was a revision or completion of a draft that Shakespeare had left in an unfinished state. Advocates of the first alternative, that Shakespeare had grafted on an already existing play, are: G. C. Verplanck, who suggested Heywood as the second writer; Nicolaus Delius, who suggested an anonymous playwright without attempting to identify him;[8] J. M. Robertson, who gave the inferior parts to Chapman;[9] William Wells, who was the first to hold Middleton responsible for an original play on Timon that Shakespeare partially revised;[10] and H. Dugdale Sykes, who attributed the earlier drafts partly to Thomas Middleton and partly to John Day.[11] Among those who favoured a generative process in the other direction, with Shakespeare as author of the original draft, were: F. G. Fleay, who suggested Cyril Tourneur as co-author; Thomas

[1] Charles Knight, 'Introductory notice to *Timon of Athens*', pp. 331–43.
[2] Such scenes are 1.2; 2.2.50–113; most of 3.1–6; 4.2; 5.1.1–105; 5.3.
[3] *Shakespeare's Plays*, ed. G. C. Verplanck, 1844–7.
[4] *The Works of William Shakespeare*, ed. H. N. Hudson, 1880–1 (Harvard edn); *Mr William Shakespeare's Comedies Histories Tragedies and Poems*, ed. R. Grant White, 1883 (Riverside edn).
[5] Butler provides a list of passages that were thought Shakespearean or non-Shakespearean according to the divided-authorship theories of the nineteenth and beginning of the twentieth century (pp. 39–41).
[6] F. G. Fleay, 'On *Timon of Athens*', Part I (1874), Part II (1869), *Shakespeare Manual*, 1876, repr. 1970; E. H. Wright, *The Authorship of 'Timon of Athens'*, Columbia University Studies in English, 1910.
[7] See E. K. Chambers, 'The disintegration of Shakespeare', *Proceedings of the British Academy*, 1924.
[8] N. Delius, 'Über Shakespeare's *Timon of Athens*', *SJ* 2 (1867), 335–61.
[9] J. M. Robertson, *Shakespeare and Chapman*, 1917, pp. 123–81.
[10] W. Wells, '*Timon of Athens*', *N&Q* 12th ser., 6 (1920), 266–9.
[11] H. Dugdale Sykes, 'The problem of *Timon*', *N&Q* 12th ser., 13 (1923), 83–6, 105–7, 123–6, 145–9, 166–8, 188–90, 208–10; and *Sidelights on Elizabethan Drama*, 1924, pp. 1–48.

Parrott, who chose Chapman and an unidentified third writer as possible revisers;[1] and M. Dixon Wector, who developed the theory that, for political reasons, Shakespeare's play was given to Thomas Middleton for the purpose of being revised.[2]

The dual-authorship theory has lately been revived, though on more rational grounds and with more methodical procedures. Thomas Middleton turns out to be the only one still under serious consideration. In his study *The Canon of Thomas Middleton's Plays* (1975), David J. Lake devoted Appendix V to a thorough investigation into the probability of Middleton's co-authorship of *Timon of Athens*. He added further linguistic details to Wells's and Sykes's findings, such as frequency studies of contractions and elisions in Middleton and Shakespeare, which partly corroborated Wells's and Sykes's attribution of particular scenes to Middleton. Nevertheless, Lake came to the conclusion 'that the evidence available at present is inadequate to resolve the problem of authorship' and he did not go beyond voicing 'a strong suspicion of Middleton's presence'.[3] Macdonald P. Jackson increased the body of evidence by listing O-Oh spellings and analysing rare-word frequencies in Shakespeare and Middleton; his conclusions, however, are also rather low-key: 'I am sure of nothing about *Timon*, and my aims are modest – to turn some of the prevailing certainty over the play into uncertainty.'[4] The attitude of caution here may strengthen an awareness that, cogent as these patterned resemblances may be in detail, they include after all only a small percentage of the possible elements of the text. There are important features suggesting one author, Shakespeare. Hibbard, amongst others, pointed out the consistency of the play's imagery;[5] Nuttall also argued for a more cautious approach in matters of authorship and collaboration.[6]

Nevertheless, the editors of the 1986 Oxford Shakespeare attribute portions of *Timon of Athens* to Middleton with such a degree of certainty that in their *Complete Works*,[7] Shakespeare and Middleton together figure as authors of the play.[8] In the complementary volume, *A Textual Companion*,[9] they display the evidence:

(1) Image clusters: these are said to exist in Shakespeare's share of *Timon of Athens*, but not in the share attributed to Middleton.[10] Only a few examples need be cited to show the dubiousness of this evidence.

(a) The 'breeding' metaphor is to be found in 1.1.277–8 ('no gift to him / But

---

[1] T. Parrott, *The Problem of 'Timon of Athens'*, Shakespeare Association, 1923.

[2] M. Dixon Wecter, 'Shakespere's purpose in *Timon of Athens*', *PMLA* 43 (1928), 701–21.

[3] D. J. Lake, *The Canon of Thomas Middleton's Plays*, 1975, p. 285.

[4] M. P. Jackson, *Studies in Attribution: Middleton and Shakespeare*, Salzburg, 1979, pp. 215, 155–6 and 63–4.

[5] Hibbard, 'Sequestration', pp. 215–17.

[6] Nuttall, p. 39.

[7] *William Shakespeare: The Complete Works*, ed. S. Wells *et al.*, 1986.

[8] It should be noted that their attributions differ considerably from previous ones, most conspicuously in giving a lesser share of 1.1 to Middleton; in attributing 2.2.1–49 and 4.2.1–29 to Middleton; and in regarding 5.1 and 5.3 as Shakespearean.

[9] S. Wells *et al.*, *William Shakespeare: A Textual Companion*, 1987.

[10] Image clusters are defined, after Armstrong, as patterns of associations between images (*A Textual Companion*, p. 78).

breeds the giver a return . . .'), a passage attributed to Middleton; yet the same metaphor figures prominently in parts of the play definitely attributed to Shakespeare, e.g. 2.1.9–10 ('it [i.e. his horse] foals me straight / And able horses'; 4.3.1–4 ('O blessed breeding sun . . . Twinned brothers of one womb, / Whose procreation, residence, and birth . . .'); 4.3.179–81 ('Common mother, thou / Whose womb unmeasurable and infinite breast / Teems and feeds all . . .').

(b) The imagery of 'flood', 'flowing' and related words: there is a 'flood of visitors' in 1.1.43; there is furthermore 'the ebb of your estate' and a 'great flow of debts' in 2.2.135–6 – all parts of the play that are attributed to Shakespeare; yet there is also a 'flow of riot' (2.2.3), a 'tide / Of knaves' (3.4.110–11) and the phrase 'He pours it [i.e. his bounty] out' (1.1.275), all passages attributed to Middleton.

(c) Repetition: 'All studies of internal evidence, in any art form, depend upon the fact that artists repeat themselves.'[1] Here is an example: at 4.2.25–7 we have 'Let's shake our heads, and say, / As 'twere a knell unto our master's fortunes, / "We have seen better days."' This, say the Oxford editors, is Middleton. Yet in *AYLI* 2.7.113–14 we find: 'If ever you have look'd on better days, / If ever been where bells have knoll'd to church . . .' and at 2.7.120–1: 'True is it that we have seen better days, / And have with holy bell been knoll'd to church . . .'

(2) Metrical evidence: according to the Oxford editors, 'unusual mixtures of rhyme, irregular verse, and prose in the suspect scenes of *Timon*' substantiate a claim regarding authorship, since they 'resist rationalization'.[2] It is true that 1.2, which is attributed to Middleton, shows an unusual percentage of rhyming couplets, which E. H. Wright had already subsumed under 'unworthy' elements; and the intermixture of prose passages had already been pointed out by F. G. Fleay. The Oxford editors give no clue as to why these metrical anomalies, if such they be, should point towards Middleton, neither do they provide any count of metrical anomalies in those scenes which are attributed to Shakespeare. Even a rough count will show that 'metrical anomalies' (the term itself presupposes a definitive norm, which may be a misguided assumption) – i.e. long and short lines – appear interspersed throughout the play and particularly numerously in 1.1, but not only in the part attributed to Middleton, and certainly not fewer than in 1.2, which is given to Middleton. Yet many short lines, probably the greatest percentage in any scene, occur in 5.1 – a scene which the Oxford editors attribute to Shakespeare.

(3) Linguistic evidence, depending on a count of certain elisions and contractions, which has been the main body of evidence in Lake's and Jackson's studies, is not much in favour with the Oxford editors.[3]

(4) Stage directions are not seriously adduced as evidence for Middleton's share. Mention is made of an 'Enter'-formula peculiar to Middleton: 'Enter X meeting Y'.[4] This formula occurs only once in *Timon*, at 3.4.0 SD.

---

[1] *Ibid.*, p. 77.
[2] *Ibid.*, p. 79.
[3] *Ibid.*, p. 80.
[4] *Ibid.*

(5) The main ground for the Oxford editors' assertion that parts of *Timon* cannot have been written by Shakespeare is the function-words test. It is a computer-based frequency study of common words such as 'but', 'not', 'to', etc.; these words occur with a determinable consistency in an author's work and thus provide evidence, should the statistical deviation either fall considerably below or above the standard deviation typical of an author. This method may serve to exclude a work from an author's canon, but cannot with any degree of conclusiveness attribute it to a specific canon.

UNFINISHED PLAY THEORIES

Johnson's criticism of the play's structural deficiencies has also induced critical responses of a very different kind. These responses assume that Shakespeare has to be considered the sole author of the play, and that the structural weaknesses result from his incompletely realised conception of the play, so that certain incidents have never grown beyond the stage of 'false starts'. Shakespeare started a new plot aspect but did not develop it. Others have supposed that Shakespeare abandoned the play for unknown reasons at a pretty early stage of its growth, with the result that details of the plot were left unconnected and that characters were sketched but not fully developed.

Why should Shakespeare have abandoned a play at such a stage? The explanation rendered by Susan Handelman[1] proceeds on a psychoanalytic line of argument and is based on a certain assumption of what art should accomplish. She holds that the play as it stands shows 'a breakdown of all those ways in which rage, pain, and loss can somehow be accepted, made sense of, transformed into life-affirming energies'.[2] Shakespeare's awareness that the play does not meet his own expectations of what art should accomplish must supposedly have been the reason for abandoning it. Clearly, this presupposes a notion of what art should achieve, but it also shows a peculiar similarity to what Schiller said about his own abortive attempts, first with his projected Timon play, and then with his substitute project 'The Reconciled Misanthrope'.[3]

This hypothesis of *Timon* as an unfinished and abandoned play was first proposed by Wilhelm Wendlandt;[4] its most powerful and persuasive presentation was given by Una Ellis-Fermor.[5] She argued that thinking of the play text as being in different stages of completion serves much better to explain its unrelated parts and the insufficiently worked out details than assuming that there was a second hand – and would not a second hand have completed the work? Ellis-Fermor does not cover up the play's many weaknesses; she painstakingly points them out, and regards Timon himself as

[1] Handelman, pp. 45–68.
[2] *Ibid.*, p. 48.
[3] See pp. 60–1 above.
[4] W. Wendlandt, 'Shakespeare's *Timon von Athen*', *SJ* 23 (1888), 107–92.
[5] Ellis-Fermor, pp. 270–83.

the greatest and weightiest unrelated element; she goes so far as to say that he has no individuality and that his character is inadequate to the theme.[1]

Many critics before and after Ellis-Fermor believe Shakespeare is the sole author of the play.[2] Furthermore, new knowledge of forms of structural coherence other than those of plot and character involves reassessing what were called structural deficiencies.[3] A. D. Nuttall's very cautious conclusion seems cogent: '*Timon of Athens* is one play not two, superficially disfigured by technical inconsistencies but conceptually and imaginatively coherent.'[4]

[1] She sees the main inconsistencies of the plot (1) in the disconnected and therefore inexplicable appearance of the Fool (2.2); and (2) in the similarly disconnected character of the trial scene (3.5). Analysing parts of this scene and pointing out the characteristics of what she calls 'broken speeches', she persuasively argues that such a condition cannot well be imagined as being the result of second-hand interferences, but very well as the product of a man 'who was roughing out a scene' (Ellis-Fermor, p. 274) and then abandoning it and leaving it in this form. A more pragmatic, but none the less highly speculative explanation for the unfinished state of the play was given by F. W. Brownlow, who, arguing against the tendency to allot the play to Shakespeare's 'tragic period', suggested taking the author's unexpected death as a cogent reason for its having been left incomplete (Brownlow, p. 221).

[2] Among them are Chambers, *Shakespeare*, I, 480–4; Draper, 'The theme of *Timon*'; R. A. Haug, 'The authorship of *Timon of Athens*', *SAB* 15 (1940), 227–48; Greg, pp. 408–11.

[3] 'Viewed as a private fantasy, the play is complete. The details which Ellis-Fermor describes as missing are "essential" only for logical consistency and social significance, two Shakespearean goals which, in this case, seem to have been secondary to the expression of the personal myth ringing changes on the scene in which someone is being flattered' (Skura, p. 169).

[4] Nuttall, p. 39.

The Life of Timon of Athens

LIST OF CHARACTERS

TIMON OF ATHENS

FLAVIUS, *Timon's Steward*

FLAMINIUS
LUCILIUS   } *servants to Timon*
SERVILIUS

Other SERVANTS *to Timon*

ALCIBIADES, *an Athenian captain*

PHRYNIA
TIMANDRA } *mistresses to Alcibiades*

SOLDIER *of Alcibiades' army*

APEMANTUS, *a churlish philosopher*

A FOOL

A PAGE

LORDS *and* SENATORS *of Athens, some of them flattering Lords*

LUCIUS
LUCULLUS
SEMPRONIUS } *flattering Lords and false friends*
VENTIDIUS

CAPHIS, *servant to a Senator who is Timon's creditor*

ISIDORE SERVANT, *servant to one of Timon's creditors*

VARRO 1 *and* 2 SERVANT, *servants to one of Timon's creditors*

HORTENSIUS
LUCIUS
PHILOTUS } *servants to Timon's creditors*
TITUS

A POET

A PAINTER

A JEWELLER

A MERCHANT

An OLD ATHENIAN

Three BANDITTI

Three STRANGERS, *one called* HOSTILIUS

One dressed as CUPID

Ladies dressed as AMAZONS

Messengers, Attendants, Soldiers

Notes

An incomplete list of 'The Actors' Names' was given in F. The present list differs substantially from that first list as well as from subsequent ones in the assignment of names and in the groupings of characters.

Among the group of Lords and Senators of Athens there is a sub-group of Flattering Lords, partly unspecified in terms of names and figures. Within this group there is another sub-group of False Friends, i.e. those whom Timon approached for a loan. Of these only four are assigned individual names.

A separate group is that of Timon's creditors – in F called 'Usurers' – of whom only one appears briefly in person (the Senator in 2.1), whilst all the others are represented only by their servants.

Of the creditors' servants, only one has a clearly assigned individual name (Caphis). Equally clearly, Isidore's and Varro's servants take on the names of their masters. With the other four servants to Timon's creditors, the naming problem cannot be finally resolved.

The identity of the master to the servant Lucius is discussed at pp. 186–7 below.

Most of the names in *Timon* stem from North's Plutarch. Shakespeare found Timon, Alcibiades and Apemantus in 'The Life of Marcus Antonius'; six other names – Lucius, Hortensius, Ventidius, Flavius, Lucilius and Philotus – occur in the parts of 'The Life of Marcus Antonius' that do not deal with Timon. The name Timandra is to be found in 'The Life of Alcibiades'. Phrynia is not mentioned in Plutarch; she was an exquisite Athenian courtesan and artist's model.

Some of the names are etymologically significant:

Timon may be derived from the Greek *timé*, denoting 'honour', 'value', 'worth' (see Murray J. Levith, *What's in Shakespeare's Names*, 1978, p. 65).

Apemantus means 'to be free from misery and not to be affected by the evils of the world' (Bradbrook, *Craftsman*, p. 157).

Timandra denotes 'man-honour' (M. Nussbaum, *The Fragility of Goodness*, 1986, p. 177).

THE LIFE OF TIMON OF ATHENS

[1.1] *Enter* POET, PAINTER, JEWELLER, MERCHANT, *at several doors*

POET Good day, sir.
PAINTER   I am glad y'are well.
POET I have not seen you long, how goes the world?
PAINTER It wears, sir, as it grows.
POET   Ay, that's well known.
　　　　But what particular rarity? What strange,
　　　　Which manifold record not matches? See   5
　　　　Magic of bounty, all these spirits thy power
　　　　Hath conjured to attend! I know the merchant.
PAINTER I know them both; th'other's a jeweller.
MERCHANT O, 'tis a worthy lord.
JEWELLER   Nay, that's most fixed.
MERCHANT A most incomparable man, breathed, as it were,   10

Title] The Life of Tymon of Athens. F   Act 1, Scene 1   1.1] *Actus Primus. Scoena Prima.* F   0 SD MERCHANT] *Johnson;*
Merchant, and Mercer F   5 matches?] *Pope;* matches: F   7] *Pope;* Hath . . . attend. / I . . . Merchant. F

Act 1, Scene 1

1.1 After the initial *Actus Primus. Scoena Prima* F does not provide any further act or scene divisions.

0 SD F adds a *Mercer*, perhaps misinterpreting the Merchant's speech heading, given in F as *Mer.*

0 SD *at . . . doors* In a theatre with three doors, the central door could have been used by Timon, the side doors by the 'confluence' and 'flood' of visitors (43).

2 **long** for a long time.

3 **It . . . grows** It wears away, sir, as it grows larger and older. The theory that the world has been in steady decline since the Fall, and is 'worn', was a commonplace; see *Lear* 4.6.134–5: 'This great world / Shall so wear out to nought', and John Donne, 'The First Anniversary. An Anatomy of the World', 201: 'So did the world from the first houre decay' (*The Complete English Poems*, ed. C. A. Patrides, 1985). A paradox is involved, that growth

carries the stigma of decay – an early foreshadowing of what Timon's 'world' is like.

4 **What strange** What is strange.

5 **record** Accented on the second syllable.

5–7 **See . . . attend** According to the poet, Timon's liberality gathers attendants around him, just as the art of the magician conjures up spirits. The question is, are these good or evil spirits? In Jacobean stage performance, entrances 'at several doors' could be made as if resulting from a magical summons. M. C. Bradbrook observes that '*Good* spirits were not conjur'd into a circle' (*Pageant*, p. 7). Alternatively, the 'magic' and 'power' are projected upon Timon by his followers and admirers.

6 **bounty** liberality. For a discussion of this frequently used term, see Supplementary Note, p. 175 below.

9 **fixed** certain.

10 **breathed** 'so trained as not to be wearied' (Johnson).

To an untirable and continuate goodness;
He passes.
JEWELLER I have a jewel here.
MERCHANT O, pray let's see't. For the Lord Timon, sir?
JEWELLER If he will touch the estimate. But for that –   15
POET When we for recompense have praised the vile,
It stains the glory in that happy verse
Which aptly sings the good.
MERCHANT   'Tis a good form.
JEWELLER And rich. Here is a water, look ye.
PAINTER You are rapt, sir, in some work, some dedication   20
To the great lord.
POET   A thing slipp'd idly from me.
Our poesy is as a gown which uses
From whence 'tis nourished. The fire i'th'flint
Shows not till it be struck. Our gentle flame
Provokes itself, and like the current flies   25
Each bound it chases. What have you there?

---

16 vile] *Pope;* vild F   20–1 You . . . lord.] *Pope; prose* F   21 idly] F2; idlely F   22 gown] F, gum *Pope*   22 uses] F; issues *Pope;* oozes *Johnson*   26 chases] F; chafes *Theobald*

11 **untirable** indefatigable.

11 **continuate** long-continued.

11–12 **goodness . . . passes** 'he is of surpassing virtue' or 'he is financially sound'. Compare *MV* 1.3.15–17: 'my meaning in saying he is a good man is to have you understand me that he is sufficient'.

15 **touch the estimate** come up to the estimated price.

16–18 'If we poets sacrifice truth for money in praising the vile, we damage even good poems praising the truly good.' Many editors since Warburton have used quotation marks to suggest that the Poet is reciting from his own work.

18 **form** shape (the Merchant continues to examine the jewel).

19 **water** 'the transparency and lustre characteristic of a diamond or a pearl' (*OED* Water *sb* 20).

20 **rapt** (1) wholly absorbed or engrossed (as a form of concentration on something), (2) transported with some emotion, ravished (with the implication that one is being carried away and lifted out of oneself). The second meaning unfolds in the Poet's 'free drift' passage (46–51). In *Temp.* Prospero speaks of being 'transported / And rapt in secret studies' (1.2.76–7).

21 **idly** casually.

22–6 I follow the F reading with Hulme (p. 12), who would rather stick to 'an *Elizabethan* perplexity' than follow 'eighteenth-century certainties'. The problematic first simile apparently combines two ideas: (1) poetry is like a gown hanging on its patron, which, as time passes, wears out (for the proverbial background see Tilley G387 and Hulme, p. 82); and (2) the interest poetry once generated in the patron, who originally nourished it, consumes itself. This process of something being 'Consum'd with that which it was nourish'd by' is explored on different grounds in Sonnet 73; it also has a striking analogue in Volumnia's 'I sup upon myself, / And so shall starve with feeding' (*Cor.* 4.2.50–1). If one accepted the emendation 'gum' for 'gown' and 'oozes' for 'uses' one could agree with Seamus Heaney that here Shakespeare is 'glossing the abundance and naturalness of his own art' in the Poet's words (*Preoccupations*, 1980, p. 79). There then follow two straightforward comparisons: unlike the fire in the flint, which has to be produced by striking (see Tilley F371: 'In the coldest flint there is hot fire'), the flame of poetic inspiration is self-generating; and poetry is like a current that both heads for and overleaps boundary after boundary.

PAINTER   A picture, sir. When comes your book forth?
POET   Upon the heels of my presentment, sir.
                    Let's see your piece.
PAINTER   'Tis a good piece.
POET   So 'tis. This comes off well, and excellent.   30
PAINTER   Indifferent.
POET   Admirable! How this grace
            Speaks his own standing! What a mental power
            This eye shoots forth! How big imagination
            Moves in this lip! To th'dumbness of the gesture
            One might interpret.   35
PAINTER   It is a pretty mocking of the life.
            Here is a touch; is't good?
POET   I will say of it,
            It tutors nature; artificial strife
            Lives in these touches, livelier than life.

            Enter certain SENATORS [*and pass over the stage*]

PAINTER   How this lord is followed.   40
POET   The senators of Athens, happy men.
PAINTER   Look moe!

---

34 lip! To] *Johnson/Steevens*⁵; Lip, to F   39 SD *and pass over*] *Capell; not in* F

28 **Upon . . . presentment** As soon as it has
been presented.
29–35 Whether the Painter's picture ('piece') is a
portrait of Timon remains an open question.
30 **well, and excellent** excellently well.
31 **Indifferent** Tolerably.
31–2 **How . . . standing** How this man's
graceful appearance expresses his dignity.
33–4 **How big . . . lip** How powerfully the
imagination of this man comes alive in his lip. The
poet emphasises the depiction of speech, of imagination naturally proceeding from a person's lips.
34–5 **To th'dumbness . . . interpret** Although
the painted gesture (of the lip) is silent, it is so
expressive that a poet might give words to it (Riverside). The Renaissance commonplace, originally
ascribed to Simonides, held that 'Painting is a
dumme Poesie, and a Poesie is a speaking painting'
(G. G. Smith (ed.), *Elizabethan Critical Essays*,
1904, I, 342). For an exposition of the *paragone*
problem in Shakespeare's time, see Supplementary
Notes, p. 175 below.
36 **mocking . . . life** counterfeiting of the living
person, suggesting both the sense of imitation
(without deceit) and of feigning (with the intention
to deceive).

37 **touch** A stroke of a pencil or a brush (see also
39).
38 **tutors nature** tells nature what it could or
should be like.
38 **artificial strife** (1) the striving of art to outdo
nature or life, (2) striving that is 'artful, cunning,
deceitful' (*OED* Artificial II.9). Taken with line 39's
'Lives . . . livelier than life' the Poet at once praises
the Painter for transfusing nature with art, and con-
demns him for contrived and false ('artificial') exag-
geration ('livelier than life'). The Poet subtly avoids
the commendatory terms of *WT* 4.4.95–7 where art
and nature harmoniously combine: 'This is an art /
Which does mend Nature . . . but / The art itself is
Nature.'
39 **livelier** (1) more lifelike, (2) more energetic;
see *OED* Lively *a* 3 and 4a.
39 SD Capell was the first to add *and pass over*,
indicating that 'persons of the rank of those *Senators*
pass to Timon's apartment, and pay their court to
him there' (*Notes and Various Readings to Shakespeare*, II, 1780).
41 **happy men** This F reading suggests that
the Poet envies the Senators' privileged access to
Timon.
42 **moe** more.

POET You see this confluence, this great flood of visitors.
    I have in this rough work shaped out a man
    Whom this beneath world doth embrace and hug   45
    With amplest entertainment. My free drift
    Halts not particularly, but moves itself
    In a wide sea of wax; no levelled malice
    Infects one comma in the course I hold,
    But flies an eagle flight, bold, and forth on,   50
    Leaving no tract behind.
PAINTER How shall I understand you?
POET I will unbolt to you.
    You see how all conditions, how all minds,
    As well of glib and slipp'ry creatures, as   55
    Of grave and austere quality, tender down
    Their services to Lord Timon. His large fortune,
    Upon his good and gracious nature hanging,
    Subdues and properties to his love and tendance

---

48 wax] F; tax *Alexander*

44 rough unpolished, without refinement. In view of the Poet's role this need not be read as self-denigration, but rather as spoken with a touch of false modesty.

45 this beneath world this earthly world beneath heaven.

46–7 My free . . . particularly My free poetic impulse does not linger over particulars.

47–8 but moves . . . wax The reading 'sea of wax' is disputed: 'wax' means the soft material (capable of melting to a fluid) formerly used for moulding and writing (as the coating of a waxen tablet); hence moving in a 'wide sea of wax' could suggest a freely ranging inspiration not to be confined in a single tablet of wax. 'Wax' as a verb means 'grow' (as in *Cor.* 2.2.99: 'he waxed like a sea'); the word could then subliminally suggest the swelling inspiration of poetic impulse. As A. D. Nuttall notes, there is a parallel with 5.4.65–9 where the word 'wax' occurs close to the word 'sea' and 'the poetry is working strongly with notions of hardness and softness, and then of formlessness' (pp. 9–11).

48–9 no . . . hold there are no intended malicious hints in the poetic line I follow; 'levelled' suggests 'aimed', the archer's arrow fledged with feathers, just as the Jacobean poet wrote with a quill, a sharpened feather, the poet's weapon. As Nuttall points out (p. 11), 'comma' is a small group of words, 'infects' means affects.

50 an eagle flight The soaring eagle is an emblem of noble thought. See Tilley E7, who quotes

from Sidney, *Arcadia:* 'Eagles we see fly alone, and they are but sheepe, which alwaies heard together.' See also Webster, *The Duchess of Malfi* 5.2.30–1: 'Eagles commonly fly alone. They are crows, daws, and starlings that flock together' (ed. Elizabeth M. Brennan, 1993); and *Tro.* 1.2.243–4: 'the eagles are gone; crows and daws . . .'

51 Leaving . . . behind His free drift is so bold that it cannot be traced in its course, and thus it outdoes the mundane way of writing which leaves traces (particularly if written on waxen tablets). Nuttall (p. 11), writing about lines 46–51, follows Armstrong in seeing a reference to the myth of Icarus, to be applied, in the final analysis, not to the Poet and his soaring imagination, but to Timon, as later in 2.1.30–2.

53 unbolt explain.

54 all conditions people of different social positions and moral dispositions.

56 tender down offer; with the connotation 'to lay down in payment' (*OED* Tender *v*[1] 1b); related to 'tendance' in 59 and 83 meaning the bestowal of personal attention.

57–60 His . . . hearts The image of wealth as clothing (his fortune is 'hanging' on him) suggests that it is not himself but his possession of wealth that binds other people to him, and that it is weighing him down. The verbs, 'Subdues and properties', suggest oppressive submission and possession, but ostensibly relate here to his 'love and tendance'.

All sorts of hearts; yea, from the glass-faced flatterer   60
To Apemantus, that few things loves better
Than to abhor himself; even he drops down
The knee before him, and returns in peace
Most rich in Timon's nod.

PAINTER I saw them speak together.   65

POET Sir, I have upon a high and pleasant hill
Feigned Fortune to be throned. The base o'th'mount
Is ranked with all deserts, all kind of natures
That labour on the bosom of this sphere
To propagate their states. Amongst them all,   70
Whose eyes are on this sovereign lady fixed,
One do I personate of Lord Timon's frame,
Whom Fortune with her ivory hand wafts to her,
Whose present grace to present slaves and servants
Translates his rivals.

PAINTER   'Tis conceived to scope.   75
This throne, this Fortune, and this hill, methinks,
With one man beckoned from the rest below,
Bowing his head against the steepy mount
To climb his happiness, would be well expressed

---

67 *Rowe;* Feign'd . . . thron'd. / The . . . Mount F   75 conceived to scope.] *Johnson;* conceyu'd, to scope F

60 glass-faced flatterer The notion of 'flatterer' as 'mirror' was proverbial (Dent G132.1); the mirror functions as a standard emblem of pride. See *R2* 4.1.279–81: 'O flatt'ring glass, / Like to my followers in prosperity, / Thou dost beguile me!'

61–2 Apemantus . . . himself The Poet's explanation of Apemantus's demeanour is highly doubtful. Hanmer's conjecture, 'to make himself abhorr'd', is closer to Apemantus's real behaviour.

64 rich . . . nod feeling himself most amply rewarded by Timon's merest sign of recognition.

66–97 For the concept of Fortune, see p. 1 above.

68 ranked . . . deserts occupied by people of different merit.

69 on . . . sphere on the surface of this earth. See *John* 4.1.2–3: 'When I strike my foot / Upon the bosom of the ground'; entry 2 in *OED* Bosom *sb* says 'Applied to the surface of the sea . . . or the ground'. In more recent criticism, 'bosom' is taken as belonging to the play's 'core fantasy' of the 'nurturing mother', especially when taken with line 70's 'propagate'; see p. 31 above.

70 propagate increase, multiply (*OED* Propagate *v* 2a).

70 their states their condition or position in life (*OED* State *sb* 15).

72 personate represent.

72 frame physical and mental nature.

73 ivory hand 'as white as ivory' is proverbial (see Tilley 1109). S. C. Chew (*Pilgrimage*, p. 50) comments: 'is it not implied that her other hand is of ebony?' – which, if true, would underline the fickle nature of Fortune.

74–5 Whose . . . rivals Fortune's favours presently bestowed on Timon instantly transform his rivals for these favours into slaves and servants (Riverside). The emphasis on 'present' brings out Fortune's changeability and arbitrary suddenness (see Patch, p. 55).

75 to scope fittingly.

79–80 would . . . condition would find an appropriate expression in our art (of painting). The phrase 'in our condition' has been interpreted as referring to the human condition but this is less likely in view of the Painter's eagerness to play his own art off against the Poet's.

    In our condition.

POET   Nay, sir, but hear me on: 80
All those which were his fellows but of late,
Some better than his value, on the moment
Follow his strides, his lobbies fill with tendance,
Rain sacrificial whisperings in his ear,
Make sacred even his stirrup, and through him   85
Drink the free air.

PAINTER   Ay marry, what of these?

POET When Fortune in her shift and change of mood
Spurns down her late beloved, all his dependants
Which laboured after him to the mountain's top
Even on their knees and hands, let him slip down,   90
Not one accompanying his declining foot.

PAINTER 'Tis common:
A thousand moral paintings I can show,
That shall demonstrate these quick blows of Fortune's
More pregnantly than words. Yet you do well,   95
To show Lord Timon that mean eyes have seen
The foot above the head.

Trumpets sound. Enter LORD TIMON, *addressing himself courteously to every*
suitor; [*a* MESSENGER *from Ventidius;* LUCILIUS *and other servants*
following]

---

90 hands] F2; hand F   90 slip] *Rowe;* sit F; fall *Sisson*   94 Fortune's] *Malone;* Fortunes F; Fortune F2–4   97 SD.2 *a*
MESSENGER *from Ventidius*] Capell subst.; not in F   97 SD.2–3 LUCILIUS . . . *following*] Cam.²; not in F

82 **his value** his moral standing, his economic solvency, and his rank in society.

83 **his lobbies . . . tendance** crowd into his house to attend upon him.

84 **Rain . . . ear** Shower him with whispered expressions of adoration.

85–6 **through . . . air** Since, if the air is free, no man depends upon another's will to breathe it, this is an impossibly hyperbolic expression exposing the absurd degree of flattery and implying an almost overt cynicism in the flatterers, as well as Timon's wilful need to be deceived.

90* **slip** Rowe's emendation is more in line with the movement described than is F's 'sit'.

93–5 The Painter claims the superiority of painting over poetry and thus brings the rivalry of the verbal and visual arts to the fore. See Supplementary Note 1.1.30–1.

93 **moral paintings** paintings pointing out a moral – for instance, by allegory.

96 **mean eyes** common people's eyes (with a suggestion of small-mindedness and malice).

97 **The foot . . . head** The foot of Fortune ready to spurn the climber; or 'the great man falling head-long', as suggested in Riverside. See Dent (F562) for a proverbial version of this phrase.

97 SD The stage direction in F has only Lord Timon enter, *addressing himself courteously to every suitor.* From the dialogue it is clear that the messenger from Ventidius is necessary. The SD *Lucilius and other servants following* is adopted from Cam.², so that he should be present when Timon calls for him in 118. Shakespeare's stagecraft provides an image of Timon dispensing generously, which the preceding dialogue has already subjected to complex inspection. The dialogue opens with Timon talking to Ventidius's messenger; he addresses the other suitors in the course of the scene. The F stage direction is not practicable, but is (perhaps) an au-

TIMON Imprisoned is he, say you?
MESSENGER Ay, my good lord, five talents is his debt,
        His means most short, his creditors most strait.   100
        Your honourable letter he desires
        To those have shut him up, which failing
        Periods his comfort.
TIMON   Noble Ventidius! Well,
        I am not of that feather to shake off
        My friend when he must need me. I do know him   105
        A gentleman, that well deserves a help,
        Which he shall have. I'll pay the debt, and free him.
MESSENGER Your lordship ever binds him.
TIMON Commend me to him; I will send his ransom,
        And being enfranchised, bid him come to me;   110
        'Tis not enough to help the feeble up,
        But to support him after. Fare you well.
MESSENGER All happiness to your honour!   *Exit*

Enter an OLD ATHENIAN

OLD ATHENIAN Lord Timon, hear me speak.
TIMON   Freely, good father.
OLD ATHENIAN Thou hast a servant named Lucilius.   115
TIMON I have so. What of him?
OLD ATHENIAN Most noble Timon, call the man before thee.
TIMON Attends he here, or no? Lucilius!
LUCILIUS Here, at your lordship's service.
OLD ATHENIAN This fellow here, Lord Timon, this thy creature,   120
        By night frequents my house. I am a man

---

105 must need] F; most needs F3–4   114 SH OLD ATHENIAN] F4 *subst.*; Oldm. / *or* / Old. F (*throughout scene*)

thor's note indicating what Lord Timon's role should be generally here, an authorial reminder of how to structure the scene. (Dessen, p. 56, uses the term 'fictional signals' for notes that 'show the dramatist thinking out loud in the process of writing . . .') If the printer's copy was authorial, not marked up for performance, this might also explain why there is no mention of the messenger's entrance, nor of Lucilius's. See the Textual Analysis, p. 188 below.

99 five talents For a discussion of the inconsistent handling of the number of talents, see p. 177 below.

100 strait severe, exacting.

101 Your . . . letter A letter from your honour.

102 which failing the lack of which.

103 Periods Puts an end to.

104 feather character. See also 2.1.30.

105 when . . . me 'when he cannot but want my assistance' (Malone).

108 binds obliges. But Timon's gesture of generosity unwittingly involves oppression.

110 enfranchised released from confinement.

112 But . . . after But it is also necessary to support him afterwards.

118 Attends he Is he in attendance.

120 creature dependant; not necessarily in a contemptuous sense (quoted *OED* Creature 5).

120–1 The emphasis is on 'thy' and 'my'.

That from my first have been inclined to thrift,
And my estate deserves an heir more raised
Than one which holds a trencher.

TIMON   Well; what further?

OLD ATHENIAN One only daughter have I, no kin else,   125
On whom I may confer what I have got.
The maid is fair, a'th'youngest for a bride,
And I have bred her at my dearest cost
In qualities of the best. This man of thine
Attempts her love; I prithee, noble lord,   130
Join with me to forbid him her resort,
Myself have spoke in vain.

TIMON The man is honest.

OLD ATHENIAN   Therefore he will be, Timon.
His honesty rewards him in itself,
It must not bear my daughter.   135

TIMON Does she love him?

OLD ATHENIAN   She is young and apt;
Our own precedent passions do instruct us
What levity's in youth.

TIMON [*To Lucilius*]   Love you the maid?

LUCILIUS Ay, my good lord, and she accepts of it.

OLD ATHENIAN If in her marriage my consent be missing,   140
I call the gods to witness, I will choose
Mine heir from forth the beggars of the world,
And dispossess her all.

TIMON   How shall she be endowed,
If she be mated with an equal husband?

133] *This edn;* The . . . honest. / Therefore . . . *Timon,* F   133 be, Timon.] F4; be *Timon,* F   136] *Oliver;* Does . . . him? / She . . . apt: F   138 levity's] F3–4; leuities F, F2   138 SD] *Johnson subst.; not in* F   143] *Johnson/Steevens⁵;* And . . . all. / How . . . endowed, F

122 thrift economy, frugality (as the speaker's conscious meaning); but thrift could include profit-making as well as niggardliness (see *OED* Thrift *sb¹* 3).

124 holds a trencher waits at table.

127 a'th'youngest . . . bride of the youngest age – i.e. just old enough – to marry.

128–9 bred her . . . best spared no effort or expense in bringing her up.

129 qualities accomplishments.

130 Attempts Is trying to attain.

131 her resort access to her.

133–5 Therefore . . . daughter If he really is honest he will continue to be so; honesty is its own

reward: it does not require the added reward of my daughter in marriage. For the proverb 'Virtue is its own reward' see Dent v81.

135 bear win as a prize (as in *JC* 1.2.131: 'bear the palm alone').

136 apt 'susceptible to impressions' (*OED* Apt *a* 5), but with a sexual undercurrent (see Colman, p. 183).

137 precedent former. The accent is on the second syllable.

143 all completely.

143 How . . . endowed What dowry shall she have.

144 equal of equal social rank and wealth.

OLD ATHENIAN Three talents on the present, in future, all.   145
TIMON This gentleman of mine hath served me long;
    To build his fortune, I will strain a little,
    For 'tis a bond in men. Give him thy daughter;
    What you bestow, in him I'll counterpoise,
    And make him weigh with her.
OLD ATHENIAN   Most noble lord,   150
    Pawn me to this your honour, she is his.
TIMON My hand to thee, mine honour on my promise.
LUCILIUS Humbly I thank your lordship, never may
    That state or fortune fall into my keeping,
    Which is not owed to you.   155

                     Exit [with Old Athenian]

POET Vouchsafe my labour, and long live your lordship.
TIMON I thank you, you shall hear from me anon.
    Go not away. What have you there, my friend?
PAINTER A piece of painting, which I do beseech
    Your lordship to accept.
TIMON   Painting is welcome.   160
    The painting is almost the natural man;
    For since dishonour traffics with man's nature,
    He is but outside; these pencilled figures are
    Even such as they give out. I like your work,
    And you shall find I like it. Wait attendance   165

146] *Rowe;* This . . . mine / Hath . . . long: F   152] *Pope;* My . . . thee, / Mine . . . promise. F   155 SD *with Old Athenian*] *Theobald subst.; not in* F   156] *Pope;* Vouchsafe . . . Labour, / And . . . Lordship. F   163 outside] *Warburton;* out-side F

145 all i.e. everything I have.

146 gentleman Attendant of a person of rank (as in *Lear* 1.3.1–2: 'Did my father strike my gentleman for chiding of his Fool?').

148 bond bond of loyalty and moral obligation; also a constraint that binds people to all kinds of issues (as e.g. legal or financial bonds).

149–50 counterpoise . . . weigh with her Timon uses the metaphor of a pair of scales, as if each young person were a weight of gold, to be balanced equally.

151 Pawn . . . honour Give me your honour as a surety to this offer. The Old Athenian continues the mercenary language; honour cannot, of course, properly be pawned.

153–5 never . . . you 'let me never henceforth consider any thing that I possess, but as *owed* or *due* to you; held for your service, and at your disposal' (Johnson).

156 Vouchsafe Deign to accept.

161–4 Man dishonestly appears to be what inwardly he is not. He lives by outward seeming. The painting, depicting outward appearance, does so honestly. Dr Johnson paraphrases: 'Pictures have no hypocrisy; they are what they profess to be.' See Supplementary Notes, p. 177 below.

162 traffics to have dealings with (either commercial dealings or dealings of an illicit or secret character: see *OED* Traffic *v* 1 and 2b).

163 but outside His external appearance is the only indication we have of his nature, and this is not reliable. Maxwell adds: 'Shakespeare almost always uses "outside" with an implication of false semblance.'

164 give out show. Shakespeare usually employs the phrase to suggest a wilfully deceiving attitude (as in *R3* 4.2.56–7: 'I say again, give out / That Anne, my queen, is sick'), but he can also, as here, apply it in a neutral sense.

Till you hear further from me.

PAINTER   The gods preserve ye.

TIMON Well fare you, gentleman; give me your hand.
We must needs dine together. Sir, your jewel
Hath suffered under praise.

JEWELLER What, my lord, dispraise?   170

TIMON A mere satiety of commendations;
If I should pay you for't as 'tis extolled,
It would unclew me quite.

JEWELLER   My lord, 'tis rated
As those which sell would give; but you well know,
Things of like value differing in the owners,   175
Are prizèd by their masters. Believe't, dear lord,
You mend the jewel by the wearing it.

TIMON Well mocked.

Enter APEMANTUS

MERCHANT No, my good lord, he speaks the common tongue
Which all men speak with him.   180

TIMON Look who comes here; will you be chid?

JEWELLER We'll bear with your lordship.

MERCHANT   He'll spare none.

169–70 F; Hath . . . dispraise? (*one line*) *Johnson/Steevens*⁴   171 satiety] F4; saciety F   178 SD APEMANTUS] F4;
Apermantus F, F2–3 (*and throughout*)   182 We'll bear with] F; We'll bear it with *Pope*

168–9 your . . . praise The jewel has been much
praised and, in consequence, has been given a high
market value, which from the purchaser's point of
view is a disadvantage. The Jeweller misunder-
stands, thinking Timon meant 'underpraise' (=
dispraise).

171 mere complete, absolute.

173 unclew ruin, undo (literally: unwind a ball of
thread).

174 As . . . give At cost price.

176 Are . . . masters Different values will be
placed on them by different owners. A similar suggestion is made by Troilus: 'What's aught but as 'tis
valued?' (*Tro.* 2.2.52), and in Sonnet 96: 'As on the
finger of a thronèd queen / The basest jewel will be
well esteem'd . . .' (5–6).

177 mend increase its value.

178 Well mocked A good mimicking of an
ingenious argument (Timon is both appreciative
and ironic).

178 SD I retain F's early placing of Apemantus's
entrance. The large size of the Elizabethan stage

meant that an actor might enter at a door in the
tiring-house but not be part of the action played
towards the forward edge of the thrust-stage; the
actor would have to take several paces when he
did join the action. Here I suppose Apemantus is
noticed first by the audience and only later, when
he moves slowly forward (182), by Timon and his
visitors. See also below 5.1.0 SD and n.

179–80 he . . . him he only says what everyone
else would say.

181 will . . . chid do you have a mind to be
scolded? This, together with the Jeweller's and
Merchant's answers, indicates that Timon and his
friends distance themselves from Apemantus, brace
themselves to meet him playfully. In a similar,
perhaps somewhat more accommodating way Duke
Senior and his friends prepare to meet Jacques, who
is also an outsider: 'I love to cope him in these sullen
fits . . .' (*AYLI* 2.1.67).

182* We'll . . . lordship We'll endure (the
scolding of Apemantus) together with your lordship.

TIMON   Good morrow to thee, gentle Apemantus.

APEMANTUS   Till I be gentle, stay thou for thy good morrow.

When thou art Timon's dog, and these knaves honest.   185

TIMON   Why dost thou call them knaves? Thou know'st them not.

APEMANTUS   Are they not Athenians?

TIMON   Yes.

APEMANTUS   Then I repent not.

JEWELLER   You know me, Apemantus?   190

APEMANTUS   Thou know'st I do, I call'd thee by thy name.

TIMON   Thou art proud, Apemantus.

APEMANTUS   Of nothing so much, as that I am not like Timon.

TIMON   Whither art going?

APEMANTUS   To knock out an honest Athenian's brains.   195

TIMON   That's a deed thou'lt die for.

APEMANTUS   Right, if doing nothing be death by th'law.

TIMON   How lik'st thou this picture, Apemantus?

APEMANTUS   The best, for the innocence.

TIMON   Wrought he not well that painted it?   200

APEMANTUS   He wrought better that made the painter, and yet he's but
a filthy piece of work.

PAINTER   Y'are a dog.

APEMANTUS   Thy mother's of my generation; what's she, if I be a dog?

183] *Rowe;* Good . . . thee, / Gentle *Apermantus.* F   **183** Apemantus] F4; *Apermantus* F, F2–3 *(and throughout)*   **194** Whither] F4; Whether F, F2–3

184–5 Till . . . honest You can wait for your good morrow until I am gentle and until you are Timon's dog and these knaves honest (that is, you can wait for ever). Since the word 'cynic' derives from the Greek word for 'dog', this seems to be, in view of Timon's invectives in Act 4, a cryptic foreshadowing of future developments.

185–6 The bitter banter between Apemantus and the group around Timon has certain structural and verbal resemblances to *Lear* 2.2. Apemantus's naming of his opposites as 'knaves' is followed by Timon's question 'Why dost thou call them knaves?'; Kent's naming of Oswald as 'knave' is followed by Cornwall's question 'Why dost thou call him knave?' (*Lear* 2.2.88–9). The Painter calls Apemantus a dog, and with the same term Kent rails against Oswald (*Lear* 2.2.80); Apemantus's denigration of the Painter (202–3) has an equivalent in Kent's abusive description of Oswald as the bad work of a painter (*Lear* 2.2.58–60).

191 thy name i.e. knave.

192–3 Compare this sequence with 4.3.284, where the speakers' roles are inverted.

195–7 Apemantus plays a witty trick on Timon by referring to an 'honest' Athenian who, in his view, of course, does not exist.

199 innocence Judging by 202–3 this can in no way be intended as praise; 'ignorance' or 'silliness' (*OED* Innocence 3) is a more likely interpretation.

201–3 Compare Kent's bickering with Oswald in *Lear* 2.2.54–60 and, in addition, Beckett's variation on the idea of God's and man's creative competence in Nagg's story of the Tailor (*Endgame*, in *The Complete Dramatic Works*, 1986, pp. 101–3).

204 generation (1) breed, (2) age.

204 what's . . . dog Apemantus turns the insult against the Painter: his mother would be called (1) a bitch, (2) a cynic, with the implication that she must have been cynical about having given birth to a son like the Painter.

TIMON Wilt dine with me, Apemantus?   205
APEMANTUS No; I eat not lords.
TIMON And thou shouldst, thou'dst anger ladies.
APEMANTUS O, they eat lords; so they come by great bellies.
TIMON That's a lascivious apprehension.
APEMANTUS So thou apprehend'st it, take it for thy labour.   210
TIMON How dost thou like this jewel, Apemantus?
APEMANTUS Not so well as plain-dealing, which will not cast a man a
    doit.
TIMON What dost thou think 'tis worth?
APEMANTUS Not worth my thinking. How now, poet?   215
POET How now, philosopher?
APEMANTUS Thou liest.
POET Art not one?
APEMANTUS Yes.
POET Then I lie not.   220
APEMANTUS Art not a poet?
POET Yes.
APEMANTUS Then thou liest: look in thy last work, where thou hast
    feigned him a worthy fellow.
POET That's not feigned, he is so.   225
APEMANTUS Yes, he is worthy of thee, and to pay thee for thy labour.
    He that loves to be flattered is worthy o'th'flatterer. Heavens, that I
    were a lord!
TIMON What wouldst do then, Apemantus?
APEMANTUS E'en as Apemantus does now: hate a lord with my heart.   230

208] Pope; O . . . Lords; / So . . . bellies. F   210] Pope; So . . . it, / Take . . . labour. F   212 cast] F; cost F3   215] Pope;
Not . . . thinking. / How . . . Poet? F   225 feigned] F2; fegin'd F   226 Yes, he] F4; Yes he F

206–8 The eating-images within their larger context are discussed at pp. 26–8 above.
206 I . . . lords I do not consume their wealth.
207 And If.
208 they eat lords Taking up Timon's remark,
Apemantus plays on the sexual meaning of 'eat'
('use up sexually', Colman, p. 192; 'enjoy sexually',
Williams). This is part of a preoccupation with
cannibalism running through the play's imagery.
209 apprehension (1) way of perceiving, (2)
grasping in the physical sense. Timon may not be
aware of the ambiguity, but Apemantus certainly is,
as he shows in his repartee.
210 So . . . labour Provided that (1) you perceive it this way, (2) you seize the opportunity of a
sexual encounter, take it for your pains.

212–13 cast . . . doit The F reading (plain-
dealing will not render a man a doit) recalls the
proverb 'Plain dealing is a jewel, but they that use it
die beggars' (Dent P382). The F3 reading 'which
will not cost a man a doit', adopted by many editors,
is also in keeping with Apemantus's jibes at the
values of this society, but it is an easier reading and
from a non-authoritative text.
212–25 Apemantus is playing with the conventional charge that poets are liars (compare Smith, I,
p. xxviii). The standard arguments against this
accusation are either that, since the poet does not
affirm anything to be true, he cannot be accused of
lying (see Sidney, *Apology*, in Smith, I, 184–5), or
that 'the truest poetry is the most feigning' (*AYLI*
3.3.19–20).

TIMON What, thyself?

APEMANTUS Ay.

TIMON Wherefore?

APEMANTUS That I had no angry wit to be a lord. Art not thou a
merchant?   235

MERCHANT Ay, Apemantus.

APEMANTUS Traffic confound thee, if the gods will not.

MERCHANT If traffic do it, the gods do it.

APEMANTUS Traffic's thy god, and thy god confound thee.

Trumpet sounds. Enter a MESSENGER

TIMON What trumpet's that?   240

MESSENGER 'Tis Alcibiades, and some twenty horse,
All of companionship.

TIMON Pray entertain them, give them guide to us.

[*Exeunt some Attendants*]

You must needs dine with me; go not you hence
Till I have thanked you; when dinner's done   245
Show me this piece. I am joyful of your sights.

Enter ALCIBIADES *with the rest*

Most welcome, sir.

APEMANTUS So, so; there! Aches contract and starve your supple
joints! That there should be small love amongst these sweet knaves,
and all this courtesy! The strain of man's bred out into baboon and   250
monkey.

234–5] *Capell;* That . . . Lord. / Art . . . Merchant? F   243 SD] *Capell; not in* F   248–51] F; *as verse,* Capell
248 *So . . . there!*] Capell; So, so; their F

234–5 'I hate myself for not having had the angry
wit to be a lord, so that I could have hated myself
properly.' Theobald, Warburton and Johnson
suppose that Apemantus retracts his former wish
to be a lord – now. More recent editors explain
Apemantus's words as an expression of regret that
he had no ampler wit than to be a lord (see Maxwell).

237 **Traffic** Trade, business.

239 SD The announcement of Alcibiades' arrival
by a trumpet is in accordance with the ceremonial
character of the scene.

242 **All of companionship** All coming in a
body.

244–5 **You . . . you . . . you** With the first 'you'
Timon may be addressing the Merchant and the
Jeweller, with the second and third, the Poet and
the Painter.

246 **Show . . . piece** Most likely the painting.
This would suggest that when the painting was presented to him earlier (159–60), he did not even
deign to look at it; that his expressions of liking
(164–5) were patronising gestures; and that his
deliberations on painting and man's nature are very
general indeed.

246 SD The unspecified stage direction in F *Enter
Alcibiades with the rest* needs to be restricted to fewer
than the twenty announced in 241.

248 **So, so; there!** Apemantus mocks the ceremony of greeting.

248 **Aches** Pronounced as two syllables.

248 **contract and starve** cripple and disable.

249 **sweet** i.e. feigning kindness.

250 **strain** race, line (*OED* Strain *sb*¹ 6).

250 **bred out** degenerated.

ALCIBIADES Sir, you have saved my longing and I feed
    Most hungerly on your sight.
TIMON   Right welcome, sir!
    Ere we depart, we'll share a bounteous time
    In different pleasures. Pray you let us in.   255

                      Exeunt [all but Apemantus]

             Enter two LORDS

FIRST LORD What time o'day is't, Apemantus?
APEMANTUS Time to be honest.
FIRST LORD That time serves still.
APEMANTUS The most accursèd thou that still omit'st it.
SECOND LORD Thou art going to Lord Timon's feast?   260
APEMANTUS Ay, to see meat fill knaves, and wine heat fools.
SECOND LORD Fare thee well, fare thee well.
APEMANTUS Thou art a fool to bid me farewell twice.
SECOND LORD Why, Apemantus?
APEMANTUS Shouldst have kept one to thyself, for I mean to give thee   265
    none.
FIRST LORD Hang thyself!
APEMANTUS No, I will do nothing at thy bidding; make thy requests to
    thy friend.
SECOND LORD Away, unpeaceable dog, or I'll spurn thee hence.   270
APEMANTUS I will fly like a dog, the heels o'th'ass.   *[Exit]*
FIRST LORD He's opposite to humanity.
    Come, shall we in, and taste Lord Timon's bounty?
    He outgoes the very heart of kindness.
SECOND LORD He pours it out; Plutus, the god of gold,   275

---

255 *Rowe;* In . . . pleasures. / Pray . . . in. F   255 SD.1 *all but Apemantus*] *Capell; not in* F   255 SD.2 *Enter two* LORDS] F;
Enter Lucius *and* Lucullus *Rowe*   268–9] *Pope;* No . . . bidding: / Make . . . Friend. F   270] *Pope;* Away . . . Dogge, /
Or . . . hence. F   271 o'th'ass] *Rowe;* a'th'Asse. F   271 SD] *Hanmer subst.; not in* F   273 Come] F2; Comes F   273 taste]
F2; raste F   273–4] *Pope;* Comes . . . in, / And . . . out-goes / The . . . kindnesse. F

252 **saved my longing** prevented me from
merely longing to see you. According to Dent
this was a common phrase and not restricted to
'Woman's longing' (L422.1).
  253 **hungerly** hungrily.
  257 **Time . . . honest** It is characteristic of
Shakespeare's technique here to have Apemantus
answer the most common of questions with one of
the key terms of the play.
  259 **omit'st** neglect, leave unregarded.
  261 **knaves . . . fools** The 'fool and knave' combination is common in proverbs – see Dent (F506.1).

270 **unpeaceable** quarrelsome (the only instance
in Shakespeare: the play is remarkable for the
number of words not found elsewhere in
Shakespeare).
  272 **opposite** antagonistic, adverse.
  274 **outgoes** exceeds.
  275 **He . . . out** An ambiguous phrase, suggesting both his magnanimity and his prodigality.
  275 **Plutus . . . gold** Plutus is often emblemati-
cally depicted as a boy with a cornucopia; he is
reputed to 'pour out' his wealth indiscriminately
(see A. Henkel and A. Schöne (eds.), *Emblemata.*

    Is but his steward; no meed but he repays
    Sevenfold above itself; no gift to him
    But breeds the giver a return exceeding
    All use of quittance.
FIRST LORD   The noblest mind he carries
    That ever governed man.   280
SECOND LORD Long may he live in fortunes! Shall we in?
    I'll keep you company.

                                Exeunt

[1.2] *Hautboys playing loud music. A great banquet served in,* [FLAVIUS *and*
SERVANTS *attending;*] *and then enter* LORD TIMON, *the States, the Athenian*
LORDS [ALCIBIADES, *and*] VENTIDIUS, *which Timon redeemed from prison.*
Then comes, dropping after all, APEMANTUS, *discontentedly like himself*

VENTIDIUS Most honoured Timon,
    It hath pleased the gods to remember my father's age,
    And call him to long peace.
    He is gone happy, and has left me rich.
    Then, as in grateful virtue I am bound   5
    To your free heart, I do return those talents,

Act 1, Scene 2   1.2] *Capell; not in* F 0 SD.1–2 FLAVIUS *and* SERVANTS *attending*] *Capell; not in* F 0 SD.3 ALCIBIADES
and] *Johnson; not in* F 0 SD.3 VENTIDIUS] F4; *Ventigius* F 1 SH VENTIDIUS] F4; *Ventig.* F

Handbuch zur Sinnbildkunst des XVI. und XVII.
Jahrhunderts, 1967, pp. 1565–6). C. Davidson
quotes from Abraham Fraunce, *The Third Part*
of the Countesse of Pembrokes Yvychurch (1592):
'Pluto *was accompted the Lord of riches and*
treasure . . . Plutos *in Greeke, signifieth riches*'
(Davidson, p. 192).

276 meed deserved praise, merit.

277–8 no . . . return The idea that a gift will
'breed' a multiplicity of further gifts springs from
the idea of a likeness between material (and
monetary) generation and sexual generation; it is
resumed in 2.1.5–10. In *MV* it is problematised in a
contention between Shylock and Antonio, Shylock
arguing for the naturalness of the 'use' of gold and
silver: 'I make it breed as fast' (1.3.96) – that is, as
fast as the natural generation of lambs referred to
earlier (1.3.76–90).

279 All . . . quittance 'All the customary
returns made in discharge of obligations'
(Warburton).

279 carries bears.

Act 1, Scene 2

0 SD Several features in this stage direction indicate the unfinished state of the manuscript. Flavius
and servants are omitted in F, although they are
required for serving the banquet; Alcibiades is not
mentioned but must be present since Timon gives
him an invitation and converses with him at 210–15.
Unspecific announcements, such as *the States*
(probably the governing body of a town; in the
present case, the Senators) and *the Athenian Lords*,
stand side by side with over-explanatory directions,
such as the reminder concerning Ventidius, and the
descriptive form in introducing Apemantus. Three
of *the Athenian Lords* have speaking parts in this
scene; they remain unidentified in F. So Rowe
(anticipating 2.2.181–3) names them Lucius,
Lucullus and Sempronius. However, the messages
and gifts from two of them, delivered by servants,
speak against their being or having been present.

5–6 I am . . . heart Ventidius later rejects
Timon's suit (3.3.4–11).

6 free (1) generous, (2) free from obligations.

Doubled with thanks and service, from whose help
I derived liberty.
TIMON   O by no means,
Honest Ventidius. You mistake my love;
I gave it freely ever, and there's none   10
Can truly say he gives, if he receives.
If our betters play at that game, we must not dare
To imitate them; faults that are rich are fair.
VENTIDIUS A noble spirit!
TIMON   Nay, my lords,
Ceremony was but devised at first   15
To set a gloss on faint deeds, hollow welcomes,
Recanting goodness, sorry ere 'tis shown;
But where there is true friendship, there needs none.
Pray sit, more welcome are ye to my fortunes
Than my fortunes to me.   20
                         [*Guests sit*]
FIRST LORD My lord, we always have confessed it.
APEMANTUS Ho, ho, confessed it? Hanged it, have you not?
TIMON O Apemantus, you are welcome.
APEMANTUS No, you shall not make me welcome;
I come to have thee thrust me out of doors.   25
TIMON Fie, th'art a churl, y'have got a humour there
Does not become a man; 'tis much to blame.
They say, my lords, *Ira furor brevis est*,

---

9 Ventidius] F4; *Ventigius* F   14 SH VENTIDIUS] F4; *Vint.* F   14–15] *Malone;* A . . . spirit. / Nay . . . first F   20 SD]
Rowe; not in F   21 SH FIRST LORD] F; *Luc*[*ius*] *Rowe* (*throughout scene*)   22 Hanged] F2; Handg'd F   26 y'have] *Kittredge;*
ye'haue F

7 **service** 'a term of mere courtesy' (Schmidt).
8 **derived** gained (see 3.4.64).
10–11 **there's . . . receives** There are two biblical references to the ethics of giving and receiving, which are more specific and less radical. Luke 6.34 denounces the attitude of giving with the hope of receiving: '. . . if ye lend to them of whom ye hope to receive, what thank have ye?' Acts 20.35 does not make a claim for a radical exclusion: 'It is more blessed to give than to receive.'
15–18 **Ceremony . . . none** Timon starts his harangue on the abuses of ceremony without having been prompted to it by occasion. Johnson tries to mitigate this abruptness by inserting a stage direction '*They all stand ceremoniously looking on* Timon.' His unprovoked outburst takes place in the midst of a highly ceremonious banquet which he is

about to celebrate with the still more ceremonial masque.
16 **set . . . on** give a fair (here: specious) appearance to.
17 **Recanting goodness** Unsaying one's good offers.
21 **confessed** avowed.
22 **confessed . . . not** Apemantus alludes to the proverb 'Confess and be hanged' (Tilley C587), where 'confess' means 'admit to a crime'. If the proverb is taken to be a ruder form of saying 'You lie' (see *OED* Confess *v* 10), Apemantus, in a witty way, is giving the lie to 1 Lord.
26 **humour** disposition, cast of mind.
28 *Ira furor brevis est* Anger is short madness (Horace, *Epistles* 1.2.62). See Burton, *Anatomy of Melancholy*, I, 311 ('On Anger'), and Dent A246.

But yond man is very angry.
Go, let him have a table by himself;   30
For he does neither affect company,
Nor is he fit for't indeed.

APEMANTUS Let me stay at thine apperil, Timon;
I come to observe, I give thee warning on't.

TIMON I take no heed of thee; th'art an Athenian, therefore welcome; I   35
myself would have no power, prithee let my meat make thee silent.

APEMANTUS I scorn thy meat; 'twould choke me, for I should ne'er
flatter thee.

[Sits at a table by himself]

O you gods! What a number of men eats Timon, and he sees 'em
not! It grieves me to see so many dip their meat in one man's blood,   40
and all the madness is, he cheers them up too.
I wonder men dare trust themselves with men.
Methinks they should invite them without knives,
Good for their meat, and safer for their lives.
There's much example for't; the fellow that sits next him, now parts   45
bread with him, pledges the breath of him in a divided draught, is
the readiest man to kill him. 'T'as been proved; if I were a huge
man, I should fear to drink at meals,
Lest they should spy my windpipe's dangerous notes;
Great men should drink with harness on their throats.   50

---

38 SD] *This edn; not in* F   49–50] *Rowe³; prose* F

29 **very angry** i.e. as opposed to being short, the anger is very intense. Rowe's emendation 'ever An-gry' focuses a different opposition. On a wider view of anger and man's nature see 3.5.58 and note.

31 **affect** like.

33 **apperil** risk.

35–6 **I . . . power** I myself refuse to have any power (in view of my role as host) to make you silent.

37–8 **'twould . . . thee** Capell mentions the vulgar saying 'that grudg'd meat choaks the person that eats of it' (*Notes*); applied to Apemantus: the meat would choke him since, not being a flatterer himself, it would have been given him under incorrect assumptions.

39–40 **O . . . blood** The imagery suggests the Last Supper; more concretely, it suggests a parody of the idea of sacrifice by turning it into a bestial cannibalistic feast (Matt. 26.23). It would be misleading, however, to deduce from these allusions that Timon should be seen as a Christ figure, or that this kind of imagery is intended to compel sympa-

thy for Timon. This is a further reference to Lucian's *The Dialogue of Timon*, where Timon's flatterers are described in parasitic terms (Bullough, VI, 265). See also note 1.2.72–3.

41 **all the madness** the maddest thing of all.

41 **all . . . too** Apemantus points out the bewildering insensitivity of Timon, who fails to perceive a perspective other than his own.

43 **invite . . . knives** It was a custom in Shakespeare's time for every guest to bring his own knife.

44 **Good . . . meat** They would eat less meat.

45 **much example** Referring to the custom mentioned in 43.

45 **parts** shares.

46 **pledges . . . draught** drinks his health from the shared cup.

49 'Dangerous' does not refer to 'notes' but to the spying: as done with a dangerous intention (the rhetorical figure hypallage, in which relations are reversed).

50 **harness** armour.

TIMON My lord, in heart; and let the health go round.
SECOND LORD Let it flow this way, my good lord.
APEMANTUS Flow this way? A brave fellow! He keeps his tides well.
　　Those healths will make thee and thy state look ill, Timon.
　　　　Here's that which is too weak to be a sinner,   55
　　　　Honest water, which ne'er left man i'th'mire.
　　　　This and my food are equals, there's no odds;
　　　　Feasts are too proud to give thanks to the gods.
　　　　　　　　　Apemantus' Grace
　　　　　　Immortal gods, I crave no pelf,
　　　　　　I pray for no man but myself;   60
　　　　　　Grant I may never prove so fond,
　　　　　　To trust man on his oath or bond;
　　　　　　Or a harlot for her weeping,
　　　　　　Or a dog that seems a–sleeping,
　　　　　　Or a keeper with my freedom,   65
　　　　　　Or my friends, if I should need 'em.
　　　　　　Amen. So fall to't;
　　　　　　Rich men sin, and I eat root.
　　　　Much good dich thy good heart, Apemantus.
TIMON Captain Alcibiades, your heart's in the field now.   70
ALCIBIADES My heart is ever at your service, my lord.

---

52 SH SECOND LORD] F; *Lucul[lus] Rowe*   70 Captain Alcibiades] *Hanmer;* Captaine, / *Alcibiades* F

51 My lord . . . round Timon is pledging one of the Lords 'my Lord's health with sincerity' (Johnson) and asks for the cup to go round.

53 Flow Further uses of 'flow' and 'flood' in the play imply superabundance, excess (1.1.43; 2.2.3; 2.2.136).

53 tides (1) time, season, (2) ebb and flow of the sea. Calculatingly, the Lord benefits from Timon's surges of generous giving.

54 Those . . . ill As so often, Apemantus uses proverbial wisdom in his arguments: 'To drink health is to drink sickness' (Tilley H292). Timon takes up a similar idea in 4.3.196–7: 'ingrateful man with liquorish draughts / . . . greases his pure mind'.

54 state situation, circumstances of fortune.

55 Here's that Apemantus drinks a toast with a cup of water.

55 sinner cause of sin.

56 which . . . mire Again proverbial: 'to leave (lie) in the mire' (Tilley M989).

57 odds difference in the way of benefit or detriment (*OED* Odds *sb* 2c).

58 Feasts Partakers of feasts (the figure metonymy).

58 proud arrogant, supercilious (*OED* Proud *a* B1).

58 *Apemantus' Grace* Presumably not meant to be spoken by Apemantus, but a caption for the ensuing prayer.

59–68 Apemantus's grace contains the traditional elements of saying grace, but in negative form.

59 *pelf* wealth, riches.

61 *fond* foolish.

65 *keeper* jailer.

69 dich Either a corruption of 'do it' (*OED* Dich) or an obsolete and dialect form of 'ditch' = smear, daub (*OED* Ditch *v²* *dial.*).

70 heart mind.

71 heart As the seat of love or affection (*OED* Heart *sb* 10).

TIMON You had rather be at a breakfast of enemies than a dinner of
friends.

ALCIBIADES So they were bleeding new, my lord, there's no meat like
'em; I could wish my best friend at such a feast.   75

APEMANTUS Would all those flatterers were thine enemies then, that
then thou mightst kill 'em – and bid me to 'em.

FIRST LORD Might we but have that happiness, my lord, that you
would once use our hearts, whereby we might express some part of
our zeals, we should think ourselves for ever perfect.   80

TIMON O, no doubt, my good friends, but the gods themselves have
provided that I shall have much help from you; how had you been
my friends else? Why have you that charitable title from thousands,
did not you chiefly belong to my heart? I have told more of you to
myself than you can with modesty speak in your own behalf; and   85
thus far I confirm you. O you gods, think I, what need we have any

---

72–3 You . . . friends 'breakfast of enemies' can
mean a breakfasting group of hostile persons
(*genetivus subjectivus*); but, taken by Apemantus as it
is here as *genetivus objectivus*, it means that the enemies are being breakfasted on. Alcibiades openly
plays upon this cannibalistic sense in his rejoinder
(74–5): the idea of slaughter can apply equally to
butchering animals and to slaying men in battle, and
death is said to feast on his victims. In *1H4* 2.4.102–
3 it is said of Hotspur 'he that kills me some six or
seven dozen of Scots at a breakfast'; in *Cor.* 1.9.10–
11 overcoming enemies is likened to eating: 'Yet
cam'st thou to a morsel of this feast, / Having fully
din'd before.' Correspondingly, 'a dinner of friends'
means a group of friends dining together, but in this
ironic context it also suggests the idea of feasting on
friends, i.e. of devouring (metaphorically: exploit-
ing, living at somebody else's expense) or being
devoured. In Lucian's account of Timon we find
the metaphor 'When they had finally eaten him
down to the bone, and sucked the marrow, they left
him dry and stripped from top to toe' (Bullough, VI,
265). Throughout Acts 1–3, associations are made
between eating, voracity and cannibalism, a proximity between the ideas of devouring and of civilised
social behaviour. (See also pp. 26–8 above)

74 So Provided that, if only.

77 bid invite.

79 use our hearts make use of our affection;
with an undercurrent of insinuation that he will
have to pay interest for it (see 1.1.274–9). This
rather vague offer by 1 Lord of his good services
gives Timon the clue for his ensuing speech.

80 perfect satisfied, happy.

83 charitable tender-hearted; loving, kindly
(*OED* Charitable *a* 2 *obs*).

83 from thousands from among thousands.

84 my heart my inmost being (*OED* Heart *sb*
6).

84–5 I . . . myself (1) I have made a broader picture of you to myself (quantitatively), (2) I have
spoken more highly of you (qualitatively). Both
senses conjoin in suggesting that the picture could
have fantasy elements in it that may not be endorsed
by what his friends 'really' are.

86 confirm you acknowledge your friendship.

86–8 In this part of his speech on friendship,
Timon repeatedly speaks of 'need', and finally of
'use'. Staunton suggests that either 'if we should
ne'er have need of 'em' or 'should we ne'er have use
for 'em' was intended to be cancelled. However,
these phrases may, rather than being redundant,
shed more light on Timon's idea of friendship.
Timon asks what friends are for, whether they are
needed; having need of friends is one of the purposes of having them at all. Being without friendship is the state of not being needed or wanted, of
being dispensable. To be in need of a friend is, on
the one hand, to desire a social bond but, on the
other, to subject others to one's own 'use' (which
carries the connotation of 'usury', see pp. 13–17
above); to be a 'needless creature' is undesirable – to
be dispensable, without social bonds; but it also
suggests autonomous existence, not being made
'use' of.

86 what for what purpose.

friends, if we should ne'er have need of 'em? They were the most
needless creatures living, should we ne'er have use for 'em, and
would most resemble sweet instruments hung up in cases, that
keeps their sounds to themselves. Why, I have often wished myself   90
poorer, that I might come nearer to you. We are born to do benefits;
and what better or properer can we call our own than the riches of
our friends? O what a precious comfort 'tis to have so many like
brothers commanding one another's fortunes. O joy's e'en made
away ere't can be born! Mine eyes cannot hold out water, methinks.   95
To forget their faults, I drink to you.
APEMANTUS Thou weep'st to make them drink, Timon.
SECOND LORD Joy had the like conception in our eyes,
    And at that instant like a babe sprung up.
APEMANTUS Ho, ho! I laugh to think that babe a bastard.   100
THIRD LORD I promise you, my lord, you moved me much.
APEMANTUS Much!

                    Sound tucket

---

94 joy's e'en] *Kittredge;* ioyes, e'ne F   96 faults, I] *Rowe;* Faults. I F   102 SD] *Rowe subst.; Sound Tucket. Enter the Maskers
of Amazons, with Lutes in their hands, dauncing and playing.* F

89–90 would most . . . themselves This comparison between 'needless' friends and instruments
hung up, keeping their sounds to themselves, may
recall Psalm 137.1–4: 'By the rivers of Babylon,
there we sat down, yea, we wept, when we remembered Zion. We hanged our harps upon the willows
in the midst thereof. For there they that carried us
away captive required of us a song; and they that
wasted us required of us mirth, saying, Sing us one
of the songs of Zion. How shall we sing the Lord's
song in a strange land?' But Timon's idea itself
recalls the most famous passage on the talents (as in
MM 1.1.32–5).

90 keeps Sixteenth-century writers including
Shakespeare used the third person plural with an -*s*
ending. See Abbott 235–7, and Franz 155.

91 nearer to you 'nearer in love to you, by being
made a receiver' (Capell, *Notes*); perhaps also 'closer
in social standing'.

92 properer Related to 'propriety' and 'property' (see Nuttall, p. 42).

92–3 riches of our friends 'the riches that
our friends possess' and 'being rich in having
friends'.

94 commanding having at one's disposal and
service.

94–5* O . . . born I follow Kittredge's emendation: Joy is completely destroyed before it comes
into existence; Capell (*Notes*) adds: by 'wearing

grief's badge, i.e. tears', which is elaborated in the
following sentence.

95 Mine . . . water My eyes cannot keep dry.

96 To . . . faults Preferably to be read as 'To
make you forget their faults' (i.e. my eyes' weakness). Many verbs in Shakespeare's time like
'cease', 'expire', 'fear', 'fall', 'lose' and others admit
of causative usage. See 2.1.16–17: 'be not ceased /
With slight denial' (compare Franz 630).

97 Thou . . . drink Timon proposes a toast to
the Lords to make them forget his weakness of
weeping but Apemantus says that Timon weeps
(i.e. gives in to his eyes' weakness) in order to make
the Lords drink (i.e. take advantage of his weakness
and exploit him). Apemantus implies ironically that
Timon's weakness is the direct cause of his being
exploited by his lordly friends.

98–9 Joy . . . sprung up Joy was first formed in
our eyes in the same way (as with you) and at that
moment leapt up like a babe (probably with an allusion to Luke 1.44). The metaphor of eyes conceiv-
ing is Shakespearean, and Hebrew has the same
word for both 'eye' and 'spring' or 'well' (contribution by Angela Stock, privately).

100 I . . . bastard Apemantus quibbles on the
birth metaphor.

101 promise assure.

102–17 SDS In F the stage directions are confused.
Rowe eliminates the early entrance of the *Maskers of*

TIMON What means that trump?

Enter SERVANT

How now?

SERVANT Please you, my lord, there are certain ladies most desirous of
    admittance.   105

TIMON Ladies? What are their wills?

SERVANT There comes with them a forerunner, my lord, which bears
    that office to signify their pleasures.

TIMON I pray let them be admitted.

[Exit Servant]

Enter CUPID

CUPID Hail to thee, worthy Timon, and to all that of his bounties taste!   110
    The five best senses acknowledge thee their patron, and come freely
    to gratulate thy plenteous bosom.
        There taste, touch, all, pleased from thy table rise;
    They only now come but to feast thine eyes.

TIMON They're welcome all, let 'em have kind admittance.   115
    Music, make their welcome.

[Exit Cupid]

FIRST LORD You see, my lord, how ample y'are beloved.

[Music]

---

103 SD] *Dyce; after* How now F   104–5] *Pope;* Please . . . Ladies / Most . . . admittance. F   109 SD.1] *Kittredge; not in*
F   109 SD.2] *Capell; Enter Cupid with the Maske of Ladies.* F   113 There] F; Th'Ear *Theobald* (*suggested by*
Warburton)   113 touch, all] *Rowe;* touch all F; Touch, Smell *Theobald* (*and Warburton*); touch, smell, all *Malone*   115–16]
F3; *prose* F   116 SD] *Capell; not in* F   117 SH FIRST LORD] *Capell; Luc.* F   117 SD] *Capell; see 102 SD and 109 SD.2 for* F

Amazons in F, since it corresponds neither with the
subsequent announcement of the servant (104–5)
nor with Cupid's announcement of the Ladies as
the five best senses (111). Capell interferes with the
second direction in F (*Enter Cupid with the Maske of*
Ladies) and separates Cupid's entrance from that of
the maskers. Although it leaves Timon's command
for the admission of the group ('them' (109)) partly
unanswered as well as entailing an awkward follow-
up of *Exit* and immediate re-entry on Cupid's part
(116 and 118), neither of which is warranted by F, it
has received editorial approval ever since. The inconsistencies in explicit and implicit stage directions could be a sign that this part of the scene has
not been thoroughly worked out; Ann Pasternak
Slater's opinion is that 'the masque is an afterthought' (*Shakespeare the Director*, 1982, p. 229).
    107–8 which . . . office whose task it is.
    108 signify announce.
    109 SD.2 Cupid functions as a 'forerunner' or

presenter of the masque. It was conventional for
Cupid to appear in such a role; cf. *Rom.* 1.4.4ff.,
where the intruding maskers refuse to consider
having a Cupid to introduce them. On contexts for
the banquet and masque see Supplementary Notes,
p. 178 below.
    112 gratulate (1) greet, (2) show gratitude
for, express gratitude to (*OED* Gratulate *v* 4; *Tit.*
1.1.221: 'And gratulate his safe return to Rome').
    112 plenteous bosom generous heart; metony-
mically: sumptuous tables. In recent psychoanalytic
criticism, 'bosom' is regarded as specially referring
to 'the nurturant qualities of the female body'
(Adelman, pp. 167–8).
    113 There . . . rise The senses 'taste' and
'touch', together with the three other senses (as
indicated in 113) should have been gratified by the
banquet. Theobald emends 'There' to 'Th'Ear' and
replaces 'all' by 'Smell'. Line 114 would then name
the fifth sense with 'eyes'.

Enter [CUPID *with the masque of* LADIES *as*] *Amazons, with lutes in their hands, dancing and playing*

APEMANTUS Hoy-day,
What a sweep of vanity comes this way.
They dance? They are madwomen.   120
Like madness is the glory of this life,
As this pomp shows to a little oil and root.
We make ourselves fools to disport ourselves,
And spend our flatteries to drink those men
Upon whose age we void it up again   125
With poisonous spite and envy.
Who lives that's not depravèd or depraves?
Who dies that bears not one spurn to their graves
Of their friends' gift?
I should fear those that dance before me now   130
Would one day stamp upon me. 'T'as been done;
Men shut their doors against a setting sun.

The Lords rise from table, with much adoring of Timon, and to show their loves
each single out an Amazon, and all dance, men with women, a lofty strain or
two to the hautboys, and cease

TIMON You have done our pleasures much grace, fair ladies,
Set a fair fashion on our entertainment,
Which was not half so beautiful and kind;   135

133] *Pope;* You . . . pleasures / Much . . . Ladies) F

118 **Hoy-day** 'An exclamation of contemptuous surprise' (Schmidt).

119 **sweep** motion of dancers 'with a magnificent or impressive air' (*OED* Sweep *sb* 2).

122 **to . . . root** in comparison with feeding in the simplest way on a little oil and root.

123 **disport** amuse.

124 **drink** (1) 'drink (the health of)' (Sisson, *Readings*, p. 168), (2) swallow, consume. Sisson's reading seems more convincing in view of 125 ('we void it up again' meaning 'we regurgitate those pledges as bitter spite'), and also in relation to the banquet.

125 **age** old age, and probably in a more concrete sense, decay of fortune (Warburton).

126 **envy** malice.

127 **depravèd** (1) ill-spoken of, (2) rendered corrupt. The first meaning is the more likely one in view of 128–9.

127 **depraves** vilifies, slanders.

128 **spurn** hurt, insult.

129 **gift** giving, donation (as in 3.4.19: 'And he wears jewels now of Timon's gift').

130–1 Apemantus takes up elements of the Poet's vision given in 1.1.90–1.

132 **Men . . . sun** This passage has a sententious undertone, cf. Tilley and Dent: 'The rising, not the setting, sun is worshipped by most men' (s979). The image is elaborated further in Sonnet 7, 9–12.

132 SD The coming together of the banqueters and the maskers in a dance apparently signifying harmony marks the climax of the ceremonial banquet, centring on the chief figure, Timon, who is reverenced.

133 **You . . . grace** You have added grace to our pleasures (but 'pleasures' also means the indulgence of the appetites, sensual gratification (*OED* Pleasure *sb* B1c). Essentially the sense is 'You have greatly increased our sensual appetites.'

135 **kind** as it ought to be.

> You have added worth unto't and lustre,
> And entertained me with mine own device.
> I am to thank you for't.

FIRST LADY My lord, you take us even at the best.

APEMANTUS Faith, for the worst is filthy, and would not hold taking, I   140
    doubt me.

TIMON Ladies, there is an idle banquet attends you,
> Please you to dispose yourselves.

ALL LADIES Most thankfully, my lord.

> > > > *Exeunt [Cupid and Ladies]*

TIMON Flavius!   145

FLAVIUS My lord?

TIMON The little casket bring me hither.

FLAVIUS Yes, my lord. [*Aside*] More jewels yet?
> There is no crossing him in's humour,
> Else I should tell him well, i'faith I should,   150
> When all's spent, he'd be crossed then, and he could.
> 'Tis pity bounty had not eyes behind,
> That man might ne'er be wretched for his mind.   *Exit*

---

139 SH FIRST LADY] *Johnson/Steevens; 1 Lord* F   144 SD *Cupid and Ladies*] *Capell; not in* F   148 SD] *Johnson subst.; not in* F   150 tell him well, i'faith] F; tell him – well – i'faith *Rowe;* tell him – well – i'faith, *Theobald;* tell him well (i'faith, . . .) *Kittredge*

137 device 'faculty of devising' (*OED* Device 1). Ever since Johnson, editors have taken Timon's utterance to mean that the masque was designed by Timon himself, probably to surprise his guests; but this would imply that from its first announcement (104 ff.) Timon was playing the hypocrite in order to celebrate his own honour more effectively. This would place him on the same level of ceremonial hollowness as his so-called friends. I do not assent to this interpretation.

138 I . . . thank I ought to and wish to thank.

139 SH FIRST LADY In view of Apemantus's rejoinder, it seems beyond doubt that the speaker is a woman (see collation).

139 you . . . best you estimate us to our advantage, in the best possible way. To explain it thus takes no account of the double entendre brought out by Apemantus's next remark.

140 for the worst . . . taking if you took them (sexually) at their worst, which is foul and diseased, they would prove intolerable. Apemantus quibbles on 'take' meaning have sexually, 'the worst' meaning physically foul and diseased; he identifies beneath their surface courtesy the ferocity, destructiveness and sexual

obsession which, though hidden, are inherent in this world.

140–1 I doubt me I fear (see Franz 307).

142 idle banquet trifling or simple repast (a polite understatement).

149 crossing . . . humour opposing him in this mood.

150 tell him well Not recorded in *OED* and the only occurrence in Shakespeare; this may account for the alternative punctuation which editors clung to until recently. Recent suggestions: 'use plain language' (H. Craig, Bevington); 'tell him forthrightly' (Riverside).

151 he'd . . . could he would receive money if only he could. Theobald refers to the old usage 'that he would have his Hand *cross'd*, as we say, with Money' (see also *OED* Cross v 2b). Oliver, referring to Deighton, suggests 'crossed off a list of debtors'.

152 had . . . behind was not wary (proverbial; see Tilley and Dent E236); see *TN* 2.5.136–8: 'Ay, and you had any eye behind you, you might see more detraction at your heels than fortunes before you.'

153 for his mind for his moral disposition (to be bounteous).

FIRST LORD Where be our men?
SERVANT Here, my lord, in readiness.   155
SECOND LORD Our horses!

Enter FLAVIUS [*with the casket*]

TIMON   O my friends, I have one word
        To say to you. Look you, my good lord,
        I must entreat you honour me so much
        As to advance this jewel; accept it and wear it,
        Kind my lord.   160
FIRST LORD I am so far already in your gifts.
ALL LORDS So are we all.

Enter a SERVANT

SERVANT My lord, there are certain nobles of the senate newly alighted,
        and come to visit you.
TIMON They are fairly welcome.   165
                                        [*Exit Servant*]
FLAVIUS I beseech your honour, vouchsafe me a word, it does concern
        you near.
TIMON Near? Why then another time I'll hear thee. I prithee let's be
        provided to show them entertainment.
FLAVIUS I scarce know how.   170

Enter another SERVANT

SECOND SERVANT May it please your honour, Lord Lucius,
        Out of his free love, hath presented to you

156–7] *Oliver; Our Horses. / O . . . Friends: / I . . . good L.* F   156 SD *Enter* FLAVIUS] *Globe; in* F *placed after 165*   156
SD *with the casket*] *Capell; not in* F   162 SH LORDS] *Capell; not in* F   165 SD] *Kittredge; not in* F   171 SH SECOND SERVANT]
Rowe; Ser. F

159 advance raise in value (by wearing the jewel).

161 in your gifts under an obligation for having accepted your gifts. To have something 'in one's gift' means that one has the power to bestow or give away something (a privilege, a position, a favour); the ironic implication is that the Lords are no more than disposable assets: Timon's wealth is so powerful that autonomous human beings are reduced to tokens.

163 nobles of the senate Although they never appear on stage, they may have been intended to add to the impressiveness of the 'great flood of visitors' (1.1.43).

165 fairly kindly, courteously – but the sense 'justly', as in an equitable exchange or bargain, is

picked up in 174 and 180, as Nuttall, pp. 43–4, observes.

166 vouchsafe grant (indicating submissiveness and expecting a condescending reply).

168 Near . . . hear thee i.e. Timon disdains any selfish concern, he is all magnanimity.

170 This speech can be delivered as an aside. Honigmann ('Stage direction', pp. 117–26, 120) would not agree, and points out Flavius's later remark: 'You would not hear me' (2.2.121), but this may just as well refer to Flavius's request at 166 for a word with Timon, as to his remark at 170. Either interpretation is valid, Shakespeare's text open. Flavius's two other speeches (148 ff. and 180 ff.) are more clearly marked as asides by his using the third person pronoun in referring to Timon.

Four milk-white horses, trapped in silver.
TIMON I shall accept them fairly, let the presents
       Be worthily entertained.

                                      [*Exit Second Servant*]

                    Enter a third SERVANT

                         How now? What news?   175
THIRD SERVANT Please you, my lord, that honourable gentleman,
       Lord Lucullus, entreats your company tomorrow to hunt with him,
       and has sent your honour two brace of greyhounds.
TIMON I'll hunt with him, and let them be received,
       Not without fair reward.
FLAVIUS [*Aside*]   What will this come to?   180
       He commands us to provide, and give great gifts,
       And all out of an empty coffer;
       Nor will he know his purse, or yield me this,
       To show him what a beggar his heart is,
       Being of no power to make his wishes good.   185
       His promises fly so beyond his state
       That what he speaks is all in debt; he owes for ev'ry word;
       He is so kind that he now pays interest for't;
       His land's put to their books. Well, would I were
       Gently put out of office, before I were forced out!   190
       Happier is he that has no friend to feed
       Than such that do e'en enemies exceed.
       I bleed inwardly for my lord.   *Exit*
TIMON You do yourselves much wrong,
       You bate too much of your own merits.   195

175] *Capell;* Be . . . entertain'd. / How . . . newes? F   175 SD.1] *Kittredge; not in* F   179–80] *Hanmer;* Ile . . . him, /
And . . . Reward. / What . . . to? F   180 SD] *Johnson; not in* F   181–2] *Johnson/Steevens; one line* F

173 trapped in silver with silver harnesses.
175 entertained received.
176–8 This hunt is later confirmed as having taken place (2.2.182–3).
180 fair 'good, generous', with the subsidiary sense 'just, equal' which raises the issue of measure in gauging exchange.
183 yield grant or allow.
185 Being The most likely antecedent is 'his heart' (184) as the seat of his generosity.
185 make . . . good put into effect.
186 state wealth, fortune.
188 He . . . for't He pays interest for being so kind. The language displays the stressful contradiction between financial and moral considerations;

further complexity is felt in the double senses of 'kind', humanely generous (as men should by nature be) and, for Timon, characteristically prodigal to extremes, as they actually are. See 4.1.36 n.
189 put . . . books entered in their account books as being mortgaged.
192 Than . . . exceed Than to feed such friends as are worse than enemies.
193 bleed Proverbial expression for deep sorrow: 'To have one's heart bleed or weep' (Dent BB12).
195 bate An aphetic form of 'abate' (*OED* Bate *v*²) meaning to bring down in value. Timon tells them they should value themselves more highly; apparently he does not recognise their hyperbolic flattery for what it is.

Here, my lord, a trifle of our love.
SECOND LORD With more than common thanks I will receive it.
THIRD LORD O he's the very soul of bounty.
TIMON And now I remember, my lord, you gave good words the other
      day of a bay courser I rode on. 'Tis yours because you liked it.   200
THIRD LORD O, I beseech you pardon me, my lord, in that.
TIMON You may take my word, my lord; I know no man
      Can justly praise but what he does affect.
      I weigh my friends' affection with mine own.
      I'll tell you true, I'll call to you.   205
ALL LORDS O none so welcome.
TIMON I take all and your several visitations
      So kind to heart, 'tis not enough to give;
      Methinks I could deal kingdoms to my friends,
      And ne'er be weary. Alcibiades,   210
      Thou art a soldier, therefore seldom rich;
      It comes in charity to thee; for all thy living
      Is 'mongst the dead, and all the lands thou hast
      Lie in a pitched field.
ALCIBIADES Ay, defiled land, my lord.   215

197] *Pope;* With . . . thankes / I . . . it. F **201** SH THIRD LORD] *Rann; 1. L.* F; *2 Lord / Rowe* **202–5**] *Johnson; prose*
F **204** friends'] *Harbage;* Friends F; friend's *Warburton* **207** all and] *Capell;* all, and F **214–15**] F; Lie . . . lord. *Johnson/*
*Steevens*⁵ **215** Ay,] *Malone;* I, F; In *Johnson/Steevens*²

199 gave good words spoke well.
200 courser racehorse.
201 pardon . . . that i.e. pardon me for having given you the impression that I wanted it.
203 affect like, be fond of (*OED* Affect *v*¹ 2); it is not clear whether Timon intends an ironic play on another sense, to seek to obtain (*OED* Affect *v*¹ 1).
204 I weigh . . . affection The metaphor of the pair of scales, used in weighing for commercial purposes, but also the emblem of justice, adds ironic undertones; as if unconsciously, touching on the heartless calculating of the Lords.
207 I take . . . your visitations, altogether and individually.
208 kind kindly (for the substitution of adjective for adverb, see Franz 241).
208 'tis . . . give there is no way of responding in equal measure; ''tis' means there is (as in ''tis doubt' in *R2* 1.4.20 and 3.4.69). Timon's expression blurs the difference between requiting a moral attitude, kindness, and giving material reward.
209 deal . . . to bestow . . . on. According to

Honigmann, Timon's penchant for royal gestures which are in no way backed up by reality may be related to Shakespeare's interest in another figure in Plutarch, Mark Antony, whose grand gestures of giving away whole realms ('Antonius did easely geve away great seigniories, realmes, and mighty nations': *North's Plutarch*, ed. G. Wyndham, 6 vols., 1895–6, VI, 36–7) may have informed Shakespeare's creation of Timon.
212 in charity (1) as acts of charity, (2) out of a charitable heart.
212 living income, way of making a living. Alcibiades' way of life is dealing death in battle, an honest open trade compared to financiers, merchants, courtiers and other parasites.
215–21 The fashion for creating blank verse lines in such cases, as seen in editions since Capell, has no convincing basis. I follow the layout of F.
214 pitched field battle-ground.
215 defiled land A play on words referring to Ecclus. 13.1: 'He that toucheth pitch shall be defiled with it' (see Tilley P358). A blood-soaked field of battle may well be spoken of as defiled.

FIRST LORD We are so virtuously bound –
TIMON And so am I to you.
SECOND LORD So infinitely endeared –
TIMON All to you. Lights, more lights!
FIRST LORD The best of happiness, honour and fortunes   220
          Keep with you, Lord Timon.
TIMON Ready for his friends.
                    Exeunt Lords [and others. Apemantus and Timon remain]
APEMANTUS   What a coil's here,
          Serving of becks and jutting-out of bums!
          I doubt whether their legs be worth the sums
          That are given for 'em. Friendship's full of dregs;   225
          Methinks false hearts should never have sound legs.
          Thus honest fools lay out their wealth on curtsies.
TIMON Now, Apemantus, if thou wert not sullen,
          I would be good to thee.
APEMANTUS No, I'll nothing; for if I should be bribed too, there would   230
          be none left to rail upon thee, and then thou wouldst sin the faster.
          Thou giv'st so long, Timon, I fear me thou wilt give away thyself in
          paper shortly. What needs these feasts, pomps, and vainglories?
TIMON Nay, and you begin to rail on society once, I am sworn not to
          give regard to you. Farewell, and come with better music.   *Exit*   235
APEMANTUS So; thou wilt not hear me now, thou shalt not then.

---

216 bound –] *Pope;* bound. F   218 endeared –] *Rowe;* endeer'd. F   222 SD] *Cam.; Exeunt Lords* F   222–5 What . . . 'em.]
Rowe; prose F

216 **virtuously** Another play on meanings: 'virtue' as power, and as moral quality.

216 **bound** With the double meaning of being grateful and being compelled (which latter implies a lack of virtue).

218 **endeared** Also with a twofold meaning: (1) obliged and (2) raised in price. The language witnesses to the pressure of contradictions bearing down on the speakers; they presumably do not consciously make this word-play, for if we assumed they did it consciously, this would have to mean grossly brazen contempt for Timon, to his face, which even he, vain as he is, might be expected to recognise.

219 **All to you** All the obligation is on my part.

222 **coil** turmoil, fuss.

223 **Serving of becks** bowing of heads (Johnson), and see *OED* Beck *sb²* 3.

224 **legs** Punning on the noun (leg = a limb) and

the verb meaning bend the knee in obeisance (see *OED* Leg *sb* 4).

227 **lay . . . curtsies** expend, use up their wealth on acts of courtesy; with allusion to the sense of 'courtesy' = a bow.

232–3 **in paper** in written securities.

233 **What needs** What necessity is there for.

234 **and . . . once** if ever you begin to rail against company, companionship. For this more general sense of 'society', see *AYLI* 3.2.255–6: 'I thank you too for your society' and throughout Shakespeare; for the sense of 'once' as 'ever', 'indeed' see *OED* Once B2, and later on 5.1.47.

235 **come . . . music** change your tune. A proverbial expression, in Dent: 'To change one's note' (N248) and 'To sing another song' (S637).

236 **thou shalt not then** 'thou shalt not have the opportunity hereafter' (Collier), i.e. when he is ruined.

I'll lock thy heaven from thee.
O that men's ears should be
To counsel deaf, but not to flattery.   *Exit*

[2.1] *Enter a* SENATOR

SENATOR And late five thousand; to Varro and to Isidore
He owes nine thousand, besides my former sum,
Which makes it five and twenty. Still in motion
Of raging waste? It cannot hold, it will not.
If I want gold, steal but a beggar's dog   5
And give it Timon, why, the dog coins gold.
If I would sell my horse and buy twenty more
Better than he, why, give my horse to Timon,
Ask nothing, give it him, it foals me straight
And able horses. No porter at his gate,   10
But rather one that smiles and still invites
All that pass by. It cannot hold, no reason
Can sound his state in safety. Caphis, ho!
Caphis, I say!

Enter CAPHIS

CAPHIS   Here, sir, what is your pleasure?
SENATOR Get on your cloak, and haste you to Lord Timon;   15
Importune him for my moneys; be not ceased

Act 2, Scene 1   2.1] *Rowe; not in* F

237–9 'thy heaven' is usually explained as good advice by which he might have saved Timon from ruin. Consequently, his subsequent advice is highly abusive. I arrange these lines as a triplet; they acquire an almost mechanical rhythmic beat, by which they take on the character of an evil curse. Hulme, on whose interpretation of the passage my reading is partly based, thinks this passage to be unfinished (see Hulme, pp. 86–7).

Act 2, Scene 1

1 late lately (the Senator is calculating Timon's debts).
3 in motion in a state of commotion.
4 hold continue.
5 steal but I have only to steal.
9 it foals me it bears foals ('me' is the ethic dative: see Franz 294). The 'yield' or generous return on investing in Timon is compared to natural

fecundity, which is also farmed; cf. the discussion in *AYLI* 3.2.73–85.
9 straight immediately.
10 And able And not only that but full-grown (Riverside).
10 porter Whose duty it is to keep out strangers and the uninvited.
11 still constantly.
12–13 no ... safety 'No reason, by *sounding*, fathoming, or trying, *his state*, can find it safe' (Johnson).
16 moneys This plural form is repeatedly used by Shylock in *MV* 1.3 (108, 116, 119, 129, 141); in this scene he also alludes to the breeding potential of gold (95–6).
16 ceased put off.
16–19 Timon acts out an imaginary scene for his servant's benefit.

With slight denial, nor then silenced when
'Commend me to your master' and the cap
Plays in the right hand, thus; but tell him
My uses cry to me; I must serve my turn   20
Out of mine own; his days and times are past,
And my reliances on his fracted dates
Have smit my credit. I love and honour him,
But must not break my back to heal his finger.
Immediate are my needs, and my relief   25
Must not be tossed and turned to me in words,
But find supply immediate. Get you gone,
Put on a most importunate aspect,
A visage of demand; for I do fear,
When every feather sticks in his own wing,   30
Lord Timon will be left a naked gull,
Which flashes now a phoenix. Get you gone.
CAPHIS I go, sir.
SENATOR Ay, go, sir; take the bonds along with you,
And have the dates in. Come.
CAPHIS   I will, sir.
SENATOR   Go.   35
                                                Exeunt

---

17 when] F; then F2; with *Rowe*   18 'Commend ... master'] *Johnson;* Commend ... Master, F   34 Ay, go, sir;] *Pope (subst.);* I go sir? F; *not in Dyce*   34 Ay ... you,] *Pope;* I ... sir? / Take ... you, F   35 in. Come] F; in Compt *Theobald;* in count *Hanmer*

20 **uses** financial needs.
20–1 **I ... own** I must meet claims made against me out of my own resources.
21 **his ... past** the deadlines for repaying his loans have expired.
22 **reliances** trust; not used elsewhere by Shakespeare.
22 **fracted** broken.
23 **smit** damaged (an uncommon form of past participle, the only instance in Shakespeare).
25 **Immediate** Directly touching me.
26 **tossed and turned** hit back to me (a metaphor from tennis).
27 **immediate** with nothing intervening.
30 **When ... wing** When every creditor has restored to him what is his due. This alludes to the fable of the crow decking itself with borrowed plumes. (Robert Greene described Shakespeare as 'an upstart Crow, beautified with our feathers ...':

Greens Groats-worth of Wit, 1592, in *The Life and Complete Works in Prose and Verse of Robert Greene*, 15 vols., 1964, p. 144.) The feather image appears variously in the play; see 1.1.104 and 2.2.71.
30 **his** its.
31 **naked** mere (but also with the senses 'exposed' and 'helpless').
31 **gull** (1) unfledged bird, (2) dupe.
32 **phoenix** The mythical Arabian bird always reviving in the flames burning it to ashes.
34* **Ay, go, sir** I follow Pope's emendation and Mason's explanation (see Johnson/Steevens⁵) that the Senator, already impatient and agitated, reacts in irritation to Caphis. Some editors delete, assuming a compositor's error.
35 **And ... Come** i.e. Caphis should put in the exact dates to make clear that the bonds are either overdue (Oliver) or will be due shortly (Charney).

[2.2] *Enter Steward* FLAVIUS, *with many bills in his hand*

FLAVIUS No care, no stop, so senseless of expense,
        That he will neither know how to maintain it,
        Nor cease his flow of riot. Takes no accompt
        How things go from him, nor resumes no care
        Of what is to continue. Never mind   5
        Was to be so unwise, to be so kind.
        What shall be done, he will not hear, till feel.
        I must be round with him, now he comes from hunting.
        Fie, fie, fie, fie!

        Enter CAPHIS [*and the* SERVANTS *of*] ISIDORE *and* VARRO

CAPHIS Good even, Varro; what, you come for money?   10
VARRO SERVANT Is't not your business too?
CAPHIS It is; and yours too, Isidore?
ISIDORE SERVANT It is so.
CAPHIS Would we were all discharged.
VARRO SERVANT I fear it.   15
CAPHIS Here comes the lord.

        Enter TIMON *and his train* [*with* ALCIBIADES]

TIMON So soon as dinner's done, we'll forth again,
        My Alcibiades. [*To Caphis*] With me? What is your will?
CAPHIS My lord, here is a note of certain dues.
TIMON Dues? Whence are you?   20
CAPHIS Of Athens here, my lord.

Act 2, Scene 2   2.2] *Rowe; not in* F   0 SD *Steward* FLAVIUS] *Rowe; Steward* F   1 SH FLAVIUS] *Rowe; Stew.* F (*throughout scene*)   4 resumes] *Rowe;* resume F   9 SD *and the* SERVANTS *of*] *Hanmer; not in* F   11 SH VARRO SERVANT] *Malone; Var.* F (*throughout scene*)   13 SH ISIDORE SERVANT] *Malone; Isid.* F (*throughout scene*)   16 SD *with* ALCIBIADES] *Capell; not in* F   18 SD] *Oliver; not in* F

Act 2, Scene 2
1 **of** with respect to.
2 **know** learn.
3 **riot** extravagance.
3 **accompt** An alternative form of 'account'.
4 **nor . . . care** has no concern. In Elizabethan English the double or multiple negative need not signify affirmation.
5 **what . . . continue** what is to serve future needs.
5–6 **Never . . . kind** Never was man so fated to be so unwise in the attempt to be (1) so generous, (2) so humane.
7 **till feel** until he feels it.
8 **round** frank.
9 **Fie** Expressing dislike or impatience.
9 SD The servants of Isidore and Varro are here named after their masters (see 31–2). For the problem of assigning names to servants, see p. 69 above.
14 **discharged** paid.
15 **I fear it** I fear that is not going to happen.
17 **we'll forth** we'll go out hunting.

TIMON   Go to my steward.

CAPHIS   Please it your lordship, he hath put me off
          To the succession of new days this month.
          My master is awaked by great occasion   25
          To call upon his own, and humbly prays you
          That with your other noble parts you'll suit
          In giving him his right.

TIMON   Mine honest friend,
          I prithee but repair to me next morning.

CAPHIS   Nay, good my lord –

TIMON   Contain thyself, good friend.   30

VARRO SERVANT   One Varro's servant, my good lord –

ISIDORE SERVANT   From Isidore; he humbly prays your speedy
          payment.

CAPHIS   If you did know, my lord, my master's wants –

VARRO SERVANT   'Twas due on forfeiture, my lord, six weeks and past.

ISIDORE SERVANT   Your steward puts me off, my lord, and I   35
          Am sent expressly to your lordship.

TIMON   Give me breath!
          I do beseech you, good my lords, keep on,
          I'll wait upon you instantly.

                              [*Exeunt Alcibiades and Timon's train*]
          [*To Flavius*]   Come hither. Pray you
          How goes the world, that I am thus encountered   40
          With clamorous demands of debt, broken bonds,
          And the detention of long since due debts
          Against my honour?

FLAVIUS   [*To Servants*]   Please you, gentlemen,

---

39 SD.1] *Staunton; not in* F   39 SD.2] *Johnson; not in* F   41 of debt, broken] F; *of broken* Hanmer; *of date-broken*
Malone   43 SD] *Oliver; not in* F

24 To . . . month From one day to the next all
month (Riverside).

25 awaked . . . occasion prompted by very
pressing circumstances.

26 call . . . own demand what is due to him.

27–8 That . . . giving That in a manner consistent with your other noble qualities, you will give.

29 repair return.

30 Contain Restrain.

32 prays requests.

34 'Twas . . . forfeiture It was due under pen-
alty of confiscation of your securities, for non-
payment.

34 and past and longer.

38 lords This is an unusual form for addressing
servants. At 48 he calls them 'friends'.

38 keep on continue on your way, proceed.

39 I'll . . . you I'll join you.

41 demands . . . bonds The F reading has been
retained; the repetition of 'debt' in the next line and
the rough metre persuade some editors to omit
'debt'.

42 detention withholding.

43 Against my honour Damaging (or marring)
my reputation.

The time is unagreeable to this business.
Your importunacy cease till after dinner,   45
That I may make his lordship understand
Wherefore you are not paid.

TIMON Do so, my friends. [*To Flavius*] See them well entertained.

[*Exit*]

FLAVIUS Pray draw near.   *Exit*

Enter APEMANTUS *and* FOOL

CAPHIS Stay, stay, here comes the fool with Apemantus; let's ha' some   50
      sport with 'em.

VARRO SERVANT Hang him, he'll abuse us.

ISIDORE SERVANT A plague upon him, dog!

VARRO SERVANT How dost, fool?

APEMANTUS Dost dialogue with thy shadow?   55

VARRO SERVANT I speak not to thee.

APEMANTUS No, 'tis to thyself. [*To Fool*] Come away.

ISIDORE SERVANT [*To Varro's Servant*] There's the fool hangs on your
      back already.

APEMANTUS No, thou stand'st single, th'art not on him yet.   60

CAPHIS Where's the fool now?

APEMANTUS He last asked the question. Poor rogues, and usurers'
      men, bawds between gold and want.

ALL SERVANTS What are we, Apemantus?

APEMANTUS Asses.   65

ALL SERVANTS Why?

APEMANTUS That you ask me what you are, and do not know your-
      selves. Speak to 'em, fool.

---

48 SD.1] *Oxford; not in* F   48 SD.2] *Pope; not in* F   57 SD] *Johnson; not in* F   58 SD] *Malone; not in* F   64 SH ALL SERVANTS]
Malone; F *varies* / *Al.* / *or* / *All.* / *throughout scene*

44 **unagreeable to** unsuitable for.
45 **Your . . . cease** Suspend your demands.
49 **draw near** come this way.
49 SD.2 FOOL The passage 50–112 is the only
one where the Fool is present. For discussion of
this as a possible 'false start', see pp. 65–6
above.
50–1 **let's . . . 'em** The group of servants adopt
an attitude to Apemantus similar to that taken by
the group of Timon, Jeweller and Merchant in
1.1.181–2.
54–62 In this first round of the verbal contest
with Apemantus, the label 'fool' is fastened in turn

on Varro, on Isidore, and then on Caphis, before
they grasp the rules of the game.
55 **Dost . . . shadow** i.e. do you speak with yourself? In the following seven lines all three are called
fool.
62–3 **usurers' . . . want** The desire for gold and
for sex is equated, as in Timon's invectives against
Phrynia and Timandra in 4.3.135–67. See also *MM*
3.2.5–7: ''Twas never merry world since of two
usuries the merriest was put down, and the worser
allow'd by order of law.'
64–70 For protection the servants now speak in
chorus.

FOOL   How do you, gentlemen?

ALL SERVANTS   Gramercies, good fool. How does your mistress?   70

FOOL   She's e'en setting on water to scald such chickens as you are.
Would we could see you at Corinth!

APEMANTUS   Good, gramercy.

Enter PAGE

FOOL   Look you, here comes my master's page.

PAGE   [*To Fool*] Why, how now, captain? What do you in this wise   75
company? How dost thou, Apemantus?

APEMANTUS   Would I had a rod in my mouth, that I might answer thee
profitably.

PAGE   Prithee, Apemantus, read me the superscription of these letters, I
know not which is which.   80

APEMANTUS   Canst not read?

PAGE   No.

APEMANTUS   There will little learning die then that day thou art
hanged. This is to Lord Timon, this to Alcibiades. Go, thou wast
born a bastard, and thou'lt die a bawd.   85

PAGE   Thou wast whelped a dog, and thou shalt famish a dog's death.
Answer not, I am gone.   *Exit*

APEMANTUS   E'en so thou outrun'st grace. Fool, I will go with you to
Lord Timon's.

FOOL   Will you leave me there?   90

APEMANTUS   If Timon stay at home. You three serve three usurers?

ALL SERVANTS   Ay, would they served us.

70] *Pope;* Gramercies . . . Foole: / How . . . Mistris? F   **74** master's] F; mistress's *Theobald*   **75** SD] *Johnson; not in* F   **76**
company? How] *Pope;* Company. / How F   **76** Apemantus] F4; *Apermantus* F, F2–3   **79** SH PAGE] F4; *Boy* F, F2–3   **86**–
7 death. Answer] *Pope;* death. / Answer F   **88** grace. Fool] *Capell;* Grace, / Foole F   **91** home. You] *Capell;* home. / You
F   **92** Ay, would] *Capell;* I would F

70 Gramercies Great thanks.

71–2 She's . . . Corinth Chickens are scalded in
boiling water so that their feathers can be removed
(see 2.1.31, the image of the 'naked gull'); but 'scald'
also means to infect with venereal disease (see
Partridge, s.v. 'scald' and 'burn', and Williams);
thus, visitors to this brothel are likely to lose their
shirts (be gulled of their money) and get a dose of
the pox.

74 my . . . page Many editors follow Theobald's
emendation 'mistress's', on the grounds that in 96
the Fool speaks of his mistress. In 98–9, however,
he refers again to his 'master's house'. The Fool and
the Page could have had both master and mistress.

Malone conjectured that 'M' in the manuscript
served for both 'master' and 'mistress'.

77 rod Instrument used for chastisement.

78 profitably in a manner fit to instruct and
improve (Schmidt).

79 superscription address.

84 This . . . Alcibiades Nothing is ever learnt
about what is communicated in these letters.

86 famish . . . death die by starving like a dog;
'famish' is used with an accusative denoting the
result (see Schmidt).

88 E'en . . . grace Indeed by doing so you run
away from the instruction that might save you
(Riverside).

APEMANTUS So would I – as good a trick as ever hangman served thief.

FOOL Are you three usurers' men?

ALL SERVANTS Ay, fool.   95

FOOL I think no usurer but has a fool to his servant. My mistress is one,
  and I am her fool. When men come to borrow of your masters, they
  approach sadly, and go away merry; but they enter my master's
  house merrily, and go away sadly. The reason of this?

VARRO SERVANT I could render one.   100

APEMANTUS Do it then, that we may account thee a whoremaster and
  a knave, which notwithstanding, thou shalt be no less esteemed.

VARRO SERVANT What is a whoremaster, fool?

FOOL A fool in good clothes, and something like thee. 'Tis a spirit;
  sometime 't appears like a lord, sometime like a lawyer, sometime   105
  like a philosopher, with two stones moe than's artificial one. He is
  very often like a knight; and generally in all shapes that man goes up
  and down in, from fourscore to thirteen, this spirit walks in.

VARRO SERVANT Thou art not altogether a fool.

FOOL Nor thou altogether a wise man; as much foolery as I have, so   110
  much wit thou lack'st.

APEMANTUS That answer might have become Apemantus.

ALL SERVANTS Aside, aside, here comes Lord Timon.

          Enter TIMON *and Steward* [FLAVIUS]

APEMANTUS Come with me, fool, come.

FOOL I do not always follow lover, elder brother, and woman; sometime 115
  the philosopher.

                              [*Exeunt Apemantus and Fool*]

FLAVIUS [*To Servants*] Pray you, walk near, I'll speak with you anon.

                              Exeunt [*Servants*]

TIMON You make me marvel wherefore ere this time
  Had you not fully laid my state before me,
  That I might so have rated my expense   120

---

93 I – as] *Pope;* I: / As F   98 master's] F; mistress's *Theobald*   110 man; as] *Pope (prose);* man, / As F   116 SD] *Capell;*
Exeunt F *after 117*   117 SD.1] *Oxford; not in* F   117] *Pope;* Pray . . . neere, / Ile . . . anon. F   117 SD.2] *Capell; Exeunt* F

101 **whoremaster** fornicator, whoremonger,
procurer (Williams).

102 **which . . . esteemed** despite which you will
be respected no less than before (because you were
already so little respected).

106 **stones** testicles; with an allusion to the philosopher's stone, supposedly capable of converting
any metal into gold.

112 **become** done credit to.

115–16 **I . . . philosopher** I as a fool do not always associate with those who are proverbially considered foolish. (For the folly of the lover see Tilley
L558 or L517; the 'elder brother' may be considered
as the counterpart to the proverbially wiser younger
brother (Tilley B687); on the folly of women as a
proverbial theme, Tilley B179, F605, W698 and
more.)

120 **rated** estimated.

                As I had leave of means.
FLAVIUS   You would not hear me;
                At many leisures I proposed –
TIMON   Go to!
                Perchance some single vantages you took,
                When my indisposition put you back,
                And that unaptness made your minister   125
                Thus to excuse yourself.
FLAVIUS   O my good lord,
                At many times I brought in my accompts,
                Laid them before you; you would throw them off,
                And say you found them in mine honesty.
                When for some trifling present you have bid me   130
                Return so much, I have shook my head, and wept;
                Yea, 'gainst th'authority of manners, prayed you
                To hold your hand more close. I did endure
                Not seldom, nor no slight checks, when I have
                Prompted you in the ebb of your estate   135
                And your great flow of debts. My loved lord,
                Though you hear now, too late, yet now's a time:
                The greatest of your having lacks a half
                To pay your present debts.
TIMON   Let all my land be sold.
FLAVIUS 'Tis all engaged, some forfeited and gone,   140
                And what remains will hardly stop the mouth
                Of present dues. The future comes apace;
                What shall defend the interim, and at length
                How goes our reck'ning?
TIMON To Lacedaemon did my land extend.   145

---

122 proposed –] F2; propose. F   129 found] F2; sound F

122 **leisures** convenient times.
123 **vantages** advantageous opportunities.
124 **indisposition** unwillingness to discuss this topic.
125 **And . . . minister** And made that disinclination your excuse.
129 **found . . . honesty** relied on my honesty for their truth.
131 **so much** a certain amount.
132 **th'authority of manners** what good manners would require.
133–4 **I . . . checks** i.e. I suffered frequent severe rebukes.

137 **yet . . . time** yet now is at last a time to make this clear to you.
138–9 **The . . . debts** At its highest estimate, your property would not cover half the debts now due.
140 **engaged** mortgaged, pawned.
143 **What . . . interim** How shall we survive in the interim.
143 **at length** in the longer perspective.
145 **Lacedaemon** Sparta, the capital of Laconia in the south-east of the Peloponnesus.

FLAVIUS O my good lord, the world is but a word;
           Were it all yours, to give it in a breath,
           How quickly were it gone.
TIMON   You tell me true.
FLAVIUS If you suspect my husbandry or falsehood,
           Call me before th'exactest auditors,   150
           And set me on the proof. So the gods bless me,
           When all our offices have been oppressed
           With riotous feeders, when our vaults have wept
           With drunken spilth of wine, when every room
           Hath blazed with lights, and brayed with minstrelsy,   155
           I have retired me to a wasteful cock,
           And set mine eyes at flow.
TIMON   Prithee no more.
FLAVIUS Heavens, have I said, the bounty of this lord!
           How many prodigal bits have slaves and peasants
           This night englutted! Who is not Timon's?   160
           What heart, head, sword, force, means, but is Lord
             Timon's?
           Great Timon, noble, worthy, royal Timon!
           Ah, when the means are gone that buy this praise,
           The breath is gone whereof this praise is made.
           Feast-won, fast-lost; one cloud of winter showers,   165
           These flies are couched.
TIMON   Come, sermon me no further.

---

161 Lord] *Rowe;* L. F   165 Feast-won] *Pope;* Feast won F   165 fast-lost] *Theobald;* fast lost F

146–8 the world ... gone 'as the world itself may be comprised in a word, you might give it all away in a breath' (Warburton).

149 suspect ... falsehood suspect my household management to be dishonest or me of falsehood. Some editors emend to the simpler substitution 'of' for 'or'.

151 set me on put me to.

152 offices Parts of the household concerned with food (*OED* Office *sb* 9). Here and in what follows, parts of the building are metaphorically personified as being oppressed, weeping, braying.

152 oppressed over-stretched.

153 riotous feeders unruly guests demanding to be fed.

154 spilth spillage.

155 brayed with minstrelsy resounded with raucous music and coarse singing (as bad as donkeys braying).

156 retired me retired; ethic dative, expressive of the agent's subjective interest in the doing (see Franz 294).

156 wasteful cock spigot of a cask open and running with wine (reminiscent of the prodigal's attitude).

157 eyes at flow The flow of tears, stimulated by the wasted flow of wine, is associated with the 'flow of debts' (136) and 'flow of riot' (3).

159 prodigal bits bits provided prodigally; the rhetorical figure hypallage.

165 Feast-won, fast-lost A punning phrase: what is won by giving feasts is lost again (1) by a fast (going without food), and (2) quickly.

166 couched gone into hiding.

No villainous bounty yet hath passed my heart;
Unwisely, not ignobly, have I given.
Why dost thou weep? Canst thou the conscience lack
To think I shall lack friends? Secure thy heart;   170
If I would broach the vessels of my love,
And try the argument of hearts, by borrowing,
Men and men's fortunes could I frankly use
As I can bid thee speak.

FLAVIUS   Assurance bless your thoughts.
TIMON   And in some sort these wants of mine are crowned,   175
That I account them blessings. For by these
Shall I try friends. You shall perceive how you
Mistake my fortunes; I am wealthy in my friends.
Within there! Flaminius! Servilius!

Enter three SERVANTS [FLAMINIUS, SERVILIUS, *and another*]

SERVANTS My lord, my lord.   180
TIMON I will dispatch you severally. [*To Servilius*] You to Lord Lucius;
[*To Flaminius*] to Lord Lucullus you; I hunted with his honour today; [*To the other*] you to Sempronius. Commend me to their loves;
and I am proud, say, that my occasions have found time to use 'em
toward a supply of money. Let the request be fifty talents.   185
FLAMINIUS As you have said, my lord.

                                                    [*Exeunt Servants*]

FLAVIUS Lord Lucius and Lucullus? Humh!
TIMON [*To Flavius*] Go you, sir, to the senators,

177–8] *Johnson; Shall . . . perceive / How . . . Fortunes: / I . . . Friends.* F   **179** Flaminius] *Rowe; Flauius* F   **179** SD]
Kittredge; Enter three Seruants. F   **181** severally. You] *Capell; seuerally. / You* F   **181** SD] *Dyce²; not in* F   **182** SD] *Dyce²;
not in* F   **183** SD] *Dyce²; not in* F   **186** SD] *Dyce²; not in* F   **188** SD] *Rowe; not in* F

167 villainous bounty bounty extended to villains, bounty with villainous consequences.

168 Unwisely . . . given Nuttall (p. 52) compares Othello's 'one that lov'd not wisely but too
well' (*Oth.* 5.2.344) and remarks that 'the speaker is
still not able fully to perceive or understand the
truth he acknowledges'.

169 conscience good sense, understanding
(*OED* Conscience 3, with this reference given).

170 Secure thy heart Take heart.

171 broach tap; the metaphor is of love as wine,
set flowing from its store in his friends.

172 try . . . hearts test the avowals of love. This
connects with the Lord's plea to Timon in 1.2.78–9
'that you would once use our hearts'.

173 frankly without restraint.

174 Assurance . . . thoughts May what you
think be blessed by proving true.

175 crowned given dignity (Riverside).

178 Mistake Misjudge.

181 dispatch you severally send you on different errands.

184 occasions needs.

184 time occasion. Timon apparently takes pride
in using his friends at last.

185 fifty talents Timon is inconsistent in making requests for money (compare 1.1.99 and
2.2.191).

Of whom, even to the state's best health, I have
Deserved this hearing; bid 'em send o'th'instant   190
A thousand talents to me.
FLAVIUS   I have been bold,
For that I knew it the most general way,
To them to use your signet and your name;
But they do shake their heads, and I am here
No richer in return.
TIMON   Is't true? Can't be?   195
FLAVIUS They answer in a joint and corporate voice
That now they are at fall, want treasure, cannot
Do what they would, are sorry; you are honourable,
But yet they could have wished – they know not –
Something hath been amiss; a noble nature   200
May catch a wrench – would all were well – 'tis pity –
And so, intending other serious matters,
After distasteful looks, and these hard fractions,
With certain half-caps and cold-moving nods
They froze me into silence.
TIMON   You gods reward them!   205
Prithee, man, look cheerly. These old fellows
Have their ingratitude in them hereditary;
Their blood is caked, 'tis cold, it seldom flows;
'Tis lack of kindly warmth they are not kind;
And nature, as it grows again toward earth,   210
Is fashioned for the journey, dull and heavy.
Go to Ventidius. Prithee, be not sad,
Thou art true and honest; ingeniously I speak,

---

197 treasure] F2; Treature F   204 cold-moving] *Theobald;* cold mouing F   212, 214 Ventidius] F2; *Ventiddius* F

189 **to . . . health** for my services to the welfare of the state. Perhaps another parallel with Othello: 'I have done the state some service, and they know't' (5.2.339).

192 **general way** '*compendious*, the way to try many at a time' (Johnson).

193 **signet** seal (as proof of authority).

197 **at fall** at a low ebb (Riverside).

201 **catch a wrench** be twisted from its natural course.

202 **intending . . . matters** busying (or affecting to busy) themselves with serious matters.

203 **distasteful looks** looks showing distaste.

203 **hard fractions** '*broken* hints, *interrupted* sentences, *abrupt* remarks' (Johnson).

204 **half-caps** 'half-courteous salute[s], shown by a slight movement only of the cap' (*OED* Half-cap 1).

204 **cold-moving** stiff (as if with benumbed muscles); conveying coldness (Riverside).

208 **caked** clotted.

209 **'Tis . . . kind** For lack of (1) natural, (2) generous warmth they are not (1) as they naturally ought to be, (2) friendly.

210 **nature** the life of man.

213 **ingeniously** honestly, straightforwardly. 'Ingenious' and 'ingenuous' were used indiscriminately; see Schmidt.

No blame belongs to thee. Ventidius lately
Buried his father, by whose death he's stepped   215
Into a great estate. When he was poor,
Imprisoned, and in scarcity of friends,
I cleared him with five talents. Greet him from me,
Bid him suppose some good necessity
Touches his friend, which craves to be remembered   220
With those five talents. That had, give't these fellows
To whom 'tis instant due. Ne'er speak or think
That Timon's fortunes 'mong his friends can sink.

FLAVIUS I would I could not think it.
That thought is bounty's foe;   225
Being free itself, it thinks all others so.

Exeunt

[**3.1**] FLAMINIUS *waiting to speak with Lord* LUCULLUS *from his master.*
Enters a SERVANT *to him*

SERVANT I have told my lord of you; he is coming down to you.
FLAMINIUS I thank you, sir.

Enter LUCULLUS

SERVANT Here's my lord.
LUCULLUS [*Aside*] One of Lord Timon's men? A gift, I warrant. Why,
this hits right; I dreamt of a silver basin and ewer tonight. –   5
Flaminius, honest Flaminius, you are very respectively welcome,
sir. – Fill me some wine.

[*Exit Servant*]

And how does that honourable, complete, free-hearted gentleman
of Athens, thy very bountiful good lord and master?

Act 3, Scene 1   3.1] *Rowe; not in* F   0 SD.1 *with Lord* LUCULLUS] *Kittredge; with a Lord* F   0 SD.1–2 *master. Enters*] *Rowe;*
Master, enters F   4 SD] *Johnson; not in* F   5 tonight. –] *Capell (subst.); to night.* F   7 SD] *Capell; not in* F

219 some good necessity (1) some want arising
from an honest need, (2) some want which might
provide (for Ventidius) an opportunity for doing
good.
221 had received.
225 bounty assumes all others to give generously,
freely, doing so itself.

Act 3, Scene 1
5 ewer 'A pitcher with a wide spout, used to
bring water for washing the hands' (*OED* Ewer² 1).
6 respectively especially.
8 complete accomplished.

FLAMINIUS His health is well, sir.   10
LUCULLUS I am right glad that his health is well, sir; and what hast thou
    there under thy cloak, pretty Flaminius?
FLAMINIUS Faith, nothing but an empty box, sir, which, in my lord's
    behalf, I come to entreat your honour to supply; who, having great
    and instant occasion to use fifty talents, hath sent to your lordship   15
    to furnish him, nothing doubting your present assistance therein.
LUCULLUS La, la, la, la! 'Nothing doubting', says he? Alas, good lord;
    a noble gentleman 'tis, if he would not keep so good a house. Many
    a time and often I ha' dined with him, and told him on't, and come
    again to supper to him of purpose to have him spend less, and yet he   20
    would embrace no counsel, take no warning by my coming. Every
    man has his fault, and honesty is his. I ha' told him on't, but I could
    ne'er get him from't.

Enter SERVANT *with wine*

SERVANT Please your lordship, here is the wine.
LUCULLUS Flaminius, I have noted thee always wise. Here's to thee.   25
FLAMINIUS Your lordship speaks your pleasure.
LUCULLUS I have observed thee always for a towardly prompt spirit,
    give thee thy due, and one that knows what belongs to reason; and
    canst use the time well, if the time use thee well. Good parts in thee.
    [*To Servant*] Get you gone, sirrah.   30

                                       [*Exit Servant*]

---

30 SD.1 *To Servant*] Pope; *not in* F   30 SD.2 *Exit Servant*] Theobald; *not in* F

14 supply fill.
15 instant occasion urgent want.
16 nothing not at all.
16 present immediate.
18 if if only.
18 keep … house offer such extravagant hospitality.
20 of purpose … him purposely, with the intention of making him.
21–2 Every … fault A proverbial expression (see Tilley M116), but here absurdly applied, making honesty, with a subsidiary sense, generosity (*OED* Honesty *sb* 3c), a fault. The bland tone of Lucullus has a pomposity worthy of a Dickens character. There are several other occasions where the word is equivocally used – see e.g. 1.2.227 when Apemantus speaks of 'honest fools' or 4.3.115 when Timon says of the 'counterfeit matron' that 'It is her habit only that is honest', or when he addresses Poet

and Painter sarcastically as 'honest men' (5.1.47, 62, 64).

25 wise discreet.
25 Lucullus drinks the wine himself; his original intention when ordering his servant 'Fill me some wine' could have been to offer it to Flaminius. Hibbard so interprets it and considers it a 'very neat dramatic reversal'.

26 speaks your pleasure i.e. is pleased to say so.
27 towardly genial.
27 prompt alert.
29 canst use … thee well The most obvious meaning of Lucullus's commendatory remarks is: if time is friendly disposed toward you, you will be able to make good use of opportunities provided by it.

29 parts quantities, abilities.
30 sirrah A term of address used to inferiors.

Draw nearer, honest Flaminius. Thy lord's a bountiful gentleman,
but thou art wise, and thou know'st well enough, although thou
com'st to me, that this is no time to lend money, especially upon
bare friendship without security. Here's three solidares for thee;
good boy, wink at me, and say thou saw'st me not. Fare thee well.   35
FLAMINIUS Is't possible the world should so much differ,
    And we alive that lived? Fly, damnèd baseness,
    To him that worships thee. [*Throwing back the money*]
LUCULLUS Ha! Now I see thou art a fool, and fit for thy master.
                                         Exit Lucullus

FLAMINIUS May these add to the number that may scald thee!   40
    Let molten coin be thy damnation,
    Thou disease of a friend, and not himself!
    Has friendship such a faint and milky heart,
    It turns in less than two nights? O you gods!
    I feel my master's passion. This slave unto his honour   45
    Has my lord's meat in him;
    Why should it thrive and turn to nutriment
    When he is turned to poison?
    O may diseases only work upon't,
    And when he's sick to death, let not that part of nature   50
    Which my lord paid for, be of any power
    To expel sickness, but prolong his hour!   *Exit*

[3.2] *Enter* LUCIUS *with three* STRANGERS

LUCIUS Who, the Lord Timon? He is my very good friend and an
    honourable gentleman.

---

38 SD] *Rowe; not in* F   39 SD] F2; *Exit L.* F   45 his honour] F; *this hour Pope*   Act 3, Scene 2   3.2] *Pope; not in* F   0 SD]
F; *Enter* LUCIUS, *with* HOSTILIUS *and two other* STRANGERS *Sisson*

34 bare mere.
34 solidares Coins of Shakespeare's invention,
perhaps after the Roman 'solidus' or the Italian
'solido'.
35 wink shut your eyes.
36 differ be other than before – that is, when
money was indeed lent 'upon bare friendship'.
37 And . . . lived i.e. in a single lifetime: we who
knew it as it was are still alive to see it so changed.
40 these these coins.
41 Let . . . damnation Usurers in medieval tradition were boiled in molten lead when sent to hell.
This is the ironic fate suffered in this world by
Barabas the usurer in Marlowe's *The Jew of Malta.*

42 disease of a friend sick image of a friend.
43 milky weak.
44 turns turns sour.
45 passion (1) suffering (possibly with biblical
undertones), (2) anger.
45–6 This slave . . . him Though a lord,
Lucullus shows himself a slave: my lord's meat in
him honours him. Some editors accept Pope's conjecture 'Unto this hour', which substitutes a plain
formulation for a complex one.
50 that . . . nature that part of his bodily
system.
52 prolong his hour lengthen his hour of sickness and death.

FIRST STRANGER We know him for no less, though we are but strangers to him. But I can tell you one thing, my lord, and which I hear from common rumours, now Lord Timon's happy hours are done 5
and past, and his estate shrinks from him.

LUCIUS Fie, no, do not believe it; he cannot want for money.

SECOND STRANGER But believe you this, my lord, that not long ago one of his men was with the Lord Lucullus, to borrow so many talents, nay, urged extremely for't, and showed what necessity be- 10
longed to't, and yet was denied.

LUCIUS How?

SECOND STRANGER I tell you, denied, my lord.

LUCIUS What a strange case was that! Now before the gods, I am ashamed on't. Denied that honourable man? There was very little honour 15
showed in't. For my own part, I must needs confess, I have received some small kindnesses from him, as money, plate, jewels, and such like trifles; nothing comparing to his; yet had he mistook him and sent to me, I should ne'er have denied his occasion so many talents.

Enter SERVILIUS

SERVILIUS See, by good hap, yonder's my lord; I have sweat to see his 20
honour. My honoured lord!

LUCIUS Servilius? You are kindly met, sir. Fare thee well, commend me to thy honourable virtuous lord, my very exquisite friend.

SERVILIUS May it please your honour, my lord hath sent –

LUCIUS Ha? What has he sent? I am so much endeared to that lord; he's 25
ever sending. How shall I thank him, think'st thou? And what has he sent now?

SERVILIUS H'as only sent his present occasion now, my lord; requesting your lordship to supply his instant use with so many talents.

---

3 SH FIRST STRANGER] *Rowe;* 1 F (*throughout scene*) 8 SH SECOND STRANGER] *Rowe;* 2 F; HOSTILIUS *Sisson* (*throughout scene*) 25 has] F2; ha's F 29 so many talents] F; fifty Talents *Rowe*

Act 3, Scene 2

3 **We . . . less** '*we know him* by report to be *no less* than you represent him' (Johnson).

6 **his estate . . . him** his wealth is dwindling.

7 **want for** be short of.

18 **his** i.e. Lucullus.

18–19 **had . . . me** had he by mistake sent to me. The reflexive use of 'mistake' in 'mistook him' meaning '(had he) mistaken himself' is obsolete and the only instance in Shakespeare.

19 **his occasion** him in his need. See *OED* Occasion *sb*[1] 5b.

20 **hap** luck.

20 **sweat** made great efforts.

25 **endeared** obliged; perhaps also punning with the literal meaning 'render costly', 'enhance the price of' (*OED* Endear *v* 1).

28 **his . . . occasion** what he urgently needs now.

29 **to supply . . . use** to supply him for his immediate use.

LUCIUS I know his lordship is but merry with me,   30
      He cannot want fifty – five hundred talents.

SERVILIUS But in the mean time he wants less, my lord.
      If his occasion were not virtuous,
      I should not urge it half so faithfully.

LUCIUS Dost thou speak seriously, Servilius?   35

SERVILIUS Upon my soul, 'tis true, sir.

LUCIUS What a wicked beast was I to disfurnish myself against such a
good time, when I might ha' shown myself honourable! How
unluckily it happened, that I should purchase the day before for a
little part, and undo a great deal of honour! Servilius, now before   40
the gods, I am not able to do – the more beast, I say – I was sending
to use Lord Timon myself, these gentlemen can witness; but I
would not, for the wealth of Athens, I had done't now. Commend
me bountifully to his good lordship, and I hope his honour will
conceive the fairest of me, because I have no power to be kind. And   45
tell him this from me, I count it one of my greatest afflictions, say,
that I cannot pleasure such an honourable gentleman. Good
Servilius, will you befriend me so far as to use mine own words to
him?

SERVILIUS Yes, sir, I shall.   *Exit Servilius*   50

LUCIUS [*Calling after him*] I'll look you out a good turn, Servilius. –
      True, as you said, Timon is shrunk indeed,
      And he that's once denied, will hardly speed.   *Exit*

FIRST STRANGER Do you observe this, Hostilius?

SECOND STRANGER Ay, too well.   55

FIRST STRANGER Why, this is the world's soul,
      And just of the same piece
      Is every flatterer's sport. Who can call him his friend

---

31 fifty – five] *Oliver;* fifty five F   41 beast, I say] *Theobald;* beast I say F; beast I, I say *Collier²*   50 SD] F; *after 51 in Johnson*   51 SD] *Oliver; not in* F   51 Servilius. –] *Pope; Seruilius.* F   58 sport] F; *spirit Theobald*

30 is . . . me is but playing a joke on me.

31 want Punning on both meanings: 'lack' and 'desire' (the same in 32).

31 fifty . . . talents I follow F but amend punctuation (like Riverside), leaving several options for how the actor speaks the line. Capell prints 'fifty-five hundred'; Oliver follows the theory that Shakespeare put down two alternative numbers expecting to settle on one later. (See p. 177 below.)

33 If . . . virtuous If his need were not brought about by virtuous causes (honesty or generosity).

34 faithfully earnestly.

42 use borrow from.

44 bountifully Ironic in view of his refusal; the word is earlier associated with Timon as 'Magic of bounty' (1.1.6) and 'soul of bounty' (1.2.198).

45 conceive . . . me think the best of me.

51 I'll . . . turn I'll do you a good turn.

53 speed thrive.

54 Hostilius This is the only mention of the Second Stranger by name.

57 of . . . piece of the same kind.

That dips in the same dish? For in my knowing
Timon has been this lord's father,   60
And kept his credit with his purse;
Supported his estate; nay, Timon's money
Has paid his men their wages. He ne'er drinks
But Timon's silver treads upon his lip;
And yet – O see the monstrousness of man,   65
When he looks out in an ungrateful shape! –
He does deny him, in respect of his,
What charitable men afford to beggars
THIRD STRANGER Religion groans at it.
FIRST STRANGER   For mine own part,
I never tasted Timon in my life,   70
Nor came any of his bounties over me,
To mark me for his friend. Yet I protest,
For his right noble mind, illustrious virtue,
And honourable carriage,
Had his necessity made use of me,   75
I would have put my wealth into donation,
And the best half should have returned to him,
So much I love his heart. But I perceive
Men must learn now with pity to dispense,
For policy sits above conscience.   80

                                                  Exeunt

59 **That . . . dish** By this scriptural allusion (Matt. 26.23) Lord Lucius is referred to as a kind of Judas; see also Apemantus's railings against Timon's flatterers, 1.2.39–41.

61 **kept . . . purse** sustained Lucius's credit (i.e. his financial solvency and, in a more general sense, his reputation) with his own money.

64 **treads upon** presses upon; 'tread' is used here in an uncommon way; usually it refers only to the pressure of one's feet, even if used figuratively. A punning use, or even misprint, of 'trades' cannot be excluded.

65 **monstrousness** See *Cor.* 2.3.9 ('Ingratitude is monstrous'). The noun form 'monstrousness' is the only instance in Shakespeare.

66 **When . . . out** When he shows himself.

67–8 **He . . . beggars** 'what *Lucius* denies to *Timon* is in proportion to what *Lucius* possesses, less than the usual alms given by good men to beggars' (Johnson).

70 **I . . . Timon** I never got the opportunity to benefit from Timon's generosity.

71–2 **Nor . . . friend** Ironically, he reveals a parasitical attitude: being marked for a friend is made dependent on Timon's showering of 'bounties'.

74 **carriage** conduct.

76 **I . . . donation** 'I would have *supposed* my whole fortune to have been a *gift* from him' (Malone, after Steevens). This reading is supported by 'returned' in the next line, which implies that something is put back from where it came. His manner of speaking is contrived to the point of obscurity.

80 **policy** shrewd course of action, but (remembering the term's association with the Machiavels of Elizabethan drama) also expedient (*OED* Policy *sb*¹ 5).

80 **sits above** takes precedence over.

[**3.3**] *Enter* [*Timon's*] *third* SERVANT *with* SEMPRONIUS, *another of Timon's friends*

SEMPRONIUS Must he needs trouble me in't? Humh!
　　　　　　'Bove all others?
　　　　　　He might have tried Lord Lucius or Lucullus;
　　　　　　And now Ventidius is wealthy too,
　　　　　　Whom he redeemed from prison. All these　　　　　5
　　　　　　Owes their estates unto him.
SERVANT　　　　　　　　　　　　　　　My lord,
　　　　　　They have all been touched and found base metal,
　　　　　　For they have all denied him.
SEMPRONIUS How? Have they denied him?
　　　　　　Has Ventidius and Lucullus denied him,　　　　　10
　　　　　　And does he send to me? Three? Humh?
　　　　　　It shows but little love or judgement in him.
　　　　　　Must I be his last refuge? His friends, like physicians,
　　　　　　Thrive, give him over; must I take th'cure upon me?
　　　　　　H'as much disgraced me in't, I'm angry at him　　　15
　　　　　　That might have known my place. I see no sense for't,
　　　　　　But his occasions might have wooed me first;
　　　　　　For, in my conscience, I was the first man
　　　　　　That e'er received gift from him.
　　　　　　And does he think so backwardly of me now,　　　20
　　　　　　That I'll requite it last? No!
　　　　　　So it may prove an argument of laughter
　　　　　　To th'rest, and 'mongst lords I be thought a fool.
　　　　　　I'd rather than the worth of thrice the sum
　　　　　　H'ad sent to me first, but for my mind's sake;　　　25

Act 3, Scene 3　3.3] *Pope; not in* F　0 SD *Timon's third* SERVANT] *Capell; a third seruant* F　4 Ventidius] F2; Ventidgius F (*throughout scene*)　14 Thrive,] F; That thriv'd, F2–4; Three *Pope;* Tried *Hanmer;* Thrice *conj. Johnson*　15 H'as] *Rowe;* Has F　23 I] F2; *not in* F　25 H'ad] F4; Had F

Act 3, Scene 3

6 Owes The third person plural *-s* is common in Elizabethan English (see Franz 679a).

7 touched tested with the touchstone (to distinguish pure metal from base).

10 Has A similar case to the one in 6.

14 Thrive . . . over Prosper and declare his situation hopeless, do not help him. The F reading gains some support from its closeness to the proverbial saying 'Physicians enriched give over their patients.' Another example, from Webster's *Duchess of Malfi*, is cited by Dent P264.11.

16 That . . . place Who should have known my position (as first) in the order of his friends.

16–17 I . . . first I see no reason why in his need he did not approach me first (Riverside).

20 does . . . backwardly does he think of me as being late or last in the order of his friends (perhaps also, 'as an afterthought').

21 That . . . last That I am the last one to be asked to pay.

22 argument of laughter reason to laugh at me.

25 but . . . sake for the sake of my good will to him.

I'd such a courage to do him good. But now return,
And with their faint reply this answer join:
Who bates mine honour shall not know my coin.   *Exit*
SERVANT Excellent! Your lordship's a goodly villain. The devil knew   30
not what he did, when he made man politic; he crossed himself by't;
and I cannot think but, in the end, the villainies of man will set him
clear. How fairly this lord strives to appear foul! Takes virtuous
copies to be wicked; like those that under hot ardent zeal would set
whole realms on fire; of such a nature is his politic love.
  This was my lord's best hope; now all are fled   35
Save only the gods. Now his friends are dead,
Doors that were ne'er acquainted with their wards
Many a bounteous year, must be employed
Now to guard sure their master.
And this is all a liberal course allows;   40
Who cannot keep his wealth must keep his house.   *Exit*

[3.4] *Enter* VARRO'*s* [*two* SERVANTS], *meeting others, all* [*servants of*]
Timon's creditors, to wait for his coming out. Then enter [TITUS], LUCIUS *and*
HORTENSIUS

FIRST VARRO SERVANT Well met, good morrow, Titus and
   Hortensius.
TITUS The like to you, kind Varro.
HORTENSIUS   Lucius!

Act 3, Scene 4 3.4] *Pope; not in* F   0 SD.1 VARRO'S *two* SERVANTS] *Capell; Varro's man* F   0 SD.1–2 *all
servants . . . creditors*] *Rowe; All Timons Creditors* F   0 SD.2 TITUS] *Rowe; not in* F   1 SH FIRST VARRO SERVANT] *Capell;
Var. man.* F   2–4] *Capell; The . . . Varro. / Lucius . . . together? / I . . . all* F

26 **courage** desire.
28 **bates** diminishes.
30 **politic** crafty, cunning (*OED* Politic A2d).
(Compare 3.2.80 n.)
 30 **crossed** thwarted.
31–2 **will . . . clear** 'him' is the devil, who by
contrast with man will appear innocent: the basic
proposition in Ben Jonson's 1616 comedy *The Devil
Is An Ass.*
32 **How fairly** With what an appearance of
decency.
32–3 **Takes . . . wicked** Models himself on the
virtuous in order to be wicked (Riverside).
33–4 **under . . . fire** under the cloak of religious
devotion would cause wars and civil strife – like
Puritans (Warburton) or Jesuits (Maxwell).

37 **Doors . . . wards** Doors that have always
been left unbolted.
39 **sure** securely.
40 **liberal** generous.
41 **must . . . house** must stay indoors (with a
pun on 'maintain a household', to keep one's house
open).

Act 3, Scene 4
 0 SD F's 'permissive' SDs give names for only three
of the creditors' servants whereas two more speak in
the dialogue: but how many altogether are on stage?
The SDs may be evidence that the MS. at this point
was not finally revised by the author.
 1–16 For a discussion of the metrical problems (as
documented in the collation) see pp. 194–5 below.

                    What, do we meet together?
LUCIUS   Ay, and I think
             One business does command us all;
             For mine is money.
TITUS   So is theirs and ours.   5

                        Enter PHILOTUS

LUCIUS And Sir Philotus too!
PHILOTUS   Good day at once.
LUCIUS Welcome, good brother. What do you think the hour?
PHILOTUS Labouring for nine.
LUCIUS So much?
PHILOTUS   Is not my lord seen yet?
LUCIUS   Not yet.
PHILOTUS I wonder on't; he was wont to shine at seven.   10
LUCIUS Ay, but the days are waxed shorter with him;
             You must consider that a prodigal course
             Is like the sun's, but not like his recoverable, I fear.
             'Tis deepest winter in Lord Timon's purse;
             That is, one may reach deep enough, and yet   15
             Find little.
PHILOTUS   I am of your fear for that.
TITUS I'll show you how t'observe a strange event.
             Your lord sends now for money?
HORTENSIUS   Most true, he does.
TITUS And he wears jewels now of Timon's gift,

---

3 SH LUCIUS] F (*Luci.* / alternating with / *Luc.* / throughout scene); *Luc. Serv.* / *Malone*   **3–5**] *Maxwell;* I . . . all. / For . . . money. / So . . . ours. / F   **6** And . . . too] F; And Sir Philo's too *Rowe;* And, sir, Philotus too *Collier²*   **7**] *Pope;* Welcome . . . Brother. / What . . . houre? F   **9**] *Johnson/Steevens¹;* So much? / Is . . . yet? / Not yet. F   **14–16** 'Tis . . . little.] *Pope; prose* F

6 And . . . too I follow F. Rowe links this line with the previous remarks of Lucius and Titus (4–5) about their common 'business', i.e. money, and, with Philotus having just entered the scene, it would mean 'this is also the newcomer's business'. I regard this as possible but not compelling. Collier, followed by Oliver and Riverside, has different punctuation, to avoid the impropriety of a servant being addressed as 'Sir'.
  6 at once to you all.
  10 shine The first of a sequence of sun images.
  11 waxed grown.
  12–13 a prodigal . . . sun's a prodigal's course is like the seasonal course of the sun. The prodigal

myth is used by Flavius at 2.2.151–7 and plays a role in the banter between Timon and Apemantus in 4.3.285–6.
  13 not . . . recoverable i.e. the sun moves lower in the sky in winter but regains height in summer; but unlike the sun, the prodigal cannot regain his height of fortune once it is lost.
  14 'Tis . . . purse The winter metaphor (as Steevens explains) is continued in 14–16, referring to animals digging deep in the snow for food (Johnson/Steevens⁵).
  16 I . . . fear I share your fear.
  19 of . . . gift given by Timon.

          For which I wait for money.   20
HORTENSIUS It is against my heart.
LUCIUS Mark how strange it shows,
          Timon in this should pay more than he owes;
          And e'en as if your lord should wear rich jewels,
          And send for money for 'em.   25
HORTENSIUS I'm weary of this charge, the gods can witness;
          I know my lord hath spent of Timon's wealth,
          And now ingratitude makes it worse than stealth.
FIRST VARRO SERVANT Yes, mine's three thousand crowns; what's
          yours?
LUCIUS Five thousand mine.   30
FIRST VARRO SERVANT 'Tis much deep, and it should seem by
          th'sum,
          Your master's confidence was above mine,
          Else, surely, his had equalled.

                    Enter FLAMINIUS

TITUS One of Lord Timon's men.
LUCIUS Flaminius? Sir, a word. Pray is my lord ready to come forth?   35
FLAMINIUS No, indeed he is not.
TITUS We attend his lordship; pray signify so much.
FLAMINIUS I need not tell him that; he knows you are too diligent.
                                                              [*Exit*]

          Enter Steward [FLAVIUS] *in a cloak, muffled*

LUCIUS Ha! Is not that his steward muffled so?
          He goes away in a cloud. Call him, call him.   40
TITUS Do you hear, sir?
SECOND VARRO SERVANT By your leave, sir –
FLAVIUS What do ye ask of me, my friend?

21–2] F; *one line in Johnson/Steevens⁵*   26] *Rowe;* I'me . . . Charge, / The . . . witnesse: F   29] *Pope;* Yes . . . Crownes: /
What's yours? F   38 SD.1 *Exit] Malone; not in* F   38 SD.2 FLAVIUS] *Rowe; not in* F   42 sir –] *Capell;* sir. F   43 SH
FLAVIUS] *Rowe;* Stew. F (*throughout scene*)

20 For . . . money To buy which, Timon borrowed money that he cannot now repay.
21 against my heart against my feelings.
26 charge commission, employment.
28 stealth stealing.
31 much deep very heavy.
32 above mine greater than my master's
confidence.

33 his had equalled my master's loan would
have equalled yours.
37 attend (1) wait for, (2) expect (in a more
demanding sense).
40 in a cloud (1) gloomily, (2) as if covered in a
cloud; this suggests a dissimulating purpose. See
Dent C443.1.

TITUS We wait for certain money here, sir.

FLAVIUS   Ay,
If money were as certain as your waiting,   45
'Twere sure enough.
Why then preferred you not your sums and bills,
When your false masters eat of my lord's meat?
Then they could smile and fawn upon his debts,
And take down th'int'rest into their glutt'nous maws.   50
You do yourselves but wrong to stir me up;
Let me pass quietly.
Believe't, my lord and I have made an end;
I have no more to reckon, he to spend.

LUCIUS Ay, but this answer will not serve.   55

FLAVIUS If 'twill not serve, 'tis not so base as you,
For you serve knaves.   [*Exit*]

FIRST VARRO SERVANT How? What does his cashiered worship mutter?

SECOND VARRO SERVANT No matter what; he's poor, and that's
revenge enough. Who can speak broader than he that has no house   60
to put his head in? Such may rail against great buildings.

Enter SERVILIUS

TITUS O, here's Servilius; now we shall know some answer.

SERVILIUS If I might beseech you, gentlemen, to repair some other
hour, I should derive much from't; for, take't of my soul, my lord
leans wondrously to discontent. His comfortable temper has for-   65
sook him; he's much out of health, and keeps his chamber.

44–5 Ay . . . waiting] *Capell; one line in* F   56 If 'twill] F4; If't 'twill F; Ift twill F2–3   57 SD] *Rowe; not in* F

44 certain money (1) a specified sum of money, (2) money which we are sure is owed and is sure to be paid. Since nothing is less certain, the tone could be menacing or it could be unsure. Flavius mockingly repeats the word.

47 preferred presented.

49 fawn upon behave in a servile manner, like a dog.

50 maws stomachs.

51 You . . . up You only injure your cause by rousing my temper.

54 no more In the senses of quantity of money or of time ('no longer').

54 reckon count up, keep account of.

55 serve avail.

58 cashiered discarded from service.

60 speak broader be more plain-spoken ('often in a bad sense' – *OED* Broad *a* 6, where meanings such as 'coarse', 'gross' and 'indecent' are registered).

60–1 This may be read as a foreshadowing of Timon's changed condition from the beginning of Act 4 on.

60–1 house . . . in The Fool in *Lear* uses the phrase when mocking Lear for the folly of having given away all to his daughters (1.5.27–31).

63 repair return.

64 derive gain.

64 take't . . . soul accept it as my sincere conviction; 'soul' is the seat of real, not only professed, sentiments.

65 comfortable cheerful.

LUCIUS Many do keep their chambers are not sick;
    And if it be so far beyond his health,
    Methinks he should the sooner pay his debts,
    And make a clear way to the gods.
SERVILIUS   Good gods!   70
TITUS We cannot take this for answer, sir.
FLAMINIUS (*Within*) Servilius, help! My lord, my lord!

Enter TIMON *in a rage*

TIMON What, are my doors opposed against my passage?
    Have I been ever free, and must my house
    Be my retentive enemy? My gaol?   75
    The place which I have feasted, does it now,
    Like all mankind, show me an iron heart?
LUCIUS Put in now, Titus.
TITUS My lord, here is my bill.
LUCIUS Here's mine.   80
HORTENSIUS And mine, my lord.
FIRST *and* SECOND VARRO SERVANTS And ours, my lord.
PHILOTUS All our bills.
TIMON Knock me down with 'em, cleave me to the girdle.
LUCIUS Alas, my lord –   85
TIMON Cut my heart in sums.
TITUS Mine, fifty talents.
TIMON Tell out my blood.
LUCIUS Five thousand crowns, my lord.
TIMON Five thousand drops pays that. What yours? And yours?   90
FIRST VARRO SERVANT My lord –
SECOND VARRO SERVANT My lord –

81 SH HORTENSIUS] *Capell; 1 Var.* F   82 SH FIRST *and* . . . SERVANTS] *Capell; 2. Var.* F   85 lord –] *Capell;* Lord. F   90]
Dyce; Fiue . . . that. / What . . . yours? F   91 lord –] *Rowe;* Lord. F   92 lord –] *Rowe;* Lord. F

67 are who are.
68 if . . . health if he is past his days of health (i.e. nearing death).
70 clear cleared from obligations, so that nothing impedes entry to heaven.
71 Many editors since Rowe insert 'an' before 'answer' to improve metrical smoothness but rough lines are frequent in the play.
74 free (1) unrestrained, (2) generous.
75 retentive restraining, confining.
76 feasted made festive (?), feasted in (?).
77 iron heart As opposed to the 'heart of kind-

ness' connected with 'Plutus, the god of gold' (1.1.275–6).
78 Put in Advance your claim.
81–2 SHS The speech headings in F are *1. Var.* for 81 and *2. Var.* for 82. Since this arrangement does not make sense, I follow Capell's emendation, assigning 81 to Hortensius and 82 to the two servants of Varro as joint speakers.
84 Timon puns on the sense of 'bill' meaning halberd, since these demands for payment bring him down. The idea is developed in the metaphor of butchering, dividing him into pieces.
88 Tell out Count.

TIMON Tear me, take me, and the gods fall upon you!   *Exit Timon*

HORTENSIUS Faith, I perceive our masters may throw their caps at
    their money; these debts may well be called desperate ones, for a   95
    madman owes 'em.

                                                             Exeunt

Enter TIMON [*and* FLAVIUS]

TIMON They have e'en put my breath from me, the slaves. Creditors?
    Devils!

FLAVIUS My dear lord –

TIMON What if it should be so?   100

FLAVIUS My lord –

TIMON I'll have it so. My steward!

FLAVIUS Here, my lord.

TIMON So fitly? Go, bid all my friends again,
    Lucius, Lucullus, and Sempronius – all.   105
    I'll once more feast the rascals.

FLAVIUS   O my lord,
    You only speak from your distracted soul;
    There's not so much left to furnish out
    A moderate table.

TIMON   Be it not in thy care;
    Go, I charge thee, invite them all, let in the tide   110
    Of knaves once more; my cook and I'll provide.

                                                             Exeunt

---

96 SD.2 *and* FLAVIUS] *Rowe; not in* F   99 lord –] *Johnson;* Lord. F   101 lord –] *Johnson;* Lord. F   105 Sempronius] F3; *Semprovius* [*or / Sempronius*] *Vllorxa* F   106–9 O . . . table] *Pope; prose* F

94–5 throw . . . money give up their money as
lost (proverbial – see Dent c62).

95 desperate having the effect of making desperate. Hulme explains: 'Debts . . . were reckoned
"sperate" or "desperate", having some hope of being paid or else irrecoverable' (p. 164). See also J. C.
Maxwell, 'Desperate debts', *N&Q* 212 (1967), 141.

97 put . . . me put me out of breath (with angry
speech).

100 What . . . so? The idea of the banquet begins
to take shape in Timon's mind (as we see from what
follows).

104 fitly pat, opportunely.

105 Sempronius – all F has the name *Vllorxa*
added to Sempronius; for this, no intelligible explanation has been found. Sisson supposes an inter-
linear misreading by the compositor (*Readings*,
pp. 171–2).

108 to furnish out as to supply.

110–11 tide / Of knaves This metaphor recalls
the 'great flood of visitors' in 1.1.43.

[**3.5**] *Enter three* SENATORS *at one door*, ALCIBIADES *meeting them,*
with Attendants

FIRST SENATOR My lord, you have my voice to't; the fault's bloody;
　　　　'Tis necessary he should die;
　　　　Nothing emboldens sin so much as mercy.
SECOND SENATOR Most true; the law shall bruise 'em.
ALCIBIADES Honour, health and compassion to the senate!　　　　　　5
FIRST SENATOR Now, captain?
ALCIBIADES I am an humble suitor to your virtues;
　　　　For pity is the virtue of the law,
　　　　And none but tyrants use it cruelly.
　　　　It pleases time and fortune to lie heavy　　　　　　　　　　10
　　　　Upon a friend of mine, who in hot blood
　　　　Hath stepped into the law, which is past depth
　　　　To those that, without heed, do plunge into't.
　　　　He is a man, setting his fate aside,
　　　　Of comely virtues;　　　　　　　　　　　　　　　　　　15
　　　　Nor did he soil the fact with cowardice –
　　　　An honour in him which buys out his fault –
　　　　But with a noble fury and fair spirit,
　　　　Seeing his reputation touched to death,
　　　　He did oppose his foe;　　　　　　　　　　　　　　　20
　　　　And with such sober and unnoted passion

Act 3, Scene 5 1] *Rowe;* My . . . too't. / The . . . Bloody: F　4 'em] F; him *Hanmer*　14 fate] F; fault *Pope;* feat
Oxford　14–15] *Johnson; one line in* F　17 An] *Johnson;* And F

Act 3, Scene 5

1 **voice** vote.

3 **Nothing . . . mercy** Proverbial; see Dent:
'Pardon makes offenders' (P50). Escalus in *MM* argues similarly (2.1.284).

4 **'em** them, i.e. those to whom the above
mentioned saying can be applied. Hanmer's emendation 'him', accepted by many editors, is an unnecessary restriction.

7 **your virtues** your virtuous selves.

8 **the virtue . . . law** excellence, merit
(Riverside).

12 **Hath . . . depth** The metaphor is of entering
water and going unexpectedly out of one's depth.

14 **setting . . . aside** apart from his ill fate.
Alcibiades' rhetorical strategy shifts the liability to
metaphysical entities; see 10: 'It pleases time and
fortune . . .'

16 **fact** deed.

17 **buys out** redeems.

19 **touched to death** threatened with fatal
damage.

21–3 The impression which Alcibiades gives
of his friend's conduct contradicts the earlier one
in 11–12; rhetorical effect prevails over truth,
presumably.

21 **unnoted** imperceptible.

He did behove his anger, ere 'twas spent,
As if he had but proved an argument.
FIRST SENATOR You undergo too strict a paradox,
  Striving to make an ugly deed look fair.   25
  Your words have took such pains as if they laboured
  To bring manslaughter into form, and set quarrelling
  Upon the head of valour; which indeed
  Is valour misbegot, and came into the world
  When sects and factions were newly born.   30
  He's truly valiant that can wisely suffer
  The worst that man can breathe,
  And make his wrongs his outsides,
  To wear them like his raiment, carelessly,
  And ne'er prefer his injuries to his heart,   35
  To bring it into danger.
  If wrongs be evils and enforce us kill,
  What folly 'tis to hazard life for ill!
ALCIBIADES My lord –
FIRST SENATOR   You cannot make gross sins look clear;
  To revenge is no valour, but to bear.   40
ALCIBIADES My lords, then, under favour, pardon me,
  If I speak like a captain.
  Why do fond men expose themselves to battle,
  And not endure all threats? Sleep upon't,
  And let the foes quietly cut their throats   45
  Without repugnancy? If there be
  Such valour in the bearing, what make we
  Abroad? Why then, women are more valiant

---

22 behove] *Alexander;* behooue F*;* behave *Rowe* 39 lord –] *Rowe;* Lord. F

22 behove moderate, control. I do not accept Rowe's emendation 'behave'; for a discussion see Hulme, pp. 249–52.

24 undergo too strict undertake too forced.

27 bring . . . form set up manslaughter as a formal or lawful procedure (*OED* Form *sb* 11).

27–8 set . . . valour regard quarrelling as a category of valour; 'head' means 'category': *OED* Head *sb* 27 citing this passage.

28 which Refers to 'set quarrelling / Upon . . .'

32 breathe speak.

33 make . . . outsides treat the injustice inflicted upon him as something external, not vital.

34 carelessly casually.

35 prefer present.

37 enforce us kill compel us to kill.

38 for ill for an evil cause.

39 clear innocent.

40 bear put up with wrongs.

41 under favour by your leave.

42 captain soldier; military law differs from civilian in recognising killing (in battle) as honourable.

43 Why . . . themselves Why do men foolishly expose themselves.

46 repugnancy resistance.

47 we soldiers (speaking like a captain).

48 Abroad Away from home.

That stay at home, if bearing carry it;
And the ass more captain than the lion,   50
The fellow loaden with irons wiser than the judge,
If wisdom be in suffering. O my lords,
As you are great, be pitifully good.
Who cannot condemn rashness in cold blood?
To kill, I grant, is sin's extremest gust,   55
But in defence, by mercy, 'tis most just.
To be in anger is impiety,
But who is man that is not angry?
Weigh but the crime with this.

SECOND SENATOR You breathe in vain.

ALCIBIADES   In vain? His service done   60
At Lacedaemon and Byzantium
Were a sufficient briber for his life.

FIRST SENATOR What's that?

ALCIBIADES Why I say, my lords, h'as done fair service,
And slain in fight many of your enemies;   65
How full of valour did he bear himself
In the last conflict, and made plenteous wounds!

SECOND SENATOR He has made too much plenty with 'em;
He's a sworn rioter; he has a sin
That often drowns him and takes his valour prisoner.   70
If there were no foes, that were enough
To overcome him. In that beastly fury
He has been known to commit outrages

---

51 fellow] F; felon *conj. Johnson*   60–1] *Pope;* You . . . vaine. / In vaine? / His . . . Byzantium, F   64 Why I] F2; Why F
68 'em] F2; him F

49 **bearing** (1) undergoing sexual intercourse, (2) putting up with wrongs, (3) bearing children.
50 **more captain** more captainlike, i.e. valorous.
51 **loaden with irons** confined with shackles.
53 **be . . . good** be good in showing pity.
54 **Who . . . blood** Who, when his blood is cold, cannot condemn hot-headed rashness.
55 **sin's . . . gust** (1) the utmost degree of appetite for sin (Johnson), (2) a violent outburst of sin.
56 **by mercy** mercifully interpreted; possibly, short for 'by God's mercy'.
58 **who . . . angry** i.e. anger is part of human nature. On the Aristotelian background of this concept of virtue, see Martha C. Nussbaum, *The Fragility of Goodness*, 1986: 'each salient Aristotelian

virtue seems inseparable from a risk of harm' (p. 420). See also 1.2.28–9.
60 **breathe** speak.
61 **At . . . Byzantium** The reference is too vague for certain explanation. In 411 BC Byzantium revolted against Athens, in 408 it was recaptured.
62 **briber** giver of bribes (Riverside).
66 **bear himself** conduct himself.
68 **He . . . 'em** 'Plenty' can connote excess: hence he is accused of behaving riotously after his victories in battle, through a cheap pun on 'plenty'.
69 **sworn** inveterate.
69–70 **a sin . . . drowns him** i.e. drunkenness that overpowers him.
71 **If** Even if.

And cherish factions. 'Tis inferred to us,
His days are foul and his drink dangerous.   75
FIRST SENATOR He dies.
ALCIBIADES   Hard fate! He might have died in war.
My lords, if not for any parts in him –
Though his right arm might purchase his own time
And be in debt to none – yet more to move you,
Take my deserts to his, and join 'em both;   80
And for I know your reverend ages love security,
I'll pawn my victories, all my honour to you,
Upon his good returns.
If by this crime he owes the law his life,
Why, let the war receive't in valiant gore,   85
For law is strict, and war is nothing more.
FIRST SENATOR We are for law; he dies; urge it no more
On height of our displeasure. Friend or brother,
He forfeits his own blood that spills another.
ALCIBIADES Must it be so? It must not be.   90
My lords, I do beseech you know me.
SECOND SENATOR   How?
ALCIBIADES Call me to your remembrances.
THIRD SENATOR   What?
ALCIBIADES I cannot think but your age has forgot me;
It could not else be I should prove so base
To sue and be denied such common grace.   95
My wounds ache at you.
FIRST SENATOR   Do you dare our anger?

91] *Oliver;* My . . . mee. / How? F   92] *Johnson/Steevens*[4]*;* Call . . . remembrances. / What. F

74 **cherish factions** foster factious conduct in people.
74 **inferred** alleged.
77 **parts** merits.
78 **right arm** valorous feats.
78 **purchase . . . time** merit him his natural span of life. Moral obligations are here presented in terms of financial dealing.
81 **for** because.
81 **your reverend ages** you in your reverend age.
81 **security** (1) safety, (2) suretyship, collateral for a loan. The second meaning is enhanced by 'pawn' (82) and 'good returns' (83).

83 **Upon . . . returns** (1) that his future conduct will be more civilised, (2) that his future conduct will yield a profit for you.
85 **let . . . gore** let him give his life in battle.
86 **law . . . more** war is as rigorous (opposed to being lenient) in its consequences as law is.
88 **On . . . our** On pain of our highest (Riverside).
89 **another** another's.
91 **know me** recognise me for all I am.
93 **your age . . . me** i.e. because of your age you have forgotten my achievements.
95 **common grace** favour you could grant to anybody.

'Tis in few words, but spacious in effect:
We banish thee for ever.
ALCIBIADES   Banish me?
Banish your dotage, banish usury,
That makes the senate ugly.   100
FIRST SENATOR If after two days' shine Athens contain thee,
Attend our weightier judgement.
And not to swell our spirit,
He shall be executed presently.

                                            Exeunt [Senators]

ALCIBIADES Now the gods keep you old enough, that you may live   105
Only in bone, that none may look on you!
I'm worse than mad; I have kept back their foes,
While they have told their money, and let out
Their coin upon large interest; I myself
Rich only in large hurts. All those, for this?   110
Is this the balsam that the usuring senate
Pours into captains' wounds? Banishment!
It comes not ill. I hate not to be banished,
It is a cause worthy my spleen and fury,
That I may strike at Athens. I'll cheer up   115
My discontented troops, and lay for hearts.
'Tis honour with most lands to be at odds;
Soldiers should brook as little wrongs as gods.   *Exit*

---

103 our spirit] F; your spirit *Warburton*   104 SD *Senators*] *Capell; not in* F   105] *Johnson/Steevens*¹; Now ... enough, /
That ... liue F   117 most] F; worst *Hibbard*   117 lands] F; hands *Warburton*

97 **few ... spacious** The Senator's word-play is
mocking; the words are short, but they will propel
Alcibiades a long way, into exile.
102 **Attend ... judgement** expect a severer
sentence.
103 **not ... spirit** not to allow our anger to
grow.
104 **presently** at once.
106 **in bone** as mere skeletons.
107–10 Alcibiades sees that he has been exploited: while they have invested their money at
high interest, his rewards for protecting them have

been all heavy losses, wounds in war and now
banishment.
111 **balsam** healing ointment, balm (the only
instance in Shakespeare of this word).
114 **spleen and fury** An instance of the rhetorical figure hendiadys ('one through two') to lend
emphasis to a statement.
116 **lay for hearts** win their affection.
117–18 i.e. soldiers (proudly dedicated to honour, unlike civilian politicians) should be like gods
in not putting up with wrongs.

[**3.6**] [*Music.*] *Enter divers* [*of Timon's*] *friends,* [LORDS *and Senators*] *at several doors*

FIRST LORD The good time of day to you, sir.

SECOND LORD I also wish it to you. I think this honourable lord did but try us this other day.

FIRST LORD Upon that were my thoughts tiring when we encount'red. I hope it is not so low with him as he made it seem in the trial of his   5
several friends.

SECOND LORD It should not be, by the persuasion of his new feasting.

FIRST LORD I should think so. He hath sent me an earnest inviting, which many my near occasions did urge me to put off; but he hath conjured me beyond them, and I must needs appear.   10

SECOND LORD In like manner was I in debt to my importunate business, but he would not hear my excuse. I am sorry, when he sent to borrow of me, that my provision was out.

FIRST LORD I am sick of that grief too, as I understand how all things go.

SECOND LORD Every man here's so. What would he have borrowed of   15
you?

FIRST LORD A thousand pieces.

Act 3, Scene 6   3.6] *Capell; not in* F   0 SD.1 *Music*] *Capell; not in* F   0 SD.1–2 *Enter . . . doors*] *Kittredge; Enter diuers Friends at seuerall doores.* F   1 SH FIRST LORD] *Capell;* 1 F; *1 Sen. / Rowe; First Friend / Chambers;* LUCULLUS *Sisson* (*throughout scene*)   2 SH SECOND LORD] *Capell;* 2 F; *2 Sen. / Rowe; Second Friend / Chambers;* LUCIUS *Sisson* (*throughout scene*)   15 here's] F4; *heares* F

Act 3, Scene 6

0 SD Further stage directions in F (20, 74, 92) make it clear that the *divers friends* cannot be restricted to the three Lords mentioned in 3.4.105, but that – paralleling 1.1. and 1.2 – others are involved, including Senators. On names for Lords, see p. 69 above.

4 **tiring** feeding greedily (figuratively applied to persons: see *OED* Tire *v*² 2); the term 'tiring' (Old French *tirer*) was used in falconry (of the hawk): 'to pull or tear with the beak . . . that it may exercise itself'.

7 **by the persuasion** on the evidence.

8–14 Bayley (pp. 81–2) points out the self-approving and hypocritical tone of the Lords' speeches and suggests they be heard as an echo of Timon's own way of speaking in 1.1.103 ff.

9 **many . . . occasions** many pressing obligations of mine.

9 **put off** decline.

9–10 **he . . . appear** he has summoned me with an overriding urgency. Bradbrook (*Pageant*, pp. 13–

14) points out that Timon's summons is exercised with a magical irresistibility similar to that shown in 1.1.5–7, so that his guests 'must needs appear'.

11 **in debt** under obligation.

13 **my provision was out** my store of money was exhausted.

14 **sick of** troubled, afflicted by.

14 **grief** grievance.

14 The irony is in the word 'grief': now that Timon appears capable of generous giving once again, the Lord grieves, not because he could not help Timon in his hour of need but because he showed Timon hard-faced ungenerosity and may now forfeit the chance of more gifts from him; the Lord grieves not for Timon but for himself.

15 **here's** The F reading 'heares' is another (rare) spelling of 'here's'.

17 **thousand pieces** Evidently a large sum, the worth of which cannot be settled. See p. 177 below. If one identifies 1 Lord with Lucullus, as Sisson does, then the amount differs from the one actually demanded in 3.1.15.

SECOND LORD A thousand pieces?
FIRST LORD What of you?
SECOND LORD He sent to me, sir – Here he comes.   20

Enter TIMON *and Attendants*

TIMON With all my heart, gentlemen both; and how fare you?
FIRST LORD Ever at the best, hearing well of your lordship.
SECOND LORD The swallow follows not summer more willing than we
    your lordship.
TIMON Nor more willingly leaves winter; such summer birds are men.   25
    – Gentlemen, our dinner will not recompense this long stay; feast
    your ears with the music awhile, if they will fare so harshly o'th'
    trumpet's sound; we shall to't presently.
FIRST LORD I hope it remains not unkindly with your lordship that I
    returned you an empty messenger.   30
TIMON O sir, let it not trouble you.
SECOND LORD My noble lord –
TIMON Ah, my good friend, what cheer?
            The banquet brought in
SECOND LORD My most honourable lord, I am e'en sick of shame, that
    when your lordship this other day sent to me, I was so unfortunate   35
    a beggar.
TIMON Think not on't, sir.
SECOND LORD If you had sent but two hours before –
TIMON Let it not cumber your better remembrance. – Come bring in all
    together.   40
SECOND LORD All covered dishes.
FIRST LORD Royal cheer, I warrant you.

---

32 lord –] *Hanmer;* Lord. F   38 before –] F4; before. F

21 **With . . . heart** My cordial greetings.

22 **hearing . . . lordship** hearing that things are
well with your lordship.

23–5 **The swallow . . . men** The Lord aims to
sound pleasant but Timon detects the underlying
irony, as in the proverb 'Swallows, like false friends,
fly away upon the approach of winter' (Dent s1026).
Most editors since Johnson have marked the first
sentence of Timon's speech as an aside. I prefer to
leave the options open: if Timon speaks directly to
them, then his guests show their inattentiveness or
slow uptake, which is confirmed by their reactions
in 73–4.

26 **stay** wait.

27–8 **if . . . sound** if they (your ears) are prepared to feed on music which is repugnantly rough.
The music contrasts with that of the first banquet
(see stage directions 1.2.0, 1.2.117). The metaphor
of music as food recalls *TN* 1.1.1.

28 **we shall to't** we shall sit down to eat.

29 **it remains . . . lordship** i.e. that your lordship does not hold it against me.

33 **what cheer** how are you (*OED* Cheer *sb* 3b).

35–6 **unfortunate a beggar** unlucky as to be out
of money (Riverside).

39 **cumber . . . remembrance** burden your
happier memories.

42 **Royal cheer** A feast fit for a king.

THIRD LORD Doubt not that, if money and the season can yield it.

FIRST LORD How do you? What's the news?

THIRD LORD Alcibiades is banished; hear you of it?   45

FIRST *and* SECOND LORDS Alcibiades banished?

THIRD LORD 'Tis so, be sure of it.

FIRST LORD How? How?

SECOND LORD I pray you, upon what?

TIMON My worthy friends, will you draw near?   50

THIRD LORD I'll tell you more anon. Here's a noble feast toward.

SECOND LORD This is the old man still.

THIRD LORD Will't hold? Will't hold?

SECOND LORD It does; but time will – and so –

THIRD LORD I do conceive.   55

TIMON Each man to his stool, with that spur as he would to the lip of his
mistress; your diet shall be in all places alike. Make not a city feast
of it, to let the meat cool ere we can agree upon the first place. Sit,
sit. The gods require our thanks.

You great benefactors, sprinkle our society with thankfulness.   60
For your own gifts, make yourselves praised; but reserve still to
give, lest your deities be despised. Lend to each man enough, that
one need not lend to another; for were your godheads to borrow of
men, men would forsake the gods. Make the meat be beloved, more
than the man that gives it. Let no assembly of twenty be without a   65
score of villains. If there sit twelve women at the table, let a dozen
of them be as they are. The rest of your fees, O gods – the senators
of Athens, together with the common leg of people – what is amiss

43 SH THIRD LORD] *Capell;* 3 F; 3 Sen. / *Rowe; Third Friend / Chambers;* SEMPRONIUS *Sisson*   46 SH *and* SECOND
LORDS] *Malone; Both.* F   54 will –] *Capell;* will, F   54 so –] F4; so. F   67 be as] F; be – as *Johnson/Steevens*⁵   67 fees]
F; foes *Hanmer*   67 O gods –] *Capell;* O Gods, F   68 leg] F4; *legge* F; lag *Rowe;* tag *Collier*²   68 people –] *Capell;
People,* F

49 upon what for what reason.

51 toward ready to begin.

53 hold last.

55 conceive understand.

56–72 Compared with his manner at the previous
banquet in 1.2, Timon here adopts an overtly mocking and disrespectful tone.

56 spur eagerness.

57 your . . . alike the same food is provided for
you wherever you sit.

57 city feast formal city banquet, where seating
is according to rank.

59 require request, deserve (*WT* 2.3.189–90: 'be
prosperous / In more than this deed does require').

60 sprinkle Often used in ritual or religious contexts; see e.g. the Timon passage in Plutarch's 'Life

of Marcus Antonius', Bullough, VI, 251 ('they
celebrated . . . the feasts of the dead, where they
made sprincklings and sacrifices for the dead').

61 reserve still keep back something
(Riverside).

67 The rest . . . fees Riverside suggests that
'fees' means 'those holding their lives in fee from
you'. This makes sense, whereas if 'fees' means
'tributary payment', the grammar is not clear, and
one would have to suppose a sudden fracture, a new
statement beginning with 'the senators'. Hulme (p.
86) cites *Tro.* 3.3.48–9: 'for supple knees / Feed
arrogance and are the proud man's fees'. A proposed emendation ('foes') is unnecessary.

68 common . . . people Hulme explains: 'the
common people who kneel, or make a leg'.

in them, you gods, make suitable for destruction. For these my
present friends, as they are to me nothing, so in nothing bless them,   70
and to nothing are they welcome.

      Uncover, dogs, and lap.

      [*The dishes are uncovered and seen to be full of warm water*]

Some [LORDS] *speak* What does his lordship mean?

Some other LORDS I know not.

TIMON May you a better feast never behold,   75
      You knot of mouth-friends! Smoke and lukewarm water
      Is your perfection. This is Timon's last,
      Who, stuck and spangled with your flatteries,
      Washes it off, and sprinkles in your faces
      Your reeking villainy.

                [*Throwing water in their faces*]
                  Live loathed and long,   80
      Most smiling, smooth, detested parasites,
      Courteous destroyers, affable wolves, meek bears,
      You fools of fortune, trencher-friends, time's flies,
      Cap-and-knee slaves, vapours, and minute-jacks!

---

72 SD] *Johnson; not in* F   78 with your flatteries] *Hanmer;* you with Flatteries F   80 SD] *Johnson; not in* F   84 minute-jacks!]
Rann; Minute Iackes. F; Minute Iackes F2; minute-jacks *Pope*

69 For As for.

72 Uncover Remove the covers of the dishes.

72 SD Several editors add stones as contents of
the dishes, on the authority of 105. Together with
the diamonds, with which they are paired, they may
also be considered as a metonymy for valuables and
worthless trash. In the academic Timon play,
'stones painted like to [Artichokes]' are expressly
mentioned as contained in the dishes, and this is
followed by Timon's accusation, 'Yee are a stony
generation / Or harder . . .' (4.5.2065 and 2080–1).

76 mouth-friends friends professing friendship
only verbally.

76–7 Smoke . . . perfection You perfect the
qualities associated with vapour, hot air and lukewarm water. There is also word-play: 'Smoke',
which could mean vapours (see *Mac.* 1.2.18) in
Shakespeare's time, was also used figuratively for
'foolish brag' (*OED* Vapour *sb* 4) or 'empty talk'
(Berry, p. 107). 'Water' is associated with duplicity
and hypocrisy, as in *Oth.* 5.2.134: 'She was false as
water.' There is a biblical allusion in 'lukewarm'
('because thou art lukewarm, and neither cold nor
hot, I will spue thee out of my mouth' (Rev. 3.16)).

77 Timon's last Timon's final dealing with you.

79–80 He washes himself clean of the dirt of their
flatteries, and by sprinkling their faces with the water thus befouled (an inversion of the ritual of bap-
tism) he returns their villainy on their own heads.

80 Live . . . long The idea is that the longer they
live the more they suffer from being loathed.

82 Courteous . . . bears These oxymorons may
be contrasted to the different tone of Romeo (*Rom.*
1.1.176 ff.).

83 fools of fortune duped by fortune; again contrast the situation of Romeo finding himself victimised by fortune: 'O, I am fortune's fool' (*Rom.*
3.1.136).

83 trencher-friends i.e. their friendship is
assumed for as long as invitations to dine are
forthcoming.

83 time's flies ephemerae, fair-weather insects.

84 Cap-and-knee slaves 'The gesture of "cap
and knee" . . . is a conventional token of submission
to authority' (David Bevington, *Action is Eloquence*,
1984, p. 163).

84 vapours worthless or empty fellows.

84 minute-jacks A 'jack' is a figure striking the
bell in a clock; here, not just making the quarters
but every minute, an exaggerated servility.

Of man and beast the infinite malady   85
Crust you quite o'er! What, dost thou go?
Soft, take thy physic first; thou too, and thou;
   [*Threatening them physically, so that they turn to leave*]
Stay, I will lend thee money, borrow none.
What, all in motion?

                       [*Exeunt Lords and Senators*]
            Henceforth be no feast,
Whereat a villain's not a welcome guest.   90
Burn, house! Sink, Athens! Henceforth hated be
Of Timon, man and all humanity.   *Exit*

        Enter the Senators with other LORDS

FIRST LORD How now, my lords?
SECOND LORD Know you the quality of Lord Timon's fury?
THIRD LORD Push, did you see my cap?   95
FOURTH LORD I have lost my gown.
FIRST LORD He's but a mad lord, and nought but humours sways him.
    He gave me a jewel th'other day, and now he has beat it out of my
    hat. Did you see my jewel?
SECOND LORD Did you see my cap?   100
THIRD LORD Here 'tis.
FOURTH LORD Here lies my gown.
FIRST LORD Let's make no stay.
SECOND LORD Lord Timon's mad.
THIRD LORD   I feel't upon my bones.
FOURTH LORD One day he gives us diamonds, next day stones.   105
                  Exeunt the Senators [*and Lords*]

---

87 SD] *Rowe; not in* F   89 SD] *This edn; not in* F   96 SH FOURTH LORD] *Capell;* 4 F; *4 Sen. / Rowe; Fourth Friend /*
Chambers; VENTIDIUS *Sisson (throughout scene)*   100 SH SECOND LORD] F; 3. *L. / Capell;* 4 *Lord / Malone;* SEMPRONIUS
Sisson   101 SH THIRD LORD] F; 2. *L. / Capell;* LUCIUS *Sisson*   105 SD *and Lords*] *Riverside; not in* F

85 **the infinite** absolutely every imaginable.
87 **Soft** Not so fast.
87 **physic** medicine.
92 **Of** By.
93–105 The sequence of speech headings is
marked in F as 1–2–3–4, and this is repeated twice.
Editors since Rowe have completed these headings
by either adding 'Senator' or 'Lord' or individual
names. Capell suggests reversing the sequence of
speakers in 100–1, in order to have Third Lord
repeat his quest for his cap of 95 and make Second
Lord answer his query. If there is no firmer ground
for changing the speech headings I prefer to retain F.

94 **the quality . . . fury** why Timon is furious.
95 **Push** An exclamation expressing impatience
(amongst other things). In *OED* listed as an obsolete
form of 'pish' (*OED* Pish *int* (*sb*)); not used by
Shakespeare anywhere else, but used frequently by
Middleton.
97 **a mad lord** 'defining Timon's condition by
that simple label which deprives him at once of civil
rights and human status – madness' (Bradbrook,
Craftsman, p. 153).
97 **humours** whims, caprices.
97 **sways** governs (plural subject with singular
verb is common Elizabethan usage).

[4.1] *Enter* TIMON

TIMON Let me look back upon thee. O thou wall
     That girdles in those wolves, dive in the earth
     And fence not Athens! Matrons, turn incontinent!
     Obedience, fail in children! Slaves and fools,
     Pluck the grave wrinkled senate from the bench,   5
     And minister in their steads! To general filths
     Convert o'th'instant green virginity!
     Do't in your parents' eyes! Bankrupts, hold fast;
     Rather than render back, out with your knives,
     And cut your trusters' throats! Bound servants, steal!   10
     Large-handed robbers your grave masters are,
     And pill by law. Maid, to thy master's bed,
     Thy mistress is o'th'brothel. Son of sixteen,
     Pluck the lined crutch from thy old limping sire,
     With it beat out his brains! Piety, and fear,   15
     Religion to the gods, peace, justice, truth,
     Domestic awe, night-rest, and neighbourhood,
     Instruction, manners, mysteries, and trades,

Act 4, Scene 1   4.1] *Rowe; not in* F   3 incontinent!] *Knight;* incontinent, F   4 Obedience, fail] *Alexander, Riverside;* Obedience fayle F   4 fools,] *Capell;* Fooles F   6 steads! To general filths] *Capell;* steeds, to generall Filthes. F   7 virginity!] *Theobald;* Virginity, F   8 fast;] *Theobald;* fast F   9 back,] *Theobald;* backe; F   13 Son] F4; Some F

Act 4, Scene 1

2 girdles This irregular grammatical form is explained either by the dropping of *-t* in the second person (Franz 152 explains it as originating in the wish to simplify the pronunciation), or as the third person, in agreement with 'wall' instead of 'thou'.

3 incontinent sexually profligate (*OED* Incontinent *a* 1).

4 A comma after 'obedience' (as in Riverside) indicates the imperative mood, which is repeated at lines 5 ('Pluck'), 6 ('minister'), 7 ('Convert') and 8 ('Do't').

4–5 Slaves . . . Pluck This edition deviates from the punctuation in F; the comma after 'fools', first suggested by Capell, indicates the imperative character of 'pluck'.

6–7* To general . . . virginity! F places 'general filths' as the object of 'minister'. Capell interprets 'convert' as intransitive, with the sense 'may young virgins turn to general filth'.

8 hold fast keep whatever you have in your grasp (after Schmidt, sv hold 2a).

8–10* According to the punctuation in F, 'hold fast' and 'render back' are syntactically linked together in a tautological statement. Theobald's correction relates 'render back' with the imperatives that follow.

9 render back repay.

10 trusters In this context, presumably 'creditors' rather than the ordinary meaning 'one who trusts'.

10 Bound Having entered into a contract binding to service (*OED* Bound *ppl a*^{2} 7b).

11 Large-handed The reference to robbers indicates that this is the now obsolete meaning 'grasping', 'rapacious' (see *OED* Large-handed *a* 1).

12 pill steal.

13 o'th'brothel i.e. a whore.

14 lined padded.

15 fear awe (*OED* Fear *sb* 3d).

16 Religion to Reverence for.

17 Domestic awe Respect for domestic superiors, e.g. master, mistress or father, mother.

17 neighbourhood neighbourliness.

18 mysteries trades and crafts.

Degrees, observances, customs, and laws,
Decline to your confounding contraries;   20
And yet confusion live! Plagues incident to men,
Your potent and infectious fevers heap
On Athens ripe for stroke! Thou cold sciatica,
Cripple our senators, that their limbs may halt
As lamely as their manners! Lust, and liberty,   25
Creep in the minds and marrows of our youth,
That 'gainst the stream of virtue they may strive,
And drown themselves in riot! Itches, blains,
Sow all th'Athenian bosoms, and their crop
Be general leprosy! Breath infect breath,   30
That their society, as their friendship, may
Be merely poison! Nothing I'll bear from thee
But nakedness, thou detestable town!
Take thou that too, with multiplying bans!
Timon will to the woods, where he shall find   35
Th'unkindest beast more kinder than mankind.
The gods confound – hear me, you good gods all –
Th'Athenians both within and out that wall!
And grant, as Timon grows, his hate may grow
To the whole race of mankind, high and low!   40
Amen.   *Exit*

21 yet] F *;* let *Hanmer*   33 town!] *Pope;* Towne, F

19 Degrees Social ranks.
19 observances rules of practice.
20 confounding contraries mutually destructive opposites.
21 confusion live let the workings of confusion go on.
21 incident to men to which men are susceptible.
23 for stroke for being stricken (with the plague); Maxwell suggests that 'stroke' refers to Jove's thunderbolt.
23 cold sciatica hip-gout, considered as a symptom of syphilis (see *MM* 1.2.58–9: 'which of your hips has the most profound sciatica?').
24 halt limp.
25 liberty licentiousness.
28 riot dissolute behaviour.
28 blains boils or blisters; in this context (together with 'itches') suggesting symptoms of venereal disease (Colman).
29 Sow Sow yourselves (like seed, as an image of infection).
30 leprosy Also used as a term for venereal diseases (see Partridge and Colman). Williams

(II, 802) describes it as an 'emblem of sexual depravity'.
31 their i.e. the Athenians'.
31 society association with one another (Riverside) (see *OED* Society 3).
32 merely solely.
34 that Presumably Timon tears off clothing here. Perhaps a parallel with King Lear's raging (*Lear* 3.4.108–9): 'Off, off, you lendings!'
34 bans curses ('With Hecat's ban thrice blasted, thrice infected': *Ham.* 3.2.258).
36 unkindest beast In *Lear* there is word-play on two senses of 'kind': (1) behaviour characteristic of a given animal species or 'kind' – man, tiger, bear, dog, etc.; (2) solicitous and loving behaviour by a person. Strictly speaking, a tiger or bear when it kills cruelly is acting 'kindly', that is, according to the nature of its species; a person, on the other hand, ought to be naturally gentle and solicitous, 'kind' in both senses but mainly in the second sense. Timon, however, uses 'unkindest' and 'kinder' only in the second sense, 'gentle and solicitous'. A *man* who is cruel is 'unkind', untrue to his better nature and also the opposite of loving.

[4.2] *Enter Steward* [FLAVIUS] *with two or three* SERVANTS

FIRST SERVANT Hear you, master steward, where's our master?
　　　　　Are we undone, cast off, nothing remaining?
FLAVIUS Alack, my fellows, what should I say to you?
　　　　　Let me be recorded by the righteous gods,
　　　　　I am as poor as you.
FIRST SERVANT　　　　　　　Such a house broke?　　　　　5
　　　　　So noble a master fall'n, all gone, and not
　　　　　One friend to take his fortune by the arm,
　　　　　And go along with him.
SECOND SERVANT　　　　　　As we do turn our backs
　　　　　From our companion thrown into his grave,
　　　　　So his familiars to his buried fortunes　　　　10
　　　　　Slink all away, leave their false vows with him,
　　　　　Like empty purses picked; and his poor self,
　　　　　A dedicated beggar to the air,
　　　　　With his disease of all-shunned poverty,
　　　　　Walks like contempt alone. More of our fellows.　　　15

Enter other SERVANTS

FLAVIUS All broken implements of a ruined house.
THIRD SERVANT Yet do our hearts wear Timon's livery,
　　　　　That see I by our faces; we are fellows still,
　　　　　Serving alike in sorrow. Leaked is our bark,
　　　　　And we poor mates stand on the dying deck,　　　　20

Act 4, Scene 2   4.2] *Rowe; not in* F   0 SD *Steward* FLAVIUS] *Rowe; Steward* F   3 SH FLAVIUS] *Rowe; Stew.* F (*throughout scene*)

Act 4, Scene 2

5 broke bankrupt.

7 take . . . arm i.e. support him and hence improve his fortune.

10 his familiars . . . fortunes 'those who were familiar to his [now] buried fortunes, who in the most ample manner participated of them' (Malone).

11–12 false vows . . . purses picked A strained expression: the connection between 'vows' and 'purses' hinges on the idea of emptiness; 'purses picked' adds the implication that Timon has been robbed.

13 A dedicated . . . air A beggar dedicated to life in the open air.

15 Walks . . . alone 'Contempt' can mean 'the action of contemning' and also 'the condition of

being contemned' (see *OED* Contempt *sb* 1 and 2). In the mind of the servant, Timon is himself the epitome of contemptibility; yet he also shows utter contempt for others.

16–32 The magnanimous action of Flavius in sharing his money with the servants is a strong positive amongst so much cynical venality. The phrase in line 19 about the leaking bark recalls Enobarbus's comment on Antony's ill fortune (*Ant.* 3.13.63) and the inevitability of leaving his master.

17 Yet . . . livery Yet we are faithfully attached to our master.

18 fellows companions in Timon's service (recurring at 22 and 25).

20 the dying deck the deck on which we are going to die.

     Hearing the surges threat; we must all part
     Into this sea of air.
FLAVIUS   Good fellows all,
     The latest of my wealth I'll share amongst you.
     Wherever we shall meet, for Timon's sake
     Let's yet be fellows. Let's shake our heads, and say,   25
     As 'twere a knell unto our master's fortunes,
     'We have seen better days.' Let each take some;
          [*Gives money*]
     Nay, put out all your hands. Not one word more;
     Thus part we rich in sorrow, parting poor.
        Embrace and part several ways
     O the fierce wretchedness that glory brings us!   30
     Who would not wish to be from wealth exempt,
     Since riches point to misery and contempt?
     Who would be so mocked with glory, or to live
     But in a dream of friendship,
     To have his pomp, and all what state compounds,   35
     But only painted like his varnished friends?
     Poor honest lord, brought low by his own heart,
     Undone by goodness; strange, unusual blood,
     When man's worst sin is, he does too much good.
     Who then dares to be half so kind again?   40
     For bounty, that makes gods, do still mar men.
     My dearest lord, blest to be most accursed,

---

27 SD] *Johnson; not in* F 33 or to] F; *as to Rowe* 35 compounds] F; comprehends *Collier²* 41 do] F; does F4

22 sea of air Winds or storms, in connection with seafaring, are frequently associated with 'fortune' ('winds of Fortune': see Patch, p. 103).

23 latest last (now archaic and poetical); see *OED* Latest *a¹* 1, and Schmidt sv last: 'beyond which is no more'.

30 fierce violent (Steevens), excessive.

32 riches . . . contempt Another example of proverbial wisdom which tends to oversimplify.

35 all . . . compounds all that constitutes splendour.

35 state pomp, splendour.

38 blood disposition, constitution.

40 again on future occasions.

41 bounty . . . men It is only appropriate for the gods to give bounty; for men it is detrimental. G. K. Hunter remarks that Timon 'thinks that it is his privilege to move through society like an earthly god', and that his conduct 'is certainly magnificent; but it is also inhuman' (*Dramatic Identities and Cultural Tradition: Studies in Shakespeare and his Contemporaries*, 1978, p. 255). Flavius is taken by the idea that the human condition does not allow for too much bounty, since the person on the receiving end will invariably exploit it. It is only the gods who are above getting implicated in these perverse interactions. Flavius's speech abounds in notions of such perversity: 'man's worst sin is, he does too much good' (39); 'Rich only to be wretched' (43); 'thy great fortunes / Are made thy chief afflictions' (43–4).

41 do The verb is plural though the subject is singular: such pluralisation based on an adjacent noun was a characteristic feature of spoken language in Shakespeare's time (see Franz 671 and Abbott 412).

Rich only to be wretched; thy great fortunes
Are made thy chief afflictions. Alas, kind lord,
He's flung in rage from this ingrateful seat   45
Of monstrous friends;
Nor has he with him to supply his life,
Or that which can command it.
I'll follow and enquire him out.
I'll ever serve his mind with my best will;   50
Whilst I have gold I'll be his steward still.   *Exit*

[4.3] *Enter* TIMON *in the woods*

TIMON   O blessed breeding sun, draw from the earth
          Rotten humidity; below thy sister's orb
          Infect the air! Twinned brothers of one womb,
          Whose procreation, residence, and birth
          Scarce is dividant; touch them with several fortunes,   5

47 has] F3; ha's F   Act 4, Scene 3   4.3] *Rowe; not in* F   3 Twinned] *Chambers;* Twin'd F

45–6 The ideas expressed by 'ingrateful' and
'monstrous' are frequently joined together: see
3.2.65–6; *Cor.* 2.3.9–11; *Lear* 1.4.259–61, 1.5.39–40.
45 flung rushed (intransitive).
45 seat place of residence, abode.
47 to . . . life the means to sustain life.
48 that . . . command it that which can procure
his sustenance, i.e. gold.
49 enquire him out find out where he goes.

Act 4, Scene 3
0 SD In 4.1.35 Timon expresses his desire to leave
Athens for 'the woods', evidently a wilderness governed by no authority, civil or military, and not a
forest, as understood by the Elizabethans (on this
see R. Marienstras, *New Perspectives on the Shakespearean World*, 1985, pp. 15 ff.). F's SD here, *in the
woods*, may be compared to the later direction *cave*
in SDs in 5.1.23 and later; 'the very hem o'th'sea' is
mentioned in 5.4.66: 'wood' and 'cave' are Shakespeare's additions to the Timon legend. Soellner, p.
152, suggests an analogy with Spenser's Cave of
Despair (*Faerie Queene* I.ix.44).
1–2 draw . . . humidity This great cursing

speech offers parallels to several of similar universal
scope in *Lear* (e.g. *Lear* 1.4, 3.2, 4.6). The earth is
the 'common whore of mankind' (43); as a consequence of being impregnated by the sun ('breeding
sun') she secretes 'rotten humidity' indicative of,
and itself the cause of, a wasting disease (see also
Partridge sv 'rotten' and Colman, p. 212; elsewhere
in Shakespeare these vapours are clearly venereal
disease). Caliban's curse in *Temp.* 2.2.1–2 consists
of similar ingredients: 'All the infections that the
sun sucks up / From bogs, fens, flats, on Prosper
fall'; Titania in *MND* 2.1.88–90 declares: 'the
winds . . . have suck'd up from the sea / Contagious
fogs'. Marlowe's Bajazeth in *I Tamburlaine* 4.2.5–6
cries: 'Make . . . every fixed star / To suck up
poison from the moorish fens.'
2 thy sister's orb i.e. the moon. In mythology,
the moon goddess Diana is the sister of Apollo, the
sun god.
3–6 i.e. take the instance of brothers born as
twins: if their fortunes differ, the more fortunate
scorns the less fortunate.
5 dividant separable, divisible.
5 touch test (as by a touchstone).

The greater scorns the lesser. Not nature,
To whom all sores lay siege, can bear great fortune
But by contempt of nature.
Raise me this beggar, and deny't that lord,
The senator shall bear contempt hereditary,   10
The beggar native honour.
It is the pasture lards the brother's sides,
The want that makes him lean. Who dares, who dares
In purity of manhood stand upright
And say this man's a flatterer? If one be,   15
So are they all; for every grise of fortune
Is smoothed by that below. The learned pate
Ducks to the golden fool. All's obliquy;
There's nothing level in our cursèd natures
But direct villainy. Therefore be abhorred   20

---

9 deny't] F; denude *Theobald;* degrade *Hanmer;* deject *Maxwell*   10 senator] *Rowe;* Senators F   12 pasture] *Rowe;* Pastour F; Pastor F2–4   12 lards] *Rowe;* Lards, F; Lords, F2–4   12 brother's] *Johnson;* Brothers F; Beggar's *Rowe;* Weather's *Theobald (conj. Warburton);* rother's *Collier (conj. Singer)*   13 lean] F2; leaue F   16 grise] *Collier;* grize F; greeze *Pope*   18 All's obliquy] F *subst.;* All's Obloquy *Rowe;* All is oblique *Pope*

6–8 Not nature . . . contempt of nature i.e. a man raised by fortune out of the normal miseries of nature despises those who continue in them (Riverside).

9 Raise me Promote in wealth or standing; 'me' as dative of interest (*OED* Me 2b) expresses the speaker's emphatic interest in what is being done; see also 114, 'Strike me the counterfeit matron.'

9 deny't that lord deny promotion to that lord.

10* The senator . . . hereditary The senator will be treated with contempt, as though he had inherited it as proper to his position. (The placing of the adjective lends an air of legal phraseology – Franz 685.) Rowe's emendation lends consistency to Timon's train of thought: from line 3 on, it outlines the picture of a society in which human interaction is based not upon the 'natural' qualities of individuals, but rather on social rank and material wealth.

11 native naturally befitting; it is as if the beggar were born of honourable rank.

12–13* It . . . lean An obscure passage; the most convincing reading is: 'The amount of respect a man enjoys is in direct proportion to the extent to which he was himself fattened ("lards") on life's pastures.' Rowe modernises the spelling of F's 'Pastour' to 'pasture'. Two conjectures about 'brothers' suppose a congruence with 'pasture': Warburton suggests 'Weather's' and Singer (after Collier) 'rother's' (meaning ox's). The latter makes

excellent sense and is tempting. The reading 'brother's', which is basically F, is to be preferred because it adds a fresh variation to the argument that material wealth is the criterion for mutual esteem among men.

16 grise Variant form of 'grece': a single step or stair in a flight of stairs (*OED* Grece 2c).

17 smoothed i.e. flattery smooths the way in a social system's graduated hierarchy.

17 learned pate man of learning.

18 Ducks Bows his head (as a gesture of deference).

18 golden fool fool favoured with riches.

18 obliquy In *OED* (Obliquie) defined as 'probable misprint for oblique', with this line as the sole instance of its use; Rowe reads it as 'obloquy', meaning 'evil-speaking' as well as 'the condition of being spoken against' (*OED* Obloquy 1 and 1b). Deighton conjectures that 'obliquy' could stand for 'obliquity', i.e. moral and mechanical deviation.

19 level straight (*not* oblique).

20 direct downright.

20 abhorred Adelman sees a pun on 'ab/whored' and another on 'hoar' / 'whore' (36 and 156), and finds the notion of 'whore' and 'whoring' a focus of the play (Adelman, p. 170). In *Oth.* 4.2.161–2, the pun 'whore' / 'abhor' is expressly suggested: 'I cannot say "whore". / It does abhor me now I speak the word.'

All feasts, societies, and throngs of men.
His semblable, yea himself, Timon disdains;
Destruction fang mankind! Earth, yield me roots.

[*Digs*]

Who seeks for better of thee, sauce his palate
With thy most operant poison. What is here?   25
Gold? Yellow, glittering, precious gold?
No, gods, I am no idle votarist.
Roots, you clear heavens! Thus much of this will make
Black, white; foul, fair; wrong, right;
Base, noble; old, young; coward, valiant.   30
Ha, you gods! Why this? What this, you gods? Why, this
Will lug your priests and servants from your sides,
Pluck stout men's pillows from below their heads.
This yellow slave
Will knit and break religions, bless th'accursed,   35
Make the hoar leprosy adored, place thieves,
And give them title, knee, and approbation
With senators on the bench. This is it
That makes the wappened widow wed again;

---

23 fang] *Johnson;* phang F   23 SD] *Rowe; not in* F   39 wappened] F; wained *conj. Johnson;* weeping *conj. Johnson/Steevens³;* wappered *conj. Mason, 'Comments' (1785) and conj. Singer*

22 His semblable Anything resembling him, i.e. his fellow man; a word in use since Chaucer's time.

23 fang seize, lay hold of. If seen as an extension of the dog imagery (as suggested by Spurgeon), it could also mean: sink one's fangs into.

24 of thee from thee (i.e. the earth).

24 sauce tickle.

25 operant potent, effective.

26 precious Depending on the underlying value structure, the meaning can oscillate between 'having a high value' (*OED* Precious *a* 1) and 'of little worth' (*OED* Precious *a* 4b), especially in ironical contexts such as 'Precious villain!' (*Oth.* 5.2.235) or 'you precious pandar!' (*Cym.* 3.5.81).

27 No ... votarist Presumably with the implication that he realises he has, for a moment, been caught up in the conventional idea of the great value of gold.

27 idle votarist One who makes a vow without meaning to keep it.

28 clear The natural simplicity of raw roots contrasted to the evil effects culture produces from gold.

29–30 Black ... valiant i.e. if a man is seized by desire for gold it sweeps away all moral scruples, he will swear black is white, espouse any base, immoral or unnatural thing in his quest for gold. See also Jonson, *Volpone* 5.2.100–2: 'It [gold] transforms / The most deformed, and restores 'em lovely, / As 'twere the strange poetical girdle.'

33 Pluck ... heads 'This alludes to an old custom of drawing away the pillow from under the heads of men in their last agonies, to make their departure the easier' (Warburton).

34 slave Gold is itself a slave (a term of abuse and contempt) and is the cause of others being enslaved.

36 hoar leprosy A disease which causes shining white scales to form on the skin. Leprosy was also thought of as a venereal infection; this makes it probable that 'hoar' puns on 'whore', as Colman (p. 198) and Partridge (sv whore) suggest. See also 156.

36 place give office to.

37–8 give ... senators give them the same honours, in name, in kneeling to them, and in according them respect, as are given to senators.

39 wappened (sexually) exhausted, fatigued. *OED* Wappened *a* gives this line as the only refer-

She whom the spital-house and ulcerous sores   40
Would cast the gorge at, this embalms and spices
To th'April day again. Come, damnèd earth,
Thou common whore of mankind, that puts odds
Among the rout of nations, I will make thee
Do thy right nature.
                        March afar off
                        Ha? A drum? Th'art quick,   45
But yet I'll bury thee. Thou'lt go, strong thief,
When gouty keepers of thee cannot stand.
Nay, stay thou out for earnest. [*Keeps some gold*]

Enter ALCIBIADES, *with drum and fife, in warlike manner, and* PHRYNIA *and*
TIMANDRA

ALCIBIADES   What art thou there? Speak.

TIMON   A beast as thou art. The canker gnaw thy heart   50
For showing me again the eyes of man!

ALCIBIADES   What is thy name? Is man so hateful to thee,
That art thyself a man?

---

43 puts] F *subst.;* puttest *Rowe;* putt'st *Pope*   45 Do . . . quick] *Pope;* Do . . . Nature. / Ha . . . quicke F   48 SD.1 *Keeps some gold*] *Pope; not in* F

ence and says the origin and meaning of the term are obscure, but refers to Singer's conjectural reading 'wappered', a dialect term meaning 'fatigued', 'wearied'; its negative form 'unwapper'd' occurs in *TNK* 5.4.10. For further references see Williams, sv wap. Conjectures such as 'wained' for 'decayed by time' (Johnson) or 'weeping' (Steevens) are unconvincing.

40–1 She . . . spices 'She', placed at the beginning of the sentence for emphasis, is actually the object of the sentence: 'She at whose sight people in hospitals with ulcerous sores would vomit – gold embalms and spices this woman.' Franz (287g) finds this anacoluthon frequent in Shakespeare.

41 this this gold.

41 embalms and spices As is done with corpses.

42 damnèd earth Probably the gold contained in the earth.

43–4 Thou . . . nations Gold makes nations quarrel over its possession, just as men quarrel over whores.

43 puts Instead of 'puttest' – the same grammatical problem as in 4.1.2.

43 odds quarrel, discord (Schmidt, p. 5).

45 Do . . . nature Act according to your true nature (i.e. as a common whore).

45 quick Punning on the senses (1) alive (as suggested by the context of death and rebirth in 41–2), (2) fast (in acting according to its 'right nature').

46 But . . . thee The burying of gold, like the rituals in 40–2, may be viewed as a phase in the death and rebirth circle.

46–7 go . . . stand Gold's inherent power will keep it effective, even though those who possess it (keepers) grow old and infirm.

48 for earnest for token payments; a deposit to secure goods or services.

48 SD.2 PHRYNIA The only name among the dramatis personae which is not found in Plutarch; there was, however, a renowned Greek courtesan named Phryne.

48 SD.3 TIMANDRA Appears in North's translation of Plutarch as Alcibiades' concubine. This strangely stylised episode, in which an isolated and persecuted hero is visited by a trio, recalls *Titus* and the visit of Tamora and her sons, representing revenge and murder, to the defiantly nihilistic Titus, who is also mad.

50 canker ulcerous growth.

TIMON I am Misanthropos, and hate mankind.

    For thy part, I do wish thou wert a dog,   55

    That I might love thee something.

ALCIBIADES   I know thee well;

    But in thy fortunes am unlearned and strange.

TIMON I know thee too, and more than that I know thee

    I not desire to know. Follow thy drum;

    With man's blood paint the ground, gules, gules.   60

    Religious canons, civil laws are cruel;

    Then what should war be? This fell whore of thine

    Hath in her more destruction than thy sword,

    For all her cherubin look.

PHRYNIA   Thy lips rot off.

TIMON I will not kiss thee, then the rot returns   65

    To thine own lips again.

ALCIBIADES How came the noble Timon to this change?

TIMON As the moon does, by wanting light to give.

    But then renew I could not like the moon;

    There were no suns to borrow of.   70

ALCIBIADES Noble Timon, what friendship may I do thee?

TIMON None, but to maintain my opinion.

ALCIBIADES What is it, Timon?

TIMON Promise me friendship, but perform none. If thou wilt not

---

74–5 wilt not promise] F: wilt promise *Hibbard, Oxford*

54 **I am Misanthropos** I am Hater of Man. Bullough follows Deighton in thinking Lucian to be the source of this self-characterisation, while other editors since Malone attribute it to a marginal note in North's Plutarch ('Life of Antony'). See pp. 52–8 above.

55–6 **I . . . something** 'The implication . . . is that the dog is a low creature but still better than Alcibiades' (Farnham, 'Beast theme', p. 53). Timon's reaction seems to be tinged with madness.

56 **something** somewhat, a little.

57 **unlearned and strange** uninformed and ignorant. It has been pointed out that this partly contradicts Alcibiades' statement in 93–6.

60 **gules** Heraldic name for red; compare Hamlet's 'rugged Pyrrhus' speech: 'Now is he total gules' (*Ham.* 2.2.457).

62 **fell** ruthless, destructive.

65 **rot** Williams (III, 1172) comments that this is 'venereal disease, combining notions of physical and moral corruption'.

67 **noble Timon** Alcibiades carries on the 'noble

Timon' idea of the previous acts, although the circumstances are completely changed.

68 **wanting** lacking.

68–70 For the notion of the moon borrowing light from the sun see Marlowe, *I Tamburlaine* 1.1.69: 'Before the moon renew her borrowed light'. Here in *Timon* it is hard not to hear the financial aspect of 'borrow', to bleakly ironic effect.

69 **renew** Used intransitively: 'grow afresh, become new again' (*OED* Renew v¹ 9).

72 **maintain** support or act according to.

74–5 In an attempt to improve the logic of what Timon is saying, Hibbard and Oxford move 'not' from 74 to 75; what results, however, is a redundant version of Timon's first statement. It might be clearer to delete 74's 'not' altogether, but in any case F makes sense: if you will not promise, may the gods plague you for being a man (also, because usually men promise falsely, and not to do so is therefore perverse in you); if you do perform as well as promising, damn you, for being a man (being a man in itself is enough to earn damnation anyway).

promise, the gods plague thee, for thou art a man; if thou dost   75
perform, confound thee, for thou art a man.

ALCIBIADES I have heard in some sort of thy miseries.

TIMON Thou saw'st them when I had prosperity.

ALCIBIADES I see them now, then was a blessed time.

TIMON As thine is now, held with a brace of harlots.   80

TIMANDRA Is this th'Athenian minion, whom the world
      Voiced so regardfully?

TIMON   Art thou Timandra?

TIMANDRA Yes.

TIMON Be a whore still; they love thee not that use thee; give them
    diseases, leaving with thee their lust. Make use of thy salt hours;   85
    season the slaves for tubs and baths; bring down rose-cheeked
    youth to the tub-fast and the diet.

TIMANDRA Hang thee, monster!

ALCIBIADES Pardon him, sweet Timandra, for his wits
    Are drowned and lost in his calamities.   90
    I have but little gold of late, brave Timon,
    The want whereof doth daily make revolt
    In my penurious band. I have heard and grieved
    How cursèd Athens, mindless of thy worth,
    Forgetting thy great deeds, when neighbour states,   95
    But for thy sword and fortune, trod upon them –

75–6 dost perform] F; dost not perform *Hibbard, Oxford*   87 tub-fast] *Theobald* (*conj. Warburton*); Fubfast F   96 them –]
Rowe; them. F

---

77 **in some sort** to some extent.

77–9 Alcibiades thinks that Timon's present condition is a state of misery and that his period of prosperity was a 'blessed time'; Timon's understanding is that this 'blessed time' was in fact a time of misery, and that in his prosperity he was as much the dupe of Fortune as Alcibiades is now with his 'brace of harlots'.

80 **held with** carried on with.

81 **minion** 'the "idol" of a people, a community' (*OED* Minion *sb*¹ 1b), with reference to 'minion of fortune', used in a contemptuous sense.

82 **Voiced so regardfully** Spoke of with so much respect.

84 **Be ... still** Proverbial (Dent W321: 'Once a whore and ever a whore'); the phrase is repeated in 141.

84–5 **they ... lust** i.e. they leave their lust with you, so you should leave your diseases with them. (Another option is to read 'leaving' as 'levying' – *OED* Leave *v*³.)

85 **salt** lecherous.

86 **season** prepare (*OED* Season *v* 4d).

86 **tubs and baths** Treatments for venereal disease.

87 **tub-fast . . . diet** Fasting or a strict diet was a treatment for venereal diseases.

89–90 Despite the evident difficulty Alcibiades has in comprehending Timon's extremity of misanthropy, it is possible to share his impression that Timon is partly deranged.

93 **penurious** poverty-stricken.

93–7 These references to Timon's former public (and apparently military) role in support of Athens are repeated more vaguely in 5.1.137 and hinted at in 2.2.186–90. There seems to be a parallel with *Titus*, as if Shakespeare were half-consciously recalling the early tragedy here (conscious or unconscious parallels with *Titus* are quite frequent in *Timon* – as this Commentary indicates).

96 **trod** would have trodden.

TIMON I prithee beat thy drum, and get thee gone.
ALCIBIADES I am thy friend, and pity thee, dear Timon.
TIMON How dost thou pity him whom thou dost trouble?
     I had rather be alone.   100
ALCIBIADES Why, fare thee well; here is some gold for thee.
TIMON Keep it, I cannot eat it.
ALCIBIADES When I have laid proud Athens on a heap –
TIMON Warr'st thou 'gainst Athens?
ALCIBIADES   Ay, Timon, and have cause.
TIMON The gods confound them all in thy conquest,   105
     And thee after, when thou hast conquered.
ALCIBIADES Why me, Timon?
TIMON   That by killing of villains
     Thou wast born to conquer my country.
     Put up thy gold. Go on, here's gold, go on;
     Be as a planetary plague, when Jove   110
     Will o'er some high-viced city hang his poison
     In the sick air; let not thy sword skip one;
     Pity not honoured age for his white beard;
     He is an usurer. Strike me the counterfeit matron;
     It is her habit only that is honest,   115
     Herself's a bawd. Let not the virgin's cheek
     Make soft thy trenchant sword; for those milk-paps,
     That through the window-bars bore at men's eyes,
     Are not within the leaf of pity writ,
     But set them down horrible traitors. Spare not the babe   120
     Whose dimpled smiles from fools exhaust their mercy;
     Think it a bastard, whom the oracle

---

101 Why . . . for thee] *This edn;* Why . . . well: / Heere . . . thee F   103 heap –] *Rowe³;* heape. F   107 Why . . . villains]
Collier; Why . . . Timon? / That . . . Villaines F   118 window-bars] *Conj. Johnson;* window Barne F; window-lawn
Warburton; window, bared, *Hibbard*

103 on a heap 'in a prostrate mass' (*OED* Heap
sb 5c), in ruins.
  109 Put up Put away.
  110 planetary caused by a malignant planet.
  111 Will Resolves to.
  112 sick infected, infectious.
  113 age aged man.
  114 Strike me Strike (dative of interest: see 4.3.9
n.).
  114 counterfeit matron A married woman of
deceptively respectable appearance.
  115 habit Not only 'dress' but also 'bearing',
'demeanour'.

117 trenchant cutting, having a keen edge.
  118* window-bars This widely accepted conjecture by Johnson means either the lattice-work
of her window or the open-work squares of her
bodice. The metaphor in *A Lover's Complaint*, line
14 ('Some beauty peep'd through lettice of sear'd
age'), strengthens the plausibility of Johnson's
emendation.
  119 leaf of pity The list of names or things to be
spared out of pity.
  120 traitors betrayers (of men).
  121 exhaust draw forth.

Hath doubtfully pronounced the throat shall cut,
And mince it sans remorse. Swear against objects;
Put armour on thine ears and on thine eyes,   125
Whose proof nor yells of mothers, maids, nor babes,
Nor sight of priests in holy vestments bleeding,
Shall pierce a jot. There's gold to pay thy soldiers;
Make large confusion; and thy fury spent,
Confounded be thyself. Speak not, be gone.   130

ALCIBIADES Hast thou gold yet, I'll take the gold thou givest me,
Not all thy counsel.

TIMON Dost thou or dost thou not, heaven's curse upon thee.

PHRYNIA, TIMANDRA Give us some gold, good Timon; hast thou
more?

TIMON Enough to make a whore forswear her trade,   135
And to make whores, a bawd. Hold up, you sluts,
Your aprons mountant; you are not oathable,
Although I know you'll swear, terribly swear
Into strong shudders and to heavenly agues
Th'immortal gods that hear you. Spare your oaths;   140
I'll trust to your conditions, be whores still.
And he whose pious breath seeks to convert you,
Be strong in whore, allure him, burn him up,

---

123 the throat] F; thy throat *Pope*   131–2] *Capell; prose* F   134, 150, 168 SH PHRYNIA, TIMANDRA] *Johnson/Steevens²;
Both.* F

123 **doubtfully** obscurely or ambiguously.
124 **sans remorse** without pity.
124 **Swear against objects** Curse objects of
compassion. Mason (*Comments* (1785), p. 301) suggests that 'objects' means 'objects of charity and
compassion', for which *OED* gives ample evidence
(Object *sb* 3b; see also *Lear* 5.3.239). Sisson (*Readings*, II, 174) thinks that 'the sense of *objects* is simply
"objections"' which is plausible in the light of line
125, although there are no other supporting instances in Shakespeare.
126 **Whose proof** Whose (referring to 'armour'
at 125) proved or tested strength, impenetrability.
129 **large confusion** extensive destruction.
131 **Hast** If you have.
133 **Dost . . . not** Whether you do or not.
135 **forswear** give up.
135–40 Brownlow (p. 229) sees this as a parody of
Zeus's appearance to Danae in a golden shower.
136 **And . . . bawd** 'And to make a bawd (forswear) making whores' (Sisson, *Readings*, II, 174,
following Johnson).

136–7 **Hold . . . mountant** This command
'suggests a metaphorical rape by the gold he pours
into their laps, a grotesque parody of what Jove did
to Danae' (M. Hattaway, 'Fleshing his will in the
spoil of her honour: desire, misogyny and the perils
of chivalry', *S.Sur.* 46 (1994), 130).
137 **aprons   mountant** rising   aprons;
'mountant' is a coinage based on such heraldic
terms as 'couchant', 'rampant'. There are also
sexual connotations in 'mountant': see F. H. Mares
(ed.), *Ado* 1.1.23 and n.
137 **oathable** fit to be trusted even on oath.
138–9 **swear / Into** swear so violently as to
throw into.
139 **heavenly agues** agues as felt by gods.
141 **conditions** characters.
141 **still** forever.
143 **burn him up** (1) inflame him with love, (2)
infect him with venereal disease.

Let your close fire predominate his smoke,
And be no turncoats; yet may your pains six months   145
Be quite contrary; and thatch your poor thin roofs
With burthens of the dead – some that were hanged –
No matter; wear them, betray with them; whore still;
Paint till a horse may mire upon your face.
A pox of wrinkles!
PHRYNIA, TIMANDRA   Well, more gold! What then?   150
Believe't that we'll do anything for gold.
TIMON Consumptions sow
In hollow bones of man; strike their sharp shins,
And mar men's spurring. Crack the lawyer's voice,
That he may never more false title plead,   155
Nor sound his quillets shrilly. Hoar the flamen,
That scolds against the quality of flesh,
And not believes himself. Down with the nose,

145 your pains six months] F; your pains exterior *Hanmer;* your pains, six months, *Capell;* your paint-siz'd mouths *conj. Deighton;* your pain-sick months *Oxford* 146–8] *Capell;* Be . . . Thatch / Your . . . dead, / (Some . . . matter: / Weare . . . still, F 157 scolds] *Rowe;* scold'st F

144 **predominate** overmaster.
144 **smoke** Smoke screen of pious words.
145 **pains six months** This passage resists clear elucidation: lines 143–4 are about venereal disease, so 'pains' might refer to this, or to the *effort* required over six months to infect their victim properly. Warburton suggests 'six months' as a period of severe discipline and cure; Steevens as a period of punishment inflicted upon them in a house of correction; Oliver and Riverside explain this period as one of abnormal menstrual pain. Hulme would see an allusion to Persephone, who Zeus ruled should spend six months of the year in the underworld.
146–7 **thatch . . . dead** replace your hair (lost by disease) with wigs of hair from the dead.
148 'wear' and 'betray' refer in the first place to the wigs, but Timon may play upon the sense of 'wear' as 'possess or enjoy sexually', in which case 'with them' would refer to the dead (not the wigs); but Timon's main idea is that whores deceive and betray, they *paint*, they are false and dedicated to disease and death.
149 **Paint** Put cosmetics on with a view to dissembling and as a sign for having a harlot's mind. See Claudius's reflections: 'The harlot's cheek, beautied with plast'ring art . . .' and 'my most painted word' (*Ham.* 3.1.50–2).
149 **Paint . . . face** 'Slap on the paint until it's thick enough for a horse to get bogged down in it';

'mire' also means 'defecate', suggesting a possible additional meaning.
152–3 The connection between hollow bones and venereal diseases is conspicuously prevalent in *MM* 1.2, and so is the connection between disease and money in the puns there on 'dolors' as 'pains' and 'dollars'.
152–65 There are parallel notions and phrasings in *Lear* and *Timon* about how the destruction of mankind should be effected. See *Lear* 3.2.1–8 with the verbs 'strike', 'flat', 'crack'; but in *Lear* the destruction is envisaged in cosmic terms, in *Timon* venereal diseases are called upon (Adelman, pp. 171–2, 332).
152 **Consumptions** Any wasting disease, including syphilis.
152 **sow** The verb is imperative.
153 **hollow bones** Caused by the disease.
154 **spurring** Literally, the action of stimulating; in this context also as a sexual innuendo. Williams (III, 1295) explains it as 'symbolic of sexual riding'.
156 **quillets** verbal quibbles.
156 **Hoar the flamen** Whiten the priest with disease (with a quibble on 'whore' as in 36).
157 **That . . . flesh** Who preaches against carnal desires.
158 **Down . . . nose** An effect of syphilis; at the same time the ground for the image of 'smelling' in 161.

Down with it flat, take the bridge quite away
Of him that, his particular to foresee,   160
Smells from the general weal. Make curled-pate ruffians
    bald,
And let the unscarred braggarts of the war
Derive some pain from you. Plague all,
That your activity may defeat and quell
The source of all erection. There's more gold.   165
Do you damn others, and let this damn you,
And ditches grave you all!

PHRYNIA, TIMANDRA More counsel with more money, bounteous
    Timon.

TIMON More whore, more mischief first; I have given you earnest.

ALCIBIADES Strike up the drum towards Athens! Farewell, Timon;   170
    If I thrive well, I'll visit thee again.

TIMON If I hope well, I'll never see thee more.

ALCIBIADES I never did thee harm.

TIMON Yes, thou spok'st well of me.

ALCIBIADES   Call'st thou that harm?

TIMON Men daily find it. Get thee away,   175
    And take thy beagles with thee.

ALCIBIADES We but offend him. Strike!
      [*Drum beats.*] *Exeunt* [*Alcibiades, Phrynia and Timandra*]

TIMON [*Digging*] That nature being sick of man's unkindness
    Should yet be hungry! Common mother, thou
    Whose womb unmeasurable and infinite breast   180
    Teems and feeds all; whose self-same mettle,
    Whereof thy proud child, arrogant man, is puffed,

170–1 Strike . . . again] *Rowe³; prose* F   177 SD *Drum beats*] *Johnson; not in* F   177 SD *Alcibiades . . . Timandra*] *Theobald; not in* F   178 SD] *Johnson; not in* F

160 **his . . . foresee** to provide for his personal advantage (see *OED Particular a* and *sb* B6).

161 **Smells from** loses the scent of (Johnson points out the hunting metaphor). The imagery leads from the syphilitic decay of the nasal bone to the deficiency of the sense of smell, which makes man lose the scent, so that he finds himself on the wrong track.

161 **weal** welfare.

162 **unscarred . . . war** Those who boast what they did in war but cannot show any scars.

164 **quell** destroy.

165 **erection** constructive activity (with a play on sexual arousal).

167 **grave** be a grave for.

169 **earnest** a down payment, a first instalment to secure their services.

176 **beagles** hunting dogs (taking up the hunting metaphor in 158–61).

179 **Common mother** To speak of the earth as 'common mother' was a commonplace; see Dent E28.1.

181 **Teems** Bears.

181 **mettle** spirit.

Engenders the black toad and adder blue,
The gilded newt and eyeless venomed worm,
With all th'abhorrèd births below crisp heaven   185
Whereon Hyperion's quick'ning fire doth shine;
Yield him, who all the human sons do hate,
From forth thy plenteous bosom, one poor root.
Ensear thy fertile and conceptious womb,
Let it no more bring out ingrateful man.   190
Go great with tigers, dragons, wolves and bears,
Teem with new monsters, whom thy upward face
Hath to the marbled mansion all above
Never presented. O, a root, dear thanks!
Dry up thy marrows, vines, and plough-torn leas,   195
Whereof ingrateful man with liquorish draughts
And morsels unctuous greases his pure mind,
That from it all consideration slips –

Enter APEMANTUS

More man? Plague, plague!

187 do] F; do's *Rowe;* doth *Capell*   195 vines] F; Veins *Rowe*   197 unctuous] *Johnson;* Vnctious F

183–4 toad . . . adder . . . newt . . . worm In
Shakespeare, considered venomous; compare 'like
the toad, ugly and venomous' (*AYLI* 2.1.13); for
the adder see *MND* 3.2.71, and for newts and blind-
worms *MND* 2.2.11. Compare *R2* 3.2.12–20.
  185 crisp (1) shining, clear (*OED* Crisp *a* 4, citing this passage); (2) having a curled or wrinkled
surface (*OED* Crisp *a* 2), as with curled clouds.
  186 Hyperion Sun (god).
  186 quick'ning life-giving.
  187 who . . . hate A grammatical incongruity,
which leaves two optional readings: (1) 'who does
hate all the human sons', (2) '*whom* all the human
sons do hate'. Within the general context of the play
either reading is possible, with a preference for (1).
  188 plenteous bosom fertile soil.
  189 Ensear Dry up, as in *Lear* 1.4.279: 'Dry up
in her the organs of increase'; en- as a prefix to
nouns or adjectives is meant 'to put a person or
thing in a specified situation' (G. L. Brook, *The
Language of Shakespeare*, 1976, p. 131); in this case:
put into a state of being sear (or sere).
  189 conceptious apt to conceive; neither
'ensear' nor 'conceptious' is used by Shakespeare
anywhere else.
  191 Go great Become pregnant.
  192 Teem with Give birth to.
  192 upward face Usually (since Warburton)

explained as 'surface' of the earth; also the female
posture when giving birth.
  193 marbled mansion sky, heaven; the same
phrase appears in *Cym.* 5.4.87; *Oth.* 3.3.460 has
'marble heaven'. A metatheatrical reference to the
'Heavens ceiling' painted to imitate marble (see C.
Walter Hodges, *The Globe Restored*, 1953, p. 77);
but 'marble skies' is in Studley's translation of
Seneca's *Oetaeus* and frequently in Studley's and
Heywood's translations (so Gordon Braden, *Renaissance Tragedy and the Senecan Tradition*, 1985, p.
176 with note 32).
  195 marrows Figuratively, the vital strength of
the earth, when imagined as a female body (although the proximity of 'vines' and 'leas' might
suggest vegetables, vines and corn, major life-
sustaining crops).
  195 leas fields.
  196 liquorish As pointed out in *OED*, a punning
or etymologically false use of 'lickerish', which
means 'lecherous'. See also Williams, II, 819.
  197 morsels bits of food; also figuratively of persons, as in *Ant.* 3.13.116: 'I found you as a morsel'.
  197 unctuous An adjective modifying 'morsels'.
  197 greases makes greasy (Partridge sv 'grease'
notes the figurative sense 'obscene').
  198 consideration reflection (i.e. the glutton
thinks of nothing but gratification).

APEMANTUS I was directed hither. Men report   200
     Thou dost affect my manners, and dost use them.
TIMON 'Tis then, because thou dost not keep a dog
     Whom I would imitate. Consumption catch thee!
APEMANTUS This is in thee a nature but infected,
     A poor unmanly melancholy sprung   205
     From change of future. Why this spade? This place?
     This slave-like habit, and these looks of care?
     Thy flatterers yet wear silk, drink wine, lie soft,
     Hug their diseased perfumes, and have forgot
     That ever Timon was. Shame not these woods   210
     By putting on the cunning of a carper.
     Be thou a flatterer now, and seek to thrive
     By that which has undone thee; hinge thy knee,
     And let his very breath whom thou'lt observe
     Blow off thy cap; praise his most vicious strain,   215
     And call it excellent. Thou wast told thus.
     Thou gav'st thine ears, like tapsters that bade welcome,
     To knaves, and all approachers. 'Tis most just
     That thou turn rascal; hadst thou wealth again,
     Rascals should have't. Do not assume my likeness.   220
TIMON Were I like thee, I'd throw away myself.
APEMANTUS Thou hast cast away thyself, being like thyself
     A madman so long, now a fool. What, think'st
     That the bleak air, thy boisterous chamberlain,
     Will put thy shirt on warm? Will these moist trees,   225

---

206 future] F; *Fortune Rowe*   217 bade] *Knight;* bad F; bid F2   225 moist] F; moss'd *Hanmer*

201 **affect** imitate.
202–3 Timon would rather imitate his dog because a dog is preferable to any man.
207 **habit** dress.
207 **care** anxiety, misery.
209 **perfumes** perfumed mistresses and perhaps luxury generally (Malone).
210 **Shame . . . woods** The woods are the pure state of nature.
211 **cunning** craft.
211 **carper** cynic, caviller.
214 **observe** do homage to.
216 **Thou . . . thus** This is what you used to be told (Riverside).
217 **gav'st thine ears** listened readily.
217 **like . . . welcome** Tapsters were proverbially undiscriminating in their welcome to customers.

219 **rascal** (1) rogue, (2) deer in poor condition (also sexually, see Williams, sv).
222–33 This lesson that Apemantus delivers for Timon about Nature's adversities recalls not only *Lear* 3.4 but also Duke Senior's speech in *AYLI* 2.1. Duke Senior's message is that 'the uses of [Nature's] adversity' are 'sweet' as compared with the 'painted pomp' of 'the envious court' (*AYLI* 2.1.2–4), but Apemantus insists that Nature's adversities are relentless and will prove unacceptable to Timon because of his spoilt and fastidious nature.
224 **chamberlain** servant.
225 **moist trees** Assuming this is an emphasis on great age, F. P. Wilson ('Shakespeare and the diction of common life', *Proceedings of the British Academy* 27 (1941), 167–97) reads 'moist' as 'full of sap', 'pithy'. Hulme supposes 'wet trees, in seventeenth-century proverbial idiom, were thought

That have outlived the eagle, page thy heels
And skip when thou point'st out? Will the cold brook,
Candied with ice, caudle thy morning taste
To cure thy o'ernight's surfeit? Call the creatures
Whose naked natures live in all the spite   230
Of wreakful heaven, whose bare unhousèd trunks,
To the conflicting elements exposed,
Answer mere nature; bid them flatter thee.
O thou shalt find –

TIMON   A fool of thee. Depart.
APEMANTUS I love thee better now than e'er I did.   235
TIMON I hate thee worse.
APEMANTUS Why?
TIMON Thou flatter'st misery.
APEMANTUS I flatter not, but say thou art a caitiff.
TIMON Why dost thou seek me out?   240
APEMANTUS To vex thee.
TIMON Always a villain's office, or a fool's.
        Dost please thyself in't?
APEMANTUS Ay.
TIMON What, a knave too?   245
APEMANTUS If thou didst put this sour cold habit on
        To castigate thy pride, 'twere well; but thou
        Dost it enforcedly. Thou'dst courtier be again
        Wert thou not beggar. Willing misery
        Outlives incertain pomp, is crowned before;   250

---

234 find –] *Rowe;* finde. F   250 Outlives incertain] *Rowe;* Out-liues: incertaine F

of as affording less than no shelter' (p. 83). Some
editors follow Hanmer and read 'moss'd', but J.
Lawlor compares Falstaff, whose 'moist eye' (*2H4*
1.2.180) functions as a sign of rheum and old age
(*The Tragic Sense in Shakespeare*, 1960, p. 134).
    226 eagle The eagle's old age was proverbial
(Tilley E5).
    226 page . . . out follow at your heels like a page.
    228 Candied crusted, as if sugared. Timon also
speaks of 'sugar'd game' (266) and of the world
being his 'confectionary' (267), referring to flattery,
deceiving others and self-deceit. So Hamlet says:
'let the candied tongue lick absurd pomp' (*Ham.*
3.2.60); in *Temp.* Antonio says: 'Twenty con-
sciences, / . . . candied be they, / And melt ere they
molest!' (2.1.278–80).
    228–9 caudle . . . surfeit provide a soothing
warm drink as a cure for the previous night's glut-

tony. *OED* Caudle *sb* 1 gives this recipe: 'A warm
drink consisting of thin gruel, mixed with wine or
ale, sweetened and spiced, given chiefly to sick
people . . .'
    230 naked natures natural nakedness.
    231 wreakful revengeful.
    231 trunks bodies.
    233 Answer . . . nature 'cope with nature in all
its stark rigour' (Deighton).
    234 thou . . . thee you will find – that you are a
fool (Abbott 172 and Franz 515).
    239 caitiff wretch.
    246 habit manner.
    248 enforcedly under compulsion.
    249 Willing misery Voluntary poverty.
    250 Outlives Outlasts.
    250 incertain not proof against change.
    250 crowned before achieves its desires sooner.

The one is filling still, never complete;
The other, at high wish. Best state, contentless,
Hath a distracted and most wretched being,
Worse than the worst, content.
Thou shouldst desire to die, being miserable.   255
TIMON   Not by his breath that is more miserable.
Thou art a slave, whom Fortune's tender arm
With favour never clasped, but bred a dog.
Hadst thou like us from our first swath proceeded
The sweet degrees that this brief world affords   260
To such as may the passive drugs of it
Freely command, thou wouldst have plunged thyself
In general riot, melted down thy youth
In different beds of lust, and never learned
The icy precepts of respect, but followed   265
The sugar'd game before thee. But myself,
Who had the world as my confectionary,
The mouths, the tongues, the eyes and hearts of men
At duty, more than I could frame employment;
That numberless upon me stuck, as leaves   270
Do on the oak, have with one winter's brush
Fell from their boughs, and left me open, bare,
For every storm that blows. I to bear this,
That never knew but better, is some burthen.

261 drugs] F4; drugges F; drudges *conj. Mason, 'Comments'* (*1797*)   262 command] *Rowe;* command'st F   266 sugar'd]
Pope; Sugred F

251 **The one** Referring to 'incertain pomp'.

251 **is . . . complete** is always adding further items of pomp and thereby missing completion.

252 **at high wish** at the height of one's wishes.

252–4 **Best . . . content** Man's best state, if it does not bring content, is more wretched than his worst, if he feels content with the worst.

255–6 What Apemantus has in mind is Timon's wretched state as an involuntary outcast; what Timon has in mind is Apemantus's low birth and his never having been favoured by Fortune.

256 **breath** advice.

258 **bred a dog** Treated like a dog. Not all dog references are allusions to the Cynic school of philosophy, nor is Apemantus the only character to be called a dog.

259 **swath** swaddling clothes.

259–60 **proceeded . . . degrees** advanced up the steps.

261 **passive drugs** Since the spelling of 'drugs'

was not stable and since it is also an obsolete form for 'drudge' (see *OED* Drudge *sb* and Sisson, *Readings*, II, 175), the meaning is twofold: (1) 'things in passive subserviency to salutary as well as pernicious purposes' (Schmidt); (2) submissive menial servants.

263 **riot** dissoluteness.

265 **icy . . . respect** cold admonitions of reason.

266 **sugar'd game** sweetly desirable (sexual) quarry; 'game' signifies 'woman as sexual quarry' (Williams, II, 572).

267 **confectionary** place where sweets are made.

269 **At duty** Awaiting orders.

271 **winter's brush** brush of a wintry storm.

272 **Fell** Fallen (see Franz 167 for the use of the preterite form as past participle).

273 **I . . . this** For me to bear this.

274 **That . . . better** Who have always known better circumstances; 'but' = except.

Thy nature did commence in sufferance, time   275
Hath made thee hard in't. Why shouldst thou hate men?
They never flattered thee. What hast thou given?
If thou wilt curse, thy father, that poor rag,
Must be thy subject; who in spite put stuff
To some she-beggar and compounded thee   280
Poor rogue hereditary. Hence, be gone!
If thou hadst not been born the worst of men,
Thou hadst been a knave and flatterer.

APEMANTUS Art thou proud yet?

TIMON   Ay, that I am not thee.

APEMANTUS I, that I was no prodigal.   285

TIMON I, that I am one now.
            Were all the wealth I have shut up in thee,
            I'd give thee leave to hang it. Get thee gone.
            That the whole life of Athens were in this!
            Thus would I eat it.
                              [*Eats a root*]

APEMANTUS   Here, I will mend thy feast.   290
                              [*Offers food*]

TIMON First mend thy company, take away thyself.

APEMANTUS So I shall mend mine own, by th'lack of thine.

TIMON 'Tis not well mended so, it is but botched;
            If not, I would it were.

APEMANTUS What wouldst thou have to Athens?   295

---

278 rag] F4; ragge F; rogue *conj. Johnson*   284 Art ... thee] *Knight;* Art ... yet / I ... thee F   290 SD.1 *Eats a root*] *Rowe;*
not in F   290 SD.2 *Offers food*] *Johnson; not in* F   291 thy] F; my *Rowe and editors*

275 **Thy ... sufferance** Your experience has
been from the beginnning one of suffering.
276 **Hath ... in't** Hardened you to it.
279 **stuff** semen.
280 **compounded** begot.
281 **hereditary** by inheritance.
282 **worst** lowest in social position.
284 Apemantus returns to the question which
Timon had put to him in 1.1.192, and Timon's
answer also corresponds to what Apemantus had
said in 1.1.193, but this dispute takes place on a
more equal footing.
287 **shut up** enclosed, summed up.
290 **mend** improve.
291 **First ... thyself** First improve the company you provide by taking away yourself. Most

editors follow Rowe's emendation 'my' for 'thy',
giving the sense: 'That will mend *my* own company,
you being absent' (Sisson, *Readings*, II, 176).
292 **So ... thine** I shall improve my own company by not having you as a companion. A feeble
rejoinder; Apemantus is clearly on the defensive.
293 **botched** bungled, badly mended.
294 No convincing explanation of this remark has
been found. This whole piece of banter very much
resembles Feste's and Olivia's repartee in *TN*
1.5.38–54, even to the point of using words like
'mend', 'patch' and 'botcher'. Seen in this perspective, Timon assumes the more aggressive role of the
'fool' here.
295 **What ... Athens** What would you like to be
sent to Athens.

TIMON Thee thither in a whirlwind. If thou wilt
    Tell them there I have gold; look, so I have.
APEMANTUS Here is no use for gold.
TIMON   The best and truest;
    For here it sleeps, and does no hired harm.
APEMANTUS Where liest a nights, Timon?   300
TIMON Under that's above me.
    Where feed'st thou a days, Apemantus?
APEMANTUS Where my stomach finds meat; or, rather, where I eat it.
TIMON Would poison were obedient, and knew my mind!
APEMANTUS Where wouldst thou send it?   305
TIMON To sauce thy dishes.
APEMANTUS The middle of humanity thou never knewest, but the
    extremity of both ends. When thou wast in thy gilt and thy per-
    fume, they mocked thee for too much curiosity; in thy rags thou
    know'st none, but art despised for the contrary. There's a medlar   310
    for thee, eat it.
TIMON On what I hate I feed not.
APEMANTUS Dost hate a medlar?
TIMON Ay, though it look like thee.
APEMANTUS And th'hadst hated meddlers sooner, thou shouldst have   315
    loved thyself better now. What man didst thou ever know unthrift
    that was beloved after his means?

---

300 a nights] F; a-nights *Pope;* o'nights *Theobald*   302 a days] F2; a-dayes F; o'days *Theobald*   310 medlar] *Theobald;* medler F   313 medlar] *Theobald;* Medler F   315 meddlers] *Knight;* Medlers F

299 hired harm harm through being used as a means to corrupt or as a bribe (see *OED* Hire *v* 1b).
  301 that's that which is.
  303 meat food in general.
  306 sauce season.
  307–8 The middle ... ends Perhaps alluding to Aristotle's concept of the 'mean' as the characteristic measure of human virtue (see *Nichomachean Ethics*, Loeb Classical Library, 1956, II, vi and vii). Aristotle defines 'liberality' as 'the observance of the mean in relation to wealth', with 'Prodigality' and 'Meanness' as its corresponding modes of excess (iv, 1). (For the proverb see Tilley and Dent.) It is surprising that many critics take these words as a guide to understanding the play (see John Holloway, *The Story of the Night*, 1961, p. 132), although in the play's first half, Apemantus is far from being accepted as reliable by these critics.
  309 curiosity 'finical delicacy' (Warburton); fastidiousness (*OED* Curiosity 4a).

310–16 Punning on 'medlar' (i.e. the fruit of the medlar tree) which is eaten only when decayed to a soft pulpy state and is proverbial for being never good till rotten (Tilley M863); and 'meddler', one who busies himself with the concerns of others (*OED* Meddle *v* 8) or one who over-indulges in sexual matters. F spells 'medler' throughout, which according to *OED* (Medle(e), Medler) is an obsolete spelling for 'medlar'. I retain the ambiguity by spelling 'medlar' until line 315, where only one meaning obtains. A further pun is on 'eat' and 'hate'. This is phonological: initial 'h' was commonly silent and the vowel quality in 'eat' and 'hate' was the same (see H. Kökeritz, 'Five Shakespeare notes', *RES* 23 (1947), 312–13). This explains why 'eat' in 311 is the cue for 'hate' in 312, and why the answer to the question in 313 is introduced by 'though' in 314 (313 takes 'hate' to mean 'eat').
  317 after (1) in accordance with, (2) after the loss of (Riverside).

TIMON Who, without those means thou talk'st of, didst thou ever know beloved?

APEMANTUS Myself.   320

TIMON I understand thee; thou hadst some means to keep a dog.

APEMANTUS What things in the world canst thou nearest compare to thy flatterers?

TIMON Women nearest, but men – men are the things themselves. What wouldst thou do with the world, Apemantus, if it lay in thy power?   325

APEMANTUS Give it the beasts, to be rid of the men.

TIMON Wouldst thou have thyself fall in the confusion of men, and remain a beast with the beasts?

APEMANTUS Ay, Timon.

TIMON A beastly ambition, which the gods grant thee t'attain to. If thou   330
wert the lion, the fox would beguile thee; if thou wert the lamb, the fox would eat thee; if thou wert the fox, the lion would suspect thee, when peradventure thou wert accused by the ass; if thou wert the ass, thy dullness would torment thee, and still thou liv'dst but as a breakfast to the wolf. If thou wert the wolf, thy greediness would   335
afflict thee, and oft thou shouldst hazard thy life for thy dinner. Wert thou the unicorn, pride and wrath would confound thee and make thine own self the conquest of thy fury. Wert thou a bear, thou wouldst be killed by the horse; wert thou a horse, thou wouldst be seized by the leopard; wert thou a leopard, thou wert germane to   340
the lion, and the spots of thy kindred were jurors on thy life. All thy safety were remotion, and thy defence absence. What beast couldst thou be that were not subject to a beast? And what a beast art thou already, that seest not thy loss in transformation!

321 thou . . . dog you had just enough to keep a dog (and only a dog could love you).

324 Women . . . themselves 'Apart from men, women are the nearest to being flatterers; but in fact men are not *near-flatterers*, they are the thing itself' (Sisson, *Readings*, II, 176).

327 fall be degraded; possibly alluding to the Fall of Man.

327 confusion overthrow; see 4.1.21.

334 liv'dst wouldst live.

337–8 unicorn . . . fury The unicorn's fierceness is recorded in Pliny, *Natural History*, VIII, 31; Hanmer supplies a story of the unicorn's pro-verbial wrath taken from Konrad Gesner, *Historia animalium*: 'that he and the Lion being enemies by nature, as soon as the Lion sees the Unicorn he betakes himself to a tree: The Unicorn in his

fury . . . running at him sticks his horn fast in the tree . . .' In *JC* 2.1.204 Decius mentions a similar story of the unicorn, but only as food for Caesar's superstition.

338–41 The argument is that Apemantus cannot evade being victimised, whatever beast he may identify with. The word-play on 'spots', meaning physical markings as well as moral stains, is prefigured in *R2* 1.1.174–5.

340 germane closely related, akin (*OED* Ger-man, germane *a*¹ and *sb*¹ 3 marks this meaning as obsolete, with this instance given as reference).

342 remotion removal of yourself (to some other place).

344 loss . . . transformation what you would lose by being changed into an animal. In *AYLI* (2.7.1–2) Duke Senior thinks of Jacques in similar

APEMANTUS If thou couldst please me with speaking to me, thou   345
mightst have hit upon it here. The commonwealth of Athens is
become a forest of beasts.

TIMON How has the ass broke the wall, that thou art out of the city?

APEMANTUS Yonder comes a poet and a painter; the plague of company light upon thee! I will fear to catch it, and give way. When I   350
know not what else to do, I'll see thee again.

TIMON When there is nothing living but thee, thou shalt be welcome. I
had rather be a beggar's dog than Apemantus.

APEMANTUS Thou art the cap of all the fools alive.

TIMON Would thou wert clean enough to spit upon.   355

APEMANTUS A plague on thee, thou art too bad to curse.

TIMON All villains that do stand by thee are pure.

APEMANTUS There is no leprosy but what thou speak'st.

TIMON If I name thee.
  I'll beat thee, but I should infect my hands.   360

APEMANTUS I would my tongue could rot them off.

TIMON Away thou issue of a mangy dog!
  Choler does kill me that thou art alive;
  I swound to see thee.

APEMANTUS Would thou wouldst burst!   365

345–7] *Pope;* If . . . please me / With . . . might'st / Have . . . heere. / The . . . become / A . . . Beasts. F   **349–51**] *Theobald;* Yonder . . . Painter: / The . . . thee: / I . . . way. / When . . . do, / Ile . . . againe. F   **352–3**] *Johnson;* When . . . thee, / Thou . . . welcome. / I . . . Dogge, / Then *Apemantus.* F   **354–8**] *Pope;* Thou . . . Cap / Of . . . aliue. / Would . . . enough / To spit vpon. / A . . . thee, / Thou . . . curse. / All Villaines / That . . . pure. / There . . . Leprosie, / But . . . speak'st. F   **359** thee.] *Theobald;* thee, F   **360** I'll . . . hands] *Capell;* Ile . . . thee; / But . . . hands F   **361** *Pope;* I . . . tongue / Could . . . off. F   **363–4**] *Rowe;* Choller . . . me, / That . . . thee F   **364** swound] F4; swoond F; swoon *Pope*

terms: 'I think he be transform'd into a beast, / For
I can no where find him like a man.' The idea of
'transformation' in *Timon* will recur at 5.4.19, and is
also addressed in the concept 'alchemist' (5.1.104).

346–7 commonwealth . . . beasts Recalling
Titus, and his appalled recognition that 'Rome is a
wilderness of tigers.'

349 Yonder . . . painter Their appearance actually occurs almost 200 lines later, in 5.1, after the
visits of the Bandits and Steward Flavius. Perhaps
Shakespeare changed his mind but forgot to delete
this early announcement; possibly, therefore, this is
another piece of evidence that the compositors used
authorial manuscript, not prepared for playhouse
use. See 5.1.0 SD n., and Textual Analysis, pp. 188–
90 below.

350 give way yield, leave the place to them.

354 cap top, chief. *OED* Cap *sb*[1] 4h gives this
passage as the only reference.

357 that do . . . pure i.e. compared to you, they
are pure.

359–60 Neither the punctuation nor the lineation
in F makes sense. Theobald's replacement of F's
comma after 'name thee' by a full stop makes it clear
that this first phrase of Timon's speech is meant to
be an answer to Apemantus's previous jibe.

360 I'll beat thee, but I would beat you except
that.

361 rot The transitive use of 'rot' is noted in
OED (Rot *v* 4), especially its use in 'imprecations
against a person' (Rot *v* 6).

364 swound Archaic and dialectic form of
'swoon'.

TIMON Away, thou tedious rogue, I am sorry I shall lose a stone by thee.

[*Throws a stone*]

APEMANTUS Beast!

TIMON Slave!

APEMANTUS Toad!

TIMON Rogue, rogue, rogue!   370
    I am sick of this false world, and will love nought
    But even the mere necessities upon't.
    Then, Timon, presently prepare thy grave;
    Lie where the light foam of the sea may beat
    Thy grave-stone daily; make thine epitaph,   375
    That death in me at others' lives may laugh.
    [*Looks at the gold*] O thou sweet king-killer, and dear divorce
    'Twixt natural son and sire; thou bright defiler
    Of Hymen's purest bed, thou valiant Mars,
    Thou ever young, fresh, loved and delicate wooer,   380
    Whose blush doth thaw the consecrated snow
    That lies on Dian's lap. Thou visible god,
    That sold'rest close impossibilities,
    And mak'st them kiss; that speak'st with every tongue
    To every purpose. O thou touch of hearts,   385
    Think thy slave man rebels, and by thy virtue
    Set them into confounding odds, that beasts
    May have the world in empire.

APEMANTUS   Would 'twere so,
    But not till I am dead. I'll say th'hast gold.

---

366 SD] *Capell; not in* F   377 SD] *Pope; not in* F   378 son and sire] *Rowe;* Sunne and fire F   382] *Rowe;* That . . . lap. /
Thou . . . God, F

372 But even Save only.

372 necessities the basic imperatives. The foremost of these 'necessities' is death, which he is now going to turn his attention to.

374–5 The sense of freshness and pleasure in the phrase 'the light foam of the sea' is striking and beautiful, the more so for its contrast to the context. As in *Pericles*, the sea is associated with death and yet seems to reconcile fundamental antinomies.

378 natural son son by birth (not illegitimate).

379 Hymen God of marriage.

379 Mars God of war; caught in adultery with Venus, a sordid and ludicrous occasion, the very opposite of 'fresh' or 'delicate'.

382 Dian The goddess Diana, celebrated for chastity and beauty. On the imagery, compare *Cym.* 2.5.6–13, especially 'A pudency so rosy the sweet view on't / Might well have warmed old Saturn, that I thought her / As chaste as unsunn'd snow' (11–13) – referring to the Diana-like Imogen.

383 close closely, tightly.

383 impossibilities things or qualities that cannot be put together.

384–5 that speak'st . . . purpose Compare Jonson, *Volpone* 1.1.22: 'Riches, the dumb god, that giv'st all men tongues'.

385 touch touchstone.

386–7 by thy . . . odds by thy power set them at strife that will destroy them.

> Thou wilt be thronged to shortly.

TIMON   Thronged to?

APEMANTUS   Ay.   390

TIMON Thy back, I prithee.

APEMANTUS   Live, and love thy misery.

TIMON Long live so, and so die. I am quit.

Enter the BANDITTI

APEMANTUS Moe things like men; eat, Timon, and abhor them.

                                                    Exit Apemantus

FIRST BANDIT Where should he have this gold? It is some poor frag-
    ment, some slender ort of his remainder. The mere want of gold, and   395
    the falling-from of his friends, drove him into this melancholy.

SECOND BANDIT It is noised he hath a mass of treasure.

THIRD BANDIT Let us make the assay upon him; if he care not for't, he
    will supply us easily; if he covetously reserve it, how shall's get it?

SECOND BANDIT True; for he bears it not about him; 'tis hid.   400

FIRST BANDIT Is not this he?

ALL *other* BANDITTI Where?

SECOND BANDIT 'Tis his description.

THIRD BANDIT He; I know him.

ALL BANDITTI Save thee, Timon.   405

TIMON Now, thieves?

ALL BANDITTI Soldiers, not thieves.

TIMON   Both too, and women's sons.

ALL BANDITTI We are not thieves, but men that much do want.

TIMON Your greatest want is, you want much of meat.

> Why should you want? Behold, the earth hath roots;   410

---

392 SD] F4; *Enter the Bandetti.* F (*after 393*); *Enter Thieves.* / *Pope*   393] *Pope;* Mo . . . men, / Eate . . . then. F   393 them]
Rowe; then F   394 SH FIRST BANDIT] *Rowe;* 1 F (*throughout scene*)   396 falling-from] *Capell;* falling from F   397 SH
SECOND BANDIT] *Rowe;* 2 F (*throughout scene*)   397 It . . . treasure] *Pope;* It . . . nois'd / He . . . Treasure F   398 SH
THIRD BANDIT] *Rowe;* 3 F (*throughout scene*)   400] *Pope;* True . . . him: / 'Tis hid. F   402 SH ALL *other* BANDITTI]
Riverside; All F   404 He;] *Rowe;* He? F   405, 407, 408 SH ALL BANDITTI] *Riverside; All* F   407] *Deighton;*
Soldiers . . . Theeues. / Both . . . Sonnes. F   408] *Pope;* We . . . men / That . . . want. F   409 meat.] F; meet.
Theobald; . . . men. *Hanmer*

---

392 **I am quit** I have no more to do with you.

392 SD The Banditti are not immediately aware of
Timon's presence, although Timon is made aware
of them by Apemantus in line 393.

395 **slender . . . remainder** tiny scrap of the remains of his fortune.

396 **falling-from** desertion.

398 **make . . . him** put him to the test; punning
on the sense (*OED* Assay *sb* 6) 'trial to determine the
amount of precious metal in ore or alloy'.

403 His appearance corresponds to descriptions
of him.

407 **Both too, and** Both indeed, and also.

407 **women's sons** Most likely with a
misogynistic thrust.

408 **want** lack; but with an unintentional alternative meaning, 'desire', 'wish for', which in the next
line is taken up by Timon.

409 **Your . . . meat** Your greatest lack is caused
by your greedy desire for food.

      Within this mile break forth a hundred springs;
      The oaks bear mast, the briers scarlet hips;
      The bounteous housewife nature on each bush
      Lays her full mess before you. Want? Why want?

FIRST BANDIT We cannot live on grass, on berries, water,   415
      As beasts and birds and fishes.

TIMON Nor on the beasts themselves, the birds and fishes;
      You must eat men. Yet thanks I must you con
      That you are thieves professed, that you work not
      In holier shapes; for there is boundless theft   420
      In limited professions. Rascal thieves,
      Here's gold. Go, suck the subtle blood o'th'grape,
      Till the high fever seethe your blood to froth,
      And so 'scape hanging. Trust not the physician,
      His antidotes are poison, and he slays   425
      Moe than you rob. Take wealth and lives together;
      Do villainy, do, since you protest to do't,
      Like workmen. I'll example you with thievery.
      The sun's a thief, and with his great attraction
      Robs the vast sea. The moon's an arrant thief,   430
      And her pale fire she snatches from the sun.
      The sea's a thief, whose liquid surge resolves
      The moon into salt tears. The earth's a thief,
      That feeds and breeds by a composture stol'n
      From gen'ral excrement; each thing's a thief.   435
      The laws, your curb and whip, in their rough power
      Has unchecked theft. Love not yourselves; away,

---

427 villainy] *Rowe;* Villaine F; villains *Riverside*   427–8 to do't, / Like workmen.] *Pope;* to doo't. / Like Workemen, F

412 **mast** acorns.
412 **hips** fruit of the rose.
414 **mess** variety of foods, meal.
418 **con** offer.
420 **shapes** disguises.
421 **limited** officially regulated.
422 **the subtle . . . grape** red wine.
423 **the high fever** the heat of intoxication (which you will die of, so escaping the punishment for theft, hanging).
424–5 **Trust . . . poison** That the physician is more dangerous than the disease was a commonplace; see Tilley P267a.
427 **protest** profess.
428 **example you with** give you examples of.
429–37 Anacreon's Ode XIX has been suggested

as an antecedent to this catalogue of precedents for thievery in nature or the cosmos. See Christopher Smart, 'On Shakespeare's learning' (1756), repr. *CH*, IV, 1976, p. 205.
432 **resolves** dissolves, melts.
434 **composture** manure.
436–7 **The laws . . . theft** The laws provide opportunity for unlimited thievery. That the laws lend themselves to wrong-doing is a recurrent idea; see the conflict between Alcibiades and the Senators in 3.5; also 4.1.12.
437 **Has** The plural subject with singular verb is frequent in Elizabethan English. This singular form is determined by the nearest noun, and not by the noun with which it is syntactically related.

Rob one another; there's more gold, cut throats:
All that you meet are thieves. To Athens go;
Break open shops; nothing can you steal   440
But thieves do lose it; steal less for this I give you,
And gold confound you howsoe'er. Amen.   [*Timon withdraws*]

THIRD BANDIT H'as almost charmed me from my profession, by
persuading me to it.

FIRST BANDIT 'Tis in the malice of mankind that he thus advises us,   445
not to have us thrive in our mystery.

SECOND BANDIT I'll believe him as an enemy, and give over my trade.

FIRST BANDIT Let us first see peace in Athens; there is no time so
miserable but a man may be true.

[*Exeunt*] *Thieves*

Enter the Steward [FLAVIUS] *to Timon*

FLAVIUS O you gods!   450
Is yond despised and ruinous man my lord?
Full of decay and failing? O monument
And wonder of good deeds evilly bestowed!
What an alteration of honour has desp'rate want made!
What viler thing upon the earth than friends,   455
Who can bring noblest minds to basest ends!
How rarely does it meet with this time's guise,
When man was wished to love his enemies!
Grant I may ever love, and rather woo
Those that would mischief me than those that do.   460

---

441 less] F; not less *Rowe;* no less *Collier²*   442 SD] *Capell; not in* F   447] *Pope;* Ile . . . Enemy, / And . . . Trade. F   448–9 Let . . . true.] F; Let . . . Athens; / SH 2 Thief . . . true. *Theobald (conj. Warburton)*   449 SD.1 Exeunt] F2; Exit F   449 SD.2 FLAVIUS] *Rowe; not in* F   450 SH FLAVIUS] *Rowe; Stew.* F *(throughout scene)*

440–1 nothing . . . lose it i.e. you cannot steal anything from honest people, there are none.

441–2 steal . . . howsoe'er 'if you steal less because of this, may gold destroy you whatever happens' (Maxwell). Maxwell explains this as use of the imperative form for stating a condition.

445 in the malice out of hatred.

446 mystery craft, profession.

447 as an enemy as I would an enemy; i.e. do the opposite of the advice given.

448–9 Let us defer giving up our trade until there is peace in Athens; there is no time so miserable that one cannot be honest. Warburton gives the second half of the sentence to the Second Bandit, and assumes he is confirming his repentance. Malone thinks it a deferral of repentance.

451 ruinous man man brought to ruin. Flavius speaks of Timon in images of a decayed house or monument; see also 4.2.16.

452–3 monument / And wonder wondrous monument (the rhetorical figure hendiadys).

454 alteration decline.

457–8 How rarely . . . enemies Flavius sarcastically equates Timon's foolish love for his false friends with the biblical doctrine 'Love your enemies.'

457 rarely very well.

457 guise fashion.

458 wished desired.

460 that would . . . that do who openly intend my harm rather than those who do actually harm me while pretending kindness. Johnson notes the

H'as caught me in his eye, I will present
My honest grief unto him; and as my lord
Still serve him with my life.

[TIMON *comes forward*]

My dearest master!
TIMON Away! What art thou?
FLAVIUS   Have you forgot me, sir?
TIMON Why dost ask that? I have forgot all men.   465
Then, if thou grant'st th'art a man,
I have forgot thee.
FLAVIUS An honest poor servant of yours.
TIMON Then I know thee not.
I never had honest man about me, I; all   470
I kept were knaves, to serve in meat to villains.
FLAVIUS The gods are witness,
Ne'er did poor steward wear a truer grief
For his undone lord than mine eyes for you.
TIMON What, dost thou weep? Come nearer, then I love thee,   475
Because thou art a woman, and disclaim'st
Flinty mankind, whose eyes do never give
But thorough lust and laughter. Pity's sleeping.
Strange times, that weep with laughing, not with weeping.
FLAVIUS I beg of you to know me, good my lord,   480
T'accept my grief, and whilst this poor wealth lasts
To entertain me as your steward still.
TIMON Had I a steward
So true, so just, and now so comfortable?
It almost turns my dangerous nature wild.   485
Let me behold thy face. Surely this man

461–3] *Pope; prose* F   463 SD] *Theobald; not in* F   466 grant'st] *Capell;* grunt'st F   470 me, I; all] *Capell*; me, I all F; me;
ay, all *Knight*   475] *Rowe;* What . . . weepe? / Come . . . thee F   485 wild] F; mild *Hanmer*

Spanish proverb, 'Defend me from my friends,
and from my enemies I will defend myself.'
    471 knaves Both servants and villains.
    471 serve in meat Again, 'meat' is used
metonymically (as in 409 and 1.2.36) for his liberality in general.
    477 give yield tears.
    478 thorough through.
    481 grief sympathy, pity.
    481 whilst while my little money lasts to employ
me.
    484 comfortable comforting.

    485 wild distracted, mad. This edition retains
F ('wilde'); editorial opinion is divided about
Hanmer's emendation 'mild'. There is no indication elsewhere that the idea of mildness even enters
Timon's mind, whereas madness is evidently close
(and parallels not only to Lear but to Titus suggest
this is Shakespeare's conception of Timon).
    486–94 Timon points to this figure as an exem-
plar to moralise on, very much like Lear viewing
Poor Tom (*Lear* 3.4 *passim*, especially 'Consider
him well . . .', 103 ff.).

Was born of woman.
Forgive my general and exceptless rashness,
You perpetual sober gods. I do proclaim
One honest man. Mistake me not, but one;   490
No more, I pray, and he's a steward.
How fain would I have hated all mankind,
And thou redeem'st thyself. But all save thee
I fell with curses.
Methinks thou art more honest now than wise;   495
For, by oppressing and betraying me,
Thou mightst have sooner got another service;
For many so arrive at second masters
Upon their first lord's neck. But tell me true –
For I must ever doubt, though ne'er so sure –   500
Is not thy kindness subtle, covetous,
If not a usuring kindness, and as rich men deal gifts,
Expecting in return twenty for one?
FLAVIUS No, my most worthy master, in whose breast
Doubt and suspect, alas, are placed too late.   505
You should have feared false times when you did feast;
Suspect still comes, where an estate is least.
That which I show, heaven knows, is merely love,
Duty and zeal to your unmatchèd mind,
Care of your food and living; and believe it,   510
My most honoured lord,
For any benefit that points to me,
Either in hope or present, I'd exchange
For this one wish, that you had power and wealth
To requite me, by making rich yourself.   515
TIMON Look thee, 'tis so. Thou singly honest man,
Here, take. The gods out of my misery
Has sent thee treasure. Go, live rich and happy;
But thus conditioned: thou shalt build from men;

---

502 If not a usuring] F; A usuring *Pope*

488 **exceptless** Making no allowance for exceptions.
499 **Upon . . . neck** By treading down their first master (Riverside).
501 **subtle** sly, devious.
502 **If . . . kindness** I retain F's 'If not'; usually, since Pope, deleted by editors on metrical grounds.

507 **Suspect** Suspicion.
508 **merely** nothing but.
512 **For** As for.
512 **points to** is destined for.
516 **singly** uniquely.
519 **from** remote from.

Hate all, curse all, show charity to none,   520
But let the famished flesh slide from the bone
Ere thou relieve the beggar. Give to dogs
What thou deniest to men. Let prisons swallow 'em,
Debts wither 'em to nothing; be men like blasted woods,
And may diseases lick up their false bloods!   525
And so farewell, and thrive.
FLAVIUS O let me stay and comfort you, my master.
TIMON If thou hat'st curses
Stay not; fly, whilst thou art blest and free;
Ne'er see thou man, and let me ne'er see thee.   530

                                                        [*Exeunt severally*]

[5.1] *Enter* POET *and* PAINTER [*Timon in his cave*]

PAINTER As I took note of the place, it cannot be far where he abides.
POET What's to be thought of him? Does the rumour hold for true that
   he's so full of gold?
PAINTER Certain. Alcibiades reports it; Phrynia and Timandra had

---

530 SD] *Theobald; Exit* F   **Act 5, Scene 1**   **5.1**] *Capell; not in* F   **0** SD *Timon . . . cave*] *Sisson; not in* F   **2–31**] *As Pope;* What's . . . him? / Does . . . true, / That . . . Gold? / Certaine. / Alcibiades . . . Timandylo / Had . . . enrich'd / Poore . . . quantity. / 'Tis . . . Steward / A . . . summe. / Then . . . his, / Ha's . . . Friends? / Nothing else: / You . . . againe, / And . . . highest: / Therefore . . . loues / To . . . his: / It . . . vs, / And . . . purposes / With . . . for, / If . . . goes / Of his hauing. / What . . . now / To . . . him? / Nothing . . . time / But . . . him / An . . . Peece. / I . . . too; / Tell . . . him. / Good . . . best. / Promising . . . Time; / It . . . Expectation. / Performance . . . acte, / And . . . people, / The . . . vse. / To . . . fashionable; / Performance . . . Testament / Which . . . iudgement / That makes it. / Excellent Workeman, / Thou . . . badde / As . . . selfe. / I am thinking / What . . . him: / It . . . himselfe: / A . . . Prosperity, / With . . . Flatteries / That . . . opulencie. / Must thou needes / Stand . . . Worke? / Wilt . . . men? / Do . . . thee. F   **4** Phrynia] *Rowe³; Phrinica* F; *Phrinia* F2   **4** Timandra] F2; *Timandylo* F

---

524 blasted blighted.

Act 5, Scene 1

0 SD The entry of Poet and Painter poses two different problems. The first is that their entry is mentioned by Apemantus back at 4.3.349, with no explanation for their non-appearance there. Moving that episode forward is not possible, since Poet and Painter mention at 5.1.3–6 that the Bandits and Flavius the Steward have already visited and got gold from Timon, which happens in 4.3. The second problem concerns Timon's entry; F has this in 5.1.23, but with no indication of how he can then

for a time go unobserved, or how his remarks pass unnoticed, by the visitors. I assume three phases. Phase one presents Timon upstage, visible to the audience, overhearing what Poet and Painter say. The second phase (23 ff.) is his coming forward and making sarcastic remarks while still remaining unnoticed by them. The third stage, finally, begins with him declaring 'Fit I meet them . . .' (45). For a discussion of the possible position of the cave, see Bevington, *Action is Eloquence*, pp. 115–16. On the question of making an entrance on the stage of Shakespeare's Globe, see above 1.1.178 SD n.

gold of him. He likewise enriched poor straggling soldiers with   5
great quantity. 'Tis said he gave unto his steward a mighty sum.

POET Then this breaking of his has been but a try for his friends.

PAINTER Nothing else. You shall see him a palm in Athens again, and
flourish with the highest. Therefore 'tis not amiss we tender our
loves to him in this supposed distress of his: it will show honestly in   10
us, and is very likely to load our purposes with what they travail for,
if it be a just and true report that goes of his having.

POET What have you now to present unto him?

PAINTER Nothing at this time but my visitation; only I will promise
him an excellent piece.   15

POET I must serve him so too, tell him of an intent that's coming toward
him.

PAINTER Good as the best. Promising is the very air o'th' time; it opens
the eyes of expectation. Performance is ever the duller for his act,
and but in the plainer and simpler kind of people the deed of saying   20
is quite out of use. To promise is most courtly and fashionable;
performance is a kind of will or testament which argues a great
sickness in his judgement that makes it.

Enter TIMON *from his cave* [*unobserved*]

TIMON Excellent workman, thou canst not paint a man so bad as is
thyself.   25

POET I am thinking what I shall say I have provided for him. It must be

---

23 SD *unobserved*] Pope; not in F   24–5, 30–1, 38] F; *marked as aside in Capell*

6 **'Tis said . . . sum** This remark shows that
Steward Flavius has been as eagerly spreading the
news of Timon's gold as the other visitors.

7 **breaking** bankruptcy.

7 **try** test.

8–9 **You shall . . . highest** Steevens notes the
biblical allusion to Psalm 92.12: 'The righteous
shall *flourish* like a *palm*-tree' (Johnson/Steevens⁵).

11 **load** reward.

11 **travail** strive.

12 **goes . . . having** is spread of his wealth.

14 **visitation** visit; Schmidt points out that
Shakespeare knew 'visit' only as a verb.

16 **intent** (1) plan, project, (2) subject, theme
(see Hulme, p. 312).

18 **air** style, fashion.

19 **for his act** in practice.

20 **deed of saying** carrying-out of a promise; but
with the subsidiary sense that saying is in itself a
kind of deed.

20–1 Contrast the proverb 'Fine words butter no
parsnips.'

24–5 SH Reasons for not marking *Aside* this and
the subsequent speeches of Timon (30, 38) are
given in the Textual Analysis, p. 190 below.
Nevertheless, these speeches are not heard by the
others on stage.

24–5 **Excellent . . . thyself** This echoes Apemantus's sarcastic remark at 1.1.201–2.

26–9 What the Poet promises to do is a satirical
piece of work setting forth what he conceives to be
the moral to be drawn from Timon's life. Similar to
his allegorical representation of Timon's rise and
downfall in 1.1.66–91, it may be seen as an example
of a restrictive and simplistic reading of Timon's
life; as such, it has to be distinguished from the
larger-scale and much more complex satiric pattern
created by the play as a whole.

a personating of himself; a satire against the softness of prosperity,
with a discovery of the infinite flatteries that follow youth and
opulency.

TIMON Must thou needs stand for a villain in thine own work? Wilt thou   30
whip thine own faults in other men? Do so, I have gold for thee.

POET Nay, let's seek him.
   Then do we sin against our own estate,
   When we may profit meet, and come too late.

PAINTER True.   35
   When the day serves, before black-cornered night,
   Find what thou want'st by free and offered light.
   Come.

TIMON   I'll meet you at the turn.
   What a god's gold, that he is worshipped
   In a baser temple than where swine feed?   40
   'Tis thou that rigg'st the bark and plough'st the foam,
   Settlest admired reverence in a slave.
   To thee be worship; and thy saints for aye
   Be crowned with plagues, that thee alone obey.
   Fit I meet them. [*Comes forward*]   45

POET Hail, worthy Timon!

PAINTER   Our late noble master!

TIMON Have I once lived to see two honest men?

POET Sir,
   Having often of your open bounty tasted,
   Hearing you were retired, your friends fall'n off,   50
   Whose thankless natures – O abhorrèd spirits!

---

38 Come . . . turn.] *This edn;* Come. / Ile . . . turne: F 43 worship] *Rowe;* worshipt F 43–4 aye / Be] *Rowe³;* aye: / Be
F 45 SD] *Capell; not in* F 47] *Rowe;* Haue . . . liu'd / To . . . men? F

27 **himself** i.e. his case and situation.

30 **stand** be the model.

30–1 **Wilt thou . . . men** Proverbial; see Dent
F107.

33 **estate** interest, affairs (Schmidt, p. 3).

36–7 Find what you want by the free, available
light of day, before darkness makes it as hard to find
as in dark corners.

36 **serves** is available.

38 **at the turn** An obscure phrase: Beckerman, p.
196, explains 'turn' as one of the posts of the stage
which acquire particular relevance in observation
scenes. Other editors suggest more figurative readings; Maxwell glosses 'play you at your own game'.

42 **admired reverence** admiring, venerating
reverence.

43 **thy saints** those who distinguish themselves
and are canonised in your service. Jonson's *Volpone*
begins with a sacrilegious veneration of gold as a
'saint' in a 'shrine'.

45 **Fit . . . them** It is the right time, or occasion,
for me to meet them.

47 **once** really, indeed (used as an intensifier; see
1.2.234).

49 **open** (1) open-handed, (2) free from
dissimulation.

Not all the whips of heaven are large enough –
What, to you,
Whose star-like nobleness gave life and influence
To their whole being! I am rapt, and cannot cover   55
The monstrous bulk of this ingratitude
With any size of words.

TIMON   Let it go
Naked, men may see't the better.
You that are honest, by being what you are,
Make them best seen and known.

PAINTER   He and myself   60
Have travailed in the great shower of your gifts,
And sweetly felt it.

TIMON   Ay, you are honest men.

PAINTER We are hither come to offer you our service.

TIMON Most honest men. Why, how shall I requite you?
Can you eat roots and drink cold water, no?   65

POET, PAINTER What we can do, we'll do to do you service.

TIMON Y'are honest men; y'have heard that I have gold;
I am sure you have; speak truth, y'are honest men.

PAINTER So it is said, my noble lord, but therefore
Came not my friend, nor I.   70

TIMON Good honest men! Thou draw'st a counterfeit
Best in all Athens; th'art indeed the best,
Thou counterfeit'st most lively.

PAINTER   So, so, my lord.

TIMON E'en so, sir, as I say. – And for thy fiction,

57] *Charney;* With . . . words. / Let it go F   62 men] F2; man F   63] *Pope;* We . . . come / To . . . seruice. F   64] *Pope;*
Most . . . men: / Why . . . you? / F   66 SH POET, PAINTER] *Hibbard; Both.* F (*throughout scene*)   66] *Pope;* What . . . do,
/ Wee'l . . . seruice. F   67] *Pope;* Y'are . . . men, / Y'have . . . Gold, F

55–7 cannot . . . words I cannot adequately
represent this ingratitude with words, however
large-dimensioned; but 'cover' (hide by putting
something on) and 'size' (a glutinous wash applied
to canvas or to paper) imply deception and disguis-
ing, which gives Timon the clue for his sarcastic
answer (57–60).

60 them Referring to 'thankless natures' (51).

61 travailed Both 'toiled' and 'travelled' (as if
battling with a storm). The two forms 'travail' and
'travel' were used indiscriminately. The Painter's
paradoxical hyperboles are too gross to deceive
anyone.

71 counterfeit imitation, but also deceit, for-
gery. For a discussion of these ideas in a wider
context see Anne Righter, *Shakespeare and the Idea
of the Play*, 1962, pp. 186 ff.

73 So, so Passably.

74 The Painter's false modesty prompts Timon
to mock him covertly in return.

74 fiction poetical invention. Shakespeare used
the term only three times, always suggesting something unreal, opposed to reality.

Why, thy verse swells with stuff so fine and smooth   75
That thou art even natural in thine art.
But, for all this, my honest-natured friends,
I must needs say you have a little fault;
Marry, 'tis not monstrous in you, neither wish I
You take much pains to mend.

POET, PAINTER   Beseech your honour   80
To make it known to us.

TIMON   You'll take it ill.

POET, PAINTER Most thankfully, my lord.

TIMON   Will you indeed?

POET, PAINTER Doubt it not, worthy lord.

TIMON There's never a one of you but trusts a knave
That mightily deceives you.

POET, PAINTER   Do we, my lord?   85

TIMON Ay, and you hear him cog, see him dissemble,
Know his gross patchery, love him, feed him,
Keep in your bosom, yet remain assured
That he's a made-up villain.

PAINTER I know none such, my lord.

POET   Nor I.   90

TIMON Look you, I love you well; I'll give you gold,
Rid me these villains from your companies;
Hang them, or stab them, drown them in a draught,
Confound them by some course, and come to me,
I'll give you gold enough.

POET, PAINTER   Name them, my lord, let's know them.   95

TIMON You that way, and you this, but two in company;
Each man apart, all single and alone,
Yet an arch-villain keeps him company.

77 honest-natured] *Rowe;* honest Natur'd F   86] *Rowe;* I . . . cogge, / See . . . dissemble, F   91] *Pope;* Looke you, /
I . . . Gold F   96] *Pope;* You . . . this: / But . . . Company: F

75 **swells** is full of; but implying that it is
inflated, rhetorically tumid, stuffed.

75 **smooth** (1) easy and elegant, (2) glib,
flattering (see 3.6.81).

84 **There's . . . knave** Each one of you trusts a
knave.

86 **cog** 'wheedle, with the associations of cheat-
ing' (B. W. Vickers, *Returning to Shakespeare*, 1989,
p. 168).

87 **patchery** trickery; a sense confirmed by the
only other use by Shakespeare, *Tro.* 2.3.71–2, where

Thersites rails: 'Here is such patchery, such jug-
gling, and such knavery!'

89 **made-up** accomplished, complete.

92 **Rid me** For my sake get rid of.

93 **draught** privy, sink (see *Tro.* 5.1.75–6,
Thersites speaking: 'Sweet draught! "Sweet",
quoth 'a! Sweet sink, sweet sewer').

96–101 In a sarcastic and riddling way Timon
tells them they are villains, though pretending
honesty.

[*To one*] If, where thou art, two villains shall not be,
Come not near him. [*To the other*] If thou wouldst not reside   100
But where one villain is, then him abandon. –
Hence, pack! There's gold; you came for gold, ye slaves.
[*To one*] You have work for me; there's payment; hence!
[*To the other*] You are an alchemist, make gold of that.
Out, rascal dogs!   105

        Exeunt [*Poet and Painter; Timon retires to his cave*]

      Enter Steward [FLAVIUS] *and two* SENATORS

FLAVIUS   It is vain that you would speak with Timon;
    For he is set so only to himself,
    That nothing but himself, which looks like man,
    Is friendly with him.

FIRST SENATOR   Bring us to his cave.
    It is our part and promise to th'Athenians   110
    To speak with Timon.

SECOND SENATOR   At all times alike
    Men are not still the same; 'twas time and griefs
    That framed him thus. Time with his fairer hand,
    Offering the fortunes of his former days,
    The former man may make him. Bring us to him,   115
    And chance it as it may.

FLAVIUS   Here is his cave.
    Peace and content be here. Lord Timon! Timon,
    Look out, and speak to friends. Th'Athenians

---

99 SD] *Oliver; not in* F   100 SD] *Oliver; not in* F   100 reside] *Rowe;* recide F   103 SD] *Charney; not in* F*; To Painter / Globe; To Poet / Oliver*   104 SD] *Charney; not in* F*; To Poet / Globe; To Painter / Oliver*   105 SD.1 *Poet . . . cave*] *Staunton; not in* F   105 SD.2 *Steward* FLAVIUS] *Rowe; Steward* F   106 SH FLAVIUS] *Rowe; Stew.* F (*throughout scene*)   116 chance] F3*;* chanc'd F*;* chanc'e F2

102 pack be off.

102 slaves A term of abuse and contempt.

104 alchemist In Sonnet 114 'alcumy' is used together with the idea of flattery.

104 make . . . that F does not provide a SD; perhaps Timon gives nothing, perhaps throws a stone or rubbish. Peter Brook, in his production at the Bouffes-du-Nord, Paris, in 1973, had Timon fling excrement.

105 rascal thin, poor, vicious; also the lowest bred.

106 It is vain F's reading makes better sense than F3's adverbial phrase 'in vain', which is more restrictive in its meaning; 'vain' may mean (1) useless, (2) foolish, (3) conceited.

107 set . . . himself preoccupied with himself.

110 our part the role we have taken upon ourselves.

111–12 At all . . . the same men are not always the same.

113–15 The Senator, a typical politician, reveals implicit cynicism in saying that a man's personality and philosophy vary according to fortune and conditions: men have no integrity, he smoothly assumes.

116 chance it let it fall out.

By two of their most reverend senate greet thee.
Speak to them, noble Timon.   120

Enter TIMON *out of his cave*

TIMON Thou sun that comforts, burn! Speak and be hanged;
For each true word, a blister, and each false
Be as a cantherising to the root o'th'tongue,
Consuming it with speaking.
FIRST SENATOR   Worthy Timon –
TIMON Of none but such as you, and you of Timon.   125
FIRST SENATOR The senators of Athens greet thee, Timon.
TIMON I thank them, and would send them back the plague,
Could I but catch it for them.
FIRST SENATOR   O forget
What we are sorry for ourselves in thee.
The senators, with one consent of love,   130
Entreat thee back to Athens, who have thought
On special dignities which vacant lie
For thy best use and wearing.
SECOND SENATOR   They confess
Toward thee forgetfulness too general gross;
Which now the public body, which doth seldom   135
Play the recanter, feeling in itself
A lack of Timon's aid, hath sense withal

121] *Hanmer;* Thou ... burne, / Speake ... hang'd: F   123 Be as a cantherising] F (Cantherizing); Be as a Catherizing F2–4; Be as a Cauterizing *Rowe;* Be cancerizing *Capell*   124 SH FIRST SENATOR] *Rowe;* 1 F (*throughout scene*)   125] *Pope;* Of ... you, / And ... Timon. F   127] *Pope;* I ... them, / And ... plague, F   133 SH SECOND SENATOR] *Rowe;* 2 F (*throughout scene*)   137 sense] *Rowe³;* since F; Since *Rowe*

121 Thou ... burn And Timon himself, once benevolent, now is malign. Lear uses the same terms when speaking to Regan: 'thine [eyes] / Do comfort, and not burn' (*Lear* 2.4.172–3).
122 For ... blister Proverbially 'a lie' is 'a blister on one's tongue' (Dent R84). Even 'each true word' is to Timon relatively diseased.
123 cantherising burning, searing. Rowe reads 'cauterizing', which is also the spelling given in *OED*, but the earliest reference in *OED* is to Robert Copland's translation of Guy de Chauliac, *The Questionary of Chirurgeons* (1542), where the word appears as 'canterising' and 'canteres' throughout. Riverside sees a connection with the action of dried Spanish fly (powder) *cantharides*, used by doctors as a caustic, and notes that Chauliac refers to

'cauterides' causing 'blysters'. Perhaps cantherise is confused with cauterise.
125 Of ... Timon i.e. Timon is deserving of them and their hateful company, and they are equally deserving of him and his hatred.
129 What ... thee What we ourselves regret when considering you.
130 one ... love one united voice of affection (Malone).
134 general gross obvious to everyone (Riverside).
135 Which ... body Hanmer's suggested substitution 'And' for 'Which' gives more clarity than a pompous politician would be likely to affect.
137* sense Rowe's emendation is necessary to make sense of the passage.

Of it own fall, restraining aid to Timon,
And send forth us, to make their sorrowed render,
Together with a recompense more fruitful   140
Than their offence can weigh down by the dram;
Ay, even such heaps and sums of love and wealth
As shall to thee blot out what wrongs were theirs,
And write in thee the figures of their love,
Ever to read them thine.

TIMON   You witch me in it;   145
Surprise me to the very brink of tears.
Lend me a fool's heart and a woman's eyes,
And I'll beweep these comforts, worthy senators.

FIRST SENATOR Therefore so please thee to return with us,
And of our Athens, thine and ours, to take   150
The captainship, thou shalt be met with thanks,
Allowed with absolute power, and thy good name
Live with authority; so soon we shall drive back
Of Alcibiades th'approaches wild,
Who like a boar too savage doth root up   155
His country's peace.

SECOND SENATOR   And shakes his threat'ning sword
Against the walls of Athens.

FIRST SENATOR   Therefore, Timon –

TIMON Well, sir, I will; therefore I will, sir, thus:
If Alcibiades kill my countrymen,
Let Alcibiades know this of Timon,   160
That Timon cares not. But if he sack fair Athens,
And take our goodly aged men by th'beards,
Giving our holy virgins to the stain
Of contumelious, beastly, mad-brained war,

---

138 it] F; it's *Rowe*; its *Pope*   138 fall] F; fail *Capell*

138 it its. The form 'it' is more frequent in
Shakespeare than 'its', which is often spelt 'it's'.
  138 fall failure in virtue and justice.
  138 restraining in holding back.
  139 render acknowledgement: figuratively, from
the term in commerce, to render an account (*OED*
Render *sb²* 4). The terms 'recompense', 'weigh',
'dram', 'heaps and sums of love and wealth', and
'figures of their love' in the subsequent lines, all
refer to account-keeping.
  140 fruitful abundant.

  141 by the dram measured to the last fraction of
an ounce ('dram' originally was the name of a coin).
  143 theirs committed by them.
  145 Ever . . . thine Eternally to your credit in a
figurative but also literal balance sheet.
  145 witch bewitch, enchant.
  152 Allowed Endowed.
  155 like . . . root up Steevens quotes from
Psalm 80.13: 'The *wild boar* out of the wood doth
root it *up*' (Johnson/Steevens⁵).
  164 contumelious insolent.

Then let him know, and tell him Timon speaks it,   165
In pity of our aged and our youth,
I cannot choose but tell him that I care not,
And let him take't at worst; for their knives care not
While you have throats to answer. For myself,
There's not a whittle in th'unruly camp   170
But I do prize it at my love before
The reverend'st throat in Athens. So I leave you
To the protection of the prosperous gods,
As thieves to keepers.

FLAVIUS   Stay not, all's in vain.

TIMON Why, I was writing of my epitaph;   175
It will be seen tomorrow. My long sickness
Of health and living now begins to mend,
And nothing brings me all things. Go, live still;
Be Alcibiades your plague, you his,
And last so long enough.

FIRST SENATOR   We speak in vain.   180

TIMON But yet I love my country, and am not
One that rejoices in the common wrack,
As common bruit doth put it.

FIRST SENATOR   That's well spoke.

TIMON Commend me to my loving countrymen.

---

172 reverend'st] F2; reuerends F   182 wrack] F3; wracke F; wreck *Hanmer*

168 for . . . not Some editors read 'for their
knives I care not', which would mean that Timon
would care if his own throat were to be cut. This
seems implausible in his present state of mind.

169 While . . . answer As long as you still have
throats to be cut.

170 whittle knife.

170 unruly.

171–2 i.e. Timon values the least knife in the
rebel army above the most reverend Athenian's
throat (and life).

173 prosperous gods gods that bring
prosperity.

174 keepers gaolers. Wealth, as Timon sees it,
imprisons men and their desires.

178 nothing . . . things Bradbrook (*Pageant*,
p. 24) points out an echo of St Paul in 2 Cor. 6. 1–
10 ('as having nothyng, and yet possessyng all
thynges'). However, it is unlikely that the spirit of

what Timon is saying is the same as what St Paul
has in mind. Timon's 'nothing' seems to be an extension of his rejection of material possessions and
social bonds, confirmation of his misanthropic
stance. To Wilson Knight ('*Timon of Athens* and
Buddhism', *EC* 30 (1980), 105–23) Timon's
'nothing' is an expression of nirvana, which in
Buddhism is a positive state, and Knight contrasts
this passage with *R2* 5.5.39–41: 'Nor I, nor any man
that but man is, / With nothing shall be pleas'd, till
he be eas'd / With being nothing.'

182 wrack retributive punishment, disaster
(*OED* Wrack *sb*[1] 1 and 2). Hanmer's 'wreck' entails
a reduction in scope, Oliver *ad loc.* and Berry (p.
114) suggest (*OED* Wrack *sb*[2] 3b) 'Weeds, rubbish,
waste, etc., . . . washed down, or ashore by, a river'.
This ties in with the image cluster of flowing water,
on which see above 2.2.3 n.

183 bruit rumour.

FIRST SENATOR These words become your lips as they pass through
   them.   185
SECOND SENATOR And enter in our ears like great triumphers
   In their applauding gates.
TIMON   Commend me to them,
   And tell them that, to ease them of their griefs,
   Their fears of hostile strokes, their achès, losses,
   Their pangs of love, with other incident throes   190
   That nature's fragile vessel doth sustain
   In life's uncertain voyage, I will some kindness do them;
   I'll teach them to prevent wild Alcibiades' wrath.
FIRST SENATOR I like this well; he will return again.
TIMON I have a tree which grows here in my close,   195
   That mine own use invites me to cut down,
   And shortly must I fell it. Tell my friends,
   Tell Athens, in the sequence of degree,
   From high to low throughout, that whoso please
   To stop affliction, let him take his haste,   200
   Come hither ere my tree hath felt the axe,
   And hang himself. I pray you do my greeting.
FLAVIUS Trouble him no further; thus you still shall find him.
TIMON Come not to me again, but say to Athens,
   Timon hath made his everlasting mansion   205
   Upon the beachèd verge of the salt flood,
   Who once a day with his embossèd froth
   The turbulent surge shall cover; thither come,
   And let my grave-stone be your oracle.

203] *Capell;* Trouble . . . shall / Finde him. F

189 achès Disyllabic; see Fausto Cercignani, *Shakespeare's Works and Elizabethan Pronunciation*, 1981, p. 324.

195–202 This story is modelled on Plutarch, 'The Life of Marcus Antonius', and is in most versions of the Timon legend; for Boiardo, see Bullough, VI, 293; for Painter, see Bullough, VI, 294; for Boaistuau, see Bullough, VI, 296. The idea of a tree transformed into a gallows is in Kyd's *Spanish Tragedy* 3.12.A.63–71. The rhetorical figure employed here, delaying the climactic 'hang himself', is called by Puttenham 'the suspender'; Philip Brockbank suggested that it could be a wry private joke on Shakespeare's part to have Timon employ 'the suspender' for this purpose.

205–8 Maxwell comments that this is the one passage 'which suggests recourse to Paynter's version': 'he ordeined himselfe to be interred vpon the

sea shore, that the waues and surges might beate and vexe his dead carcas' (*Life*, p. 166).

206 beachèd verge beach at the edge.

207 Who As grammatical object of 'cover' it refers back to both 'Timon' and 'everlasting mansion' and 'beachèd verge'; 'who' had widely replaced 'whom' (by analogy with other pronouns like 'which' and 'that'). See Franz 333.

207 embossèd foaming: the froth churned up by the sea's 'turbulent surge' and standing out as if moulded in relief; see *OED* Emboss v^1 2. Another explanation, given by Malone, is 'swollen' (*OED* Emboss v^1 1) – as in *Lear* 2.4.224, 'embossed carbuncle'. Compare 4.3.374–5.

208–9 thither . . . oracle Given what the epitaphs actually say, Timon's call for his grave to be visited and his oracles read is deeply ironic and bitter.

Lips, let four words go by and language end;   210
What is amiss, plague and infection mend.
Graves only be men's works, and death their gain;
Sun, hide thy beams, Timon hath done his reign. *Exit Timon*

FIRST SENATOR His discontents are unremovably
    Coupled to nature.   215
SECOND SENATOR Our hope in him is dead. Let us return,
    And strain what other means is left unto us
    In our dear peril.
FIRST SENATOR   It requires swift foot.

                                        Exeunt

[5.2] *Enter two other* SENATORS *with a* MESSENGER

THIRD SENATOR Thou hast painfully discovered; are his files
    As full as thy report?
MESSENGER   I have spoke the least.
    Besides his expedition promises present approach.
FOURTH SENATOR We stand much hazard if they bring not Timon.
MESSENGER I met a courier, one mine ancient friend,   5
    Whom though in general part we were opposed,
    Yet our old love made a particular force,
    And made us speak like friends. This man was riding
    From Alcibiades to Timon's cave

---

210 four] F; sour *Rowe* 214–15] *Capell subst.; one line (possibly prose)* F Act 5, Scene 2 5.2] *Dyce; not in* F 1 SH THIRD SENATOR] *Sisson;* 1 F *(throughout scene)* 4 SH FOURTH SENATOR] *Sisson;* 2 F

210 let . . . end Commentators puzzle over the 'four words'. Do they refer to the 'four words' of the primal act of Creation, 'Let there be light' (Gen. 1.3.), with Timon's un-creating act resulting in an ending of language? Or does 'four' refer to the 'four corners of the earth', 'four elements', 'four seasons', 'four winds'? Rowe's emendation 'sour' makes little sense; why should language end when 'sour words' have gone by?

215 Coupled to nature Part of his nature.

218 dear severe, dire.

Act 5, Scene 2

1 painfully discovered (1) reconnoitred painstakingly (?), (2) delivered distressing news (?) (Riverside).

1 files ranks (of Alcibiades' army).

2 have spoke the least have given the lowest estimate.

3 his expedition . . . approach his haste means he will be here soon.

4 We . . . hazard We run into great danger.

5 one . . . friend one who is an ancient friend, or: one of my ancient friends. For this type of construction, which is obsolete, see *Cym.* 1.6.64–5: 'There is a Frenchman his companion, one / An eminent monsieur.'

6 general part public quarrel.

7 particular personal.

8–12 The messenger links the cause of Alcibiades with that of Timon.

With letters of entreaty, which imported   10
His fellowship i'th'cause against your city,
In part for his sake moved.

Enter the other SENATORS

THIRD SENATOR   Here come our brothers.
FIRST SENATOR No talk of Timon, nothing of him expect,
    The enemy's drum is heard, and fearful scouring
    Doth choke the air with dust. In, and prepare;   15
    Ours is the fall, I fear, our foe's the snare.

                                                    Exeunt

[**5.3**] *Enter a* SOLDIER *in the woods seeking Timon*

SOLDIER By all description this should be the place.
    Who's here? Speak, ho! No answer? What is this?
    [*Reads*] 'Timon is dead, who hath outstretched his span;
    Some beast read this; there does not live a man.'
    Dead, sure, and this his grave. What's on this tomb   5
    I cannot read; the character I'll take with wax;
    Our captain hath in every figure skill,
    An aged interpreter, though young in days.
    Before proud Athens he's set down by this,
    Whose fall the mark of his ambition is.   *Exit*   10

13 SH FIRST SENATOR] *Capell;* 3 F   14 enemy's] *Johnson;* Enemies F; enemies *Theobald²*   16 foe's] *Johnson;* Foes F; foes'
Oliver **Act 5, Scene 3**   5.3] *Dyce; not in* F   2 Who's] F3; Whose F   3 SD] *Staunton; not in* F   4 read] F; rear'd *Theobald*
(*proposed by Warburton*)

10–11 **imported ... fellowship** conveyed a
request for his participation.
12 **In part ... moved** Partly on his (Timon's)
behalf.
14 **fearful scouring** scurrying about, out of fear
and causing fear.
16* **Ours ... snare** Our lot is the fall, our foe's
lot is to have set the snare. This reading follows

Johnson's emendation; if one keeps F's 'Foes', as
many editors do, the second half would read 'our
foes are the snare'.

Act 5, Scene 3
8 **aged** highly experienced (allowing a paradoxical play on the more usual sense, old in years).

[5.4] *Trumpets sound. Enter* ALCIBIADES *with his powers before Athens*

ALCIBIADES Sound to this coward and lascivious town
     Our terrible approach.

                   Sounds a parley

         The SENATORS *appear upon the walls*

     Till now you have gone on and filled the time
     With all licentious measure, making your wills
     The scope of justice. Till now, myself and such   5
     As slept within the shadow of your power
     Have wandered with our traversed arms, and breathed
     Our sufferance vainly. Now the time is flush,
     When crouching marrow in the bearer strong
     Cries, of itself, 'No more'. Now breathless wrong   10
     Shall sit and pant in your great chairs of ease,
     And pursy insolence shall break his wind
     With fear and horrid flight.
FIRST SENATOR   Noble and young,
     When thy first griefs were but a mere conceit,
     Ere thou hadst power, or we had cause of fear,   15
     We sent to thee, to give thy rages balm,
     To wipe out our ingratitude, with loves
     Above their quantity.
SECOND SENATOR   So did we woo

Act 5, Scene 4   5.4] *Dyce; not in* F   18 SH SECOND SENATOR] *Rowe;* 2 F *(throughout scene)*

Act 5, Scene 4
  1 lascivious (1) inclined to lust, (2) luxurious. It
is remarkable that Alcibiades charges the Athenians
with vices with which he himself may be charged.
  2 terrible terrifying.
  4 all . . . measure the extreme of licentiousness.
  5 scope measure.
  6 slept remained unawares.
  7 traversed arms Meaning uncertain: small-
arms held in a non-firing position (Riverside) or
arms folded, signifying dejection.
  7 breathed complained about.
  8 vainly in vain.
  8 flush ripe.
  9 crouching marrow strength and resolution,
hitherto subdued.

  10 breathless wrong wrongdoers breathless
with fear (the abstract concept for the concrete).
  12 pursy short of breath, flatulent; see Philip
Edwards (ed.), *Ham.* 3.4.154 n.
  12 insolence The leaders of state who, whilst
they were in power, showed arrogance and contempt to their subjects; in *Ham.* it is the 'insolence
of office' (3.1.73).
  12 shall . . . wind shall fart (or pant for breath).
  13 horrid terrified.
  14 griefs grievances.
  14 conceit idea (not yet expressed in military
action).
  18 Above their quantity Greater than your
griefs (14) and rages (16).

Transformèd Timon to our city's love
By humble message and by promised means.   20
We were not all unkind, nor all deserve
The common stroke of war.

FIRST SENATOR   These walls of ours
Were not erected by their hands from whom
You have received your grief; nor are they such
That these great towers, trophies, and schools should fall   25
For private faults in them.

SECOND SENATOR   Nor are they living
Who were the motives that you first went out;
Shame, that they wanted cunning, in excess
Hath broke their hearts. March, noble lord,
Into our city with thy banners spread;   30
By decimation and a tithèd death,
If thy revenges hunger for that food
Which nature loathes, take thou the destined tenth,
And by the hazard of the spotted die
Let die the spotted.

FIRST SENATOR   All have not offended;   35
For those that were, it is not square to take
On those that are, revenge; crimes, like lands,
Are not inherited. Then, dear countryman,
Bring in thy ranks, but leave without thy rage;

---

22 SH FIRST SENATOR] *Rowe;* I F *(throughout scene)* 24 grief] F; griefs *Theobald* 28 Shame . . . excess] *Theobald;* (Shame that they wanted, cunning in excess) F; Shame (that they wanted cunning in excess) F2

20 means money, or privileges.

24 they i.e. those who have inflicted grief upon you. Theobald emends to 'griefs', supposing this to be what 'they' refers to. But 26 indicates that persons are meant by 'they'.

27 the motives . . . out the movers of the motion banishing you (Steevens in Johnson/ Steevens⁵).

28* Shame . . . excess 'Excessive shame that they lacked low cunning (to banish you)' (Theobald (subst)). F is obscure and probably corrupt. Some editors read 'cunning in excess' (F2–4, Rowe). Is 'cunning' to be understood in a positive sense (as knowledge and understanding – see Mason, *Comments* (1785), p. 305, and Knight) or as crafty deceit (Arden, Riverside)?

31 decimation selection of every tenth for punishment. This is the only instance in Shakespeare.

Honigmann ('Timon', p. 4) points out that the reference to 'decimation' 'probably derives from Plutarch's description of Antonius' punishment of his soldiers at the siege of Phraata', taken from 'The Life of Marcus Antonius', but is an anachronism.

31 tithèd death death of every tenth person; synonymous with 'decimation'.

34 spotted die The singular form of 'dice', with spots indicating the numbers on each face of the die.

35 spotted guilty.

36–7 that were . . . that are who were alive at the time . . . who are now alive. This is one of the few hints to indicate that a considerable period of time must have elapsed since Alcibiades' banishment in 3.5.

36 square just, equitable (see *OED* Square *a* II8).

39 without outside.

Spare thy Athenian cradle and those kin   40
Which in the bluster of thy wrath must fall
With those that have offended. Like a shepherd
Approach the fold and cull th'infected forth,
But kill not all together.

SECOND SENATOR   What thou wilt,
Thou rather shalt enforce it with thy smile   45
Than hew to't with thy sword.

FIRST SENATOR   Set but thy foot
Against our rampired gates, and they shall ope;
So thou wilt send thy gentle heart before,
To say thou'lt enter friendly.

SECOND SENATOR   Throw thy glove,
Or any token of thine honour else,   50
That thou wilt use the wars as thy redress
And not as our confusion; all thy powers
Shall make their harbour in our town, till we
Have sealed thy full desire.

ALCIBIADES   Then there's my glove;
Descend and open your unchargèd ports.   55
Those enemies of Timon's and mine own
Whom you yourselves shall set out for reproof
Fall, and no more; and, to atone your fears
With my more noble meaning, not a man
Shall pass his quarter or offend the stream   60
Of regular justice in your city's bounds
But shall be remedied to your public laws
At heaviest answer.

BOTH SENATORS   'Tis most nobly spoken.

ALCIBIADES Descend, and keep your words.

Enter a MESSENGER

44 all together] F3; altogether F   55 Descend] F2; Defend F   62 remedied to] F; render'd to *Dyce*   63 SH BOTH
SENATORS] *Sisson; Both.* F

41 **bluster** boisterous storm, tempest.

43 **cull . . . forth** pick out.

47 **rampired** barricaded.

48 **So** If only.

50 **token** pledge.

52 **confusion** ruin, overthrow.

53 **make their harbour** find safe lodging.

54 **sealed . . . desire** completed and officially
confirmed all your demands.

55 **unchargèd** unassailed; in this form, the only
instance in Shakespeare.

57 **reproof** punishment.

58–9 **atone . . . meaning** appease your fears by
explaining to you my nobler intentions. *OED* Atone
v I 1: 'to set at one', 'bring into concord', 'reconcile';
as in *R2* 1.1.202: 'Since we cannot atone you'.

60 **quarter** The place where troops are stationed.

62 **remedied** handed over.

63 **At . . . answer** With severest punishment to
be applied.

64 SD The MESSENGER is most likely identical
with the SOLDIER of 5.3.0 SD.

MESSENGER My noble general, Timon is dead,   65
    Entombed upon the very hem o'th'sea,
    And on his grave-stone this insculpture, which
    With wax I brought away, whose soft impression
    Interprets for my poor ignorance.
ALCIBIADES (*Reads the Epitaph*)
    Here lies a wretched corse, of wretched soul bereft;   70
    Seek not my name; a plague consume you, wicked caitiffs left.
    Here lie I, Timon, who alive all living men did hate;
    Pass by and curse thy fill, but pass and stay not here thy gait.
    These well express in thee thy latter spirits.
    Though thou abhorredst in us our human griefs,   75
    Scornedst our brains' flow, and those our droplets which
    From niggard nature fall, yet rich conceit
    Taught thee to make vast Neptune weep for aye
    On thy low grave, on faults forgiven. Dead
    Is noble Timon, of whose memory   80
    Hereafter more. Bring me into your city,
    And I will use the olive with my sword,
    Make war breed peace, make peace stint war, make each
    Prescribe to other, as each other's leech.
    Let our drums strike.   85

                                            Exeunt

69 SH, SD] *Alcibiades reades the Epitaph.* F (*centred*)   73 *gait*] *Pope;* gate F   76 brains'] *Dyce²;* Braines F; brine's *Hanmer;* brain's *Johnson/Steevens*

67 **insculpture** inscription.
69 **Interprets** Serves as interpreter.
69 **for** in the place of.
70–3 Sisson, *Readings*, II, 179, considers these lines as two alternative epitaphs, since the 'third line names Timon, where the second adjures us not to seek his name'. Sisson thinks that Shakespeare 'rejected the first, deleted it, and wrote the second in its place, and that the compositor printed both' (pp. 179–80). But the lines have also provoked sophisticated interpretations, as a reflex of the play's and Timon's own contradictions (Lesley W. Brill, 'Truth and *Timon of Athens*', *MLQ*, 40 (1979), 26; Walter C. Foreman, *The Music of the Close*, 1978, p. 207). For a further discussion of the sources of the epitaphs see Supplementary Notes, p. 180 below.
70 *corse* Obsolete form of 'corpse'.
71 *caitiffs* wretches. This is the only term by which Shakespeare deviates from the wording in North's translation of Plutarch; but the term 'caitiff' is used in Painter's rendering of the epitaph, even though in a different context; he has Timon

speak of himself in these terms: 'My wretched caitiff days, / Expired now and past . . .' (Painter, 28th Novel).
73 *stay . . . gait* do not interrupt your walking on.
74 **latter** recent.
75–9 Alcibiades sees Neptune (the sea) as weeping over Timon's grave; Timon, by 'rich conceit', has thus made the sea his chief mourner.
76 **Scornedst . . . flow** You scorn our tears (of mourning).
77 **niggard nature** miserly nature, in that it shows little grief and few tears.
82 **olive** Emblem of peace.
83–4 **Make . . . leech** Berry sees three propositions contained in these lines: (1) 'peace and war will prescribe to each other, like physicians, for the common good'; (2) 'peace and war . . . will fasten upon each other, like bloodsuckers'; (3) 'the first and second propositions are simultaneously true. Peace and war are not exclusive states, but reactivating impulses in the symbiosis of social existence' (p. 118).

SUPPLEMENTARY NOTES

1.1.6 bounty 'Bounty', together with its derivatives 'bounteous' and 'bountiful', is very frequent in the play. ('Bounty' occurs nine times, and twice in its plural form 'bounties'; 'bounteous' is used four times, and 'bountiful(ly)' three times.) With one exception (4.3.413), it is always used in relation to Timon, but its meaning varies depending on who uses it and to what purpose.

In its most general sense, 'bounty' denotes 'Goodness in general, worth, virtue' (*OED* 1). In a more specific sense, it signifies goodness 'shown in giving, gracious liberality, munificence' (*OED* 4). Aristotle understood 'liberality' as a virtue, with the condition that 'the mean in relation to wealth' (*Nicomachean Ethics*, IV, i, 1) is observed: 'the liberal man is one who spends in proportion to his means as well as on the right objects' (IV, i, 23). If, however, liberality turns into a mode of excess, if it results in wasting one's substance, it becomes a vice and is then named 'prodigality' (IV, i, 2 and 5; as such, it is used in *Timon* at 2.2.159 by Steward Flavius; by the servant Lucius at 3.4.12; and by Apemantus at 4.3.285).

Davidson (p. 187) discusses 1.1.275 ('He pours it out') and points out that 'the pouring out from a cornucopia appears as an essential detail in both *Prodigalità* and *Pietà*'. He concludes: 'To have a liberal hand may thus be a sign of immense goodness and nobility, or it may mean unpardonable folly.'

In Timon's circle the term is used by those who enjoy the social glamour of being Timon's guests. This means that when they use 'bounty' as a term of praise (as in 1.1.6, where the Poet refers to the situation as 'Magic of bounty'; or when Third Lord refers to Timon as 'the very soul of bounty' at 1.2.198), they have their own interests uppermost in mind.

'Bounty' takes on another layer of meaning when it refers to a gift or an object that can be 'tasted'. Before going in to attend Timon's banquet, First Lord says 'Come, shall we in, and taste Lord Timon's bounty?' (1.1.273). Cupid's greeting of Timon also refers to the term in this sense: 'Hail to thee, worthy Timon, and to all that of his bounties taste!' (1.2.110), and so does the Poet's welcoming of Timon in the woods (5.1.49). Phrynia and Timandra flatter Timon by calling him 'bounteous' while at the same time unashamedly asking for more gold (4.3.168).

Steward Flavius considers Timon's spending out of proportion to his means; it has crossed the boundary between liberality and prodigality (see 2.2.159–60 and 4.2.41). Timon himself, in an attempt at self-justification, tells his Steward 'No villainous bounty yet hath passed my heart' and then goes on to declare 'Unwisely, not ignobly, have I given' (2.2.167–8). Lucullus, when dealing with Timon's request for a loan, confides to Timon's servant Flaminius: 'Thy lord's a bountiful gentleman, but thou art wise . . .' (3.1.31–2); he qualifies the term 'bountiful' by placing it in opposition to 'wise', which quality he places above bounty, in contrast to Timon. A further use is when Timon himself applies the term to nature ('The bounteous housewife nature' (4.3.413)) which connects with his earlier address to the 'Common mother . . . / Whose womb unmeasurable and infinite breast / Teems and feeds all' (4.3.179–81). According to Adelman, Nature's (i.e. female) bounty is placed in opposition to male paucity (Adelman, pp. 165–6 and p. 172). Timon's fantasy of male bounty, which amounts to taking upon himself the function of nurturance, comes to an end when he has to recognise the plenteous bosom of mother earth. For further investigation of the term in Shakespeare, see Peter Erickson, *Patriarchal Structures in Shakespeare's Drama*, 1985.

1.1.30–1 The verbal skirmishes of Poet and Painter concerning their respective crafts (in addition to this passage, see 1.1.76–80 and 92–5) may be related to the *Paragone* (i.e. 'comparison') debate. This relation was first proposed by Blunt, and is also explored by John Dixon Hunt ('Shakespeare and the *Paragone*: a reading of *Timon of Athens*', in *Images of Shakespeare*, ed. Werner Habicht *et al.*, 1988, pp. 47–63). The *Paragone* concerns the rivalry of the liberal arts between themselves and with other arts. The comparison between the arts of poetry and painting is one of the issues: can one of these arts claim to represent nature more cogently and with a higher degree of faithfulness than the other? In his *Trattato della Pittura*, which was edited at the beginning of the nineteenth century under the title *Paragone*, Leonardo da Vinci set out to compare the arts of poetry and painting, since both of them professed to be imitators of nature. In doing so he found himself within a long and ancient tradition of setting off the two arts against each other, beginning with the pronouncement by Simonides of Keos (*c.* 556–468 BC) that 'Painting is dumb Poetry, and Poetry is speaking Painting' (see Plutarch, *De Gloria Atheniensium* 346f–347c) through Plato (*Republic* X, 595bff.), Aristotle (*Poetics* I.4.1447a, II.1.1448a, VI.15.1450a), Cicero (*Brutus* XVIII.70; *Orator* II.5 and 8; *De Oratore* II.xvi.69, III.vii.26) and Quintilian (*Institutio Oratoria* II.xiii.8, V.xii.21, XII.x.1–12) to Horace (*Ars Poetica* 361: 'Ut pictura poesis' – a poem is like a picture). Leonardo makes it clear that he regards painting as closer to nature than poetry can ever be, simply by the power of its medium, since the poet has to use words which bear no direct relationship to the reality they profess to imitate: 'The eye which is said to be the window of the soul, is the principal means by which *senso comune* may so copiously and magnificently consider the infinite works of nature; and the second way is the ear, made noble by being told about things that the eye has seen . . . [P]oet, if you were to figure a narrative as if painting with your pen, the painter with his brush would more easily make it satisfying and less tedious to comprehend. If you claim that painting [is] mute poetry, then the painter could say that poetry [is] blind painting' (Claire J. Farago, *Leonardo da Vinci's 'Paragone': A Critical Interpretation with a New Edition of the Text in the 'Codex Urbinas'*, 1988, p. 209). By making the eye the chief mediator for the perception of nature and by assigning to poetry the sense of hearing which is at one further remove from the imitation of nature, he overturns the order of senses suggested by Simonides, and claims superiority for the art of painting.

This topic attracts English writers of the sixteenth and early seventeenth centuries. Sir Philip Sidney, following Aristotle, defines poetry as 'an arte of imitation . . . that is to say, a representing, counterfetting, or figuring foorth: to speake metaphorically, a speaking picture . . .' (*An Apology for Poetry*, in Smith, I, 158). Edmund Spenser, in stanza 2 of the proem to Book III of *The Faerie Queene*, reflects on how 'Chastity' can be most adequately represented; comparing painting and poetry, there is no doubt in his mind that painting must fall far short of poetry when ideas are to be represented ('Poets wit, that passeth Painter farre / In picturing the parts of beautie daint . . .'), although the terms he uses to describe the poet's potential achievements are all borrowed from pictorial representation ('in colourd showes' (stanza 3), 'in living colours' (stanza 4)), and the verb 'picture' is used for representations in words ('Ut pictura poesis'). Shakespeare brings this issue into focus in *Lucrece* when Lucrece, after having been raped, casts her eyes about for a picture which could express a grief similar to hers. Eventually she finds it in 'a piece / Of skilful painting' (1366–7) representing the siege and fall of Troy, and here it is the grief and despair of Hecuba that captures her attention. However, in the attempt to identify with Hecuba's sorrows she realises that in the painter's depiction of Hecuba's woes what is lacking is what would let her give adequate expression to her grief: words. 'And therefore Lucrece swears he [the painter] did her wrong / To give her so much grief and not a tongue' (1462–3). Ben Jonson is the most outspoken defender of the poet's superiority, and his argument is based on the notion that the human faculties addressed through the arts mirror a ranking of the arts themselves: '*Poetry*, and *picture*, are Arts of a like nature; and both are busie about imitation . . . Yet of the two, the Pen is more noble then the Pencill. For that can speake to the Understanding; the other, but to the Sense' (*Timber, or Discoveries*, in *Ben Jonson*, ed. C. H. Herford and P. and E. Simpson, 11 vols., 1947, VIII, 609–10). In several of his poems, this distinction – of poetry representing and addressing the mind and painting only the senses – is elaborated at length, most clearly in his poem 'The Mind' ('The Underwood', LXXXIV, 4). (Basing his argument on the hierarchy of mind and sense, he dismisses the painter with an arrogant gesture – 'Painter, yo'are come, but may be gone, / Now I have better thought thereon, / This worke I can performe alone; / And give you reasons more than one.' And his dominant reason is that the painter's hand, bound to represent sensuous objects only, 'will never hit, / To draw a thing that cannot sit'. So all his attempts will fall short of representing a mind faithfully and truly – 'these are like a Mind, not it'.) Another example is no. 25 of 'Ungathered Verse'. Nevertheless, Jonson sat for his portrait, self-contradictory as ever.

1.1.99 **talents** In the play, reference to talents indicates contradictory value: there are three different groups of textual references – in the first, rather low figures are mentioned, in the second rather high ones and in the third, an indefinite quantity.[1]

These apparent inconsistencies have been explained in various ways with different objectives in mind. They have been taken as evidence of the 'dual authorship' theory,[2] based on the hypothesis that Chapman produced a version of the play which Shakespeare revised, and that in this process he introduced out-of-proportion figures since he did not know the value of a talent.[3] An altogether different process of revision was suggested by T. J. B. Spencer.[4] He proposes that Shakespeare, in the course of writing the play, '(1) became aware that he did not know the value of a talent, (2) found out this piece of information from some person or some book, and (3) then in several places got his figures right'.[5] The figures given in the first group of references may be considered as Shakespeare's corrections. The indefinite figures would indicate that he had not yet made up his mind. The bizarre formulation 'fifty – five hundred talents' (3.2.31) Spencer explains as 'revealing Shakespeare's uncertainty'; 'it represents his manuscript indication for "fifty five hundred . . ."'[6]

Going back to Shakespeare's sources, Maxwell offers yet another explanation. He discovered that in money matters Lucian uses small figures, whereas Plutarch mentions large ones. 'I think it is possible that Shakespeare took his figures from Lucian in the first instance, and then got into difficulties by turning to Plutarch for an idea of debts on the grand scale.'[7]

All these explanations are based on hypotheses regarding Shakespeare's workshop, and they all agree that, in a finalised version of the play, the wide range of figures would have been harmonised. An altogether different explanation is offered by Lewis Walker.[8] He suggests that the large differences in numbers may have been intentional; 'Shakespeare might have chosen these sums to make a specific point about friendship'[9] – that is, Timon wanted to test his friends by making these extravagant claims.[10] Interesting as this suggestion is, it does not offer any clue to the indefinite number of talents.

1.1.160–5 **Painting . . . like it** 'Natural man' does not carry connotations of man in a state of nature, whether pre-lapsarian or Hobbesian ('man to man being as wolf to wolf'), but refers to *man's nature*, a

---

[1] The first group is centred around Timon's loan to Ventidius: a Messenger informs Timon about Ventidius's debt of five talents (1.1.99); Ventidius offers to repay his debt; he speaks of 'those talents' without giving a precise figure (1.2.6); finally, Timon approaches Ventidius with a view to having 'those five talents' repaid (2.2.221). Within this group of references the figures given are perfectly consistent, and even the mention of 'those talents' appears sensible in the given dialogic context. However, the figures are very different in the second group of references, when Timon sends out his servants to request loans from his friends. It is important to notice that these two groups partly overlap. Timon requests fifty talents each from three of his lordly friends (2.2.181–5). His request to the Senators is 'A thousand talents' (2.2.191). In answer to Timon's request, Lucius speaks of 'fifty – five hundred talents' (3.2.31). In the third rather compact group of references – all occurring within two dozen lines in 3.2 – an indefinite number of talents is mentioned. Second Stranger reports that Timon has tried to borrow 'so many talents' (9–10); Lucius asserts that had he been asked he would not have denied Timon 'so many talents' (19); Servilius, when conveying Timon's request to Lucius, speaks of 'so many talents' (29). This last occasion is the most surprising one, since in this situation one would expect a specific amount to be mentioned.

[2] J. M. Robertson, *Shakespeare and Chapman*, 1917, pp. 123–81.

[3] Maxwell, *Life*, gives figures for estimating the value of the talent in 1957, varying from £100 to £180; nowadays the figures would of course have to be much higher (p. 94).

[4] Spencer, 'Shakespeare learns the value of money: the dramatist at work on *Timon of Athens*', *S.Sur.* 6 (1953), 75–8.

[5] *Ibid.*, p. 76.

[6] *Ibid.*, p. 77.

[7] Maxwell, *Life*, pp. 95–6.

[8] Walker, 'Money in *Timon of Athens*', *PQ* 57 (1978), 269–71.

[9] *Ibid.*, p. 269.

[10] Walker makes reference to Cicero's *De Amicitia*, where he advises that friends can be tested by large sums.

mixing of good and bad. Oliver interprets 'the natural man' as 'man as he really is, not the man whom dishonesty makes pretend to be better than he is'. Hibbard sees a link with *Lear* 3.4.106: 'Thou art the thing itself.' In Timon's subsequent reasoning about man being 'but outside', we find no clear indication as to what the 'inside' location could be; instead we are offered as an explanation: 'dishonour traffics with man's nature'. This seems to say that man's nature is to engage in dishonourable dealings and that therefore 'He', i.e. 'man', 'is but outside', meaning that man's nature is tainted with a false semblance. (See Maxwell's persuasive reading of this line.) As to Timon's third statement about 'these pencilled figures', Dr Johnson explained that 'Pictures have no hypocrisy; they are what they profess to be'; but if this might mean that painting is honest and truthful as an art that exposes underlying truth by depicting what can be seen also truthfully, one might also argue that painting is complicit in a corrupt pleasure in false appearance, and knows that it is false. Arguing along these lines, John Dixon Hunt concluded his thoughts upon the meaning of this dark passage by asserting as Timon's 'primary meaning' that 'painting shows only the outside and none of that within which passeth show' and that 'Timon's praise of painting's meretricious signs is . . . apt' ('Shakespeare and the *Paragone*', p. 53). According to this interpretation Timon would show his tainted mind by accepting a painting as welcome even though he takes a low view of its moral value. For Johnson and his followers, who saw in painting a truthful representation of man's real (= ideal) nature, Timon's praise of the Painter's work would be perfectly congruent with their view of Timon's admirable moral nature. The passage's conceptual looseness, ambivalent terms and inconclusive logic make it impossible to choose either of these definite interpretations. One can ascribe its darkness either to the unfinished state of Shakespeare's manuscript or to the dramatic character Timon's personality and mind – his views contradictory, his conceptual positions muddled, a man far from convincing in his roles as connoisseur or patron of the arts or as moral preceptor of his society. Perhaps he should be condemned for putting on an outward show and relishing its pleasures, those of the role which everyone around him expects him to play: that of a generous patron of the arts. In this sense he is 'Even such as [he] give[s] out'. Yet the play as a whole denies any such certain judgement of Timon in his generous phase.

1.2.0 SD.I **banquet** The banquet should not be seen only in the most obvious terms as a social entertainment; we should also recognise there is a wider emblematic meaning and consider it as a Banquet of Sense. Whereas the Platonic Banquet represents an 'ascent from sense to the higher powers of the soul', the Banquet of Sense represents 'a descent from sight to the sense capable only of material gratification' (Frank Kermode, 'The Banquet of Sense', *Bulletin of the John Rylands Library* 44 (1961/2), 83). That this is Shakespeare's intention is corroborated by references to the five senses in the text: Cupid points out that the maskers (i.e. the Ladies as Amazons) are meant to gratify the senses (1.2.112–13), including those which according to the Neo-Platonic hierarchy were considered base – that is, 'taste' and 'touch', which could only function through immediate contact with their objects. When Cupid introduces the masque of Ladies, the role of patron of the five senses is attributed to Timon (1.2.111–12). Here is reason enough to assume that the banquet, an essential part of which is the masque (see Supplementary Note 1.2.117 SD.2), is like similar literary banquets, Spenser's 'The Banquet of Sin' in *The Faerie Queene* I.iv.15 ff., and Milton's description of Satan's temptation of Christ (*Paradise Regained* II, 348 ff.). Kermode concludes that 'this little entertainment is intended as part of that unspoken criticism of Timon's misconception of Honour and Nobility' ('Banquet of Sense', p. 81).

John Doebler (*Shakespeare's Speaking Pictures: Studies in Iconic Imagery*, 1974, pp. 151–2) describes the medieval roots of the concept, and judges the Renaissance Banquet of the Five Senses to be a later variation of the medieval Banquet of Sins, with the appropriate negative associations. The Neo-Platonic view of the hierarchy of the senses led people to 'associate the senses with sinful overgratification'. On the other hand, he also relates Timon's banquet to the Last Supper, since both function as occasions for betrayal. Timon's banquet serves to introduce 'the gluttony of parasites rather than the community of true friends'.

1.2.109 SD.2, 117 SD.2 **CUPID** Like the LADIES *as Amazons*, whom he introduces, Cupid is characterised by an 'iconographic doubleness' (Fulton, p. 283). As far as we can gather from the play itself, the stage audience seems to receive Cupid in a welcoming way, gladly joining in the entertainment that he provides. The only hostile critical voice is that of Apemantus (1.2.119–32). Fulton calls attention to the fact that, as in other Renaissance representations, Cupid 'probably would have appeared blindfolded' and that this condition is open to all kinds of moralistic interpretations. It may be seen as a token of man having been deprived of his moral sense (sight) or as hinting at 'the basic immorality of erotic experience' (Fulton, p. 285). Cupid's sinister potential is corroborated by negative connotations given to him in representations by Spenser, Ben Jonson and Shakespeare himself. (For detailed references, see Fulton, p. 286.)

1.2.117 SD.2 The *masque of* LADIES *as Amazons* is the highlight of Timon's entertainment; it includes an onstage audience. When *The Lords rise from table . . . and . . . each single out an Amazon, and all dance, men with women*, this festive occasion could be seen as 'the most far-reaching use of the masque as a social symbol' (Inga-Stina Ewbank, ' "These pretty devices": a study of masques in plays', in *A Book of Masques in Honour of Allardyce Nicoll*, ed. T. J. B. Spencer and Stanley Wells, 1967, pp. 407–8); it is 'tied to rules of flattery', and 'gathers to itself symbolically all the elements of Timon's earlier life: lavish expenditure, social grace, ceremony and ostentation', an 'emphatic image of the excessive adulation given to Timon' (Ewbank, 'Study', p. 418). Thomas McAlindon agrees, calling it 'treacherous entertainment', 'a ritual affirmation of love and union which turns out to be a monstrous negation of everything it affirms' (*English Renaissance Tragedy*, 1986, p. 41). As such, it is inwardly hollow and false, an empty show. Considering the use of masques in Elizabethan and Jacobean tragedy, Cyrus Hoy concludes that they 'come to function almost too conveniently as emblems for rituals gone awry' ('Masques', p. 122). Ewbank views the second banquet (3.6) as another matching show, in which Timon deliberately echoes Cupid's words; it represents the 'stripping' and rejection of flattery, as the first represented acceptance of it. The staged 'discovery' of the contents of the dishes, the throwing of water in the faces of the guests to the accompaniment of abuse, inverts the ritual of flattery in 1.2.

Amazons are often referred to in Elizabethan literature, where particular attention is paid to Hippolyta and Penthesilea (who, as Amazonian queen, assisted the Trojans). The myth of the Amazons and their literary representation have been documented by Fulton; Celeste T. Wright, 'The Amazons in Elizabethan literature', *SP* 37 (1940), 433–56; Simon Shepherd, *Amazons and Warrior Women*, 1981; and L. A. Montrose, ' "Shaping fantasies": figurations of gender and power in Elizabethan culture', in *Representing the English Renaissance*, ed. Stephen Greenblatt, 1988, pp. 31–64. Whereas classical authors tended to regard Amazons as estimable women, Elizabethan authors took a different view of them as showing political and sexual disobedience to patriarchal rules and licentious aggressiveness towards male power. 'Amazon' was at the time a cant term, meaning 'a bold prostitute', for which Williams (I, 16) and Fulton (p. 292 and n. 21) provide ample evidence. Such a view has been traced back to an anxiety about female power. Thus, in Spenser's *The Faerie Queene*, Book V, Radigund represents a type of Amazonian woman who denies obedience to men; she is full of aggressive lust and has an unbridled will. Her defeat by Britomart (representing chastity), who subdues her in order to liberate her lover Artegall (representing justice), indicates the degree to which social order depends upon female submission and women's sexual discipline. It is one of the paradoxes of the Elizabethan attitude toward Amazons that, despite disapproval of them in their relation to order and patriarchal customs, they were nevertheless regarded as 'picturesque ornaments to a pageant or a romance' ('The Amazons', Wright, p. 456). The Amazons are welcomed by Timon and well received by his guests; they are meant to 'feast' Timon's and his guests' eyes; but we also have Apemantus's devastating comments on this masque (1.2.119–32). The Amazons in their perversion of orthodox male and female roles might be similar to the perverse figures of dwarf, eunuch and androgyne in Jonson's *Volpone* and function as symbols for disorder and licentiousness.

5.1.208–9 Timon frequently impresses, if not actually imposing, on others a view of how he wishes to be seen. This penchant for directing what others should think of him manifests itself in the way he deals with his epitaphs. When the representatives of Athens, together with Flavius, visit Timon in his exile and try to win him over to their side, he tells them that he is about to write his epitaph (5.1.175) and that he wants the Athenians to know about his fate, expressly saying 'thither come' (208). The fact that his is not an invitation to celebrate a pious mourning-ritual becomes obvious when he adds 'And let my grave-stone be your oracle' (209). They are to stay away from him whilst he is still alive. Timon is as uncompromising as ever in turning away visitors, even former friends, from his self-imposed exile. Later, in 5.3.4 and more particularly in 5.4.70–4, we learn that what this self-created oracular voice has to impart is nothing but abuse of the living. The earlier invitation to visit his grave only serves the sinister purpose of making sure that his message actually reaches those for whom it is meant – which cannot be said of his long-drawn-out curses in Act 4.

As an epitaphic voice, it assumes the authority of the last word spoken. The fiction of a voice speaking from beyond the grave having been established, the living, by being exposed to it, are implicated in this state of death. They are struck dumb, as if visited by someone not human; and it is this other-than-human authority that Timon lays claim to. (Paul de Man has developed such ideas in his analysis of Wordsworth's *Essays Upon Epitaphs* ('Autobiography as de-facement', *MLN* 94,5 (1979), 919–30)). Timon's intent to make his voice an oracle for the living is not a creative act; it forestalls the possibility of communicative acts and is thus a powerful claim for language to end.

5.3.3–4 If one takes these lines as the Soldier's comment on realising that Timon must be dead, doubts are raised about the word 'read' (4), since as yet there is nothing to be read; the inscription on the tomb is only noticed later. Theobald, recognising this inconsistency, at Warburton's suggestion substitutes 'rear'd', thereby giving the deictic 'this' in line 2 a material object, 'the rude Pile of Earth heap'd up for *Timon*'s Grave'. Thus, his emendation rests on a hypothetical staging which is highly uncertain. Nevertheless, Theobald's reading was almost universally accepted in the eighteenth and the first half of the nineteenth century. Staunton (1859) was the first to suggest reading this passage as Timon's epitaph. But this reading also relied on hypothetical assumptions and scenic visualisations which are listed by the editors of Cam. (1865) as follows:

(1) 'this' in line 2 has to be identified as an inscription.
(2) The fact that the Soldier can read only one of two inscriptions is explained by assuming the use of different languages (or different language signs).
(3) To add to the plausibility of setting off a legible inscription from an illegible one, the editors attribute different locations to them.
(4) Their most important contribution, however, is to link the epitaph problem of 5.3 with the one in 5.4.70–3, where Alcibiades reads out the wax copy of the inscription which the Soldier had taken in 5.3. Faced with three inscriptions altogether, it is conceivable that 'The author may have changed his mind and forgotten to obliterate what was inconsistent with the sequel, or the text may have been tampered with by some less accomplished playwright' (Cam. note xvii).

What is merely suggested here as a possibility is radically put into effect in the Oxford text (1986): 5.3.3–4 is deleted altogether. Confronted with a situation in which f leaves all options open but implicitly calls for a more precise reading, the editor must decide what degree of emendation is justifiable. To improve on the structural deficiencies of the play cannot, I believe, be regarded as an editor's task. I consider the Oxford editors' deletion of the two lines to go too far, particularly in a play that shows many similar indeterminacies and apparent inconsistencies. I therefore let the inconsistencies stand rather than engage in what is, in effect, rewriting the text.

5.4.70–3 The source for the two epitaphs is North's translation of Plutarch's 'The Life of Marcus Antonius' (Bullough, vi, 252); the only item that deviates from North's wording is Shakespeare's 'caitiffs' (71) for 'wretches' in North's Plutarch. A possible source for 'caitiffs' is William Painter's rendering of the epitaph in his account of the Timon story (Novel 28, 'Of the Straunge and Beastlie Nature of Timon of Athens, Enemie to Mankinde, with his Death, Buriall, and Epitaphe'): 'My wretched catife dayes, / Expired now and past . . .' According to Plutarch's account, the first epitaph is reported to have been made by Timon himself, whereas the second one is passed off as the work of the poet Callimachus. This distinction reappears in Painter's version and remains unquestioned by critics and editors. On closer inspection it can, however, be seen that both epitaphs are partially modified versions of Greek epitaphs collected in Book vii of the *Greek Anthology* under the heading 'Sepulchral Epigrams'. What passes in Plutarch as Timon's own epitaph derives from an anonymous epigram with the headline 'On Timon the Misanthrope' (No. 313): 'Here I lie, having broken away from my luckless soul. My name ye shall not learn, and may ye come, bad men, to a bad end.' Plutarch's second epitaph is modelled on at least two epigrams of the same cycle – one being the first part of an epigram attributed (doubtfully) to Callimachus: 'Wish me not well, thou evil-hearted, but pass on . . .' (No. 318); the other composed by Hegesippus (No. 320): 'All around the tomb are sharp thorns and stakes; you will hurt your feet if you go near. I, Timon the misanthrope, dwell in it. But pass on – wish me all evil if you like, only pass on.' (The translation is by W. R. Paton, Loeb Classical Library, ii, 1917.)

TEXTUAL ANALYSIS

Timon of Athens was first published in the Folio edition of Shakespeare's works in 1623, with the title *The Life of Tymon of Athens*, placed between *Romeo and Juliet* and *Julius Caesar*, and occupying pp. 80–98 of the 'Tragedies' part of the volume, with an added list of 'Actors Names' printed on p. 99. The fact that there is a gap of nine pages before *Julius Caesar* begins on p. 109, together with other bibliographical evidence, reveals that *Timon* was not originally intended to occupy this place. There is further evidence that it replaced *Troilus and Cressida*, which had to be withdrawn, most likely for copyright reasons, even though the printing had already begun.[1] Since *Timon* is a shorter play by far than *Troilus and Cressida* (*Tim.* has 2607 lines and *Tro.* 3592 lines according to the numbering in the Folio reprint by Hinman), the gap in the pagination as well as in the quire arrangement can be accounted for by this fact.[2] Whether the play would have found a place in the Folio had it not been for the printer's need of a stopgap remains an open question.[3] None of the authorial manuscripts of Shakespeare's plays survive; there are only printed texts, prepared by editors and set by compositors, and the nature of the manuscript copy used by the compositors must remain speculative. Nevertheless, evidence of various kinds leads to the likelihood that the text of *Timon* printed in the First Folio is based on authorial manuscript – but probably manuscript composed of sheets at various stages of development, not an authorial fair copy and not marked up for theatrical performance – with perhaps a part transcribed by a scribe. The usual term for an authorial dramatic manuscript not fair copied is 'foul papers', but this term has been so variously interpreted that it is necessary to discriminate. W. W. Greg in 1955 thought of 'authorial foul papers' as 'a rough draft . . . representing the play more or less as the author intended it to stand'. Greg was obviously reluctant seriously to conjecture the existence of one or more rougher drafts behind this full version, preferring to assume that 'an experienced dramatist would doubtless be able to produce at once a sufficiently coherent text'. Bowers calls into question the 'single act of composition' theory, setting up instead the notion that 'a play might grow through successive drafts to its final form'.[4] Honigmann enlarges on this view and proposes using the term 'foul papers' to denote 'any kind of draft preceding the first fair copy'.[5] The idea that the term 'foul papers' can include several rough drafts has disrupted long-established editorial assumptions that textual inconsistencies and other troubling phenomena are corruptions by scribe or composi-

---

[1] See Hinman, *Printing*, II, 261.
[2] The bibliographical evidence has been established by Greg, pp. 445–6, and Hinman, *Printing*, II, 261 and 526–7.
[3] Honigmann cautions against taking it as an indication that *Timon* was never intended to be printed ('Timon', pp. 13–14).
[4] Bowers, pp. 186–7 n. 4.
[5] Honigmann, *Shakespeare's Text*, p. 18.

tor. Looking at them as possible authorial revisions has radically influenced recent study of Shakespeare's texts, especially *Hamlet* and *King Lear*; related to *Timon*, it also sheds new light on the theory (most fully developed by Ellis-Fermor on the basis of structural inconsistencies) that *Timon of Athens* is an unfinished play, 'roughed out, worked over in part and then abandoned'.[1] For, if the texts of some of Shakespeare's plays are made up of parts more or less revised, then the idea of a play being 'finished' turns out to be just as questionable as the corollary idea of a play being 'abandoned'. A play can be seen in terms of being more or less completed. Seeing *Timon* from this perspective would take away the stigma of its being an artistic failure; it would instead be read as an uncompleted draft, not finally revised. Bowers's view of the copy-text is 'that *Timon* cannot be regarded as suitable for submission for acting; but there is no reason to suppose that it is not representative of Shakespeare in the workshop and perhaps of a range of papers antecedent to the kind of copy Shakespeare would deliver to the company'.[2] Viewing the copy-text as antecedent to any kind of acting version is supported by the lack of evidence that the play was ever staged in its own time.

Another branch of textual criticism aims at differentiating authorial, scribal and compositorial errors and inconsistencies in the transmission of the text from the author's draft(s) to the printed text. Scribal interferences are claimed by Philip Williams.[3] H. J. Oliver conjectures that 'part of the copy was Shakespeare's own foul papers but that another part was a transcript – and that it was a transcript made by Ralph Crane'.[4] He bases his findings on Crane's spelling and writing habits as they can be deduced from other plays.

Studies of the printing-process – the possible influence of compositors and their peculiarities of setting type – are presented in their most complete form by Charlton Hinman.[5] He maintains that 'the whole of *Timon* was set by Compositor B' and that 'all but one page of this play was set from case y'. He bases his findings on spelling evidence[6] as well as on typographical evidence; the latter shows that signature Gg3 was not set from case y, but from case x; accordingly, one has to assume that 'Compositor B switched from case y to case x to set this page, then immediately switched back to case y to set his next page.' Hinman conjectures that Compositor E, whom he thinks less expert than the others and classes as an apprentice not to be trusted to set from manuscript copy, assisted Compositor B by distributing type into case x for B to set Gg3. Looking briefly at some of the spelling variants in *Timon*, he concludes that 'they are certainly not of printing-house origin', but that certain patterned alternatives would 'reflect peculiarities in the copy'; as to whether they are scribal or authorial, he seems to lean towards the latter.[7]

[1] Ellis-Fermor, p. 271.
[2] Bowers, p. 26. The opposite view, that *Timon* cannot be taken to throw 'much light upon Shakespeare's normal methods of working', was stated by E. K. Chambers and taken over by Greg, pp. 408–9.
[3] Williams, 'New approaches to textual problems in Shakespeare', *SB* 8 (1956), 3–14.
[4] Oliver, p. xix.
[5] Hinman, *Printing*.
[6] *Ibid.*, II, 283; I, 394.
[7] *Ibid.*, II, 283; 283–4; 285.

Spellings and abbreviations of names

The number of variant spellings and abbreviations in speech headings is unusually great. The most conspicuous example is the spelling of Apemantus. He first appears as 'Apemantus',[1] then in the stage direction in TLN 215 and in TLN 222 (gg2^r) as 'Apermantus', as well as in the catchword abbreviation 'Aper.' at the bottom of the page; the spelling then switches back to 'Apemantus' and to the speech heading 'Ape.' on gg2^v – that is, from TLN 223 to 351; on gg3^r and gg3^v (TLN 352–607) we have 'Apermantus' and 'Aper.' again. So far, the spellings vary from page to page; this, however, is not the case on gg4^r and gg4^v; here we have an extraordinary sequence of variant spellings: in TLN 611 the 'Aper.' variant is kept, but from TLN 713 on to 737 the spelling is again 'Apemantus' and the speech heading 'Ape.' In TLN 742 we have a single 'Apermantus'; in 743 we find 'Ape.', and it remains so for the rest of this scene. In 4.3 (TLN 1817–2043) the spelling 'Apemantus' and the abbreviation 'Ape.' are again consistent. A single new variant, 'Appemantus', appears only under 'The Actors Names'. Maxwell offers two alternative explanations for this extraordinary variety. His first explanation is that the spelling 'Apemantus' 'represents a correction of a MS. "Apermantus"'; if this is correct, 'no readily intelligible system can be traced'.[2] In his alternative explanation, he argues for an unspecified mixture of authorial and printing-house corrections; he attempts to pattern the changes by referring to units of e.g. a scene or an act, which, however, may not have been the units to go by, either for the author or for the compositor. By contrast, H. J. Oliver[3] relates the various spellings of Apemantus to the variant spellings of Ventidius[4] and suggests that the spellings 'Apermantus' and 'Venti(d)gius' are due to Crane (the scribe), whereas the spellings 'Apemantus' and 'Ventid(d)ius' are Shakespeare's. E. A. J. Honigmann accounts for the variant spellings by assuming 'that there is some indication for two men in the transmission'.[5] But, differing from Oliver, he assumes them to be two compositors working on the early portions of the text, since, according to him, the variants occur consistently – 'page against page, column against column'.[6] Finally, T. H. Howard-Hill, by claiming that Gg3, where Apermantus-spellings occur throughout, was set entirely by Compositor E, adds to the likelihood that at least some of the variants may be compositorial in origin. But even with this new item of knowledge, we are left guessing as to how to account for the spelling inconsistencies on the other pages (and

---

[1] Line 76, based on the successive numbering – Through Line Numbering – of the Norton Facsimile of the First Folio of Shakespeare, prepared by Charlton Hinman, 1968, signature Gg^v.

[2] Maxwell, p. 90. Since he does not assume a scribal interference in the transmission process to have taken place, the attempt at correcting the spelling – had it ever occurred – would have to be ascribed either to the author or to the compositor. Concerning the compositor, Maxwell is of the then current opinion – he refers to Hinman's findings published in *SQ* 6 (1955) – that Compositor B set the whole text.

[3] Oliver, pp. xx–xxi.

[4] As Charlton Hinman had explored in 'Cast-off copy for the First Folio of Shakespeare', *SQ* 6 (1955), 259–73, and set forth again in Hinman, *Printing*.

[5] Honigmann, 'Timon', p. 18. He also points out that Thomas Lodge in his *Wits Miserie* (1569) spells 'Apermantus' ('Timon', p. 13); and in *The Stability of Shakespeare's Text* (1965) he concedes that 'both forms may go back to Shakespeare since they go back further' (pp. 41–2).

[6] Oliver, p. 19; which is not quite correct: on gg4^v both spellings occur in the same column.

columns), and we get no further clue in the vexing problem of how to identify and delimit authorial, scribal and compositorial responsibilities.

There are other names that show variant spellings. The speech headings of 'Lucius' are a case in point.[1] In 3.2 there are two speech headings 'Luc.' (TLN 981, 1023); four 'Luci.' (TLN 994, 996, 1012, 1025); one 'Lucius' (TLN 988), and three 'Lucil.' (TLN 1007, 1018, 1041), which is obviously an erroneous reminiscence of the servant Lucil(l)ius of 1.1, whose speech heading is consistently 'Luc.' (TLN 144, 168, 186). To complicate matters further and get an inkling of the possible confusion which either the author's or the compositor's mind may have been subject to: there is in 3.1 a figure by the name of Lucullus, whose speech heading is consistently 'Luc.' (TLN 923, 931, 938, 948, 951, 965). And then there is in 3.4 a servant by the name of Lucius, whose speech heading is three times 'Luc.' (TLN 1164, 1224, 1228) and the rest of the time (i.e. thirteen times) 'Luci.' Finally, there is in F TLN 474 an unprecedented speech heading 'Luc.' (which, since Capell, has been changed to 1 Lord). These overlappings of speech headings, in which four (or even five) different persons are involved, show an extraordinary muddle, which may be either of authorial or compositorial origin, or both. Along with differently-layered complications regarding character designations,[2] I regard it as more likely that they are ditherings of the author himself and show his as yet undecided mind. The spellings of 'Ventidius', which is supposedly the normal spelling, are similarly variant. 'Ventigius' (TLN 339, 351 and in 'The Actors Names'), 'Ventidgius' (TLN 1076, 1083) and 'Ventiddius' (901, 903) are each of them consistent only within a brief paragraph. There are other names as well that show inconsistencies of the above-mentioned kind: 'Phrynia' and 'Timandra' (TLN 1653 ff.) are named as 'Phrinica' and 'Timandylo' in 2199; however, the naming may be explained as a misrepresentation by the speaker, i.e. the Painter.

Assignation of names

The assignation of names, to servants as well as to Lords, is loose and inconsistent. Servants are either assigned their functional name 'Servant', sometimes with a numeral added to it,[3] or they are assigned a proper name, or else they are called by their master's name. Three of Timon's servants belong with certainty to the group endowed with proper names: Lucilius, who is identified as such by the Old Athenian (1.1.115); Flaminius; and Servilius, whom Timon calls for to deliver an errand (2.2.175).[4] In

---

[1] I am dealing here only with the figure 'Lord Lucius' in 3.2. He has to be distinguished from a servant by the name of 'Lucius'. The problems that must be raised in determining their identities and their relation will be dealt with later.

[2] See pp. 187–8 below.

[3] As, e.g., in F TLN 1071 SD *Enter a third servant . . .* ; in the following speech headings, however, the number is not repeated.

[4] The fact that in F TLN 863 the character otherwise known as Flaminius is once named Flavius does indicate a lapse, but does not cast doubt on the clear assignation of a name to this servant, particularly in view of the speech headings in F TLN 872 and intermittently in 3.1, together with the stage direction at the beginning of the latter scene and the fact that Lord Lucullus repeatedly addresses him by that name. (Rowe's emendation of 'Flaminius' for 'Flavius' has been almost generally accepted.)

2.2.179 SD *three servants* enter, the third one, however, without a proper name. His appearance is necessary from a functional point of view, since he will be sent on an errand to Lord Sempronius (3.3). But he is still not assigned a proper name, even though the servant name Lucilius (from 1.1) would have been available. The only other case of a clear proper-name attribution for a servant is Caphis (2.1.13–14). Caphis is mentioned again in 2.2 together with a group of servants of Timon's creditors. However, he is not mentioned in the group of servants who are threatening Timon with their masters' bonds (3.4), although the F stage direction says *All Timons Creditors to wait for his comming out* (TLN 1117–18). All the other name-attributions to servants are more involved and show signs of indecisiveness (which in this matter can be nothing but authorial).[1]

The servant Titus belongs to the above-mentioned group of servants in 3.4. In the F stage direction at the beginning of 3.4, he is not mentioned by name; his entrance is as one of the unspecified 'others'.[2] His name is first mentioned by another servant in 3.4.1 and then in the dialogue. On the evidence of this dialogue, there is no doubt that Titus is one of Timon's creditors' servants. What is not so clear is whether 'Titus' is his proper name or his master's name. Lacking an alternative plausible argument, editors have considered it to be his proper name, while his master's name remains a blank. The servant by the name of Hortensius is a parallel case.

There is a group of servants who, by the evidence of their own statements in the dialogue, are named after their masters. This is the case with Isidore and Varro (2.2.31–2).[3] While Isidore (servant) is (like Caphis) not mentioned among the creditors' servants group of 3.4.0 SD, Varro (servant), on the other hand, is mentioned. In the F stage direction, he is announced this time as *Varro's man* (TLN 1117); in the ensuing speech headings, he changes from *Var.man* (TLN 1120) to *Varro* (1159), and in 1173 a *2.Varro* is added without any previous introduction; the differentiation is kept up in TLN 1189 and 1191.[4] The complications are enhanced by the fact that the two Varro servants seem to present different bonds (F TLN 1219–20); this would only be meaningful if their master had to claim more than one bond from Timon, which is highly unlikely.[5] Inconsistencies of this kind do not really affect the structural consist-

---

[1] Greg's statement that 'Character designations are not as a rule indefinite or inconsistent, but many of the characters are themselves unspecified and hard to place' needs to be looked into more closely (p. 411).

[2] Rowe was the first to include his name in the stage direction.

[3] The F stage direction TLN 666 does not give this information. Hanmer (1744) is the first editor who seems to have recognised the identification problem. He remarks in a note to the stage direction: 'The two last are but Servants to Isidore and Varro, here call'd by their Masters names as is usual among Servants with one another.' Johnson expresses doubt on this matter. His comment: 'Whether servants, in our authour's time, took the names of their masters, I know not. Perhaps it is a slip of negligence.' However, Johnson writes in the stage direction: 'Enter Caphis, with the servants of Isidore, and Varro.' Varro and Isidore are named as Timon's creditors by the Senator in 2.1.1.

[4] There is no convincing functional reason for this doubling unless it were for the sake of adding to the number of servants pressing Timon for repayment. This, however, could have been effected by reintroducing the servants who got lost along the way.

[5] Rowe and subsequent editors sought to mend this inconsistency by giving 3.4.81 to Caphis; they failed to notice, however, that Caphis does not enter the scene at all. It was Capell who noticed the inconsistency of this attribution and who gave 3.4.81 to Hortensius and the second to both Varro servants. The redistribution has been accepted by most editors.

ency of the play. If one wished to relate them to the workings of a mind, one would probably diagnose them as signs of inattentiveness to the task of fixing the identities of minor dramatic personnel – a task of tidying up that could easily be done at a later stage.

Of greater weight and structural relevance is the relationship between the servant Lucius and Lord Lucius and the identity problem of Lucius (master). A servant Lucius is mentioned by name in the F stage direction (TLN 1118) at the beginning of 3.4. Speaking with other servants (of creditors), he states that Timon owes his master five thousand crowns (3.4.30), without specifying what his master's name is. Johnson was the first to observe this blank and he concluded: 'Lucius is here again for the servant of Lucius.' This reasoning is based on the assumption that servants are sometimes called by their masters' names (such as Isidore and Varro).

Who is the master of Lucius (servant)? On the basis of Johnson's reasoning, his name would have to be 'Lucius'. There is a 'Lord Lucius' in the play, who is mentioned in 1.2.171; and there is a Lord Lucius, who in 3.2 is approached for a loan by one of Timon's servants. Can this Lord Lucius be identical with Lucius (creditor)? There is no evidence in the play that the servant Lucius's claim for 'five thousand crowns' is a claim asserted by the Lord Lucius of 1.2. The only time we hear of Lord Lucius having bestowed something on Timon is in 1.2.171–3. Considering Timon's way of presenting gifts (as described in 2.1.5–6), Lord Lucius's bestowal will not remain without consequences, and there are reasons for assuming that he is hoping for reciprocal gifts (see 3.2.25–7). In talking to the Three Strangers in 3.2, Lord Lucius gives the impression that Lord Lucullus and he are indebted to Timon, rather than Timon to them. He affirms: 'I have received some small kindnesses from him, as money, plate, jewels, and such like trifles . . .' (3.2.16–18). It would also be inconsistent with a creditor's attitude for Lord Lucius to remark, on hearing from the First Stranger that Timon is near the end of his financial resources: 'Fie, no, do not believe it; he cannot want for money' (3.2.7).[1] We hear from Sempronius that Lord Lucius (together with Lucullus and Ventidius) 'Owes . . . their estates unto him' (3.3.6). The First Stranger comments on Lord Lucius having rejected Timon's plea for a loan, describing Timon's previous generosity to him:

> For in my knowing
> Timon has been this lord's father,
> And kept his credit with his purse;
> Supported his estate; nay, Timon's money
> Has paid his men their wages. (3.2.59–63)

Whilst this gives an impression of the extent to which Lord Lucius is indebted to Timon, we are also given information about Lord Lucius's wealth by the First Stranger a few lines later:

> He [Lucius] does deny him, in respect of his,
> What charitable men afford to beggars. (3.2.67–8)

---

[1] Compare this with the quite different attitude of the 'Senator' in 2.1, who really is Timon's creditor.

According to this, Lord Lucius is so rich that Timon's request is more within the range of a charitable gift.

To sum up: it is most likely that the 'Lord Lucius' of 1.2.171 is identical with the 'Lucius' of 3.2. There is plenty of evidence in the text that this 'Lord Lucius' belongs to the group of those who give gifts to Timon and receive them from him. However, the evidence shows that he cannot be identical with the man X, who by the evidence of his servant's name 'Lucius' has been erroneously named 'Lucius' (following Johnson), and who has still more erroneously been identified with 'Lord Lucius'.

How closely can the circle of Timon's creditors, both guests and friends, be identified? Only one of the creditors appears in person: the 'Senator' in 2.1. He names Varro and Isidore as further creditors, neither of whom appears personally. He talks about the extent of Timon's debts, giving figures but not specifying the currency. (Both earlier and later, the talk is of 'talents', 'crowns' and 'pieces'.) In 2.2, the servants of creditors appear for the first time in a group: they are Caphis, Varro (servant) and Isidore (servant).

In 3.4, the group of creditors is enlarged still further by their servants; Titus, Hortensius, Philotus and Lucius increase the number to seven. Out of such a large group of people (relative to the characters of the play), only one appears in person; the others do not, and act only through intermediaries while remaining to some extent nameless.

The group of creditors should be distinguished from the flatterers known as 'Flattering Lords' and 'false Friends' in F – Lucius, Lucullus, Sempronius and Ventidius. The three Lords without names in 1.2 who receive gifts from Timon also belong to this group of flatterers. Out of this group of flatterers (seven in all), four are asked by Timon for a loan; by rejecting this request they prove themselves to be 'false Friends'.[1] Thus, the composition of the two groups – creditors and flatterers – is not identical. There is only one creditor, master to the servant Hortensius, who is said to have received gifts from Timon (3.4.19 and 27); there is no indication of any other overlapping between the two groups.

Individual or generic names

The Lords who appear in 1.1 and 1.2 have generic names in F. They are named by editors from Rowe to Johnson as Lucius and Lucullus. To make it possible for them to send their gifts to Timon (1.2.171 ff. and 176 ff.), Rowe has them leave the stage at 1.2.162, which is unwarranted by F and which leaves us with the awkward feeling that, of the two departing Lords, only one (Lucius) gets a farewell gift. The three Lords who, for the rest of 1.2, serve as dialogue partners for Timon keep their generic names. In 3.6 Dyce was the first to substitute individual names for the generic 'friends' (F) in

---

[1] The listing of this group in F is rather confused. Lucius and Lucullus are named as 'two flattering Lords'; Sempronius is added as 'another flattering Lord', and is listed again near the end, this time without any label; Ventidius (printed Ventigius) is labelled as 'one of Tymons false Friends'. There is no reason for preserving these inconsistencies of F either wholly or in part; since these four Lords belong to the same categories of flatterers and false friends, they should all be listed under these headings.

the stage direction, and Sisson follows, naming them (in the order of their appearance in 3.1–3.3) Lucullus, Lucius, Sempronius and Ventidius in the stage directions as well as in the speech headings.

This replacement of generic with individual names may be justified on the grounds of effecting a clear picture of who says what, particularly for the purposes of production, but it should also be noted that throughout this scene not a single individual name is mentioned, neither in F's speech headings nor in Timon's speeches.[1] The atmosphere generated thereby is one of group rather than individual affiliation. Without doubt, the three Lords mentioned in 3.4.104–6 will have to be of the party, but the speeches need not necessarily be assigned to them.

The most conspicuous instance is the Flavius–Steward problem. His is not an identity problem, no matter whether one gives the character the individual or the generic name; this seems to be mainly a matter of which aspect of the dramatic figure is focused on at any given point in the play. The individual name Flavius is used throughout 1.2, in a stage direction and in speech headings as well as in the text (1.2.145 ff.). From 2.2 onward until the end of the play, the generic name 'Steward' is used throughout for the same person, in stage directions and speech headings as well as in the text. In this edition, to avoid casting doubt on the identity of this dramatic figure, and to keep the reverberations of the term 'Steward', both names are given in the stage directions, whereas, for simplicity's sake, the individual name is used for the speech headings.

Stage directions

The stage directions show disparate characteristics which indicate their provisional character. Descriptive stage directions occur mainly in the first act. Greg, pp. 124 ff., lists several varieties. Alan C. Dessen calls them 'fictional' directions in which a dramatist slips into a narrative or descriptive style seemingly more suited to a reader facing a page than an actor on the stage. 'Some of these "fictional" signals show the dramatist thinking out loud in the process of writing (so that the details anticipate what will be evident in the forthcoming action)' (p. 56). This applies particularly to 1.1.97 SD. The most conspicuous ones are:[2]

1.1.97: *Enter Lord Timon, addressing himself courteously to every suitor.* In view of the details of the scene this reads like an author's note.[3]

1.2.0: *Hautboys playing loud music. A great banquet served in; and then, enter Lord Timon, the States, the Athenian Lords, Ventigius which Timon redeemed from prison. Then comes, dropping after all Apemantus discontentedly like himself.* Here there are opposing tendencies – towards over-explaining on the one hand (the reminder concerning Ventidius is repeated by Sempronius in 3.3.4–5), and, on the other hand, a lack of

---

[1] Timon's order to Flavius in 3.4.104–6 is taken as the main authority for assigning individual names; the assignment of Lord Lucius carries the greatest conviction.

[2] In the following, the stage directions are quoted according to F; the lineation follows this edition.

[3] For a detailed discussion see Commentary to 1.1.97 SD.

necessary information, as well as the use of indefinite directions (as 'the States', 'the Athenian Lords').

1.2.132: *The Lords rise from table, with much adoring of Timon, and to show their loves each single out an Amazon, and all dance, men with women, a lofty strain or two to the hautboys, and cease.* Unique among Shakespeare's stage directions are descriptive elements like 'adoring', 'single out', 'a lofty strain'.

Indefinite stage directions[1] showing a form of vagueness 'in the mention of unspecified groups'[2] occur frequently throughout the whole play:

1.1.39: *Enter certain Senators.* These are not assigned a speaking role and cannot therefore be numbered.

1.1.246: *Enter Alcibiades with the rest.* This probably refers to the before mentioned 'twenty horse / All of companionship' – i.e. his train.[3]

This form of vagueness is not peculiar to *Timon* and does not allow conclusions to be drawn regarding the state of the copy-text. It is, however, a different matter with another kind of vagueness, which occurs when an identifiable number of figures is given in a scene, but an indefinite formula is used in the initial direction. One might explain it by saying that the author has not yet made up his mind about the exact number of speakers (figures) required for the occasion. In 3.6.0, the stage direction is *Enter divers Friends at several doors.* The number of 'Friends' eventually needed is four, as is indicated by the speech headings.[4] A similar case is the stage direction 3.4.0, where the terms *meeting others* and *All Timon's creditors* (meaning 'All servants of Timon's creditors') suggest a vagueness about numbers, which during the ensuing scene are specified as six (two servants of Varro, Titus, Hortensius, Lucius Servant, Philotus). Again, the conclusion to be drawn is that it was only in the course of working out the details of the scene that the author realised the number of servants he needed.[5]

Even this reasoning is not quite conclusive: when we attempt to determine the number of Senators in 5.1, 5.2 and 5.4, we find in 5.1.105 *two Senators* meeting Timon before his cave. In 5.2.0 we have *two other Senators* meeting a messenger and then meeting the two Senators previously mentioned. All have speaking roles. In 5.4.2 we only have *The Senators* appearing on the wall, and only two of them have speaking roles, but one would have to assume that at least the aforementioned four are present,[6] maybe even more, so that the number of speaking roles is not always a reliable measure for filling up unspecified stage directions.

[1] See Greg, pp. 135 ff.

[2] Greg, p. 135.

[3] The formula 'with his/her/their train' is a very common way of indicating social status by requiring an unspecified number of followers. How many of them eventually appear on stage is not an editorial problem. In 2.2.16 we have *Enter Timon and his train*; in 3.6.20 *Enter Timon and Attendants*; and similarly in 5.4.0 *Enter Alcibiades with his powers before Athens.*

[4] The term 'divers' occurs six more times in stage directions in Shakespeare's plays to indicate an unspecified number. But only once (apart from the example in *Timon*) is it a term that is specified later on in the scene (*AWW* 2.1.0). In all other incidents it signifies an unspecifiable group (*Temp.* 4.1.254; *AWW* 1.2.0; *R3* 5.5.0; *H8* 1.4.0; *Mac.* 1.7.0).

[5] This view is supported by the change of 'Varro's man' in the stage direction into 'two servants of Varro'.

[6] In the trial scene (3.5) three Senators are present; in 3.6.8 SD the number of Senators cannot be identified (see above).

There are also indefinite or unspecific assignations of speech headings. 'All' speeches:

> All Ladies 1.2.144
> All [Lords] 1.2.162
> All Lords 1.2.206
> All [Servants] 2.2.64, 66, 70, 92, 95, 113

'Both' speeches:

> with regard to 'Lords': 3.6.46
> with regard to 'Senators': 5.4.63
> with regard to Poet and Painter: 5.1.66, 80, 85, 95

Not all of them, however, present an editorial problem in the sense of being a provisional and not a definitive assignation from the author. The chorus-character of 'Both' speeches seems to be clear for Phrynia/Timandra as well as for the Poet/ Painter. There is also a good case to be made for a choric speech of the two 'Lords' in 3.6.46, whereas the 'Senators'' reply in 5.4.63, if it is to be regarded as choric, should include all of them. Honigmann argues that 'Both' speeches 'may signify nothing more than the author's hasty composition. This must often be so, I think, in *Timon* . . .'¹ With regard to the 'All' speeches, only 'All Ladies' (1.2.144) may be regarded as assigned to an indefinite number of speakers. In all other cases, the number is determined by the number of speakers, the Lords in 1.2 and the Servants in 2.2.² There are permissive speech headings³ in 3.6.73–4 – 'Some speak' and 'Some other' (referring to the 'Friends'). Of all the speech headings, they seem to be the clearest example of provisional practice.⁴

Asides

There are no asides in the Folio text of *Timon*. Johnson (1765) introduced five, Capell (1768) four, and most of these have been generally accepted. Subsequently, editors have tended to create an overabundance of aside directions, professing to help readers but often rendering character interactions needlessly unequivocal, when, without such interference, they might have retained, for both reader and actor, a richer variety of multi-layered relationships. An aside is unambiguous if it occurs in a situation in which the character is no longer engaged in the dialogue, when the character he passes judgement on is spoken of in the third person and when his aside speech ends with his exit (Flavius at 1.2.148–53 and 1.2.180–93). The case is equally definite when it is

¹ Honigmann, 'Stage direction', p. 122.
² Honigmann makes the interesting point that 'All' speeches 'could be divided between two or more consecutive or simultaneous speakers' ('Stage direction', p. 122). This would rescue the banter between Apemantus, Fool and Servants in 2.2 from an overdone mechanical representation.
³ An instance of permissive stage direction occurs in 4.2.0 with *Enter Steward with two or three Servants*.
⁴ Honigmann points out that in the part of *Sir Thomas More* ascribed to Shakespeare four speeches assigned to 'other' occur ('Stage direction', p. 121).

clearly not in the speaker's interest to be overheard (Lucullus at 3.1.4–5; the end of the aside is marked by a dash). Borderline cases are those in which the speaker's comment on what others are negotiating may be meant to be overheard by them, so that, judged by the speaker's supposed intention, his speech is not an aside; however, the potential listeners may be liable not to grasp what is being said, and may, in fact, completely ignore it. I prefer not to add an aside in these cases – Flavius's comment in 2.2.187 and Timon's comment in 3.6.25 – to strengthen the impression of the listeners' inattentiveness.[1]

An almost unambiguous case along the same lines is Flavius's remark in 1.2.170.[2] Timon's remarks in 5.1.24–45, which he makes while he is being approached by the Poet and Painter but is still unobserved by them, are not asides in the sense mentioned above. Here, the situation itself makes it physically unlikely that the remarks on both sides are addressed to each other. To save an editor the laborious task of assigning asides to both groups – Timon on the one hand and the Poet and Painter on the other (to assign the asides only to Timon is illogical) – it should suffice to have the additional entry 'unobserved' in the stage direction 5.1.23.

Act and scene divisions

Apart from 'Actus Primus. Scoena Prima.' there is neither act nor scene division in *Timon*.[3] Rowe is the father of the now dominant model of act divisions for *Timon*, with only a few adoptions from Theobald and Capell with regard to scene divisions.[4]

Act 1 with its division into two scenes goes back to Theobald (and later Capell), who place the break after TLN 336 (F lineation), which is the line where Pope divided Scene 4 from Scene 5.

Act 2 and its division into two scenes is adopted from Rowe and has been generally accepted since Capell.

Act 3 (TLN 916–1502) is adopted from Rowe; the division into six scenes is taken over from Capell, who in turn adopted most of the scene divisions from Pope (except for Scene 4, which is a contraction of Pope's Scenes 4 and 5).

Act 4 (TLN 1503–2191) and its scene divisions are adopted partly from Rowe (Scenes 1 and 2) and partly from Capell, who extended Scene 3 to 589 lines (F lineation) by including Timon's meeting with Flavius. Nevertheless, both Rowe's and Capell's endings for Scene 3 are arbitrary and unsatisfactory, since the procession of visitors to Timon's cave continues on through the whole of 5.1.

Act 5, with its division into four scenes, is mostly derived from Capell, who in his turn adopted most of Pope's divisions, except for Pope's 5.1 and the two passages (TLN

---

[1] Bernard Beckerman comes close to what I am describing; one type of what he calls the 'solo aside' works under the conditions as we have them in the two examples given above; whereas he, however, aims at regularising or conventionalising the situation by saying 'This kind of solo aside relies heavily upon the convention of unheard speech' (p. 189), I prefer not to tie the speech up into a convention, so that its impact remains potentially multi-faceted.

[2] Particularly in this case, Honigmann's reasoning in 'Stage direction', pp. 119–20, has been most helpful.

[3] There are three other plays among the Tragedies that have no division at all: *Tro.*, *Rom.* and *Ant.*

[4] Pope tends to introduce new scenes whenever a major and plot-relevant character enters.

2496–506 and 2548–9) that Pope found detestable and banished into the footnotes. The only difference from Capell's divisions in modern editions is that Scenes 1 and 2 have been contracted (to my knowledge, first done by Howard Staunton in 1859).

Metrical analysis and lineation problems

Timon's dramatic verse is, compared to Elizabethan norms, rough, and some critics see this as evidence that the play is unfinished or too carelessly composed to be the finished work of Shakespeare.[1] Yet to take this view of *Timon*'s verse is to ignore the statistics concerning metrical deviations in Shakespeare's late plays. The tables of 'deviant' lines furnished by E. K. Chambers[2] and corrected by G. T. Wright[3] show that *Timon* figures in the top group of rough-verse plays, but that it cannot be rated as excessively rough, either in the figures for hexameter lines (one hexameter every 23 lines), or in the percentage for short and shared lines (20.89%).

Recent metrical studies no longer judge Shakespeare's verse by applying a rigid pentameter norm, taking deviations as metrical anomalies; they find that, above all in his later plays, Shakespeare departed more and more resourcefully from the rigid pentameter line and developed new verse patterns: 'just as in every other aspect of theatrical performance the play must shift from one speed to another, break its tempo, change its characters, its mood, its pace, so the language of the play is required to change its nature from time to time – not only from prose to verse but from standard iambic pentameter to lines of more curious character'.[4]

Long lines

Lines with six stresses (hexameters) make up the largest number of long lines.[5] They are variously structured. There are lines with a clear iambic rhythm which divide into two equal halves, with a caesura in the middle.[6] This is the most frequent pattern; it could be read as a double trimeter.

Deviations from a strict iambic line occur as 'headless' lines and 'broken-backed' lines.[7] An example of a 'headless' line is 4.3.31, which after the first truncated foot immediately reverses to an iambic rhythm. 3.5.54 is an example of a hexameter line that is both 'headless' and 'broken-backed': 'Whó cannót condémn / ráshness in cold blóod?'

There are also hexameter lines with a clearly discernible trochaic rhythm, such as 4.2.33: 'Whó would bé so mócked with glóry, ór to live'.

---

[1] Oscar James Campbell, *Shakespeare's Satire*, 1943, pp. 170–2.
[2] Chambers, *William Shakespeare: A Study of Facts and Problems*, II, Appendix H.
[3] Wright, *Shakespeare's Metrical Art*, 1988, Appendix A, B and C.
[4] *Ibid.*, p. 101.
[5] According to Wright's count there are 57 hexameter lines compared to 1,285 blank verse lines in *Timon* (*Shakespeare's Metrical Art*, Appendix B, p. 292).
[6] E.g. 3.1.45; 3.5.29.
[7] Compare Wright, *Shakespeare's Metrical Art*, pp. 175–7. A line is 'headless' when the first unstressed syllable is missing; a line is 'broken-backed' when it lacks an unstressed syllable after the mid-line caesura.

In certain cases, particularly with lines of more than six stresses, there is no clear and unambiguous borderline between verse and prose. According to G. T. Wright, 'From a formal point of view, the most notable aspect of Shakespeare's prose is that it is often hard to distinguish from verse. At many junctures prose and verse come together and for a few lines, even with the text before us, we may not be able to say with assurance whether the lines are prose or verse.'[1] 3.4.38 may serve as an example. In this edition, and in most other editions, it is printed as prose; yet it might almost be read as verse, as a line with seven, or possibly six, stresses. What made me settle on the prose option was, firstly, the resulting overlength of the verse line, and, secondly, the contiguous speeches which, with the exception of 39–40, do not seem to aspire to a clear verse pattern.

When dealing with lines of seven or more stresses, should an editor break up the line into shorter components and look for possibilities of realignment, or leave the line in its full length? In the case of 4.3.454 ('What an alteration of honour has desp'rate want made'), I opt for the second alternative, although Malone broke the line up into two, one with four, the other with three stresses, and Sisson printed the whole passage 450–4 as prose. It is a matter of discretion which alternative is chosen; even though the line is not smooth, it seems to be structured as verse; and the breaking up of the line into two short lines does not make a lot of difference to the rhythmic structure. As regards 1.2.187 ('That what he speaks is all in debt; he owes for ev'ry word'), I make a similar decision to keep the line in its full length.[2] A different decision is made concerning 3.5.14–15 ('He is a man, setting his fate aside, / Of comely virtues'). F prints this as one line of seven stresses; it is broken up by Johnson into a pentameter followed by a short line of two stresses. I follow this, since the combination of lines of 5 + 2 or 5 + 3 stresses forms a recurring pattern.[3]

Arguably the longest line in the play, 1.2.181–2 ('He commands us to provide, and give great gifts, / And all out of an empty coffer'), of nine or even ten stresses, is clearly printed not as prose in F; I follow Johnson/Steevens in breaking it into halves, one with five (or six) and the other with four stresses.

What should become clearer by looking at these examples is that there is no patent formula for printing long lines, but that it is always a matter of judgement.

Short lines

According to G. T. Wright's count there are 171 short lines compared to 1,285 blank verse lines – that is, a short line occurs in every eight lines. The number of short lines by far exceeds the number of long lines.[4]

Short lines occur in different patterns.

---

[1] Wright, *Shakespeare's Metrical Art*, p. 110.
[2] In an attempt to avoid the long line, Capell suggests a far-reaching realignment of lines 187–90, shifting the whole line pattern and ending up with four pentameters and one trimeter. Such an attempt seems to be based on the assumption that metrical regularisation is more appropriate to a Shakespearean text than metrical variation.
[3] 3.5.20; 32; 33; 36; 42; 83.
[4] Wright, *Shakespeare's Metrical Art*, Appendix B, p. 292.

(1) The most widely acknowledged pattern consists of two part lines: one as the conclusion of a speech and the other as the beginning of another character's speech. Joined together, they are a full pentameter, sometimes an hexameter line, and they are heard as being metrically complete. Johnson and Steevens's 1793 edition prints them with the second half indented.

(2) With three consecutive short lines, however, the pattern becomes more complicated. In these cases, a decision has to be made as to which of the three should be considered as 'shared lines'. According to frequency studies carried out by Fredson Bowers, in Shakespeare's plays unlinked part lines concluding a speech are much more frequent than unlinked part lines at the beginning of speeches; in fact, part lines of the last category usually occur only under special conditions, such as, for example, when there is a change of the speaker's addressee.[1] Therefore, this edition favours the principle that a part line beginning a speech should, if possible, be linked in preference to a part line ending a speech – as for example in lines 1.1.132–3 and 1.1.135–6.

(3) In the case of 1.1.143–4, 'And dispossesse her all. / How shall she be endowed, / If she be mated with an equall Husband?', the metrical conditions are slightly different, in that the third line is a complete pentameter and the linking of the two part lines results in an hexameter. To avoid the hexameter, the second part line would have to be linked with the first half of the subsequent pentameter line: 'And dispossess her all. / How shall she be endowed, if she be mated / With an equal husband?' If, however, one wished to place emphasis on the dramatic linkage between the two speakers, tightening their relationship by having them both speak within the unit of one line, one would have to link the two part lines and neglect the 'blemish' of the resulting line length. In these and similar cases, G. T. Wright speaks of 'squinting lines', which may be heard as 'one line mounted, as it were, on another'.[2] The line loses its authority as the prevailing metrical unit, which it had held in a rhetorically stylised type of dramatic speech, and yields to changing rhythmical structures. The way dramatic verses were printed in F and subsequent editions indicates that the metrically complete line was not considered as an absolute norm.

(4) A sequence of short lines of three stresses within a speech poses a different problem. Taking 3.5.102–4, the question is whether to link or not to link; linking results in an hexameter, and hexameters occur relatively frequently in this scene; not linking leaves the line as trimeters, which also occur relatively frequently. I decide against linking, since the issue of tightening a relationship between different speakers does not come up.

(5) A passage made up of independent short lines, long lines and a prose passage, as in 3.4.1–16: for the first five lines, Capell's realignment has been the most widely accepted.

The middle section is the most disputed part.[3] Widely diverging patterns have been

---

[1] Fredson Bowers, 'Establishing Shakespeare's text: notes on short lines and the problem of verse division', *SB* 33 (1980), 77 ff.

[2] Wright, *Shakespeare's Metrical Art*, p. 103.

[3] The line arrangement in F: '. . . is money. / So is theirs, and ours. / And Sir *Philotus* too. / Good day at once. / Welcome good Brother.'

suggested, such as: lines with five and six stresses by Johnson/Steevens; lines with four and five and two stresses by Delius; lines with four and three and four stresses by Staunton and Oliver; and lines with one and six and four stresses by Globe and Riverside. These variant solutions show (1) that the F arrangement has not been considered as the optimum metrical pattern; and (2) that editors make alterations according to criteria which they do not make clear.

The course I take (following Maxwell in parts) is to minimise interference with the speech rhythms as suggested by the arrangement in F, and, in doing so, to tolerate metrically incomplete lines in order to preserve the speech units.

Prose

It cannot always be decided when lines are meant to be prose. The text, as printed in F, modulates back and forth in places – e.g. 1.2.100–5. Nor can characters be divided into either prose or verse speakers. Prose passages have been rewritten as verse, mainly by eighteenth-century editors. There are no general criteria to decide which of these transmutations are acceptable. In the case of 1.2.215–21, Capell and Johnson experimented with a verse that is widely considered as unacceptable. 1.2.208–13, however, is a different case; F prints the first two sentences as prose, and then switches into partly irregular verse. Rowe transmutes the prose lines into verse and incorporates the short line of the F version into his newly conceived verse structure. An inherent rhythm here seems to have found an adequate form, and I adopt this arrangement.[1]

Some passages printed in F as verse (or what looks like verse) are altered by editors to prose. The most conspicuous example is 5.1.1–23. In F, this passage consists of a singular *mélange* of short and long lines, with a few 'regular' lines interspersed. Pope printed it as prose; others have tried their hands at reshuffling the verse, with the greatest consistency in Riverside; more half-heartedly, Knight and Harrison choose an alternation of verse and prose passages. I prefer the all-prose version, which at least avoids adding new irregularities to an already incorrigibly irregular passage.

[1] A similar decision has been made for 1.2.104–5.

APPENDIX: THE TIMON LEGEND

Many traits of Timon as a figure, and of his story, which are components of Shakespeare's play, have accrued over the centuries in treatments by different writers, of which none can rank as an immediate source of the play. Only one can with reasonable certainty be said to have served Shakespeare as an immediate source for *Timon of Athens*. This is Plutarch (*c.* AD 46–*c.* AD 120), translated by Sir Thomas North as *Lives of the Noble Grecians and Romanes* (1579); he makes casual mention of Timon in two 'Lives' that are focused on other nobles: 'The Life of Marcus Antonius' and 'The Life of Alcibiades'. However, what is mentioned in these two episodes covers very little of the treatment of Timon in the play.

For these reasons, I shall not set up hypotheses as to which treatments of the legend may be regarded as a 'source' for Shakespeare; instead, I shall give an account of the components that constitute the multi-faceted Timon legend. Three groups of treatments may be distinguished. The first consists of early references which set up a stereotypical image of Timon. There is a second group of writings in which Timon is placed within a context of philosophical concepts. In a third group Timon appears as the focal figure in narrative or dramatic treatments.

Timon stereotypes

Whether Timon can be assigned the status of a real person is not certain. Plutarch mentions him as having lived during the Peloponnesian War (431–404 BC), but cites as evidence fragmentary mentions of Timon in ancient comedies.[1] Further details regarding him are given by later writers: Lucian of Samosata (*c.* AD 115 to after AD 180) represents him as the son of Echekratides of Kollytos; Pausanias (second half of the second century AD) mentions in his *Description of Greece* that Timon had owned a tower near Academe.[2] Over and above these doubtful identifications of an historical Timon, Timon or *a* 'Timon' was referred to for long periods in antiquity before he made his appearance as a literary figure in his own right and as the main focus of attention. In these sometimes marginal and fragmentary references he had stereotypical significance.

The earliest reference is to Timon's solitariness. Phrynichus, an early Greek playwright (second half of the fifth century BC), in a dramatic fragment named *Monotropos*,[3] which means living in solitude, has a character present himself by this name, explaining his nature by saying that he leads Timon's life, the typical features

---

[1] Plutarch, 'The Life of Marcus Antonius' in Bullough, VI, 251–2.
[2] Lucian, 'Timon, or the Misanthrope', in *Lucian*, trans. A. M. Harmon, Loeb Classical Library, II, p. 383. Pausanias, *Description of Greece* I.xxx.4, trans. W. H. S. Jones, Loeb Classical Library, I, 1918, p. 167.
[3] *Poetae Comici Graeci*, ed. R. Kassel and C. Austin, VII, 1989, s.v. Phrynichus No. 19.

of which are that he is unmarried, prone to flying into a rage, inaccessible, not inclined to laughter, silent and obstinate.[1] This characteristic of solitariness is one of the features most frequently attributed to Timon. It is further elaborated in a group of tomb epigrams written at the Ptolemaic court in Alexandria in the third century BC.[2] In No. 315, Timon's desire to be solitary and his fear of not being solitary enough even when he is dead is given expression (1) by elaborating on an almost inaccessible burial place and (2) by suggesting that he fears being molested by fellow ghosts even in Hades.[3] No. 577 gives the same idea with a slightly different twist: Timon complains about having been buried in a place open to the public, because this detracts from his repose.[4]

Neanthes of Kyzikos reported that Timon's burial place was close by the sea-shore (between Piraeus and Cape Sunion) and that it became unapproachable when the sea tore off this stretch of land.[5] About fifty or so years before Plutarch's similar description of Timon's burial place, Strabo (64 BC to after AD 24) reported on Mark Antony's desire for solitude after he had lost the battle of Actium (31 BC); taking up a similar idea to the one of Timon's burial place by the sea, he mentions that Mark Antony, 'having chosen to live the life of a Timon the rest of his days', built for himself 'a royal lodge which he called Timonium' on a mole reaching far out into the harbour of Alexandria.[6] In Strabo's report Mark Antony considers himself like Timon. Plutarch, in 'The Life of Marcus Antonius', repeats Strabo's account and then inserts his brief and incidental description of Timon, in which he repeats what Neanthes said about Timon's burial place: 'He dyed in the citie of Hales, and was buried upon the sea side. Nowe it chaunced so, that the sea getting in, it compassed his tombe rounde about . . .'[7]

Views differ about whether Timon's retreat from the society of men is due to his sheer ill nature or whether his ill nature is seen as a consequence of the malicious nature of society. In Aristophanes' (*c.* 445–*c.* 385 BC) comedy *Lysistrata*, the Chorus of Women in an interchange of banter with the Chorus of Men take up the stereotype Timon-figure and pit him against a woman-hater brought forward by the Chorus of Men. Timon represents for the women someone hating males, not people in general, and in this he is 'Dear to all the womankind'.

---

[1] An evaluation of the reliability of this and other sources is given by Jeffrey Henderson (ed.), Aristophanes, *Lysistrata*, 1987, p. 172. Henderson also mentions further 'fictitious' details about Timon's life, such as the circumstances of his death: after having fallen from a pear tree, he refused to see a doctor and died from an infection.

[2] *Greek Anthology*, II, Nos. 313–20.

[3] 'Dry earth, grow a prickly thorn to twine all round me, or the wild branches of a twisting bramble, that not even a bird in spring may rest its light foot on me, but that I may repose in peace and solitude. For I, the misanthrope, Timon, who was not even beloved by my countrymen, am no genuine dead man even in Hades.'

[4] 'May he who buried me at the cross-roads come to an ill end and get no burial at all; since all the travellers tread on Timon and in death, the portion of all, I alone have no portion of repose.'

[5] Neanthes lived either in the fourth or the third century BC. The Timon reference is in a scholion to Aristophanes' *Lysistrata*, 808 (*Die Fragmente der Griechischen Historiker*, II.A, ed. F. Jacoby, Berlin, 1926, p. 201, No. 35).

[6] *The Geography of Strabo*, XVII.i.9, trans. H. L. Jones, Loeb Classical Library, VIII, 1932, p. 39.

[7] Cited after Bullough, VI, 252. In Shakespeare's *Timon* this is taken up in 5.1.205–8 and 5.4.66.

But even so, he has all the characteristics of the solitary man attributed to him: he 'Dwelt amongst the prickly thorn';[1] he 'Kept aloof from haunts of men'; he is 'Savage', 'forlorn', 'Visage-shrouded' and 'Fury-born'; he is represented as 'Cursing men' and 'Hating men [i.e. males] of evil mind', which means that he does not hate indiscriminately, but that his hatred has to be regarded as justified.[2]

Hatred of humanity, and not only of males, is a recurring characteristic of the Timon-figure. In Aristophanes' *The Birds* Prometheus explains his hatred of the gods by referring to Timon's example.[3] In an epigram Callimachus (*c.* 310–*c.* 240 BC) writes: 'Timon – for thou art no more – which is most hateful to thee, darkness or light?' 'Darkness; there are more of you in Hades.'[4] His hatred finds an outlet in his uttering abuses and curses, even after his death. The recurrent idea is that he wishes all those who pass by his grave a bad end.[5]

The only report clearly serving to justify Timon's hatred is in a letter ascribed to Plato.[6] The writer of the letter compares his own situation with Timon's and finds reasons for its justification: he hates the idea of living with other people, because they are ignorant and uncultured. He regards the city where he lives as a cage for beasts which he intends to leave. Timon, he says, was in a similar situation and cannot therefore be called a hater of mankind by nature.

These characteristics of solitariness, malice and hatred conjoin when he is labelled a 'misanthropos', which means 'hater of man'. The earliest use of this term as an epithet for Timon is probably in an epigram by Hegesippus (*c.* 300 BC): 'All around the tomb are sharp thorns and stakes; you will hurt your feet if you go near. I, Timon the misanthrope, dwell in it . . .'[7] Again, he is called by that name in one of Cicero's (106–43 BC) *Tusculan Disputations*: 'like the *hatred of all mankind* felt we are told by Timon who is termed "misanthropos" . . .'[8] North, in his translation of 'The Life of Marcus Antonius', adds in the margin: 'Plato, and Aristophanes testimony of Timon Misanthropos, what he was.'[9] Lucian has him name himself, in a flourish (similar to Shakespeare's Timon at 4.3.54): 'The name most acceptable to him, let it be "Misanthrope" . . .'[10] Diogenes Laertius (probably first half of the third century AD), referring to another authority, names both Timon and Apemantus as misanthropes.[11]

Another interesting facet is added when the Timon-figure becomes someone who

[1] A notion similar to the one expressed in the tomb epigram no. 315 (*Greek Anthology*).

[2] All quotations from the *Lysistrata* are from the translation by B. B. Rogers, *Aristophanes*, Loeb Classical Library, 3 vols., 1960–3, III, 810–19.

[3] *The Birds*, 1549, in *Aristophanes*, trans. Rogers, vol. III.

[4] *Greek Anthology*, II, no. 317.

[5] *Greek Anthology*, II, epigrams nos. 313, 314, 316. See *Tim.* 5.4.70–3 together with the Supplementary Notes, p. 180 above.

[6] The letter is inauthentic, supposedly written by a later member of the Academy. It is edited and numbered as the fourteenth letter by C. F. Hermann, *Platonis Dialogi*, VI, Leipzig, 1853, pp. 66–7.

[7] *Greek Anthology*, II, no. 320.

[8] *Tusculan Disputations*, IV.xi.25, trans. J. E. King, Loeb Classical Library, 1927.

[9] Bullough, VI, 251.

[10] *The Dialogue of Timon*; in Bullough, VI, 272.

[11] Diogenes Laertius, *Lives of Eminent Philosophers*, I.107–8, trans. R. D. Hicks, Loeb Classical Library, I, 1925.

has been wronged. This means that the failings of the people with whom he lives are considered as an important factor. Without any mention of the name Timon, Aristophanes, in his comedy *The Plutus*, sketches a relationship of deceptive friendship which is very close to what later will be regarded as a constitutive element of the Timon legend.[1] Here is the figure of the Good Man who tells the story of his eventful life which has led him from wealth to utmost need: 'For I, inheriting a fair estate, / Used it to help my comrades in their need, / Esteeming that the wisest thing to do. / . . . And I supposed that they / Whom I had succoured in their need, would now / Be glad to help me when in need myself. / But all slipped off as though they saw me not.'[2]

In both Strabo's and Plutarch's accounts, the fates of Mark Antony and Timon are presented so as to throw light on one another. Mark Antony was 'forsaken by his friends' and therefore chose 'to live the life of a Timon . . . in solitude from all those friends'.[3] Plutarch is still more explicit: 'Antonius', he writes, 'forsooke the citie and companie of his frendes, and built him a house in the sea . . . and dwelt there, as a man that banished him selfe from all mens companie: saying that he would lead Timons life, bicause he had the like wrong offered him, that was affore offered unto Timon: and that for the unthankefulnes of those he had done good unto, and whom he tooke to be his frendes, he was angry with all men, and would trust no man.'[4]

In his essay *Laelius On Friendship*, Cicero asserts that any human being, 'even if [he] were of a nature so savage and fierce as to shun and loathe the society of men – such, for example, as tradition tells us a certain Timon of Athens once was – yet even such a man could not refrain from seeking some person before whom he might pour out the venom of his embittered soul'.[5]

This urge for communication, even if seemingly contradictory to Timon's wish for solitariness, is reflected in two companions associated with him by Plutarch: Apemantus and Alcibiades. In Plutarch's account of 'The Life of Marcus Antonius', Apemantus appears as a companion of Timon, 'bicause he was much like to his nature and condicions, and also followed him in maner of life'.[6] Before Plutarch, Timon and Apemantus were jointly described as misanthropes,[7] and Apemantus's affiliation with the Cynic way of life and thought, as suggested by his name,[8] rubs off on Timon's character.[9] It may have triggered off their wit-contests about which of the two is the most authentic hater of man. Thus, Apemantus serves in different roles: being Timon's partner of communication and serving as a touchstone for concepts of misanthropy.

Unlike Apemantus, Alcibiades himself is a richly documented figure in Plutarch's

---

[1] See also Leo Salingar, *Dramatic Form in Shakespeare and the Jacobeans*, 1986, pp. 159–61.
[2] *The Plutus*, pp. 829–37, in *Aristophanes*, trans. Rogers, vol. III.
[3] *The Geography of Strabo*, XVII.i.9.
[4] Plutarch, 'The Life of Marcus Antonius', in *Lives*, XII, 72 ff.
[5] *Laelius De Amicitia*, XXIII.87, in Cicero, *De Senectute, De Amicitia, De Divinatione*, trans. W. A. Falconer, Loeb Classical Library, 1923.
[6] Bullough, VI, 251.
[7] By Aristoxenus (fourth century BC) according to Diogenes Laertius, I.107–8.
[8] Bradbrook interprets his name to mean 'feeling no pain' (*Craftsman*, p. 157).
[9] For a more detailed account of their relationship to the Cynics see below.

Lives. However, as far as his relationship with Timon is concerned, there are only two brief references. One occurs in 'The Life of Marcus Antonius', where Timon is said 'to shunne all other mens companies, but the companie of young Alcibiades, a bolde and insolent youth, whom he woulde greatly feast, and make much of, and kissed him very gladly'.[1] The second one occurs in 'The Life of Alcibiades'. Here Alcibiades gets the main narrative attention as a highly praised orator; Timon is assigned only a marginal role. He is said to have walked up to Alcibiades, who was accompanied by a great train of followers, and to have taken him by the hand, saying: 'O, thou dost well my sonne, I can thee thancke, that thou goest on, and climest up still: for if ever thou be in authoritie, woe be unto those that followe thee, for they are utterly undone.'[2] Timon both welcomes and curses Alcibiades' rise to power.

MISANTHROPY IN PHILOSOPHICAL CONTEXTS

In the *Phaedo*, Plato (427–347 BC) asserts that 'Misology and misanthropy arise from similar causes. For misanthropy arises from trusting someone implicitly without sufficient knowledge. You think the man is perfectly true and sound and trustworthy, and afterwards you find him base and false . . . By the time this has happened to a man a good many times, especially if it happens among those whom he might regard as his nearest and dearest friends, he ends by . . . hating everybody and thinking there is nothing sound in anyone at all.' This misjudgement of human relationships can only be avoided if one places trust in one's experience: 'For if he had knowledge . . . he would think that the good and the bad are both very few and those between the two are very many, for that is the case.'[3]

Cicero classifies misanthropy, together with misogyny and inhospitality, as 'sicknesses of the soul' – that is, as a kind of behavioural disorder. They 'originate in a certain fear of the things [the misanthropes] avoid and hate'. Thus, hatred of women originates in fear, just as hatred of all humanity does – and here Cicero explicitly refers to Timon 'who is termed "misanthropos"'. The effect of this type of aversion is 'an intense belief . . . which regards a thing that need not be shunned as though it ought to be shunned'.[4] Here Cicero seems to assume that fear, as well as the hate resulting from it, are unnecessary and avoidable distortions of man's judgement. It is therefore no surprise that he views these aberrant human types as fittingly represented in comedy; he mentions the comic poet Atilius with a play *Misogynos* (which is not extant), and his subsequent mention of Timon as 'misanthropos' presumably points in the same direction: that Timon is to be seen rather as a comic than as a tragic figure.[5]

Timon's misanthropy acquires a rich philosophical background[6] by being coupled

[1] Bullough, VI, 251.
[2] *Ibid.*, pp. 255–6.
[3] *Phaedo*, pp. 89–90, in *Plato*, trans. H. N. Fowler, Loeb Classical Library, I, 1914.
[4] All quotations from Cicero, *Tusculan Disputations*, IV.xi.25–6.
[5] Beside Phrynichus and Aristophanes who treated Timon or a similar type in contexts of comedy, Antiphanes, a representative of the Middle Comedy (*c.* 400–*c.* 323 BC), also has Timon as title-figure in one of his comedies (extant only in fragments).
[6] Timon the misanthrope should not be mistaken for Timon the sceptic philosopher, as Diogenes Laertius points out in IX.112.

with Apemantus, whose very name signifies his affiliation with the school of Cynics, together with its main representative, Diogenes of Sinope (*c.* 400–325 BC). The Cynics were so called from Diogenes' nickname, *kúon* (= dog), since he behaved in public like a dog, without decency. The Cynics' teaching aimed at exposing the corrupted and corrupting conditions of society, characterised by artificial and outwardly imposed value systems like wealth, pleasure and reputation. They advocated a way of life which aimed at self-sufficiency, thus allowing a person to relinquish civilisation's benefits and to lead an ascetic life.[1] These issues are relevant to Shakespeare's play. The Cynics reverse the generally accepted standards of living in their wish to achieve a closer proximity to natural living conditions, from their notion of an animal-like adaptability to whatever nature has in store for them.

In his *Lives of Eminent Philosophers*, Diogenes Laertius gives an account of Diogenes the Cynic. Detailing his way of life, he mentions his living without a proper dwelling,[2] inuring himself to hardships,[3] living on a meagre diet[4] and scorning all luxuries.[5] All this makes him free to scorn and abuse conventional human society. In Shakespeare's play the focus shifts between Timon and Apemantus as to which of the two is the more authentic Cynic and which has more fully gained the desired state of 'autarkeia'.

The most pungent remarks about Timon's misanthropy are made by Michel de Montaigne in his essay 1.50, 'Of Democritus and Heraclitus'. Montaigne balances Timon's all-encompassing hatred of men against Diogenes' cynical attitude toward life. In his judgement, Diogenes is 'a more sharp, a more bitter, and a more stinging judge' of the human condition than Timon, whose passionate concern with furthering the ruin of mankind shows his basically ambivalent attitude to this very issue, expressed by Montaigne in this maxim: 'For looke what a man hateth, the same thing he takes to hart.' The relationship of Timon and Diogenes in Montaigne's account, with Diogenes' scorn for human dealings, has certain points in common with Timon and Apemantus in Shakespeare's play; their debate in 4.3 can be seen as a contest about who has better arguments to support his position of scorn and hatred. In Montaigne's essay, the issue is concluded; in Shakespeare's play, it remains open.[6]

---

[1] For a general view of Cynicism as a school of philosophy and for further bibliographical details see P. Edwards (ed.), *The Encyclopedia of Philosophy*, II, 1967, s.v. Cynics.
[2] Diogenes Laertius VI.22.
[3] *Ibid.* VI.23 – about his living in a tub.
[4] *Ibid.* VI.37.
[5] *Ibid.* VI.26.
[6] Montaigne's *Essais* were first translated into English by John Florio and published in 1603. Edition cited: Montaigne, *The Essays*, trans. John Florio (1603), ed. George Saintsbury, vol. 1, 1892, pp. 348–51: ch. 50, p. 351. On the possible relationship between the essay and Boaistuau, see Farnham, *Frontier*, p. 66.

READING LIST

Banu, Georges. '*Timon d'Athènes* de Shakespeare et sa mise en scène par Peter Brook: l'écriture de la mise en scène', in *Les Voies de la création théâtrale*, ed. Denis Bablet and Jean Jacquot, vol. 5, 1977, pp. 59–120

Bevington, David. *Action is Eloquence*, 1984

Biggs, Murray. 'Adapting *Timon of Athens*', *Shakespeare Bulletin* 10 (1992), 5–10

Bradbrook, Muriel C. '*The Comedy of Timon*: a reveling play of the Inner Temple', *Renaissance Drama* 9 (1966), 83–103

   The Tragic Pageant of Timon of Athens: An Inaugural Lecture, 1966

Bulman, James C., Jr. 'Shakespeare's use of the "Timon" Comedy', *S. Sur.* 29 (1976), 103–16

Campbell, O. J. *Shakespeare's Satire*, 1943

Charney, Maurice. '*Coriolanus* and *Timon of Athens*', in *Shakespeare: A Bibliographical Guide*, ed. Stanley Wells, 1990, pp. 295–320

Davidson, Clifford. '*Timon of Athens*: the iconography of false friendship', *HLQ* 43 (1980), 181–200

Dillon, Janette. '"Solitariness": Shakespeare and Plutarch', *Journal of English & Germanic Philology* 78 (1979), 325–44

Ellis-Fermor, Una. '*Timon of Athens*: an unfinished play', *RES* 18 (1942), 270–83

Elton, William R., and Edward A. Rauchut. *A Selective Annotated Bibliography of Shakespeare's Timon of Athens*, 1991

Fischer, Sandra K. '"Cut my heart in sums": Shakespeare's economics and *Timon of Athens*', in *Money, Lure, Lore, and Literature*, ed. John Louis DiGaetani, 1994, pp. 187–95

Hibbard, G. R. (ed.). *The Life of Timon of Athens*, 1970 (New Penguin Shakespeare)

Honigmann, E. A. J. '*Timon of Athens*', *SQ* 12 (1961), 3–20

Hunt, John Dixon. 'Shakespeare and the Paragone: a reading of *Timon of Athens*', in *Images of Shakespeare*, ed. Werner Habicht *et al.*, 1988, pp. 47–63

Knight, G. Wilson. *The Wheel of Fire*, 1930

Lancashire, Anne. '*Timon of Athens*: Shakespeare's *Dr. Faustus*', *SQ* 21 (1970), 35–44

Marienstras, Richard. '*Timon d'Athènes* de Shakespeare et sa mise en scène par Peter Brook: la représentation et l'interprétation du texte', in *Les Voies de la création théâtrale*, ed. Denis Bablet and Jean Jacquot, vol. 5, 1977, pp. 13–59

Maxwell, J. C. (ed.). *The Life of Timon of Athens*, 1957 (New Shakespeare)

Miola, Robert S. 'Timon in Shakespeare's Athens', *SQ* 31 (1980), 21–30

Nuttall, Anthony David. *Timon of Athens*, 1989

Pasco, Richard. '*Timon of Athens*', in *Players of Shakespeare: Essays in Shakespearean Performance by Twelve Players with the Royal Shakespeare Company*, ed. Philip Brockbank, 1985, pp. 129–38

Soellner, Rolf, *Timon of Athens: Shakespeare's Pessimistic Tragedy*, 1979

Spencer, T. J. B. ' "Greeks" and "Merrygreeks": a background to *Timon of Athens* and *Troilus and Cressida*', in *Essays on Shakespeare and the Elizabethan Drama in Honor of Hardin Craig*, ed. Richard Hosley, 1962, pp. 223–33

'Shakespeare learns the value of money: the dramatist at work on *Timon of Athens*', *S. Sur.* 6 (1953), 75–8

Tobin, J. J. M. 'Apuleius and *Timon of Athens*', *Renaissance & Renascences in Western Literature* 1 (1980), 1–5

Walker, Lewis. 'Money in *Timon of Athens*', *PQ* 57 (1978), 269–71

Wallace, John M. '*Timon of Athens* and the Three Graces: Shakespeare's Senecan study', *MP* 83 (1986), 349–63